CHICKEN SOUP TEENAGE TRILOGY

CHICKEN SOUP TEENAGE TRILOGY

Stories of Life, Love and Learning

Jack Canfield
Mark Victor Hansen
Kimberly Kirberger

Health Communications, Inc.
Deerfield Beach, Florida

www.hci-online.com
www.chickensoup.com
www.teenagechickensoup.com

We would like to acknowledge the many publishers and individuals who granted us permission to reprint the cited material. (Note: The stories that were penned anonymously, that are in the public domain, or that were written by Jack Canfield, Mark Victor Hansen or Kimberly Kirberger are not included in this listing.)

Losing the "Us" and *My Story*. Reprinted by permission of Lia Gay. ©1996 Lia Gay.

After a While. Reprinted by permission of Veronica A. Shoffstall. ©1971 Veronica A. Shoffstall.

Soul Mates. Reprinted by permission of Fran Leb. ©1996 Fran Leb.

My First Kiss, and Then Some. Reprinted by permission of Mary Jane West-Delgado. ©1996 Mary Jane West-Delgado.

Changes in Life. Reprinted by permission of Sheila K. Reyman. ©1996 Sheila K. Reyman.

First Love. Reprinted by permission of Mary Ellen Klee. ©1996 Mary Ellen Klee.

A High School Love Not Forgotten and *Mrs. Virginia DeView, Where Are You?* Reprinted by permission of Diana L. Chapman. ©1996 Diana L. Chapman.

Starlight, Star Bright; The Right Thing and *The Player*. Reprinted by permission of Kelly Garnett. ©1998 Kelly Garnett.

Seven Minutes in Heaven. Reprinted by permission of Andrew Keegan. ©1998 Andrew Keegan.

Practical Application and *Pay Attention*. Reprinted by permission of Dan Clark. ©1998 Dan Clark.

A Geek, a Nerd, a Bookworm. Reprinted by permission of Kimberly Russell. ©1998 Kimberly Russell.

My Angel Has a Halo. Reprinted by permission of Amanda Johnson. ©1998 Amanda Johnson.

(Continued on page 833)

© 2001 Jack Canfield and Mark Victor Hansen
ISBN 1-55874-999-3 (hardcover)

Publisher: Health Communications, Inc.
   3201 S.W. 15th Street
   Deerfield Beach, FL 33442-8190

Cover design by Andrea Perrine Brower
Inside formatting by Lawna Patterson Oldfield

This collection is dedicated
to all the people whose
hard work make these books possible.

Contents

1. ON RELATIONSHIPS

2. ON FRIENDSHIP

3. ON LOVE AND KINDNESS

4. ON FAMILY

5. ON LEARNING AND LESSONS

6. TOUGH STUFF

7. MAKING A DIFFERENCE

8. GROWING UP AND SELF-DISCOVERY

9. LETTERS FROM READERS

Share with Us

Most of the stories in this book were written by teens like you. We would like to invite you to send us stories you would like to see published in future editions of *Chicken Soup for the Teenage Soul.*

We would also love to hear your reactions to the stories in this book. Please let us know what your favorite stories were and how they affected you.

Please send submissions to:

Chicken Soup for the Teenage Soul
P.O. Box 936
Pacific Palisades, CA 90272
fax: 310-573-3657
e-mail for stories: *stories@iam4teens.com*
e-mail for letters: *letters@iam4teens.com*

Come visit our Web site:
www.iam4teens.com

You can also visit the *Chicken Soup for the Teenage Soul* site at:
www.teenagechickensoup.com

We hope you enjoy reading this book as much as we enjoyed compiling, editing and writing it.

1

ON
RELATIONSHIPS

Love means each person is free to follow his or her own heart.

Melody Beattie

"Brian promised to love me forever. Then he told me
about a *Star Trek* episode where they scientifically
proved the possibility that forever might actually last
only a few days."

Reprinted by permission of Randy Glasbergen.

Losing the "Us"

When an emotional injury takes place,
the body begins a process
as natural as the healing
of a physical wound.

Let the process happen.
Trust that nature
will do the healing.

Know that the pain will pass,
and, when it passes,
you will be stronger,
happier, more sensitive and aware.

Mel Colgrove
from *How to Survive the Loss of a Love*

"So does this mean you want to break up?" I asked softly, hoping my question would go unanswered. That is how it all began, or I guess, ended. The months the two of us had shared were some of the happiest, hardest and most educational months I ever experienced. It seemed impossible that this was the last conversation we would have as Ben and Lia, the couple.

I had ignored the fact that the majority of high-school relationships do not last. I guess, in the back of my mind, I always thought that Ben was the only boy I would ever have these feelings for, that he was the only boy who would ever understand me. I never took into account that the last month of our relationship was one of the hardest times I had ever gone through. It just stopped being fun. It stopped being about us and started to be about everything that surrounded him and me.

The next day at school I tried looking great to make him see what he had given up. I even tried to talk to him like my heart wasn't aching, like I was better off and even happier. But inside I looked at him and could only see all the love and time I had given and all the hurt I had received. I walked around school in a complete daze and cried myself to sleep every night. He was the only thing I thought about, dreamt about and talked about. I drove my friends crazy by constantly analyzing the situation. *How could it have ended?* I found my other half when I was with him. I felt like something had been torn from me, like I was no longer whole.

One night, I couldn't stand it. I gave up and called him. I didn't last five minutes before I broke down and started crying. I told him I had forgotten how to be by myself, and that I needed him. I didn't know how to be Lia without Ben. We had been through so much together that I could not imagine getting through this on my own. He told me that he would always care for me, but that it had become impossible to love me.

For weeks I couldn't see him with other girls without thinking that they were dating. I threw myself at different guys.

I don't know at exactly what point things started to change. I began spending time with my friends. I joined clubs and made after-school plans. I was doing all I could to stay busy.

Slowly I began to have fun by myself, without Ben. Beyond that, I discovered things I liked doing, ways I could be of help. I lent a sympathetic ear to others who were hurting.

I began to smile and, finally, to laugh again. Whole days would pass without a thought of Ben. I would see him at school and wave. I was not ready to be friends with him. I was still healing. But I know I didn't cover a big wound with a Band-Aid and forget about it. I let the wound heal itself and felt enough pain to know that I had truly cared for him.

In my rebound stage, I pursued a lot of guys. Once I healed, they pursued me. The wonderful thing that happened was that I learned how to be a whole person, not half a couple. I'm in a new relationship now, and eventually we will probably break up, and it will be hard, and I will cry and feel just as much, if not more, pain. But I had to ask myself if never caring for someone so that I wouldn't feel that hurt was worth it. I know now that the famous quote is true. "Better to have loved and lost than never to have loved at all." Because no matter what, loving yourself can heal anything.

Lia Gay

"This is the '90s. You can't just dump your boyfriend
anymore. You have to recycle him."

After a While

After a while you learn the subtle difference between
    holding a hand and chaining a soul,
And you learn that love doesn't mean leaning and
    company doesn't mean security,
And you begin to learn that kisses aren't contracts
    and presents aren't promises,
And you begin to accept your defeats with your head
    up and your eyes open, with the grace of an adult,
    not the grief of a child,
And you learn to build all your roads on today
    because tomorrow's ground is too uncertain for
    plans.
After a while you learn that even sunshine burns if
    you get too much.
So plant your own garden and decorate your own
    soul, instead of waiting for someone to bring you
    flowers.
And you learn that you really can endure . . .
    that you really are strong,
    and you really do have worth.
And you learn and you learn . . .
    with every good-bye you learn. . . .

Veronica A. Shoffstall
written at age 19

Soul Mates

I have often told my daughter, Lauren, the story of how her father and I met and of our courtship. Now that she is sixteen years old, she is concerned because she realizes that her soul mate might be sitting next to her in a class or might even ask her for a date, and she is not quite ready to make the same commitment her parents made years ago.

I met Mike on October 9, 1964. Our shy eyes met from across the patio at our friend Andrea's party. We smiled and eventually found ourselves in a conversation that lasted the entire evening, to the exclusion of everyone else. I was eleven and he was twelve. We went steady three days later, which ended after a somewhat tumultuous month.

Months later, Mike still invited me to his lavish bar mitzvah and even asked me to dance. (Years later he told me that despite my braces, my skinny legs and my flipped hair, he thought I was beautiful.)

Mike and I had many mutual friends and were in the same social group at school, so our paths constantly crossed throughout the next few years. Every time I broke up with a boyfriend or had my heart broken by another, my mother would say, "Don't worry, you're going to end up with Mike Leb." I would shriek, "Never! Why would you think such a thing?" She would remind me how his name often came up in my conversations and what a nice guy he was.

Finally, I was in high school, and it was packed with new cute guys. I was ready. What did I care if Mike started dating my best friend? Why, I wondered, was this slowly driving me crazy? Why did we find ourselves talking while waiting for our buses? I will never forget the navy blue penny loafers he wore. Nobody else I knew had such great shoes. My mother's words often came to my mind, but I still wanted to erase them.

By the summer after tenth grade, Mike and I had spent more time together—in the company of his girlfriend, also known as my best friend, and others. That summer Mike left for a Spanish program in Mexico. I found I really missed seeing him. When he returned in August, he called and came by my home. He was so adorable with his tan skin and worldly demeanor. He still couldn't speak a word of Spanish but he looked so good. It was August 19, 1968, when we looked at each other outside my home and realized we had to be together. Of course, we had to wait until after the date I had that night with another guy. I told my date that I was going to start dating Mike so I had to be home early. Mike then told his on-again, off-again girlfriend it was off again for good.

We kept our relationship our little secret until we could proudly announce it at the next party. We walked in late and boldly told all of our friends that we were officially a couple. Not a soul seemed surprised as they uttered "finally."

After graduation from high school, I went away to college. I lasted ten weeks before I transferred to a closer college to be near Mike. On June 18, 1972, we were wed. I was nineteen, and Mike was twenty. We set up our love nest in married housing while we both finished our college degrees. I became a special-education teacher while Mike went on to medical school.

Now, twenty-five years later, I smile at our beautiful daughter, Lauren, and our handsome son, Alex. Although their parents' legacy causes them to look at high school relationships a bit differently, they will never have to worry about their parents saying, "Don't take it so seriously; it's only puppy love."

Fran Leb

My First Kiss, and Then Some

I was a very shy teenager, and so was my first boyfriend. We were high school sophomores in a small town. We had been dating for about six months. A lot of sweaty hand-holding, actually *watching* movies, and talking about nothing in particular. We often came close to kissing—we both knew that we wanted to be kissed—but neither of us had the courage to make the first move.

Finally, while sitting on my living room couch, he decided to go for it. We talked about the weather (really), then he leaned forward. I put a pillow up to my face to block him! He kissed the pillow.

I wanted to be kissed sooooo badly, but I was too nervous to let him get close. So I moved away, down the couch. He moved closer. We talked about the movie (who cared!), he leaned forward again. I blocked him again.

I moved to the end of the couch. He followed, we talked. He leaned . . . I stood up! (I must have had a spasm in my legs.) I walked over near the front door and stood there, leaning against the wall with my arms crossed, and said impatiently, "Well, are you going to kiss me or not?"

"Yes", he said. So I stood tall, closed my eyes tight, puckered my lips and faced upwards. I waited . . . and waited. (Why wasn't he kissing me?) I opened my eyes; he was coming right at me. I smiled.

HE KISSED MY TEETH!

I could have died.

He left.

I wondered if he had told anyone about my clumsy behavior. Since I was so extremely and painfully shy, I practically hid for the next two years, causing me to never have another date all through high school. As a matter of fact, when I walked down the hallway at school, if I saw him or any other great guy walking toward me, I quickly stepped into the nearest room until he passed. And these were boys I had known since kindergarten.

The first year at college, I was determined not to be shy any longer. I wanted to learn how to kiss with confidence and grace. I did.

In the spring, I went home. I walked into the latest hangout, and who do you suppose I see sitting at the bar, but my old kissing partner. I walked over to his bar stool and tapped him on the shoulder. Without hesitation, I took him in my arms, dipped him back over his stool, and kissed him with my most assertive kiss. I sat him up, looked at him victoriously, and said, "So there!"

He pointed to the lady next to him and said to me, "Mary Jane, I'd like you to meet my wife."

Mary Jane West-Delgado

Changes in Life

I was sixteen years old and a junior in high school, and the worst possible thing that could happen to me did. My parents decided to move our family from our Texas home to Arizona. I had two weeks to wrap up all of my "business" and move before school began. I had to leave my first job, my boyfriend and my best friend behind, and try to start a new life. I despised my parents for ruining my life.

I told everyone that I did not want to live in Arizona and would be returning to Texas the first chance I had. When I arrived in Arizona, I made sure everyone knew that I had a boyfriend and best friend waiting for me in Texas. I was determined to keep my distance from everyone; I would just be leaving soon anyway.

The first day of school came, and I was miserable. I could only think of my friends in Texas and how I wished I could be with them. For a while, I felt that my life was over. Eventually though, things got a little better.

It was in my second period accounting class where I first saw him. He was tall, trim and really good looking. He had the most beautiful blue eyes I had ever seen. He was sitting just three seats away from me in the same front row of class. Feeling I had nothing to lose, I decided to talk to him.

"Hi, my name is Sheila; what's yours?" I asked with a Texas drawl.

The guy next to him thought that I was asking *him*. "Mike."

"Oh, hi, Mike," I humored him. "What's your name?" I asked again, focusing my attention on this blue-eyed boy.

He looked behind him, not believing that I could be asking him for his name. "Chris," he responded quietly.

"Hi, Chris!" I smiled. Then I went about my work.

Chris and I became friends. We enjoyed talking to each other in class. Chris was a jock, and I was in the school band; in high school, peer pressure demanded that the two groups did not mix socially. Our paths crossed occasionally at school functions; but for the most part, our friendship remained within the four classroom walls of accounting class.

Chris graduated that year, and we went our separate ways for a while. Then one day, he came to see me while I was working in a store in the mall. I was very happy to see him. He went on my breaks with me, and we started talking again. The pressure from his jock friends had subsided, and we became very close friends. My relationship with my boyfriend in Texas had become less important to me. I felt my bond with Chris growing stronger, taking the place of my relationship in Texas.

It had been a year since I moved from Texas, and Arizona was starting to feel like home. Chris escorted me to my senior prom; we triple-dated with two of his jock friends and their dates. The night of my prom changed our relationship forever; I was accepted by his friends, and that made Chris feel more comfortable. Finally, our relationship was in the open.

Chris was a very special person to me during such a difficult time in my life. Our relationship eventually blossomed into a very powerful love. I now understand that my parents did not move the family to Arizona to hurt me, although at the time, it sure felt as though they had. I now firmly believe that everything happens for a reason. For had I not moved to Arizona, I never would have met the man of my dreams.

Sheila K. Reyman

First Love

Truly loving another means letting go of all expectations. It means full acceptance, even celebration of another's personhood.

Karen Casey

Michael and I were never really boyfriend and girl-friend. He was three-and-a-half years older than I, which was a lot when I still didn't need to wear a bathing suit top. We grew up around the pool and tennis courts of a country club. He was an excellent tennis player with sure, calm strides and a powerful stroke. When I had to take time out from swimming and diving because my lips had turned blue, I sat on the grass wrapped in a towel and watched the tennis matches. Later in the day, the guys would come to the pool and hoist the girls on their shoulders for water fights. I liked it best on Michael's shoulders, which were broad. I felt safe.

At sixteen his parents allowed him to drive during the day, and he often brought me home in his gray Dodge. The autumn after I turned fourteen, he started asking if I wanted to go to a late-afternoon movie with him. I wanted to say yes, but then I would get this jumpy feeling in my stomach and always change my mind. His dark eyes looked into mine, both pleasing and frightening me.

Gradually I stayed longer in his car, talking about things that troubled me. My older sister had lots of boyfriends, and although I worshipped her, she mostly didn't want anything to do with me. Then there were the intrigues around who was dating whom and which friends I trusted and why. A lot of my pain centered around my relationship with my parents, who had divorced when I was eleven and remarried when I was thirteen. I didn't know anyone else with a broken family, and I felt ashamed and unsure of myself, like I wasn't as good as the other kids. I could talk with Michael about all this. He was reassuring, and I began to trust him.

As time passed, I was ready to go to the movies with him. We also enjoyed hanging out at my house, where we would go down to the television room in the basement. I loved to watch TV with Michael so that I could cuddle with him on the couch. We were a strange pair. He loved sports, while I loved the arts. My sister and others made fun of his sports obsession. I guess I would have preferred it if everyone thought he was cool or if he'd been more artistic, but no one else cared about me the way he did. When he kissed me for the first time, we were at his house during a thunderstorm, watching a baseball game on television. I ran up to my sister's room when I got home. I must have looked goofy as I stood in her doorway and announced, "Michael kissed me."

"So?" she said. "Was that the first time?"

"Yeah," I nodded.

"What have you guys been doing all this time?" she demanded.

Michael dated other girls, and I went out with other boys. But I hated their sweaty palms and was horrified when a blind date tried to put his tongue in my mouth. Only Michael understood that I needed to move slowly, and he was always very patient with me. Even though Michael reassured me many times that our relationship was special by saying, "It doesn't matter whether or not I have a girlfriend or you have a boyfriend; I will always be there for you," I still got jealous when I saw him interested in someone else.

Michael got engaged to a girl from out of town when I was nineteen. I was the only unmarried, unrelated girl at the wedding. As the bride and groom said good-bye to everyone, Michael came over to me and kissed me on the cheek. "I love you," he said.

He remained true to his word. When I needed to talk to someone, he was there. I got jealous sometimes when I thought of him loving and being romantic with his wife, but that changed as she and I became friends. I moved across the country and only saw Michael occasionally, at the club when I returned to visit my family. Now we sat at the pool and watched his kids swimming. Our lives were very different. I thought I probably wouldn't have much more than a half hour's worth of conversation to share with him, but I always felt a current of love go through me when I saw him.

When I was thirty-eight, my father died. The morning before his funeral, I thought to myself, *I wonder if Michael knows.* We hadn't seen each other or spoken for years. After theservice the next day, as I was talking with the many friends and family who had come for the funeral, I felt a hand on my shoulder. I turned and saw those dark eyes.

"Are you all right?" he asked. I nodded. Putting both hands on my shoulders, he held me, looking into my eyes.

No one had ever understood the bond between us. I'm not sure that we did. But it was, and will always be, there.

Mary Ellen Klee

A High School Love Not Forgotten

When they saw him walking across our high school campus, most students couldn't help but notice Bruce. Tall and lanky, he was a thinner replica of James Dean, his hair flipped back above his forehead, and his eyebrows always cocked upward when he was in deep conversation. He was tender, thoughtful and profound. He would never hurt anyone.

I was scared of him.

I was just breaking up with my not-so-smart boyfriend, the one you stayed with and went back to thirty times out of bad habit, when Bruce headed me off at a campus pass one morning to walk with me. He helped me carry my books and made me laugh a dozen times with giddiness. I liked him. I really liked him.

He scared me because he was brilliant. But in the end, I realized I was more scared of myself than of him.

We started to walk together more at school. I would peer up at him from my stuffed locker, my heart beating rapidly, wondering if he would ever kiss me. We'd been seeing each other for several weeks and he still hadn't tried to kiss me.

Instead, he'd hold my hand, put his arm around me and send me off with one of my books to class. When I opened it, a handwritten note in his highly stylized writing would be there, speaking of love and passion in a deeper sense than I could understand at seventeen.

He would send me books, cards, notes, and would sit with me at my house for hours listening to music. He especially liked me to listen to the song, "You Brought Some Joy Inside My Tears," by Stevie Wonder.

At work one day I received a card from him that said, "I miss you when I'm sad. I miss you when I'm lonely. But most of all, I miss you when I'm happy."

I remember walking down the street of our small village, cars honking, the warm lights from stores beckoning strollers to come in from the cold, and all I could think about was, "Bruce misses me most when he's happy. What a strange thing."

I felt deeply uncomfortable to have such a romantic spirit by my side, a boy—really a man at seventeen—who thought his words out wisely, listened to every side of an argument, read poetry deep into the night and weighed his decisions carefully. I sensed a deep sadness in him but couldn't understand it. Looking back, I now think the sadness stemmed from being a person who really didn't fit into the high school plan.

Our relationship was so different from the one I'd had with my prior boyfriend. Our lives had been mostly movies and popcorn and gossip. We broke up routinely and dated other people. At times, it seemed like the whole campus was focused on the drama of our breakups, which were always intense and grand entertainment for our friends to discuss. A good soap opera.

I talked to Bruce about these things and with each story, he'd respond by putting his arm around me and telling me he'd wait while I sorted things out. And then he would read to me. He gave me the book *The Little Prince*, with the words underlined, "It's only in thy mind's eye that one can see rightly."

In response—the only way I knew how—I wrote passionate letters of love and poetry to him with an intensity I never knew before. But still I kept my walls up, keeping him at bay because I was always afraid that he'd discover I was fake, not nearly as intelligent or as deep a thinker as I found him to be.

I wanted the old habits of popcorn, movies and gossip back. It was so much easier. I remember well the day when Bruce and I stood outside in the cold and I told him I was going back to my old boyfriend. "He needs me more," I said in my girlish voice. "Old habits die hard."

Bruce looked at me with sadness, more for me than himself. He knew, and I knew then, I was making a mistake.

Years went by. Bruce went off to college first; then I did. Every time I came home for Christmas, I looked him up and went over for a visit with him and his family. I always loved his family—the warm greetings they gave me when they ushered me into their house, always happy to see me. I knew just by the way his family behaved that Bruce had forgiven me for my mistake.

One Christmas, Bruce said to me: "You were always a good writer. You were so good."

"Yes." His mother nodded in agreement. "You wrote beautifully. I hope you'll never give up your writing."

"But how do you know my writing?" I asked his mom.

"Oh, Bruce shared all the letters you wrote him with me," she said. "He and I could never get over how beautifully you wrote."

Then I saw his father's head nod, too. I sank back in my chair and blushed deeply. What exactly had I written in those letters?

I never knew Bruce had admired my writing as much as I had his intelligence.

Over the years, we lost touch. The last I heard from his father, Bruce had gone off to San Francisco and was thinking about becoming a chef. I went through dozens of bad relationships until I finally married a wonderful man—also very smart. I was more mature by then and could handle my husband's intelligence—especially when he'd remind me I had my own.

There's not one other boyfriend I ever think about with any interest, except for Bruce. Most of all, I hope he is happy. He deserves it. In many ways, I think he helped shape me, helped me learn how to accept the side of myself I refused to see amid movies, popcorn and gossip. He taught me how to see my spirit and my writer inside.

Diana L. Chapman

Starlight, Star Bright

When I was five years old, I took an extreme liking to my sister's toys. It made little difference that I had a trunk overflowing with dolls and toys of my own. Her "big girl" treasures were much easier to break, and much more appealing. Likewise, when I was ten and she was twelve, the earrings and make-up that she was slowly being permitted to experiment with held my attention, while my former obsession with catching bugs seemed to be a distant and fading memory.

It was a trend that continued year by year and, except for a few bruises and threats of terrifying "haircuts" while I was sleeping, one that my sister handled with tolerance. My mother continually reminded her, as I entered junior high wearing her new hair clips, that it was actually a compliment to her sense of style. She told her, as I started my first day of high school wearing her clothes, that one day she would laugh and remind me of how she was always the cooler of the two of us.

I had always thought that my sister had good taste, but never more than when she started bringing home guys. I had a constant parade of sixteen-year-old boys going through my house, stuffing themselves with food in the kitchen, or playing basketball on the driveway.

I had recently become very aware that boys, in fact, weren't as "icky" as I had previously thought, and that maybe their cooties weren't such a terrible thing to catch after all. But the freshman guys who were my age, whom I had spent months giggling over at football games with my friends, suddenly seemed so young. They couldn't drive and they didn't wear varsity jackets. My sister's friends were tall, they were funny, and even though my sister was persistent in getting rid of me quickly, they were always nice to me as she pushed me out the door.

Every once in a while I would luck out, and they would stop by when she wasn't home. One in particular would have long conversations with me before leaving to do whatever sixteen-year-old boys did (it was still a mystery to me). He talked to me as he talked to everyone else, not like a kid, not like his friend's little sister . . . and he always hugged me good-bye before he left.

It wasn't surprising that before long I was positively giddy about him. My friends told me I had no chance with a junior. My sister looked concerned for my potentially broken heart. But you can't help who it is that you fall in love with, whether they are older or younger, taller or shorter, completely opposite or just like you. Emotion ran me over like a Mack truck when I was with him, and I knew that it was too late to try to be sensible—I was in love.

It did not mean I didn't realize the possibility of being rejected. I knew that I was taking a big chance with my feelings and pride. If I didn't give him my heart there was no possibility that he would break it . . . but there was also no chance that he might not.

One night before he left, we sat on my front porch talking and looking for stars as they became visible. He looked at me quite seriously and asked me if I believed in wishing on stars. Surprised, but just as serious, I told him I had never tried.

"Well, then it's time you start," he said, and pointed to the sky. "Pick one out and wish for whatever you want the most." I looked and picked out the brightest star I could find. I squeezed my eyes shut and with what felt like an entire colony of butterflies in my stomach, I wished for courage. I opened my eyes and saw him smiling as he watched my tremendous wishing effort. He asked what I had wished for, and when I replied, he looked puzzled. "Courage? For what?" he questioned.

I took one last deep breath and replied, "To do this." And I kissed him—all driver's-license-holding, varsity-jacket-wearing, sixteen years of him. It was bravery I didn't know I had, strength I owed completely to my heart, which gave up on my mind and took over.

When I pulled back, I saw the astonished look in his face, a look that turned into a smile and then laughter. After searching for something to say for what seemed to me like hours, he took my hand and said, "Well, I guess we're lucky tonight. Both our wishes came true."

Kelly Garnett

Seven Minutes in Heaven

People say you change many times in the course of your teenage years, and that your time in school will teach you lessons you will never forget. I think they were referring to classrooms and football fields, but one of my greatest learning experiences began in a parking lot. It was as I was waiting to be picked up one day that I met my first girlfriend.

Her name was Brittany. She was pretty, outgoing and two years older than I was—it seemed too good to be true that she was interested in me—but not long after we met, we became an official couple. At our age, "going out" meant that we talked on the phone every night, and saw each other at school in between classes. We never really had a lot of opportunity to see each other or get to know one another very well. But, never having been in a relationship before, I thought that this was what they were like. It didn't seem like a big deal that we weren't that close, that I didn't get butterflies in my stomach when I saw her.

Not long after we got together, she called me and told me that she was going to a party with some friends, and that she wanted me to go with her. I said I would, and waited somewhat nervously that night for her to pick me up. When the small car packed with teenagers arrived, I squeezed in and wondered what I was getting myself into.

An hour into the party, I was feeling less self-conscious and a lot more comfortable. Though the people at the party were all older than me, they were people I knew, or had seen around school. It all seemed innocent enough— we just sat around eating popcorn, watching a movie and having a good time—until the movie ended.

Someone suggested a game of "Spin the Bottle," and my heart began to beat a little faster. *It can't be that bad,* I thought to myself. *It's just kissing even if it is in front of a bunch of other people.* But after a while, some people wanted to take the game a little further. I heard somebody say "Seven Minutes in Heaven," and everyone answered "Yes!" with knowing smiles. I had no idea what it was, and looked at Brittany for help, but she just smiled and agreed that it was a good idea.

After the first few couples spent their seven minutes in heaven, I figured out what the object of the game was— going into a closet and kissing. My stomach flip-flopped and I felt dizzy as I waited for the inevitable, when it would be my turn with Brittany. I was scared. I had no experience with this kind of thing, and I was about to jump into it head first with a girl two years older than I was. I didn't know what she expected, or what she would tell the other older kids when we got out. I could see a sad reputation of being a lame boyfriend looming in the near future.

I really didn't have a lot of time to think about it, because our turn came, and Brittany pulled me after her into the closet. As it turned out, she was an experienced kisser—I didn't have time to think, or react, she just kind of took over. I was relieved and glad when it was over. When she took me home later, neither one of us said much. I don't know what she was thinking about, but I was still trying to let everything sink in. It wasn't as much fun as I had thought it would be—there was no romance or feeling in it.

It was never talked about, but in the weeks that followed the party, my relationship with Brittany slowly ended, and I returned to doing normal things with kids my own age. I thought it was strange that I didn't feel sad about it. It was almost a relief to not have to worry about another party or situation where I would feel out of my league.

I was at the beach with friends several months later when I started talking to a girl. As we talked, I realized I was strangely happy just listening to her and watching her smile while she told me about her life. There was something about her that made me enjoy just being with her. With no thoughts of what it meant, I knew I wanted to see her again so we planned to meet the following week, same time, same place.

I was completely comfortable as we sat on a blanket that night filling each other in on the events of the long week that preceded our reunion. We sat next to the bonfire and laughed, and suddenly, I wanted to kiss her . . . and I did. A pure, sweet, innocent kiss, one that made me feel warm and happy. And though it was nowhere near seven minutes, it was definitely a piece of heaven.

Andrew Keegan
As told to Kimberly Kirberger

Practical Application

He's teaching her arithmetic,
He said it was his mission,
He kissed her once, he kissed her twice and said,
"Now that's addition."
And as he added smack by smack
In silent satisfaction,
She sweetly gave the kisses back and said,
"Now that's subtraction."

Then he kissed her, she kissed him,
Without an explanation,
And both together smiled and said,
"That's multiplication."
Then Dad appeared upon the scene and
Made a quick decision.
He kicked that kid three blocks away
And said, "That's long division!"

Dan Clark

A Geek, a Nerd, a Bookworm

Love is not what we become, but what we already are.

Stephen Levine

Stand straight, shoulders back, chin up, eyes forward, smile, I mumbled to myself. No, it was an impossible task. I put my glasses back on and slouched into my usual character. I immediately regretted this decision as I slid discreetly into my desk. His eyes did not even flicker at my entrance. Clearing my throat in an effort to be acknowledged seemed hopeless.

As I pulled out my organized binder neatly labeled "History," I stole a glance at him as he sat at the desk beside me. He appeared just as he had in my dream last night: flawless. Everything about him was right—his smile, the way a strand of hair always fell in his eyes and, oh, those eyes. He must have felt me staring because suddenly, he turned and looked at me. I quickly dropped my gaze back to my binder and pretended to be intently interested in finding a worksheet. I didn't dare peek to see if he was still studying me. Instead, I shifted my eyes toward the window. The light from the sun made me squint.

Ironically, I'm spending my summer in school. I didn't fail this class, unlike every other student here. I just have an incredible yearning to learn and want to get the most out of my high school career. More simply put, I am a geek. A nerd. A bookworm.

Out of the corner of my eye, I caught his hand ready to tap my shoulder. Every muscle in my body tensed. His touch was so light that I barely felt his fingers. I faced him with my eyes fixated on the tiled floor. I could not bring myself to look at him. In that instant, I just didn't feel worthy.

"The homework, from last night—did you finish it?"

Of course I finished it! I also finished tonight's assignment. Don't you know who I am? I am only the single most intelligent person in this school. Every night of the week, I spend countless hours in front of a computer screen. The force behind me is pushing me with an even greater force. Someday, I will be so far in the land of outcasts that I will want to carouse with my laptop. No, I have not entered that kingdom yet. For now, I am content knowing that there is something I don't know—what you are thinking right this second.

I cleared my throat. "Yes, I did the homework."

"Well, I was a little stumped on question thirteen. Do you know the answer?" With one smooth movement he put his pencil behind his ear.

"Me," I said.

"What? You are the answer?" he asked, confused.

"Uh, no." I could feel my cheeks burning. *Ugh! If I am such a brain, how did I just make such an error? I have practiced what I would say to him a thousand times over.* Supposedly, the conversation would lead to an invitation for a rendezvous. He would laugh at my wit and think that no one was more interesting than I.

I took a deep breath. "Franklin Roosevelt's Brain Trust."

"Thanks," he said, taking the pencil from behind his ear. I watched him sloppily jot down the answer and turn from his worksheet to the blond behind him. He tried to impress her by using his humor. She barely chuckled. I would have laughed uproariously. But then I remembered that the joke was not intended for me. I studied her body motions as she leaned forward toward him, twirling strands of her hair around her finger. Any closer and their noses would have touched. I nonchalantly pushed my pencil off the desk.

Distracted, he shifted his attention from her eyes to the floor. He bent down and picked up the pencil that was half gnawed by my nerves. He came up, his nose closer to mine than hers had been to his. My hand brushed against his as I reached for the pencil. Goosebumps ran down my arms and my heart raced. Never before had he shown so much interest.

As if that moment were just a figment of his imagination, without a word, he turned back to his beauty queen. Disappointed, I hunched forward and leaned on my hand, watching in awe as she brought out her lip balm. With much exaggeration, she moistened her lips and pressed them together firmly. He couldn't take those perfect eyes off her. I wanted to scream and shake him and make him wake up. This girl is a complete flake! Behind her beauty queen exterior is wasted, empty space.

Someday we will save each other, I silently vowed. *In an unconventional way, we are similar. Both of us are in dire need of being rescued from a fantasy world. This alone is grounds for building a relationship.*

Tonight I could go to Wal-Mart and buy hair dye and lip balm. Or maybe search around the mall until I found the halter top she was wearing. I should take advantage of the summer weather and get a bronze skin tone. Instead, I will end up doing homework.

No, tonight I will practice: practice standing straight, shoulders back, chin up and smiling. Then maybe tomorrow, he will ask me for the answer to number twelve . . . and my name.

Kimberly Russell

My Angel Has a Halo

You always were a daredevil. Flying eight or more feet through the air on your bike (your pride and joy), swinging high on a rope swing or flipping head first into the lake below.

I think that is what gives you both your wonderful character and your extraordinary inner strength. What amazes me most about you is the fact that no matter what, your determination pushes all your fears away. You never let fear stand in the way of accomplishing your goals.

But despite all your dangerous stunts, I never thought that this day would come. (Maybe in the back of my mind I did, but only there.)

You were away on a trip to the coast and I eagerly awaited your call. It came the morning of the third day of the seven days you'd be gone. Your voice was normal—but your words were not—"I broke my neck."

Right then every fear in the world hit me. My mom quickly reminded me that I needed to stay strong for you. I didn't talk much. I just quietly cried as you explained to me your ordeal and the halo you would have to wear for two months to keep your neck stabilized as it healed.

You seemed okay considering the situation, but in pain

and in low spirits. I hung up the phone and finally the tears could, and did, flow freely. Throughout this whole day I came to terms with the fact that you would be in a cast, with the exception of your arms, for two entire months. At first I was selfish and thought of how this would affect me. *He can't drive, so we'll see each other less often. He can't take me to school on the first day. I can't even give him a real hug.* But then I remembered and told myself: *Amanda, be glad that he's still alive and here for you to hug at all, no matter what form it's in. And be thankful for the fact that he can walk.*

I went and saw you tonight. You looked good but no smiles—no smiles, that is, until you saw a video of your biking stunts. I saw the determination in your eyes and it brought tears to mine. I know you're scared, but I also know that you're going to be okay. Because that determination inside of you is once again going to push those fears away, and you'll be 110 percent. You helped me be less afraid for you. I stopped thinking about what you cannot do and concentrated instead on what you can do, or what you will do again. Two months is a very short time in exchange for a lifetime of living.

I want to thank you. You have taught me more about inner strength and determination in this one day than I've learned in my whole life. I love you, Logan. We all do. Don't ever lose heart. Just let your wonderful self shine through. You're going to pull through this with flying colors, pushing yourself all the way, because that's who you are: a fighter. I feel so much better now that I'm not thinking about what I won't have and what I won't get from you. Instead, I feel grateful and so happy that you are who you are.

All I have for you now is faith and determination. I always knew that you were a blessing to me, my angel. Now, for two months, you'll have a halo to prove it.

Amanda Johnson

A Cool Drink of Water

After brushing my teeth, I stooped to drink the cool water streaming from the faucet, drifting back to that unforgettable summer. It was the summer when life began—the summer I turned sixteen. I had my own car, along with a brand-new soul. It was not the memory of a new privilege that rushed back to me, but that of him looming over me with a laughing grin painted across his lips as he watched me drink from the faucet. It was that memory that rushed back to me.

Our relationship was everything it should have been, almost as if our time together had been written for a novel. We came together through friends of ours, as do most typical high school relationships. We grew closer and closer during the school year, spending time together on weeknights rehearsing for the school's musical production and on the weekends with friends. Soon, with permission from the weather and sometimes despite it, we traveled to the beach with our friends and a cooler of colas. It was on the way home from the beach one Saturday that I realized I was falling for him. Every sign showed love. I could hardly sit still in class just anticipating the next time I would see him and the upcoming weekend we would spend together. Being in his arms were some of the happiest times I had ever experienced. I could look deep into his eyes and be enchanted forever.

Being with him changed my soul. I shared everything with him, even things I kept from my family and my best friend. I felt his love prying apart the hard shell of shyness that encircled me. His trust, his love and his support for me lifted me from the earth and gently sent me into the clouds. He cast off the chains I had given myself. Through him I learned a new insight about the world. It was as if a tall, dark mountain had stood in front of me and, out of nowhere, he provided the wings to fly over it.

Unfortunately, all good things must come to an end. Yes, even for my first love. I had matured a great deal during our time together, which possibly brought me to a clearer understanding of what true love is. Over time, the clouds floated away, replaced with a new sinking feeling that what I was doing was wrong. The eyes that had so lovingly enchanted me soon became those of a dear friend. Somehow, the spell was broken. I wished so dearly that I could return to the long summer nights we had spent together, embracing under the moonlight. But as I longed for those nights, I also longed for a new freedom. The adventure had somehow become a routine.

Sadly, we both acknowledged the separation. We held each other tighter than ever, both roughly accepting the reality that it would be best to say good-bye. He wiped away my tears and held me until it was time for him to leave. My heart was yearning to kiss him good-bye, but my mind and my lips told me no. He walked down the stairs to his black convertible and left. I watched through tear-stained eyes from the window as he pulled out of my driveway. As his headlights faded in the distance, I turned off the light to my first love.

Having satisfied my thirst, I stood up and dried my mouth and chin with the towel at my side. I smiled, once again remembering how he stood by me and protected me in more ways than one. It is impossible to sum up seven-and-one-half months of pure joy and apprentice-ship, but if there is one way to do it, a cool drink of water from the faucet would be sufficient.

Camden Watts

"He gave me a copy of *The Declaration of Independence*, then he got a tattoo that says *Give Me Liberty Or Give Me Death*. I think my boyfriend wants his freedom."

Reprinted by permission of Randy Glasbergen.

Unrequited Love

Nothing spoils the taste of peanut butter like unrequited love.

Charlie Brown
from Peanuts *by Charles Schulz*

"Guess what?"

I look at Sarah, my best friend since halfway through second grade. We've been through this routine before, and both of us know what's coming. "What?" I ask. I really don't like guessing.

We're walking home together after school. We usually do. It's freezing.

"Guess," she prompts me.

I study her face and then think for a second. What could be making her so happy? "You got another A in biology?"

"Nope."

"Your sister dropped dead?" I suggest.

"I wish," she replies, but shakes her head. "Guess again!"

"Just *tell* me!" I whine.

Her smile grows even broader, and I can see all her braces-covered teeth. "Xander kissed me."

My jaw drops and I turn to her. "Get out!" I gasp. I hit her shoulder. "Don't tell me stuff like that!" But then curiosity gets the better of me, so I meekly ask, "Lips?"

"Cheek."

I hit her shoulder again. "What's wrong with you?" she demands loudly.

I glare at her. I've liked Xander since halfway through eighth grade. Ever since he turned to me one day in class and said, "Alyson, right?" I'd given him my usual witty reply of "Yun-hun." After that we spoke, like, once or twice.

Then this year, Sarah became friends with him and his group. I never used to hang out with Sarah during recess or lunch—her friends were all straight-A students, and I was one of those has-real-potential-but-won't-apply-herself types, so I mostly got Cs. Usually I hung out with my other best friends, Darcy and Mara. But neither Darcy nor Mara had very many friends who were guys, and I wanted some. Sarah did, so I tried to spend lunch with them at least two times a week.

"Why are we still calling him 'Xander'?" she asks, her voice breaking into my thoughts. I look at her, surprised. I had almost forgotten she was there. "No one we know is around here so even if we said his real name, no one would know!"

I shrug. "It's fun."

Xander's name isn't really Xander. I came up with that as a code name for him. All my friends do that. That way they can talk about their crush in front of people and no one will know. I chose to call him "Xander" because I have a deep respect (most people call it an obsession—I can't imagine why) for the TV show *Buffy the Vampire Slayer*. Xander is the name of one of the lead characters. Only three people know that my crush is referred to as "Xander": Sarah, Mara and Darcy. I call him Xander so much, sometimes I think that's his real name. When I talk about him I sometimes have to say "Xander—the untelevised version" so my friends know I'm not talking about Xander from *Buffy the Vampire Slayer*.

"Are you coming with us to see the movie Saturday?" she asks.

I smile. "Is Xander coming?" She gives me a look but says nothing. "Then I'm there!" I say. The last time I went with them to see a movie, I ended up sitting next to Xander. For an hour and forty-three minutes, I thought I'd died and gone to heaven. Okay, maybe heaven is a bit much, but I did feel very, very happy.

But now I think of something and my smile disappears. Nervously I tuck a strand of hair behind my ear. "Sar?"

I begin to crack my knuckles, which I do whenever I'm nervous. Aw, who am I kidding? I crack my knuckles all the time. I really need to stop because it's annoying and it'll give me arthritis when I'm older. "What does he think of me?" I ask.

I hear a click as Sarah turns off her Walkman. I know she'll tell me the truth. Sar isn't the kind of friend who, when you tell her you just messed up in public speaking, says, "I'm sure nobody noticed!" Instead, she'd just laugh. At you. Mockingly. Loudly. So I nervously wait for Sarah to answer.

"He . . . he says you're kinda weird. Like, a depressed, poetry-writing nut. But, like, a nice one," she adds to make it sound better.

"Really?" I sigh, feeling as though fifty midgets have found a way into my chest and have decided to simultaneously perform cartwheels, jumping jacks and handstands on my heart.

"That's a bit harsh," she says. "Look, he likes you—he just thinks you're a bit morbid."

I try to look at the positive, "Nice is good!" I tell her. She nods her head and turns her music back on.

I begin to feel worse every time I think about what Xander had said. "Nice is good," I repeat dejectedly. I stare straight ahead for a moment and then squint because the sun is so bright it hurts my eyes. Nice but insane is probably what he meant. *I am not insane,* I tell myself, *I am depressed. There's a difference.* I kick at a bit of snow on the ground.

"You are not depressed," Mom always tells me. "Right," I reply, "I am just deeply unhappy!" "There is a difference, Alyson," she tells me, then ships me off to therapy.

I pinch Sarah the way she taught me to, back in fifth grade. It's the best way to pinch 'cause it really, really hurts. She squeals and looks at me, annoyed. "What?"

"Am I depressing?"

"Yes, you're negative, morbid, cynical. . . ."

I sigh.

She puts her arm around my shoulders, "But that's why we love you."

I'm also known around school as being depressed. That's not to say I actually *am* depressed. I'm not; I'm a complete and utter sucker for corny, happy endings (I practically live on films like *While You Were Sleeping* and *Addicted to Love*). A movie can be incredible, but if the ending is sad, I'll immediately despise it. But when people want to know about you, they usually ask certain questions, and my answers sometimes feed their "depressed poet" image of me. *Fave color?* Black. *Hobby?* Writing poetry and stories. *Oh, what kind of poetry? Sad?* Usually.

Of course, I don't exactly dissuade them from the tortured writer concept they have of me, because at least I'm known for something. Maybe it's negative, but it's better than nothing, right? So let them think me forlorn. I have my own friends and I don't really care what any of them think. Except *him.* . . .

But a long time ago, I really was depressed. I'd just been dumped by my first boyfriend and felt really crappy. I thought about death and suicide a lot. I know it was dumb, but I'd never been dumped before and it just . . . hurt. That's the only word I could think of to describe it. And I know it sounds clichéd and all, but my heart actually felt as though it had been broken in two. But I got over it (with the help of my therapist, school guidance counselor, my parents and a really long letter to Mara that I never gave her and ended up gluing into my diary). And now when I think of Xander, I feel so miserable. . . .

Sarah and I reach the street where we split. We stop and I turn to her, "This is where I get off," I say. "I'll call ya later," I begin crossing the street.

She continues on. "Alright. Bye!" she calls.

I turn onto my street and look down at the ground. The snow around here is all white and beautiful. It reminds me of cream cheese. Not like the snow in front of our school. That snow is all gray and dirty and yuck. This snow is nice. Nice. Like how he thinks of me. Nice. The chances of Xander ever liking me are about as good as me passing math. I know that!

I giggle. But hey, maybe I'll get a few poems out of this unrequited love thing. Ya think?

Rachel Rosenberg

Starting a New Path

"But I love you, Jessie," he says as we sit on the couch in my living room, his voice quivering and unstable. His pleading eyes look directly into mine, begging my forgiveness. I don't recognize these eyes that once provided me with a sense of comfort and security. The warm blue of his eyes that used to reassure me of a love that would last forever is replaced with a colder gray. I shiver and look away.

Tears cloud my eyes as I feel him breathing next to me on the edge of the couch. My mind wanders to a time a year earlier, a happier time, when I had also been acutely aware of his breathing as we sat in silence on that same couch. My heart had pounded that day as I glanced nervously into his eyes, unable to hold my stare, yet unable to look away. It was that particular day that my heart decided to surrender itself to the magic of first love. And as I sat beside him, overwhelmed by the certainty of my love for him, I struggled to say the words out loud for the first time. I wanted to scream to the world that my heart felt bigger than my whole body, that I was in love and nothing could ever take away that feeling, but no sounds came out of my mouth. As I fidgeted with the edge of a pillow, he gently placed his hand on my arm and looked directly into my eyes. His soft stare soothed my nerves. "I love you, Jessie," he told me, his eyes holding my stare. A small smile formed on my face as my heart began to beat quickly and loudly. He had known that night, just as I had—and he had felt the power of the realization of love, just like I had.

But that power is gone now, I remind myself. That returns me from that distant memory to the present moment like a slap in the face.

"Doesn't it mean anything to you that I love you?" he asks. "Please, I'm so sorry." His hand reaches for my face to brush the hair out of my eyes. I duck my head to avoid his touch. It has become too painful since I found out. He had told me two days before that he had kissed another girl. I had sat in stunned silence, unable to move or speak.

I sit now in silence, not because I don't know what to say, but because I am afraid that my voice will deceive me and begin to quiver. As I start to speak, I look into his eyes and stop myself, wondering if I will be making a mistake. *Maybe it can work,* I think, and I imagine his arms around me, hugging my head tightly to his chest, making everything okay like he had done so often in the past when I was in need of his comfort. Now, more than ever, I ache for the comfort of his arms and for the reassurance of his warm blue gaze. But it is not possible, for the trust is gone and our love has been scarred. His gaze is no longer a warm blue and his arms no longer provide comfort.

Now I struggle to find the words that I know must come out of my mouth, not like before when I knew the words would lead us to a place of magic on the path of our relationship. I now struggle to find the words that will end that path. It's not that my love for him has been taken away, it's just that I know my heart can never again feel bigger than my whole body when I am with him. When he gets up from the couch to leave, the pain in my heart feels too strong to endure, and I have to stop myself from calling after him. I know that I have done the right thing. I know that I am strong, although at this moment I feel anything but strong.

I sit frozen on the couch for a long time after he has left; the only movement in the room is the tears that run down my cheeks and soak the thighs of my jeans. I wonder how I can possibly go on when it feels like half of me is missing. And so I wait. I wait for time to heal the pain and raise me to my feet once again—so that I can start a new path, my own path, the one that will make me whole again.

Jessie Braun

Discovery

My class was two weeks away from the opening night of our play when Sherry walked into my classroom and in a hesitant voice announced that she would have to quit.

Hundreds of reasons for such a declaration rushed through my mind—tragic illness, death in the family, a terrible family crisis.

The expression on my face prompted a further explanation. Sherry stammered, "My boyfriend Dave wants me to quit. The rehearsals are taking too much time away from our being together. I bring him sandwiches after football practice."

Her boyfriend was a football player who later went on to play in the pros. He was the opposite of his brother Dan, who also played on the high school team. While Dan was easygoing, had a terrific sense of humor and was liked by nearly everyone, Dave seemed to always be angry and in need of someone to boss around.

"Sherry," I said, "we're only two weeks from opening. You're outstanding in your role. I'd never be able to replace you."

"Really?" She beamed.

"Really," I said, and I meant it. "Everyone should be

allowed to do the things they are good at. You're a good actress. Dave should realize that. I know you know how much he loves football."

"Yes," she agreed. "But I still have to quit."

"I'll bet you're his best fan."

She measured the words. "I am," she said.

"Has he ever been to a Saturday morning rehearsal to see how good you are?"

"No."

"He should," I told her. "He should be your number one fan."

The next day after sixth hour, my door flew open with a thud. Dave thundered toward me, looking twice as big as his 260 pounds. His arms dangled by his side, his large fists clenched as if around my neck.

He leaned across my desk, veins popping, face red as a beet. "You . . . you . . . you . . ." he stammered.

"Can I help you, Dave?" I asked, hoping that my voice wouldn't shake the way my knees were.

He never got beyond "you" before he turned and stomped out the door. I listened until the heavy footsteps started down the stairs to the first floor.

Sherry did continue with the play, and I can honestly say starred in her art. I also noticed that she smiled more, and I occasionally saw her interacting with other students with a great deal of poise.

Dave, I heard, found another girlfriend.

Eugene E. Beasley

Hopscotch and Tears

I watched the blue Toyota speed down my street and listened to the sound of the diesel engine fade. Tears collected in my eyes and trailed down my cheeks until I could taste them. I couldn't believe what had just happened. Making my way into the house, I quickly ran up the stairs, hoping that my brother wouldn't see the frozen look of terror in my eyes. Luckily that rainy day, his eyes were glued to the TV.

Plopping down on my unmade bed, I buried my face in my pillow. Light sniffles turned into cries, and cries into hysterics. I couldn't bear it; the pain was too strong, and my heart was broken.

We had been seeing each other for three months and two days (not that I had been counting). I had never been so happy. We had brought out the best in each other. But that day he threw it all away, out the window of his rusty blue Toyota, in a speech that still rings in my ears.

"I don't think we should see each other anymore . . ." his voice had trailed off. I wanted to ask him why, I wanted to scream at him, I wanted to hold him, but instead I whispered, "Whatever," afraid to look him in the eyes because I knew I would break down.

I lay there crying all afternoon and into the night, feeling so alone, so upset, so confused. For weeks I cried myself to sleep, but in the morning I'd put a plastic smile on my face to avoid having to talk about it. Everybody saw right through it.

My friends were concerned. I think they thought I would recover sooner than I did.

Even months after the breakup, when I heard a car drive up my street I'd jump up to the window to see if it was him. When the phone rang, a chill of hope would run down my spine. One night as I was cutting out magazine pictures and taping photos on my wall, a car came up my street, but I was too preoccupied to notice that it was the car I'd been listening for over the last two months.

"Chloe, it's me, it's . . ." It was him, calling me to come downstairs! On my way down, my heart was pounding and my thoughts were of a reconciliation. He had seen the error of his ways. When I got outside, there he stood, gorgeous as always.

"Chloe, I came to return your sweater. You left it at my house. . . . Remember?" I had forgotten all about it.

"Of course. Thank you," I lied. I hadn't seen him since the breakup and it hurt—it hurt a lot. I wanted to be able to love him again.

"Well, I guess I'll just see ya around then," he said. Then he was gone. I found myself alone in the darkness, listening to his car speed away. I slowly walked back to my room and continued to tape photos on my wall.

For weeks, I walked around like a zombie. I would stare at myself for hours in the mirror, trying to figure out what was wrong with me, trying to understand what I did wrong, searching for answers within the mirror. I'd talk to Rachel for hours. "Rachel, did you ever realize that when you fall in love, you only end up falling. . . ." I'd say before breaking down in tears. Her comforting words did little but give me a reason to feel sorry for myself.

Pretty soon my sadness turned into madness. I began to hate him and blame him for my troubles, and I believed he had ruined my life. For months I thought only of him.

Then something changed. I understood I had to go on, and every day I grew a little happier. I even began to see someone new!

One day, as I was flipping through my wallet, I came upon a picture of him. I looked at it for a few minutes, reading his face like a book, a book that I knew I had finished and had to put down. I took out the picture and stuck it in a cluttered drawer.

I smiled to myself as I realized I could do the same in my heart. Tuck him away in a special place and move on. I loved, I lost and I suffered. Now it was time to forgive and forget. I forgave myself also, because so much of my pain was feeling like I did something wrong. I know better now.

My mom used to tell me, "Chloe, there are two kinds of people in this world: those that play hopscotch and sing in the shower, and those that lie alone at night with tears in their eyes." What I came to understand is that people have a choice as to which they want to be, and that each of us is a little of both.

That same day, I went outside and played hopscotch with my sister, and that night I sang louder than ever in the shower.

Rebecca Woolf

Inside

Bottled up inside
Are the words I never said,
The feelings that I hide,
The lines you never read.

You can see it in my eyes,
Read it on my face:
Trapped inside are lies
Of the past I can't replace.

With memories that linger—
Won't seem to go away.
Why can't I be happier?
Today's a brand-new day.

Yesterdays are over,
Even though the hurting's not.
Nothing lasts forever,
I must cherish what I've got.

Don't take my love for granted,
For soon it will be gone—
All you ever wanted
Of the love you thought you'd won.

The hurt I'm feeling now
Won't disappear overnight,
But someway, somehow,
Everything will turn out all right,

No more wishing for the past.
It wasn't meant to be.
It didn't seem to last,
So I have to set him free.

Melissa Collette

Lost Love

Love is the extremely difficult realization that something other than oneself is real.

Iris Murdoch

I don't know why I should tell you this. I'm nothing special, nothing out of the ordinary. Nothing has happened to me my whole life that hasn't happened to nearly everybody else on this planet.

Except that I met Rachel.

We met at school. We were locker neighbors, sharing that same smell of fresh notebook paper and molding tennis shoes, with clips of our favorite musicians taped inside our locker doors.

She was beautiful and had that self-assurance that told me she must be going with somebody. Somebody who was somebody in school. Me—I'm struggling, trying to stay on the track team and make good enough grades to get into the college my folks went to when they were my age.

The day I met Rachel, she smiled and said hello. After looking into her warm brown eyes, I just had to get out and run like it was the first and last run of my life. I ran ten miles that day and hardly got winded.

We spent that fall talking and joking about teachers, parents and life in general, and what we were going to do when we graduated. We were both seniors, and it was great to feel like a "top dog" for a while. It turns out she wasn't dating anybody—which was amazing. She'd broken up with somebody on the swim team over the summer and wasn't going out at all.

I never knew you could really talk to somebody—a girl, I mean—the way I talked with her.

So one day my car—it's an old beat-up car my dad bought me because it could never go very fast—wouldn't start. It was one of those gray, chilly fall days, and it looked like rain. Rachel drove up beside me in the school parking lot in her old man's turquoise convertible and asked if she could take me somewhere.

I got in. She was playing the new David Byrne CD and singing along to it. Her voice was pretty, a lot prettier than Byrne's—but then, he's a skinny dude, nothing like Rachel. "So where do you want to go?" she asked, and her eyes had a twinkle like she knew something about me I didn't.

"To the house, I guess," I said, then got up the guts to add, "unless you want to stop by Sonic first."

She didn't answer yes or no, but drove straight to the drive-in restaurant. I got her something to eat and we sat and talked some more. She looked at me with those brown eyes that seemed to see everything I felt and thought. I felt her fingers on my lips and knew I would never feel any more for a girl than I did right then.

We talked and she told me about how she'd come to live in this town, how her dad had been a diplomat in Washington and then retired and wanted her, all of a sudden, to grow up like a small-town girl, but it was too late. She was sophisticated and poised and always seemed to know what to say. Not like me. But she opened up something in me.

She liked me, and suddenly I liked myself.

She pointed to her windshield. "Look," she said, laughing. "We steamed up the windows." In the fading light of day, I suddenly remembered home, parents and my car.

She drove me home and dropped me off with a "See you tomorrow" and a wave. That was enough. I had met the girl of my dreams.

After that day, we started seeing each other, but I wouldn't call them dates. We'd get together to study and always ended up talking and laughing over the same things.

Our first kiss? I wouldn't tell the guys this, because they would think it was funny, but she kissed me first. We were in my house, in the kitchen. Nobody was home. The only thing I could hear was the ticking of the kitchen clock. Oh, yeah, and my heart pounding in my ears like it was going to explode.

It was soft and brief; then she looked deep in my eyes and kissed me again, and this time it wasn't so soft and not so brief, either. I could smell her and touch her hair, and right then I knew I could die and be happy about it.

"See you tomorrow," she said then, and started to walk out the door. I couldn't say anything. I just looked at her and smiled.

We graduated and spent the summer swimming and hiking and fishing and picking berries and listening to her music. She had everything from R&B to hard rock, and even the classics like Vivaldi and Rachmaninoff. I felt alive like I never had before. Everything I saw and smelled and touched was new.

We were lying on a blanket in the park one day, looking up at the clouds, the radio playing old jazz. "We have to leave each other," she said. "It's almost time for us to go to college." She rolled over on her belly and looked at me.

"Will you miss me? Think of me, ever?" and for a nano-second I thought I saw some doubt, something unlike her usual self-assurance, in her eyes.

I kissed her and closed my eyes so I could sense only her, the way she smelled and tasted and felt. Her hair blew against my cheek in the late summer breeze. "You are me," I said. "How can I miss myself?"

But inside, it was like my guts were being dissected. She was right; every day that passed meant we were that much closer to being apart.

We tried to hold on then, and act like nothing was going to happen to change our world. She didn't talk about shopping for new clothes to take with her; I didn't talk about the new car my dad had bought for me because that would be what I drove away in. We kept acting like summer was going to last forever, that nothing would change us or our love. And I know she loved me.

It's nearly spring now. I'll be a college sophomore soon. Rachel never writes.

She said that we should leave it at that—whatever that meant. And her folks bought a house in Virginia, so I know she's not coming back here.

I listen to music more now, and I always look twice when I see a turquoise convertible, and I notice more things, like the color of the sky and the breeze as it blows through the trees.

She is me, and I am her. Wherever she is, she knows that. I'm breathing her breath and dreaming her dreams, and when I run now, I run an extra mile for Rachel.

Robby Smith
As told to T. J. Lacey

Why Guys Like Girls

One day while reading my e-mails, I came across one of those that you have to scroll down for an eternity just to get to the letter part because it is sent to hundreds of people.

Well, normally, I automatically delete those. But this one intrigued me. It was titled, "A Few Reasons Why Guys Like Girls." The instructions were to read it, add to it and then forward it to at least twenty-five people. If you did not forward it, you would have bad luck with relationships, but if you did send it to twenty-five people or more, you would be the lucky winner of romantic bliss.

After reading the reasons why guys like girls, I had an idea. If I could attain romantic bliss by sending this e-mail to twenty-five people, imagine how lucky I'd be if I sent it to millions. My husband and I are looking forward to marital perfection thanks to each and every one of you who reads this.*

[*References to chain letter results are not meant to be taken seriously.]

A Few Reasons Why Guys Like Girls

1. *They always smell good, even if it's just shampoo*
2. *The way their heads always find the right spot on your shoulder*
3. *The ease with which they fit into your arms*
4. *The way they kiss you and all of a sudden everything is right in the world*
5. *How cute they are when they eat*
6. *The way they take hours to dress, but in the end it's all worthwhile*
7. *Because they are always warm, even when it's minus thirty degrees outside*
8. *The way they look good no matter what they wear*
9. *The way they fish for compliments*
10. *How cute they are when they argue*
11. *The way their hands always find yours*
12. *The way they smile*
13. *The way you feel when you see their names on the caller ID after you just had a big fight*
14. *The way they say "Let's not fight anymore," even though you know an hour later . . .*
15. *The way they kiss when you do something nice for them*
16. *The way they kiss you when you say "I love you"*
17. *Actually, just the way they kiss you . . .*
18. *The way they fall into your arms when they cry*
19. *Then the way they apologize for crying over something silly*
20. *The way they hit you and expect it to hurt*
21. *Then the way they apologize when it does hurt (even though we don't admit it)*
22. *The way they say, "I miss you"*
23. *The way you miss them*
24. *The way their tears make you want to change the world so that it doesn't hurt them anymore*

*Yet regardless of whether you love them, hate them,
wish they would die or know that you would die without them . . . it matters not. Because once they come into
your life, whatever they are to the world, they become
everything to you. When you look them in the eyes,
traveling to the depths of their souls, and you say a million things without a trace of a sound, you know that
your own life is inevitably consumed within the rhyth-
mic beatings of their very hearts.*

*We love them for a million reasons. It is a thing not
of the mind but of the heart. A feeling. Only felt.*

Compiled by Kimberly Kirberger

"Everything about girls makes me really,
really nervous. I flunked my algebra test because
algebra has the word 'bra' in it!"

Reprinted by permission of Randy Glasbergen.

Why Girls Like Guys

In *Chicken Soup for the Teenage Soul II*, we included "A Few Reasons Why Guys Like Girls." We thought it would be fun to keep the momentum going for this book, so we asked you write to us with more reasons "Why Guys Like Girls" or even "Why Girls Like Guys." And write you did! We had such a good time reading all the imaginative and entertaining responses you came up with.

Since we heard from the guys for *Teen II*, we thought we'd let the girls have their say for this book. The following is a compilation of the sweetest lists we received from the girls:

A Few Reasons Why Girls Like Guys

1. *They always wear your favorite cologne (which happens to be the one that you bought them for their birthday)*
2. *The way they run their fingers through your hair*
3. *That look they give you that makes you just want to die right then and there*

4. *The way they kiss away your tear*
5. *The way they get mad when they can't make your problem go away*
6. *The way they show off around their friends, even though you know you would love him if he missed a basket or two*
7. *The way they make it their personal mission to ensure that you are never cold*
8. *That confused look they get on their faces when you are mad at them—guaranteed to make your heart melt and the anger fade away*
9. *The way they always let you win any game you play together*
10. *. . . . And when you point this out to them they pretend not to know what you are talking about*
11. *That smile they flash that can make your stomach drop to your feet*
12. *The way they call to apologize after you had a big fight*
13. *The way they touch and hold you so gently, as if they are afraid they will break you*
14. *The way they say, "I love you"*
15. *The way they would die before saying "I love you" in front of their friends*
16. *The way they kiss you*
17. *The way they kiss you after making up from a fight*
18. *The way they hold you when you are crying*
19. *The way they think they are your big protector*
20. *The way they say, "I miss you," even though they hate to admit it*
21. *The way you miss everything about them when they are gone*
22. *The way they comfort you when you have had a bad day*

23. *The way they write you love letters even if they think it's uncool*
24. *Regardless of whether you love them, hate them, wish they would die or know that you would die without them . . . it matters not. Because once they enter your life, whatever you were to the world, they become everything to you. When you look them in the eyes, traveling to the depths of their souls and you say a million things without even speaking, you know that your own life is consumed by their love. We love them for a million reasons; it is a thing, an indescribable feeling.*

Compiled by Kimberly Kirberger

Love Is Never Lost

If our love is only a will to possess, it is not love.

Thich Nhat Hanh

They say it's better to have loved and lost, than never to have loved at all.

That thought wouldn't be very comforting to Mike Sanders. He had just been dumped by his girlfriend. Of course, she didn't put it quite that way. She said, "I do care about you, Mike, and I hope we can still be friends." *Great,* Mike thought. *Still be friends. You, me and your new boyfriend will go to the movies together.*

Mike and Angie had been going together since they were freshmen. But over the summer, she had met someone else. Now as he entered his senior year, Mike was alone. For three years they shared the same friends and favorite hang-outs. The thought of returning to those surroundings without Angie made him feel—well, empty.

Football practice usually helped him take his mind off his troubles. Coaches have a way of running you until you are so tired, you can't really think of anything else. But lately, Mike's heart just wasn't in it. One day it caught up with him. He dropped passes he wouldn't normally miss and let himself get tackled by guys who had never been able to touch him before.

Mike knew better than to have the coach yell at him more than once, so he tried a little harder and made it through the rest of the practice. As he was running off the field, he was told to report to the coach's office. "Girl, family or school: Which one is bothering you, son?" asked his coach.

"Girl," Mike responded. "How did you guess?"

"Sanders, I've been coaching football since before you were born, and every time I've seen an all-star play like a J.V. rookie, it's been because of one of those three."

Mike nodded. "Sorry, sir. It won't happen again."

His coach patted him on the shoulder. "This is a big year for you, Mike. There's no reason why you shouldn't get a full ride to the school of your choice. Just remember to focus on what's really important. The other things will take care of themselves."

Mike knew his coach was right. He should just let Angie go and move on with his life. But he still felt hurt, even betrayed. "It just makes me so mad, Coach. I trusted in her. I opened myself up to her. I gave her all I had, and what did it get me?"

His coach pulled out some paper and a pen from his desk drawer. "That's a really good question. What did it get you?" He handed Mike the pen and paper and said, "I want you to think about the time you spent with this girl, and list as many experiences, good and bad, that you can remember. Then I want you to write down the things that you learned from each other. I'll be back in an hour." With that, the coach left Mike by himself.

Mike slumped in his chair as memories of Angie flooded his head. He recalled when he had first worked up the nerve to ask her out, and how happy he had been when she said yes. Had it not been for Angie's encouragement, Mike wouldn't have tried out for the football team.

Then he thought of the fights that they had. Though he couldn't remember all the reasons for fighting, he remembered the sense of accomplishment he got from working through their problems. He had learned to communicate and compromise. He remembered making up after the fights, too. That was always the best part.

Mike remembered all the times she made him feel strong and needed and special. He filled the paper with their history, holidays, trips with each other's family, school dances and quiet picnics together. Line by line, he wrote of the experience they shared, and he realized how she had helped shape his life. He would have become a different person without her.

When the coach returned, Mike was gone. He had left a note on the desk that simply read:

Coach,

Thanks for the lesson. I guess it's true what they say about having loved and lost, after all. See you at the practice.

David J. Murcott

David's Smile

David could make me deliriously happy or crazy with anger, quicker than anyone I'd ever known, and when he smiled everything else disappeared and I could not help but smile back. He had a million smiles, but there was one in particular that I could even hear in his voice across the phone from miles away. It was playful and knowing and cynical and sincere and secretive and assertive and a thousand other paradoxical things all at once. That smile made me laugh when I was hurting, forgive him when I was angry and believe him even when I knew he was lying. That smile made me fall in love with him—and that was the last thing I ever wanted to do.

When he was mad or hurting or thinking or listening, his face was stone. When he smiled, though, I felt like I was looking right into his soul, and when I made him smile, I felt beautiful inside and out.

David was the first guy I ever really loved. Sometimes when he held me and my head was resting on his broad shoulder I felt that he could hear my deepest, darkest thoughts. He always knew how to say exactly what I needed to hear. He would touch my face and look into my eyes and say he loved me with such warmth that I couldn't help believing.

From the first time we touched, he dominated my thoughts. I would try to concentrate on school, church, my family or my other friends, but it was no use. I would tell myself over and over again that he wasn't the kind of guy I needed in my life, but with each passing day, I only wanted him more. I felt so out of control, so scared and so excited. I would fall asleep at night thinking about his kisses and wake up in the morning with his soft, magical words ringing in my ears. Sometimes when I was near him I trembled. Then, he would put his arms around me and I would relax and feel safe again.

My instincts were in constant conflict. *Trust him. Don't trust him. Kiss him. Don't kiss him. Call him. Don't call him. Tell him how you feel. No, it will scare him off.* And then finally I would wonder if maybe that would be the very best thing that could happen.

If he was scared or insecure, I only saw it once or twice. Like the rest of his emotions, I could never tell how much was an act for my benefit and how much he really felt. He fascinated me. I would stare into his brown eyes and wonder if he had any idea how much control he had over me. If he knew, he never let it show.

Then, one day it all came crashing down around me. He was gone and, as I hurt, I wondered if he had ever really loved me. I had so many questions—and so much to tell him. It was like an alarm had gone off too soon and now my dream was over. He was gone, and all that was left of all we had shared were a few letters and some memories that I was too proud to dwell on. My heart cried out for him, but my mind warned me to move on. In the end, that is what I did.

I learned more from David than from any other guy, with the single exception of my father. When the time and the strength finally came, I was forced to take those lessons and move on without him. Time passed, life continued and I think of him less and less. But, sometimes my mind drifts back to the sweet dream of my first love, and I am haunted by images of his smile. I loved his smile.

Cambra J. Cameron

Never Been Dissed—Until Now

What can I say? Sometimes I'm a little dumb. I consider Cheetos a major food group. I play air guitar. I think burping is funny. And, worst of all, I screwed up my chance with Darcy by listening to a bunch of other jerks who were just as clueless as me.

Darcy was kinda like the Jewel CD I loved. I played that thing over and over on the way to school, but the second I pulled into the parking lot, it got stuffed under my seat for, uh, safekeeping and replaced with the Beastie Boys.

Imagine me confessing to my friends that I, captain of the basketball team, was dating Darcy, captain of the debate team. Believe me, I didn't plan on falling for the school brain. But I was blown away by the first words she ever spoke to me.

"Uh, are you lost? This is the li-brar-y. The gym is on the other side of the school, remember?" she said, enunciating the words like she was talking to a toddler. Ouch.

Even though we went to the same school, Darcy and I lived in completely different worlds. She spent her time with the Net nerds, and I roamed the halls like Moses parting the Red Sea of fans who worshipped the guys on my team. I was totally knocked for a loop when she broke the silence.

"Books. I need a book," I stammered, suddenly unable to remember my assignment. She pointed to a row of books on Thomas Edison—just the man I was looking for—and before I could turn to thank her, she was gone.

When I did catch up with her again, she was on her tippy toes reaching for an encyclopedia in the next aisle. "Need a ladder? Or how 'bout some platforms?" I asked giving her a taste of her own sarcasm.

"How about giving me a hand?" she replied. "Oh, that's right. Books are *square*, not round like a basketball. Think you can hold one?" *Cha-ching!* This girl has guts, I thought. When I started laughing, Darcy totally cracked up and started snort-laughing. The number-two pencils holding up her hair were shaking.

"I can't believe I said that to you. I can't believe you're laughing. This is so surreal," she laughed. "Oh, sorry, that's a big word. Do you need a dictionary?" More laughing, more snorting. We went on like that for a while, ripping on each other until I thought my sides would split.

For the rest of the day—okay, the rest of the *week*— every time I thought about her, I felt the same gut-socking, dizzy feeling I get before a big game. Then I found myself taking different routes to get to class just to see if I'd bump into her, and when I did . . . doh! We didn't say a word to each other, but the joke was still going. I'd innocently make gorilla noises, and she'd die laughing. Or she'd take off her glasses and bump into walls, sending her books, pen and protractor flying everywhere. She taped Brain Gum to my locker. I glued a pair of sweaty gym socks to hers. Two weeks into our secret game, Darcy asked me out. Correction: she blackmailed me into a date. I found a ransom note in my locker saying that if I ever wanted to see my lucky jockstrap again, I'd better meet her at a nearby coffee shop. What guy wouldn't love a girl with that sense of humor?

After that first date, we spent nearly every day together talking about everything—cheesy Kung Fu movies (our shared obsession), how I hated being judged as a jock despite my 3.5 GPA, why I hadn't lost my virginity—all of the things I could *never* talk about with the guys or would even think about mentioning to any of the other girls I had dated. Then again, Darcy wasn't like anyone I had ever been with before. She was a lot of firsts for me. She was the first girl who had the guts to ask me out. She was the first girl I didn't judge by her bra size or reputation. She was the first person who made me feel I had more to offer the world than a killer turnaround jumper. She was the first girl I dated who didn't obsess about her hair, her weight or what she was wearing. And she was the first girl I didn't blab about in the locker room when the guys started bragging about their weekend conquests.

It didn't take long for everyone to start wondering why I was flaking on basketball practice or missing the weekly Duke Nukem marathons at Kyle's. I had been making up *the* lamest excuses to cover for hanging out with Darcy and was feeling pretty skanky about it when the guys confronted me about it. So I told them about her.

"Who?" Steve asked.

"Not the girl in overalls and hightops?" Eric asked.

"Why are you wasting time on *that?*" Kyle asked.

I sat there as they teased me about slumming with a "geeky chick," assuming that once they exhausted all of their lame jokes about Darcy, they'd move onto their next target. Wrong. After that day, whenever I told them I was doing stuff with Darcy, they unloaded on her again. At first, I didn't let it bother me. Then one morning, Dave asked, "Have you figured out how to get her to wear a bag over her head to the prom yet?" That really pissed me off and eventually the little things turned into big things, like "accidentally" forgetting to tell me about practice or suddenly not having enough room at the lunch table for me.

After a few weeks of getting the cold shoulder from my friends, I started to doubt my own judgment. Darcy *wasn't* one of the prettiest girls in the school. Was I actually planning to take her to my senior prom? She'd probably wear number-two pencils in her hair *and* those hideous high-tops. Once I finished picking her apart, I was convinced she was totally wrong for me. Darcy didn't like basketball or my friends. She refused to go to any of the team parties. I'd been blowing off practices to be with her, and my game was totally suffering. In my mind, the relationship was doomed.

I tried to be subtle at first by taking different routes to my classes to avoid her. I'd promise to call her but never did. She finally cornered me in the hall one day and demanded an explanation, so I swore I'd meet her after school. Then I blew her off. I was hoping she'd get the hint and go away if I flaked, but she didn't let me off that easily. The next day, in front of the entire school, Darcy let me have it. She yelled at me, called me a coward, a jerk and an idiot, and, worst of all, tossed my friends a box of notes I'd written to her. I stood there speechless as they read each one aloud and laughed like hyenas. The funny thing was that for the first time (*another* first with Darcy) I didn't really care what the guys were saying or who saw me standing there like an idiot, because I knew she was right. When I looked at my friends howling and high-fiving each other, I finally realized that I was going to be the first guy in our pathetic circle to grow up.

I wish I could say there was a happy ending to the story, that I begged Darcy to take me back and she did, but it didn't happen. Well, at least not the part about her taking me back. I begged. I pleaded. I stuffed notes in her

locker. I followed her around school. I was practically
stalking her by the time I realized it was too late. She had
already gotten over slumming with a dummy.

Last I heard, Darcy graduated early and got accepted to
an out-of-state college. I still feel a little sad when I think
about her and what could have been, but I'm also grateful
that I learned what I did, when I did. I know a little bit
more about who I am—the *whole* me, not just the big man
on campus part—and who I can be, regardless of what my
friends think or say. So, Darcy, if you're reading this . . .
thanks.

Shad Powers

"This time it's *really* over, Jared. I threw out all your pictures *and* deleted all your e-mails."

Reprinted with permission of David Cooney.

Experience Is a Teacher

The true test of character is not how much we know how to do, but how we behave when we don't know what to do.

John Holt

I was shaking when I heard the car pull into the driveway. I blamed it on the chill in my house, although most likely it was because of my uncontrollable nerves. When I opened the door, Becca was standing on my porch with a smile plastered on her face.

"Hey," she said. As she stepped inside the doorway, the guys behind her became visible. "Oh, ya," she added. "This is Dan, Josh and Kevin."

"Hi," I said, and they replied the same in unison. They looked kind of like deer in headlights, standing outside the door, hands jammed in pockets, mouths half-open. As Becca made her way into the house, the guys followed her, and I felt awkwardly lost, unsure of what to say. To avoid forced conversation, I took the opportunity to jot a note to my mom, explaining where I was going.

Eventually, we made it out of the house, and I found

myself in the back seat of a navy-blue truck, wedged between Josh and Kevin, two older guys from a different school. Becca was chattering away in the passenger seat, changing the radio station and singing along. My legs began to shake, a sure indicator of my nervousness, and I had to put my hands on my thighs to steady them. We soon reached the restaurant, and I was thankful for the chance to get out of the truck.

Dan was toying with the miniature coffee creamers at the end of the table. "I don't trust these," he announced. "They've probably been sitting here since 1982."

At the opposite end of the table, next to Kevin, I giggled, probably for the eighth time since we'd sat down. I wanted to smack myself. Between my legs shaking and my ridiculous giggling, my immature nervous habits were driving me crazy, and I prayed that nobody else noticed.

Suddenly, Becca stood up. "I have to call my mom. Dan, come with me."

"Um, I'll come, too," I said. Feeling the need to elaborate, I continued, "I have to call my mom, too." I felt stupid following Becca and Dan out to the lobby, like a girl in elementary school who can't go anywhere without her best friend.

As we waited while Becca called her mom, Dan nudged me and said, "So, what do you think of Josh and Kevin?"

"Josh is pretty cute," I said, figuring that honesty was the best way to go.

"Not Kevin?" Dan's eyes sparkled, and I knew what Becca had been talking about when she said how wonderful he was.

"No . . ." I looked out the window. "But don't tell him that I said that."

"I won't." Of course he wouldn't. What did I think this was, elementary school? I felt like a child in a world of adults, unsure how to act or what to say.

"Josh thinks you're really hot," Dan continued.

His statement immediately grabbed my attention. "Oh, really?" I was flattered.

Becca hung up the phone and caught the end of our conversation, saying excitedly, "You have to sit by him when we go back to the table!"

"No," I protested. "That'll look dumb."

"No it won't," she insisted, and Dan agreed.

"Yeah, we'll just move stuff around or whatever." It was obvious that this was an argument I was not going to win.

When we returned to the table and assumed our new seats, Josh didn't say anything. I wondered if he had figured out our juvenile plan, and then I wondered if he even cared. But I quickly tried to brush the thoughts out of my head and proceeded to giggle at everything Dan said.

Next we went to the movies. Without Becca next to me in the theater, I felt completely defenseless. I gripped my knees for support, angry at myself for being nervous. Why couldn't I have more self-confidence and be as charming as other girls are? I leaned my head back against the head-rest, watching Dan and Becca out of the corner of my eye. No contact yet, I noted. I didn't know what to do with my hands, and it seemed like they took on a life of their own as they repetitiously roamed from my knees to my thighs and eventually gripped the edge of my purse.

I felt a nudge on my right arm. I looked over at Dan and watched as he mouthed the words, "Make a move." He then grinned at me and raised his eyebrows in Josh's direction.

"No!" I whispered emphatically.

"Why not?" he replied with a kind of urgency.

I half-shrugged my shoulders. "I don't know." How could I explain to him the way my mind works? I could never "make a move" on anyone; I didn't have the nerve.

My fear of rejection was too intense. Out of the corner of my eye, I saw that Becca was leaning on Dan's shoulder, and his hand was resting on her knee. I sank farther into my seat.

On the way home from the movies, Becca asked Dan if he had a piece of paper. I knew immediately what she was doing and wanted to object, but couldn't. When she handed me Josh's number on a torn piece of paper, I didn't even look at it. I just played with it between my fingers, bending the edges and running it along the folds of my jeans. Josh's reaction to the piece of paper in his hand was similar.

We pulled into my driveway, and I thought that I was finally safe at home as I said good-bye to everyone and sauntered up to my porch. But as I turned around to give a final wave good-bye, I found Josh standing on the lawn.

"Hey," he said, in a way only older guys can. "When are you going to be home tomorrow?"

"Probably all day," I managed and immediately thought of how dumb I sounded.

"Okay, then. I'll, um, call you around one."

I flashed a slight smile. "Okay. Bye!" I stepped inside my house, allowing myself to breathe only when I had closed the door and was safe inside.

I washed my face, wondering if he would think that I was "really hot" without makeup. As I curled up in bed, the phrase "If only I had . . ." crossed my mind so many times that I became exhausted. But then I remembered that experience, even if awkward and uncomfortable, or in the form of a guy named Josh, is always a teacher. With that, I gradually fell asleep, knowing tomorrow was a new day, and I could rest assured there would be more lessons to learn.

Julia Travis

A Crush

I'm not afraid of storms, for I am learning how to sail my ship.

Helen Keller

"Aaarghhhmmmmm . . . Hello?"

It was about 10:00 on a beautiful July morning, and I had just been woken up from a deep slumber by the untimely ring of the telephone. Little did I know my destiny was on the other end of the line.

"Is Leigh there?" the rich tenor voice asked.

"Yeah. This is." I sat bolt upright, smacking my head on the headboard in the process. I rubbed my forehead and stared in disbelief at the receiver in my hand.

I met Josh while we worked together at the same pizza parlor. It was love at first sight for me, and the whole restaurant knew about it. Never mind that Josh was five years older than I was or that he didn't know my name (or so I thought, until this fateful phone call proved otherwise). I was 100 percent head over heels for the guy, the guy who was at this very moment on the other end of my telephone wire, calling my name. . . .

"Leigh? Hello? Leigh?"

I regained my senses enough to answer. "Yes. I'm here. Um, hi."

"Leigh, I need to talk with you. Can I pick you up in a half hour?"

Could he? "Yeah. Sure." I responded, trying to sound casual. We hung up, and I stared at the telephone for another moment, until I realized that I had twenty-eight minutes left before the love of my life would arrive at my front door to confess his undying passion for me.

Thirty-two minutes later, I stood gazing up at Josh's figure in my doorway. This was simply too good to be true. He looked slightly uncomfortable as he stood, his tall, slim frame moving restlessly.

"Let's go," he said.

Josh led the way to his car, and we both got in. As we pulled out of my driveway, I again gazed at his beautiful face. His lips were full but firm, his nose straight and perfect, his hair sun-streaked blond (from a side job landscaping, as a little investigative research had revealed to me), and his eyes, his gorgeous, wide-set, polished mahogany eyes were . . . staring right back at me! I flushed in embarrassment, as I began to say something, but Josh interrupted me. He didn't bother with small talk, but got right down to business.

"I've been hearing some rumors at work," he began.

This was *not* the opening I had anticipated.

"What kind of rumors?" I ventured.

Josh presented me with an accusatory glance. "Oh, just that you and I are dating. That we're practically engaged. All sorts of great stuff." He gave me a pointed look. "Since I have never even *talked* to you until this morning, I don't know how anybody could have gotten that impression. Unless *somebody*," he paused dramatically, "told them."

I stared at him, shocked. I was speechless for a long

minute, my mouth attempting to form denials that wouldn't make it past my throat. A vice took hold of my heart, squeezing painfully. Finally, I managed to collect myself enough to say, "I swear, I never said anything like that. I might have had a"—my throat began to close up, but I was able to continue in a humiliated whisper—"a little crush on you, and some people knew about it, but I promise, I swear to you, I never insinuated anything else. I'm sorry."

Josh looked at me. My shock at his accusation and every ounce of my humiliation were evident on my face. After a moment, he accepted my admission for the truth that it was, and he tried to change the topic to more light-hearted chit-chat, but I was too occupied trying to keep the tears from streaming down my face, to be a good conversationalist.

After about five minutes, I requested that he take me to my friend Annette's house. As he pulled away, the tears overflowed down my cheeks. I turned to see Annette rushing outside. I ran toward her, sobs making my body shake, and she hugged me until I finally began to calm down. When my crying had diminished to random hic-cuping sighs, my best friend took my face between her hands and said softly, with wisdom beyond her years, "If it were supposed to feel good, they wouldn't call it a crush."

J. Leigh Turner

Sea Glass

We're sitting on the cold shore combing the sand around us looking for sea glass. It's windy, and the cool mist coming off the waves feels cold and charming. We're bundled up in all our layers, and he gently touches my face and kisses my lips. His blue-green eyes stare deep into mine, and I feel him looking straight into my heart.

The brilliant rays of purple, gold and turquoise start to fade as the sun finishes setting. We stand up, wipe the sand off our pants and start walking to the parking lot. I take a deep breath and smell the salt and seaweed crawling in with the tide.

On our walk home, he holds my hand, and we laugh and talk about nothing of real significance. We walk slowly to savor the moment, to savor the time we have together. The trees seem to make a tunnel, surrounding us and isolating us in our own little world.

When we get back to my house, we take the sea glass and put it in my jar. "It's almost halfway filled," he remarks, as I look at the tiny pieces filling the jar. There must be at least a hundred pieces in there, all of them different shapes and different colors. I suppose that if I counted them, there would be just as many as the days we have spent together, and the nights we have comforted each other on the phone.

Each piece of glass is a different color. I decide that they represent the ordinary days filled with insight and love. They are the most frequent ones, the everyday ones. I notice that I put in a green one today. It is a day like today that we shared together that the green ones represent. The green ones frosted with white specks represent the days in which one of us was upset and confided in the other. Although there are only a few, there are some and they're big. I think those are the ones that help the relationship grow the most. The white pieces are the biggest and the shiniest. They reflect the time one of us accomplished something or was really happy about something. One might represent him winning his car, another might be when I made the team, and yet there are so many I can't remember what each one represents. There are so few dark-brown ones. Those have the sharpest edges and cut your fingertips when you touch them. They cause tears and hurt. They're the ex-girlfriends, the not-too-long-ago crushes, the jealousy, the fights. They are the painful parts of our relationship that will never go away, but have become smoother over time.

There is one brilliant bluish-purple piece of glass. It is very small, and I know exactly what it represents. It is the first time he said those three words that before that night were just tossed around and used carelessly by other guys. It represents the time when he looked deep into my eyes, brushed back my hair and told me he loved me.

All of the pieces of sea glass are strong. No matter how hard you try (and people have tried), they won't break. They may get smoother, maybe a little smaller, but so do all memories. They are strong and will always be there and will never be lost.

Then there's a big rock, a big pink rock in the shape of a heart, down at the bottom. Its shape represents exactly what it is. It's our hearts, with all the sea glass and memories and good times to come piled on top. Our small, pink hearts, learning about each other and ourselves, piling little green days on top of big white ones, avoiding the sharp brown ones and trying to find another blue one. It's our hearts, the ones that have grown to love each other. The ones that have spent over two years piling memories on top, good and bad, to make two different, wonderful people. The glass jar will never break. The jar is our bodies that protect our hearts and memories. Like the sea glass, it is strong and even if one of us goes away, it will still be there with all the memories left behind.

Stacey Doerner

Kiss

Point your lashes down
and you can picture my face—
I'm smiling . . .

Open your mouth, speak with your heart
and you can see my soul—
I'm waiting . . .

Place your arms around my waist
and you can embrace my uncertainty—
I'm shaking . . .

Press your lips against mine
and try to catch me—
I'm falling . . .

Emily Crane

He Finally Said, "I Love You"

As I looked into his eyes
And found his longing stare
I stopped myself from saying words
That would show how much I care
I put my hand up to his face
To hold my feelings in
I wouldn't say the words again
To show my love for him
The last time I had told him
How much he meant to me
He put my hands away from his
And said to leave him be
I never spoke the words again
For fear of his deep fright
I thought it was the last time
Until that blissful night
His fingers traced around my face
Pushing hair away
And I was quite unprepared
For what he was to say
My heart beat quickly, my head raced on

I thought that I might cry
He looked as if he might faint—
Imagine this strong guy
But never would I be more impressed
With anything he'd do
Than when he took that heartfelt leap
And told me, "I love you."

Jennifer Orendach

My Childhood Sweetheart

*Love can sometimes be magic. But magic can
sometimes . . . just be an illusion.*

Javan

I met Jake when I was eleven. To me, he wasn't just "my
older brother's friend." He was a thirteen-year-old—an
older man. Jake and my brother would sit in my brother's
room, door closed, and shake their heads to the music of
Guns 'n Roses. I would desperately try to think of excuses
to knock on my brother's door, just to get a peek or a
quick smile at Jake. I found something attractive in this
geeky computer whiz. But I was just "Phil's baby sister,"
so the lines were drawn: He was the friend, and I was the
annoying little sister, two seemingly incompatible titles.

Jake went away to private school, and I missed his presence in the house, even if it had just been behind my
brother's locked door. A few months after he left, Jake
wrote a letter to Phil, and at the end of the letter, in barely
legible script, he scribbled, "Say hello to your sister for me.
Is she still cute?" I lived on that line for months; it was
enough to give me a constant flutter in my stomach.

In the summer of 1993, Jake came home. One evening, the phone rang. When I answered it, the voice on the other line responded, "Hi, Leesa, is Phil around?" I searched my memory, trying to remember the familiar voice on the other line. After a few seconds, I realized it was Jake. JAKE!

"Actually, he's not here. Where are you?" My voice shook. I couldn't believe it when he replied, "Cranbrook." He was home.

Our friendship began the instant he spoke again and said, "Well, if Phil isn't around, I guess *you* are going to have to talk to me." That night, we got together and sat in the park for hours.

I brought a friend along, with the intention of setting her up with the friend who accompanied Jake. I watched as Jake talked and laughed with my friend, Mel. I realized I wasn't going to be the one setting anyone up. Jake was obviously interested in Mel.

When Jake and Mel became a couple, my heart sank. To my selfish pleasure, I felt smug later that month when they broke up, and Jake called me to complain. We ended up talking again, and my anger toward his dating Mel wore off rather quickly. It was hard to stay mad at him.

Although he left for school again soon after that, his letters were now addressed to me, with side notes that read, "Say hi to Phil for me." Our friendship was growing stronger and stronger.

He left his school two years later, only to move farther away. I thought we would both move on, since we were so far apart, but we only grew closer. It wasn't long before I realized that I was officially in love with him. Whenever he came to visit, it was like a whole new adventure. We felt free to act like kids, but at the same time, we had endless conversations. We laughed and shared our secrets, and I always dreaded the day he had to go back home.

Every time he visited, I told myself, *This is it. I am going to tell him how I feel.* I promised myself that I would before he left, but I never got the guts to confess my true feelings.

Jake came home again a few days ago. I swore to myself that there was no more next time, that it was now or never, and that I couldn't hold it in anymore. While we had hinted at our feelings, we had never talked about them. I worked up the nerve to tell him how I felt, that I loved him and had for some time. The words just flowed out of me. He cut me off, leaned over and kissed me. I expected to feel complete bliss, but, surprisingly, I didn't. *This is Jake,* I reminded myself. *Remember? You love him!* Still, I felt nothing. When he looked at me, I could tell he felt the same. I believed that kissing Jake would be the last piece of the puzzle to complete my perfect fantasy. Yet somehow, the puzzle pieces just didn't match up.

Jake left again today, and for once, his leaving doesn't feel like a tragedy. We are best friends, nothing more, and always will be.

So maybe this isn't a storybook ending. Perhaps my childhood sweetheart will not become my fairy-tale prince, but we can still live happily ever after.

Leesa Dean

I Had to Let Him Go

"I'm sorry, I just don't really remember . . ."

His words tore through me, piercing every inch of my body and cutting jaggedly through to my heart. Just one week earlier, we had watched the sun set and held each other. He comforted me while I asked him why my best friend and I just couldn't get along anymore. But tonight, his mind was somewhere else; he couldn't remember that special night.

Why was he so distant? Was he so lost in the pain that had been haunting him for so long?

There were nights he cried himself to sleep, remembering the harsh words of his mother. He told me how much he dreaded the weekends spent with her, because it meant another seventy-two hours of being blamed for everything that went wrong. The nagging didn't stop— she harassed him because his grades were lower than his brother's and he wasn't the perfect son she wanted him to be. She said he was dumb; that he wouldn't get into college, wouldn't succeed in life. She called him a loser, a disappointment to her. His gift at art was undeniable, yet her criticism caused him to believe he had no talent, when actually, he was winning prizes for his work.

What kept him alive, he told me, was our love. Friends for years, and now dating, he needed me. He counted on me. In one letter I received from him, he said, "You're like my family. Just you. We can be a family. Do you need anyone else? I don't. Just keep loving me," he wrote, "and I'll be okay."

For a while, I believed him. I promised I would never hurt him like she had, never leave him, never stop loving him. I would be his family; the one he needed in good times and in bad, the one who held him when he was sick and cheered for him at track meets. I thought that if I held him tightly enough, his pain would disappear.

It was like a roller coaster, though, our relationship. Sometimes, he was the happiest kid I knew—laughing, joking, smiling and kissing. I always knew if he was happy by his eyes. Crystal clear and blue, they told me no lies. If he was happy, they sparkled. But if he was sad, they seemed more gray than blue. On those sad days, he didn't joke. When I tried to cheer him with a kiss, he would refuse. He wouldn't let me touch him. I couldn't show him how much I loved him. When he was hurt, all he knew was to return the hurt to those undeserving. He said things he knew were cruel, apologizing the next day. The cycle never ended—the cruelties, the apologies. Yet I knew why.

Though I loved him, I couldn't take away his pain. It stemmed from events that occurred long before I knew him. Soon I realized my love couldn't compete with his inner pain. Though it hurt, I realized that I couldn't help him; rather, he had to seek professional help. I had to let him go.

The night I told him this couldn't continue, the tears stung my eyes more painfully than ever before. He now would have to face his worst fear—to be alone to confront the real demons within him. He thought I had deceived him, that I had lied to him when I whispered the word *forever*. But I hadn't lied to anyone but myself because I believed that all he needed was my love. Right now, my love was only causing pain.

He had built a separate world, in which only he and I existed. For a while, it had been nice to dream of such a happy place, a mystical Eden for just the two of us. Before long, however, I knew the walls would crumble if he kept relying only on me. Deep down I knew it wasn't healthy for either of us. I simply couldn't hold on to us and this fantasy any longer.

Yesterday, I saw him for the first time in a year. His eyes sparkled, and the light came from within. The darkness is lifting, because he allowed other people into his life, people who helped him in more ways than I ever could have done on my own. Now, he sees the special gifts that he has, and although the painful memories will always remain, he is now beginning to believe in himself. Yesterday, I realized that even perfect love can't protect someone from himself. And, sometimes, the most loving thing you can do for someone is to let him go.

Andrea Barkoukis

Please Sign My Yearbook

The hardest of all is learning to be a well of affection, and not a fountain; to show them we love them not when we feel like it, but when they do.

Nan Fairbother

Sitting in class, I concentrated on the back of Brian's neck. Evil thoughts filled my mind; I was secretly waiting for his head to explode. It didn't, and I was forced to watch my ex-boyfriend laugh and chat with every person in the room while he blatantly ignored me.

After Brian and I broke up, third period became pure torture. While I was still nursing what I considered to be the world's worst broken heart, I was bombarded with the sight of my ex's excessive flirting, as if he were proving to me that he was so obviously over his heartache. During class, Brian would gossip loudly about his weekend, his latest party and his new car.

Maybe Brian was trying to get back at me for breaking off our six-month relationship. Maybe he thought that if he looked happy, it would hurt me more than I had hurt him.

At the end of the relationship, I let him cry on my shoulder but held a strong heart as he begged me not to go. Of course, he covered his pain very well at school, as if our tearful good-bye had never occurred.

Immediately after the breakup, Brian started dating another girl. She was graduating that spring, as if that were a big feat for a junior-year boy. She took him to the prom and announced it right beside me in math class. I, too, had a date for the prom, but it still hurt. My hurt curdled and turned to anger. It felt like he was trying to upset me, trying to rub his happiness in my face. Every time I saw them together, I wanted to scream. It felt like the pain was going to tear me in half, or at least force me to consider tearing her in half.

School was coming to an end, and I eagerly waited for summer vacation, my savior. No more Algebra Two and that gnawing feeling in my stomach each day.

One day in dreaded third period, Brian leaned over to me, and to my surprise, he asked me to sign his yearbook. I must have sat there for a full minute before I got over the shock and said yes.

I thought to myself, *This is my chance.* I could really let him have it! I could tell him that I knew what he was doing, that he was trying to hurt me, and that it wasn't fair. I could tell him that I saw through his act, that he and I both knew it was exactly that, an act. But then it hit me, what good would come of that? Would belittling him make me feel better, or would it just perpetuate the pain that we both needed to recover from?

Instead of writing of the pain I had endured, I listed all of the fun times we had shared. I wrote about the first place we had ever kissed, the gifts he had given me, the lessons I had learned—the ones he had taught me—and the first "I love you" that was whispered between us. It took up one page, and that quickly became two, until my hand was tired of writing. There were still a million more great memories crowding the corners of my mind, and I remembered many more throughout the day. It made me realize the things I learned from him and what great experiences we had shared. I finished by telling him I held no hard feelings, and I hoped he felt the same.

Maybe what I wrote in his yearbook made me look weak, maybe he thought I was pathetic for still holding onto the memories of our relationship. But writing all those things helped me; it helped me heal the wounds that still hurt in my heart. It felt liberating to let go of the grudge; I finally felt free from my anger.

I realized that Brian had taught me one final lesson: forgiveness. Someday, when he is fifty and has his own children, he may stumble upon his high school yearbook, and they will ask who Stacy was. I hope he can look back and say I was someone who really cared about him, loved him, and most importantly, that I was someone who taught him about forgiveness.

Stacy Brakebush

My Knight on His White Horse

I expected to meet my first love in a magical way. Not necessarily "Knight on White Horse" magical, but I had a definite picture in my head—tall, blond, chiseled body, deep voice, designer clothes. He would be romantic, smart and very witty. He would be perfect. One day he did come along, my perfect love, although his perfection wasn't quite there—at first.

He was five years older than I and about five inches shorter. He had a high squeaky voice, considering he was nineteen at the time, and a scrawny little body. He wasn't what you would call "good-looking."

We met at the beach. A mutual friend introduced us. He was annoying and kept cracking jokes and flirting with me. Somehow, he ended up giving my friends and me a ride home that night.

I rolled my eyes as the car pulled up to us. The brakes were shot, the door was broken, and he had to sit on a phone book to actually see over the dashboard. I could not help but laugh at the situation. *How embarrassing,* I thought. But he was far from embarrassed. He kept cracking jokes about his "trusty steed" and had us all laughing to tears. We stopped off at his house on the way home, and I asked him if I could use his bathroom. He stopped, turned and said, "Yes, but . . . those who use my bathroom must give me their phone numbers." He was grinning.

"Whatever. Here." I jotted down my number and then sought out the bathroom.

I guess you could say that was where it all started. We became friends instantly. He would take me out to dinner and to the movies. He even brought me as his date to a Halloween party and stayed by my side the whole night. That Halloween was the night I realized that Chris was more to me than just a friend. We came to the party as "hitch hikers that escaped from prison" and won the prize for most creative costume.

His creativity and silliness was what did it. That's how he won my heart. I was in love with this beautiful friend.

Did I tell him? Oh, no way! I was very proud . . . and very stubborn. I had been hurt many times before meeting Chris, and needless to say, had learned that love confessions are dangerous. But this was different; it felt real. We had been friends for almost a year and knew each other inside out. I knew that he liked me. He told me so all the time. I was confused. I didn't want to ruin the amazing friendship we had.

I hid my feelings for him for another year. It drove me crazy. He gave up on me and got a girlfriend, and I dated off and on; thus, we grew apart. I was never happy with any other guy. I compared every date and hug and voice to his. It hurt inside, and I denied my own true feelings and hid them very well until one day. . . .

He had just broken up with his girlfriend, and I called out of the blue. He asked if I wanted to come over and watch a movie, and I agreed.

"We have some catching up to do," he whispered, his voice giving me chills.

"Yeah, you're right. I've missed ya. . . . You haven't grown have you?" I joked.

"Just come over," he laughed. So I did.

It felt good to be back. I threw my arms around him immediately as I walked through the door. Our eyes met awkwardly, and I pulled away.

We talked about our lives, each other and ourselves. We talked for hours, about everything and anything, until silence interrupted our conversation.

I had always wondered how it would feel to kiss him— soft, sloppy, passionate?

And in that moment I decided that I needed to know. Our eyes met, and I leaned in and kissed him. His lips were soft, the kiss perfect. I was floating in his touch, his arms, his affection. It had been two years of flirting and friendship, and finally we were trapped in the moment, between our own true feelings.

I spilled to him the truth about my feelings. I told him how scared I was that I would lose him as a friend, but that he had become much more than that to me. I told him that I had never cared about someone this way. I told him that he was beautiful and that I was falling in love with him. I even began to cry.

He smiled and kissed me lightly on the cheek. " I love you, too," he whispered. "And I know how you feel. We go perfectly together, Becca."

"I know, Chris." At that moment he was the most beautiful person I had ever seen, every inch, up to his perfect ears. His voice was music, his touch tender. That was when our friendship became more. We were in love.

Months passed and our stability floundered. Love is a roller coaster, and I must admit sometimes all the turns and twists made me sick. But through everything we had an amazing and beautiful relationship. He taught me how to love and admired my passion for life. He instilled confidence in me and supported my individuality.

Love has a tendency to fade. Ours did. We had given each other a lot, including the confidence to grow into our own people, and, ultimately, to grow apart. One day, I just didn't see the love in his eyes any more. His kiss was different. We both felt the slow drift apart, yet neither of us really wanted to admit that our fire was blowing out. We had been together for a year-and-a-half and, secretly, I knew, no longer.

Although our relationship ended, our connection stayed strong. My friends had always warned me never to date your best friend; that you will ruin your friendship and it can never be the same again.

Three years later, he remains one of my best friends. We have changed and grown. I am involved with someone new and wonderful, and so is he. And yet we still remain major priorities in one another's lives.

The fantasy of my magical man has faded, and I no longer search for perfection. I know that it doesn't exist. What I do know is that love is mysterious, beautiful, and, oftentimes, very unexpected.

Rebecca Woolf

Fading Fast

Looking down at the interior side of my Strawberry Shortcake running shoes, I realize that his name, Forrest David, is fading. I trace my finger over his signature, remembering the day he autographed my shoe with his dad's pen as I sat in the Austin airport, tears blurring my vision.

That's what he's doing, I think, *slowly fading out of my life.* And yet, I remember everything and every moment I was with him, savoring his every move, smile and kiss. I never thought a person could be so precious to me. He was so beautiful, it hurt to look at him. But now it hurts to think of him. I memorized his face: dark eyebrows, greenish-blue eyes, tousled hair. His hands, tan and strong, could swallow my own. I had never loved anyone else the way I loved Forrest.

The first time I saw him, I stood there quietly, drinking him in. And when I finally had him, I was almost in tears because I had never felt so alive. I don't know how long I stood there holding him, breathing in his scent with my face pressed against his shirt. I knew I didn't want to let go.

I cried bitterly the day we parted, feeling utterly alone

as I watched him vanish down the airplane terminal. I tasted the salt as I wept, feeling so angry at the world and at life. I had found my love, the one I wanted to be with forever, and life had chosen to be cruel and unfair, keeping us over six hundred miles away from each other. It might as well have been 10 million. I thought my heart would break.

I sigh as I remember these painful memories, but I don't cry. I have no tears left for him.

They say real love is forever. I don't know the exact definition of it, but Forrest is as close as I've ever come to it. He's gone now, and my dreams have been shattered by the harsh reality of the situation. I thought we were meant to be together, and I dearly loved him. Two teenagers living so far away from each other usually can't make it. I thought we would be different, that we were strong enough to make it. I was wrong. When he left, he took a piece of my heart with him. It's now floating somewhere in Austin.

For a while, I couldn't eat or sleep. I felt so sick and empty. I didn't think I'd be able to go on without him. As I look back now, I see that it was a time of mourning—I was mourning the loss of a two-year relationship. I didn't think the hurt would ever end.

Then, one morning I woke up, and the sick feeling in my stomach was gone. I knew then that I was going to be okay, that I no longer needed him. I began to live again. As I look back, the only thing he ever gave me that I'll be able to carry with me forever is the discovery of my inner strength. It will carry me through all the pain, all the hurt, and I will survive. I had it in me the entire time; I just couldn't quite find it. Thank you, Forrest.

I smile as I remember him, and then I gently slip my running shoes off and let go.

Kendal Kelly

Reprinted with permission of Randy Glasbergen.

The Mirror

Her name was Jillene Jones. Jillene Jones! The alliteration just added to her mystique. To me, she was a character in the great American novel; the star of a blockbuster movie; the president of my world. She was truly the woman for me. I just knew it. Now if I could only find out something about her.

I asked around. I was Jim Rockford, Sherlock Holmes and Magnum P.I. all rolled into one. First clue: She was into heavy metal. Cool! Well, not so cool. Actually, I couldn't stand heavy metal. My hearing's a little sensitive, especially when the noise level exceeds that of a cannon blast. So what—who needs to hear? A lot of unwanted noise in this world anyway. I started listening to heavy metal.

Second clue: She liked to work out. I joined her gym. The machines in there looked like they were designed for some sort of bizarre psychological testing. Since there didn't appear to be any instruction manuals, I decided to stick to something simple like the treadmill. What fun! What a high! Actually, I felt like a hamster in a wheel. No matter. I was moving closer to my goal.

I decided to make some discreet inquiries among her

friends. The fates were truly on my side because not only did the woman of my dreams, Jillene Jones, know who I was, but she didn't find me totally repulsive. The die was cast. The plot was set. She would be mine. Even though the die was cast and the plot was set, etc., it took me another week to get up the courage to ask her out.

More research. Third clue: She loved Aramis. What an amazing coincidence! I loved Aramis, too—until I smelled it. Yikes. But surely if Jillene Jones loved Aramis, it must be an acquired taste. I bought the econo-size bottle of Aramis and began wearing it every day, everywhere I went. Every time I smelled my unique odor, I thought of Jillene Jones. And strangely enough, I began to notice a change in the way others perceived me. I always found a seat on the bus. If I had to stand in line, people would step aside and let me move to the front. Animals and small children fled in fear as I walked down the street. No matter, because I was on a quest.

A little more research and I would be ready. Clues four, five and six: She loved the color peach, bowling and sushi. I bought a peach-colored bowling shirt, found a bowling alley that served sushi and learned to throw strikes. Finally, I got up my courage and made the call. Luck was in my favor; the most popular head-banging band around was playing at our local college venue. I finagled great seats after draining my meager bank account. I put on my best Barry White baritone (which sounded more like Steve Urkel on a bad day) and asked Jillene Jones out on a date. She said yes.

The stars were aligned. All was right with the world. I saw my destiny and it had a name: Jillene Jones. The day of what would surely be the best night of my life began at the gym. Forty-five minutes on the hamster mill. I saw her out of the corner of my eye. Did she notice my Motley Crue T-shirt? I could only hope. The night finally arrived.

I put on my peach bowling shirt, drenched myself in Aramis, spiked my hair and threw in a fake nose ring for good measure.

Her eyes lit up when she saw that peach bowling shirt. "You know I was watching you today," she said. "You looked pretty cute on that treadmill. I didn't know you were a metal-head!" She saw the shirt!!! My plan was working!!! I walked her to my car and popped in a little Ozzy. She didn't seem to notice that the volume blew out all four of my speakers. She just grooved to the buzzing.

We went to the concert and I screamed at her for three hours until my ears felt like they were bleeding. Then mercifully the band finally stopped and we were able to leave. Sushi. She ordered some really slimy, expensive stuff that slid down my throat like dead goldfish. I had to pretend to use the restroom and sneak out to my car to gather all the spare change from the floorboards to pay the bill.

I drove her home and walked her to the door. She gave me a kiss that should be reserved for sailors going to sea. I had won her over. She was mine!!! Then she said the six words that I had never imagined, in my wildest fantasies, hearing: "Would you like to come in?"

Before my rational mind could answer, something came out from some part of my being that I heretofore did not know existed. "No," I said. I looked around, wondering where that had come from. She looked at me in disbelief and said good night.

I drove myself home in silence. Well, I really had no choice since my speakers were blown. I walked inside and went into the bathroom. I looked at myself in the mirror. There I was with spiky hair, a fake nose ring and wearing a peach bowling shirt. I reeked of dead fish and cheap cologne. My ears were ringing so loud I kept picking up the phone. Who was I? Jillene Jones. I remembered some

National Geographic special I had once seen on TV where the narrator described how lions hunt. "They become their prey." But starting a relationship shouldn't be a hunt. That didn't seem right.

I took off the peach bowling shirt and the nose ring. I rinsed out my hair and put on some mellow jazz. I went back into the bathroom and looked again in the mirror. There I was. Me. And somewhere out there was a woman for ME.

Every once in a while I pass an Aramis counter in a department store or smell someone wearing that potent scent and I think of Jillene Jones. The name still rolls off my tongue. I wish her well and hope she found that special peach-shirt-wearing, sushi-loving, treadmill-running, Aramis-drenched, bowling metal-head to love.

Dan Clark

I Dare You!

On the first day of my second year at California State University at Sacramento, I saw the most gorgeous guy! He was standing alone in line at the cafeteria and looked out of place. Turning to my friends, I said, "I have to meet him!"

Challenging my spontaneity, my friends reached into their purses and came up with money for a bet. They then dared me to run up to him, pretend that I knew him and convince him that he knew me. Smiling, I turned and was off to meet the cutie pie.

"Dan, Dan!" I yelled as I ran up to him. "How are you? How's your mom?" He just stood there looking at me. I could tell that he was shy. I liked him immediately.

"I'm not Dan," he said, looking a little confused.

"Sure you are!" I countered. "You lived in Sierra Hall last year, third floor! You were Bob's roommate."

"No, I lived off campus last year," this sweet man replied, still not getting it. I turned and started to leave, and he began asking me a series of questions: "Do I know you from my mom's allergy clinic?" (I hate shots.) "Were you in the parrot class I took last summer?" (I like birds only slightly more than shots.) "Do you eat at Taco Bell? I work there." (Never.)

"Well," he said, "I know I'm not Dan, and I didn't live in Sierra Hall." He reached out his hand to mine. "My name is Tim, and I'm pleased to meet you anyway."

He invited me to his fraternity party that night. I composed myself and informed him that I did not go to fraternity parties. But as I watched him walk away, I had second thoughts. That afternoon, I took the money that I'd won from the bet and bought a black miniskirt. I was going to my first fraternity party.

When I arrived there, I was a little nervous. Would he be there? When I got to the front steps of the frat house, I looked up and saw Tim sitting at the top. He looked at me and smiled.

"I was hoping you would come. I've been waiting for you." I sat down next to him and we started talking. We talked all that night—and for the next three nights—until dawn. Four months later, he asked me to marry him. Four years later, we tied the knot. This year, we celebrated the fifteenth anniversary of the day we met.

Some nights when we are snuggling together, I'm reminded that I found my soul mate on a dare. Now and then, my husband asks, "Am I Dan or Tim tonight?" Having a special place in my heart for both of them, I always laugh and reply, "You decide!"

April Kemp

The Love I'll Never Forget

The moment you have in your heart this extraordinary thing called love and feel the depth, the delight, the ecstasy of it, you will discover that the world is transformed.

J. Krishnamurti

My Minnesota hometown is a farming community of eight thousand people, tucked into the northwest corner of the state. Not a lot that is extraordinary passes through. Gretchen was an exception.

Gretchen was an Eickhof, a member of one of the town's wealthiest families. They lived in a sprawling brick place on the banks of the Red Lake River and spent summers at their vacation home on Union Lake, thirty miles away.

But there was nothing snooty about Gretchen. In sixth grade, she broke both legs skiing and for months had to be carried around by her father. After that, she taught herself to walk again. In high school, she tutored students less able than herself and was among the first to befriend new kids at school. Years later, she told me she had also been the "guardian angel" who left cookies and inspirational notes at my locker before my hockey games. She moved through the various elements of high-school society—farm kids, jocks and geeks—dispensing goodwill to all. Gretchen, the Central High Homecoming Queen of 1975, was clearly going places.

I knew her only well enough to exchange greetings when we passed in the halls. I was a good athlete and, in the parlance of the time, kind of cute. But I was insecure, especially around females. Girls were mysterious creatures, more intimidating than fastballs hurled high and tight, which may explain my bewilderment one midsummer night in 1977 when I bumped into Gretchen at a local hangout. I had just finished my freshman year at the University of North Dakota in nearby Grand Forks. Gretchen, whose horizons were much broader, was home from California after her first year at Stanford.

She greeted me happily. I remember the feel of her hand, rough as leather from hours in the waters of Union Lake, as she pulled me toward the dance floor. She was nearly as tall as I, with perfect almond skin, soft features and almost fluorescent white teeth. Honey-blond hair hung in strands past her shoulders. Her sleeveless white shirt glowed in the strobe lights, setting off arms that were brown and strong from swimming, horseback riding and canoeing.

Though not much of a dancer, Gretchen moved to the music enthusiastically, smiling dreamily. After a few dances we stood and talked, yelling to each other over the music. By the time I walked her to her car, Main Street was deserted. The traffic light blinked yellow. We held hands as we walked. When we arrived at her car, she invited me to kiss her. I was glad to oblige.

But where hometown boys were concerned, Gretchen was as elusive as mercury. As passionately as she returned some of my kisses that summer and the next, for her, I was part of the interlude between childhood and the more serious endeavors to come. I, however, was dizzy for her and had the bad habit of saying so. Each time I did, she pulled away from me. These were college summers, not the time for moony eyes and vows of undying devotion.

One night in 1978 when Gretchen and I were together, out of nowhere she spoke the words that guys in my situation dread above all.

"Tim," she said, "I think we should just be friends."

I told her I was tired of her games and was not as much of a fool as she thought. I stormed away. By morning, I had cooled off. I sent her some roses that day, with a note offering an apology and my friendship.

Gretchen and I started dating again about a month later. But this time I had learned my lesson. No more moony eyes. I could be as detached and aloof as the next guy. It worked beautifully, except that after a few weeks Gretchen asked, "What's wrong with you?"

"What do you mean, what's wrong?"

"You're not yourself," she said. "You haven't been for a long time."

"I know," I said, and let her in on my ruse. For the only time I remember, she became angry. Then she proposed a deal.

"You be who you are," she said, "and I won't go anywhere, at least for the rest of the summer."

It was a bargain I quickly accepted. She was as good as her word.

Those weeks seemed golden, a bit unreal. One time as we said good night, I discarded the final wisp of my caution and told Gretchen that I loved her. She only smiled.

I came back from college to see her off to Stanford in mid-September. While Gretchen packed, I absently shot pool at her father's table. When she finished, we took a last walk around her family's horse pasture in the gathering September chill. I thought how dramatically our lives were about to diverge and was saddened. But more than anything, I was thankful for the fine, fun times we had spent over the last two summers.

Gretchen planned to find work in California next summer. For her, the serious part of life beckoned, and I knew what that meant.

"Good-bye," I said as we stood at her front door.

"Don't say 'good-bye,'" she replied. "Say 'see you later.'"

A month later, the last of the autumn leaves were falling, but the sky was a cloudless blue, the air crisp and invigorating. Classes were done for the day.

The telephone rang the second I stepped into my dorm room. I recognized Gretchen's friend Julie's voice on the other end of the line, and my heart soared. Julie was to be married the following month, and maybe Gretchen would be returning home for the wedding after all. But hearing the uncharacteristically quiet scratch of Julie's voice, I knew before she told me that Gretchen was dead.

The previous morning Gretchen had collected one of her birthday presents from a college friend: a ride in a small plane. Shortly after takeoff, the craft lurched out of control and pitched into a marsh. Gretchen and her friend were killed instantly.

"Gretchen's parents wondered if you would be a pall-bearer," Julie said.

"I'd be honored," I heard myself reply. The word sounded strange even as it left my mouth. *Honored?* Is that what I felt?

I left my dormitory and walked aimlessly. I am told I sought out a campus priest, but eighteen years later I have no memory of that. *How does a person grieve?* I wondered, unable to cry.

The night after the funeral, I sat with my high-school buddy Joel in his Chevy Vega outside the restaurant where Gretchen's mourning friends planned to congregate.

Seeing him was the beginning of both my pain and my consolation, for as Joel spoke of Gretchen, his voice briefly failed. That tiny catch in my old friend's voice dissolved whatever stood between my sorrow and me. My torrents of grief were unleashed.

The next morning, Joel and I joined a procession from the Eickhofs' lakeside summer house into the nearby woods. Gretchen's sisters took turns carrying a small urn that contained her ashes. It was cool and sunny, and the fallen leaves crackled underfoot.

We came to a lone birch tree, its magnificent white bark standing out among the surrounding maples. Scratched into the trunk were the names of Gretchen, her father and her younger sister, as well as a date many years before.

Someone said a prayer. Gretchen's father placed the urn in the ground below the birch. Above us, wind rustled through newly barren branches.

I was among the last to leave. I emerged from the woods that day into a different world, where memories of first love linger but summers always end.

Tim Madigan

Dear Girl

Dear Girl,

I feel that the time has come for me to have a girlfriend. I know you're out there somewhere. Don't worry, I'll find you.

And when I do, I hope that you will love me because I'm Derek, not because I'm Mike's younger brother. I hope you won't be embarrassed when my clothes don't match, or be annoyed when I want to watch the Lakers on ESPN, instead of *Party of Five.*

I hope that you will remember I play soccer, not football, and that I play midfield, not defense, and that every weekend I live with my dad.

I pray that you'll love me despite my tendency to forget birthdays, and if your parents invite me to dinner, please write their names really small on my hand so I can use it as reference.

Please know that I will constantly act strong and in control, but inside I am actually lost and confused. (Just don't tell my friends.) Please don't worry if I hurt myself skateboarding. Instead, be there to mend my wounds with kisses.

Understand that loving each other means being together, but not all of the time. We should never bail on our friends. Also understand that I may at times act jealous and overly protective, but only because *I* have insecurities not because *you* are doing anything wrong.

And if we fall out of love with one another, please don't hate me. And if I cry in front of you, please don't laugh at me. Please know that I am sensitive . . . in a manly, tough kind of way.

Please be honest with me without being hurtful. After all, I am a *boy*. And I promise to always be honest with you, because you deserve honesty. And I promise to open doors for you and buy your ticket when we go to the movies.

And no, you aren't fat, so please don't constantly ask. And you don't need makeup either. Oh, and don't be upset if you cut your hair and I don't notice. I will love you even in Levi's and a T-shirt.

I hope you don't think I'm asking too much of you. I just want to be happy making you happy. I'm coming to find you, so don't go anywhere. Stay where you are, whoever you are. And by the way, my name's Derek.

Yours Always,
Derek

Derek Whittier

Dear Boy

Dear Boy,

I do not know who you are, or where or when we will meet, but I do hope it is soon.

I pray that when we meet and fall in love, you will love me, for me, and not hope for someone who is thinner or prettier. I hope you won't compare me to girls who may have brighter smiles. I hope that you will make me laugh, take care of me if I get sick, and be trustworthy.

I hope you will remember that I prefer daisies to roses, and that my favorite color changes with my mood. Please know that my eyes aren't blue, they're gray, with flecks of navy.

Please know that I might be too shy to kiss you first, but please don't be afraid to kiss me. I won't slap you or push you away. I'm sure your kisses will be perfect. When we go on a date, please don't stress about where to take me; what's important is that I'll be with you.

If I cry, please know it isn't because of you, just hold me close, and I'll heal quickly. And, if it is because of you, I'll heal just the same.

And if we decide to break up, please understand that I

may be bitter, but I'd like to be your friend if you'll let me. I promise to remember that you have feelings too, even though you'll never admit it, and when you are ready we'll have a friendship.

Please tell me if anything I do bothers you, or if something just doesn't sit right. I would like you to always be honest with me. If I have a bad day, I hope you will shower me with confidence and smiles.

I hope you don't think that I'm asking too much of you. I hope you understand that I'm a little bit nervous and very scared. I wish I could tell you how or when we will meet, and if we will be in love forever. Every relationship is a new game of cards, and . . . (sigh) . . . I've never been good at cards. But I will try my best to be kind and love you dearly for all that you are, without expecting too much from you. Thank you for listening; this is all that I ask.

Yours Always,
Sarah

Sarah Bercot

2

ON FRIENDSHIP

Some people come into our lives and quickly go. Some people stay for a while, leave footprints on our hearts, and we are never, ever the same.

Flavia Weedn

A Simple Christmas Card

A friend is a gift you give yourself.

Robert Louis Stevenson

Abbie, shy and reserved, started ninth grade in the big-city high school in the center of town. It never occurred to her that she would be lonely. But soon she found herself dreaming of her old eighth-grade class. It had been small and friendly. This new school was much too cold and unfriendly.

No one at this school seemed to care if Abbie felt welcome or not. She was a very caring person, but her shyness interfered with making friends. Oh, she had those occasional buddies—you know, the kind that took advantage of her kindness by cheating off her.

She walked the halls every day almost invisible; no one spoke to her, so her voice was never heard. It reached the point where she believed that her thoughts weren't good enough to be heard. So she continued to stay quiet, almost mute.

Her parents were very worried about her, for they feared she'd never make friends. And since they were divorced, she probably needed to talk with a friend very badly. Her parents tried everything they could to help her fit in. They bought her the clothes and the CDs, but it still didn't work.

Unfortunately, Abbie's parents didn't know Abbie was thinking of ending her life. She often cried herself to sleep, believing that no one would ever love her enough to be her real friend.

Her new pal Tammy used her to do her homework by pretending to need help. Even worse, Tammy was leaving Abbie out of the fun she was having. This only pushed Abbie closer to the edge.

Things worsened over the summer; Abbie was all alone with nothing to do but let her mind run wild. She let herself believe that this was all that life was cracked up to be. From Abbie's point of view, it wasn't worth living.

She started the tenth grade and joined a Christian youth group at a local church, hoping to make friends. She met people who on the outside seemed to welcome her, but who on the inside wished she'd stay out of their group.

By Christmastime Abbie was so upset that she was taking sleeping pills to help her sleep. It seemed as though she was slipping away from the world.

Finally, she decided that she would jump off the local bridge on Christmas Eve, while her parents were at a party. As she left her warm house for the long walk to the bridge, she decided to leave her parents a note in the mailbox. When she pulled down the door to the mailbox, she found letters already there.

She pulled the letters out to see who they were from. There was one from Grandma and Grandpa Knight, a couple from the neighbors . . . and then she saw one addressed to her. She tore it open. It was a card from one of the guys in the youth group.

Dear Abbie,

I want to apologize for not talking with you sooner, but my parents are in the middle of a divorce, so I didn't have a chance to talk with anyone. I was hoping you could help me with some questions I have about divorced kids. I think we could become friends and help each other. See you at Youth Group on Sunday!

Sincerely your friend,
Wesley Hill

She stared at the card for a while, reading it over and over again. "Become friends," she smiled, realizing that someone cared about her life and wanted plain, quiet Abbie Knight as a friend. She felt so special.

She turned around and went back to her house. As soon as she walked in the door, she called Wesley. I guess you could say he was a Christmas miracle, because friendship is the best gift you can give anyone.

Theresa Peterson

Why Rion Should Live

Believe that life is worth living and your belief will help create the fact.

William James

High school didn't frighten me. Oh sure, the endless halls and hundreds of classrooms were overwhelming, but I took it in with all the pleasure of starting a new adventure. My freshman year was full of possibilities and new people. With a class of nearly two thousand new-comers, you just couldn't go wrong. So I, still possessing the innocence of a child concealed in a touch of mascara and lipstick, set out to meet them all.

Spanish One introduced me to Rion. By the student definition, he was a "freak": the black jeans, the well-worn Metallica shirts, the wallet chains, the works. But his unique personality and family troubles drew me to him. Not a crush, more of a curiosity. He was fun to talk to, and where interrupted whispering sessions left off, hours of phone conversations picked up.

During one of these evening conversations, "it," as we like to address the incident, unfolded. We were discussing the spectacular height of Ms. Canaple's over-styled bangs when I heard Rion's dad yelling in the background. "Hold on," Rion muttered before a question could be asked. I could tell that he was trying to muffle the receiver, but you could still hear the horror as if his room were a dungeon, maximizing the bellows. Then the line went dead.

Shaking, I listened to the flatline of the phone for a minute before gently placing it in its cradle, too scared to call back for fear of what I might hear. I had grown up in an ideal family setting: a mom and a dad and an older sister as a role model. This kind of situation took me by surprise, and I felt confused and helpless at the same time. A couple of tense hours later, after his father had gone to bed, Rion called me to apologize. He told me his dad had received a letter from his ex-wife, Rion's mom, saying she refused to pay child support. Having no other scapegoat, he stumbled into Rion's room in rage.

"I can't take this anymore. All the fighting . . . it's always there. . . ." His voice had trailed off, lost in painful thought. "All I have to do is pull the trigger, and it will be over."

"No!" I screamed. "Don't talk like that! You know you have so much to live for." It was becoming clearer every second how threatening the situation was. A cold, forced chuckle came from the other end of the line. "Yeah, right," was his response. We got off the phone, but only after promising to go right to sleep.

Sleep, however, was light years away from me. I was so worried and had a feeling I was Rion's only hope. He had told me repeatedly that it was hard to open up to anyone but me. How could someone not want to live? I could literally list the reasons why I loved waking up every morning. Frantically, I racked my brain for ways to convince Rion of this. Then the lightbulb clicked on. I took a piece of notebook paper and entitled it, "Why Rion Should

Live." Below, I began listing every reason I could think of that a person had to exist. What started as a few sentences turned into twenty, then thirty-two, then forty-seven. By midnight, I had penned fifty-seven reasons for Rion to live. The last ten were as follows:

48) Six feet of earth is pretty heavy.
49) They don't play Metallica in cemeteries.
50) Braces aren't biodegradable.
51) God loves you.
52) Believe it or not, your father loves you, too.
53) Spanish One would be so boring.
54) Two words: driver's license.
55) Satan isn't exactly the type of guy you want to hang out with for eternity.
56) How could you live without Twinkies?
57) You should never regret who you are, only what you have become.

Believing that I had done my best, I crawled into bed to await tomorrow's chore: saving Rion.

I waited for him at the door to Spanish the next day and handed him the paper as he walked in. I watched him from the opposite side of the room while he read the creased sheet in his lap. I waited, but he didn't look up for the entire period. After class, I approached him, concerned, but before I could say a word, his arms were around me in a tight embrace. I hugged him for a while, tears almost blinding me. He let go, and with a soft look into my eyes, he walked out of the room. No thank you was needed, his face said it all.

A week later, Rion was transferred to another school district so that he could live with his grandmother. For weeks I heard nothing, until one night the phone rang. "Sarah, is it you?" I heard the familiar voice say. Well, it was like we had never missed a day. I updated him on Ms.

Canaple's new haircut, and he told me his grades were much better, and he was on the soccer team. He is even going to counseling with his dad to help them build a stronger relationship. "But do you know what the best part is?" I sensed true happiness in his voice. "I don't regret who I am, nor what I've become."

Sarah Barnett

[EDITORS' NOTE: *Rion was lucky. Everyone isn't as fortunate. If you are depressed or thinking about hurting yourself, (or if you think any of your friends are in this situation)*, please call for help, toll-free: **1-800-SUICIDE**. *Remember, you are not alone. People care and can help you.* **WE LOVE YOU!!**]

She Told Me It Was Okay to Cry

It takes a lot of understanding, time and trust to gain a close friendship with someone. As I approach a time of my life of complete uncertainty, my friends are my most precious asset.

Erynn Miller

I saw her last night for the first time in years. She was miserable. She had bleached her hair, trying to hide its true color, just as her rough front hid her deep unhappiness. She needed to talk, so we went for a walk. While I thought about my future, the college applications that had recently arrived, she thought about her past, the home she had recently left. Then she spoke. She told me about her love—and I saw a dependent relationship with a dominating man. She told me about the drugs—and I saw that they were her escape. She told me about her goals—and I saw unrealistic material dreams. She told me she needed a friend—and I saw hope, because at least I could give her that.

We had met in the second grade. She was missing a tooth, I was missing my friends. I had just moved across the continent to find cold metal swings and cold smirking faces outside the foreboding doors of P.S. 174, my new school. I asked her if I could see her Archie comic book, even though I didn't really like comics; she said yes, even though she didn't really like to share. Maybe we were both looking for a smile. And we found it. We found someone to giggle with late at night, someone to slurp hot chocolate with on the cold winter days when school was canceled and we would sit together by the bay window, watching the snow endlessly falling.

In the summer, at the pool, I got stung by a bee. She held my hand and told me that she was there and that it was okay to cry—so I did. In the fall, we raked the leaves into piles and took turns jumping, never afraid because we knew that the multicolored bed would break our fall.

Only now, she had fallen and there was no one to catch her. We hadn't spoken in months, we hadn't seen each other in years. I had moved to California, she had moved out of the house. Our experiences were miles apart, making our hearts much farther away from each other than the continent she had just traversed. Through her words I was alienated, but through her eyes I felt her yearning. She needed support in her search for strength and a new start. She needed my friendship now more than ever. So I took her hand and told her that I was there and that it was okay to cry—so she did.

Daphna Renan

I Just Wanted to Be Skinny

I couldn't believe that I hadn't let myself see how awful
Colleen had become. I was so ashamed of myself at that
moment, staring at her in her size zero sundress draped
loosely over her. She looked like a little girl swimming in
her mother's clothes. It was as if I was seeing her for the
first time. Her adorable round baby face had become so
gaunt, and her once bright eyes had become dull and
faded, now just slightly sunken in as if all her desire for
life had been sucked out of her. I began to panic as my
eyes frantically scanned the rest of her body. But it was no
use. With every glance, I saw skin and bone where there
should have been the beginnings of womanly curves.
Everything about her was so tiny and frail that she
reminded me of a twig that could be snapped with the
blow of a harsh winter wind. I was overwhelmed with
guilt. I was supposed to be her friend. I was supposed to
keep her from doing things like this to herself. I had
promised I would always be there for her. And right then,
I wanted to run crying from the store because I knew I
had failed. Instead, I just stood there next to her, unable to
say anything, while she critiqued herself about how fat

she looked and how tight the dress was. How had this happened?

I later found out it began in the eighth grade, which was the year when attention on being thin became emphasized. Diets became an obsession for many girls. There was a new one to try every week, each promising better results than the last. They were "in style" the same way green nail polish or jelly sandals were. Colleen was always insecure about being fat, which surprised me because she had such a healthy looking body. But seeing those stick-figured girls talk about their diets only perpetuated Colleen's insecurity.

How could I have been so dumb and so blind? How could I not have realized that her reasoning for all the missed school lunches were just excuses, that she hadn't conveniently just eaten before she came over? And all the times my friends and I invited her to eat with us, how could we not have seen the pattern in her continuous declines, saying she would love to come . . . another time?

Colleen's parents took her to see a doctor, and he confirmed everyone's worst fear: He diagnosed her as anorexic. It sounded so weird to hear her called that; even though everyone knew she was, no one had ever actually said it before. Colleen was anorexic. It was almost as if I had to say it to myself a couple of times before I could really comprehend it. She weighed only eighty-six pounds at a height of 5'4" when she was admitted, and the doctors said that had she continued the destructive pattern much longer, there was a good chance she could have died of a heart attack. Imagine that—dying of a heart attack at age fourteen.

The doctors and psychologists asked Colleen repeatedly, "What made you decide to stop eating?" And she always answered sincerely and simply, "I just wanted to be skinny." This reply frustrated them. I guess they expected to hear a huge psychological reasoning behind her anorexia, like pressure from her parents, school or sports. I'm not really sure what they wanted to hear, but they couldn't seem to accept that Colleen starved herself because she just wanted to be thinner.

It's been a little over a year now, and I'm proud to say that Colleen has only been back to the hospital once. She has worked incredibly hard to gain back her normal, stress-free life, and it's been a difficult struggle. But I know she will win this battle in the end.

It bothers me, though, that Colleen's struggle could have been prevented. What is it that makes girls feel like they must look like waifs before they are considered beautiful? Some people might blame the media, others may fault the girl's lack of self-confidence, or the parents for not providing better examples. Maybe it's a little of all three. If only there were a way to tell each young, impressionable girl that women are *supposed* to be different shapes, that it's all those dozens of unique figures that make our world beautiful. If only there were some way to tell them that it's this variety that makes every woman truly beautiful. Then, maybe, cases like Colleen's could be prevented.

Laura Bloor

The Rift

I sit perched on the edge of my bed, faint smiles drifting across my face, as I sift through all my old photographs. My sleeves pushed up over my elbows, I dig down into all the old memories. I hold each memory briefly in my hands before dropping it onto the pile in my lap and searching for the next happy moment to remember. Each picture evokes feelings long gone, but deep within me. I'm not exactly sure what has prompted this sudden trip to my past, but I feel like I need to stop, and look back.

As I continue to relive the memories, I can't help but notice one photo in particular buried deep in the box. I pluck it from the sea of snapshots and hold it in my hands. The picture at first glance is lovely. The sun was shining with not a cloud to be seen in the bright blue canopy that hung high over my head. I was sitting with my arm around a happy-looking girl, her arm rested casually on my shoulders. As I focus in on the person's face, the warm smile that covers my face is replaced by an agitated frown. It is Amy Soule, my now ex-best friend. A terrible pang of regret flashes through me, and I feel the familiar constriction in my throat.

I'm not sure exactly how, or when our decline as friends started, but it started small. A simple crack that flourished in our awkward adolescence and shameful neglect. It began with simple differences in interest. She wanted to go to the mall and scout for guys, while I wanted to spend the evening watching old movies and talking about nonsense gossip. Suddenly after-school activities took up our usual time together and weekends were spent doing other things. Soon the only time I saw her was when we exchanged a hurried hello in the busy school halls between classes. A far cry from the whispered conversations behind my half-open locker at every spare moment. No more notes were passed behind the teacher's back, and my parents' phone bill became considerably cheaper. She found a new group of friends, and so did I. Before I had a chance to patch the crack between us, she moved away from me, causing the crack to become an uncrossable rift.

I tried to make excuses for not keeping in touch. I couldn't visit, it was too far and I couldn't ask Mom to drive me all that way. I even tried to convince my nagging conscience with the notion that people change, I matured, and that is why. I knew that was not the answer, but I was too nervous to pick up the phone and call. The rift grew too large to bridge. Amy had left, and she had taken a huge chunk of my heart with her.

I stand up and stretch my cramping limbs. Pulling myself back into the now, I let the picture fall from my hand onto my cluttered desk. I glance up at my calendar and remember that Amy's birthday is around the corner. In fact, we were born in the same room, two days apart. It had always been a good-natured joke between us that she was two days older than I. We started so close, and ended up so far. This bittersweet memory causes me to smile despite my feelings of regret. I suddenly have an idea. I hastily drop to my knees and begin to rummage through my desk drawers. At last I lay my hands on an old picture frame I have had around forever. I pick up the fallen photo of Amy and me, and snap it into the frame. I quickly pen a note, and for lack of anything better to say, I simply write,

Happy Birthday Amy!
Erica

I stick the piece of white paper under the edge of the frame and search for Amy's address. I hold the frame tightly in my arms. I am not going to let this golden chance slip through my fingers. It's not much, but it is a beginning and the space between us has already gotten smaller. Maybe this time I will be strong enough to build a bridge.

Erica Thoits
Teen People *contest winner*

The Right Thing

The counselor was late for our appointment. I sat in one of the hard plastic chairs in her office that, despite a few squirming attempts to rearrange myself, continued to be uncomfortable. I glanced at the boy who sat beside me, my partner in crime. He looked upset and unsure, wounded by the decision that we had finally made out of desperation. Friends for many years, we now offered each other little comfort as we sat lost in our own thoughts and doubt.

My tingling nerves heightened my senses, and I took in everything around me. From the smell of freshly sharpened pencils to the sight of the overly organized desk, the room oozed with the aura of a disciplined junior high school counselor and I found myself again questioning our judgment in choosing this complete stranger to help save our friend.

She entered in a cloud of smiles and apologies for being late. Sitting down across from us, she looked at us expectantly. I felt as if she were waiting for us to announce that she had just won the lottery rather than tell the story of pain and frustration we had both been holding in for so long.

I was overcome for a moment by the fear that had nested in my stomach. It was hard to imagine how my best friend Suzie would react when she found out that the two people she had trusted most in the world had betrayed her. But selfishly, I was also concerned about how this betrayal would affect me. *Would she hate me? Would she even speak to me?* As much as the pain that she would feel, I contemplated whether or not I would have a best friend the next day.

"Why don't you begin, Kelly, by telling me why you're here?" the counselor suggested. I cast one more glance at my friend; his sad eyes confirmed that we were doing the right thing.

As I began to tell Suzie's story, my uncertainty gave way to a feeling of relief. Carrying the emotional burden of a friend who was slowly killing herself was a lot for a fourteen-year-old to handle, and more than I could stand any longer. Like an exhausted runner, I was passing on the baton for someone else to carry.

By way of my emotional and broken telling, Suzie's story came out. How we laughed at her strange habit of breaking all her food into tiny little pieces, not realizing that by splitting her food up, she could take more time to eat less. How we went along with her self-deprecating jokes about how overweight she was, without realizing that deep inside, she wasn't joking.

The guilt rose in my throat as I related fact after fact, knowing now that all these things should have made us aware months earlier that Suzie actually had a very serious problem. We had pushed it away as she had deteriorated a little at a time. It wasn't until it was almost too late that we had finally understood the big picture.

I explained that the depression that typically walked hand-in-hand with anorexia had closed in on Suzie a few weeks earlier. I had sat by her side, avoiding the sight of her dark-circled eyes and gaunt cheekbones as she told me that she now ate practically nothing at all, and that for no explainable reason, she would often cry for hours.

It was then that I too began to cry. I couldn't stop my tears as I explained how I hadn't known how to stop my friend's tears, either. She had reached a point that terrified me, and the terror in my voice was plain as I revealed the last thing I knew, the thing that had cemented my determination to tell someone: She was looking for an escape from the pain, sadness and feelings of inadequacy that were now constant for her. She thought that killing herself might be that way out.

My part completed, I sat back in disbelief. I had just poured out secret after secret that I had been told with the understanding that I would never speak them again. I had shattered the most sacred aspect of our friendship: trust. A trust that had taken time, love, and good and bad experiences to build had just been destroyed in ten minutes, broken out of helplessness, desperation and the burden that I could no longer bear. I felt weak. I hated myself at that moment.

So did Suzie.

She needed no explanation when she was called to the office. She looked at me, at her boyfriend sitting at my side, at the concerned look of the counselor. The tears of fury that welled up in her eyes said that she understood. As she began to cry out of anger and relief, the counselor gently sent Aaron and me back to class, shutting the door behind us.

I didn't go back to class right away, but instead walked the hallways of the school trying to make sense of the emotional ramblings going through my head. Though I had just possibly saved my friend's life, I felt less than heroic.

I still can recall the overwhelming sadness and fear that

surrounded me, as I was sure that my actions had just cost me one of the best friends I'd ever had. But an hour later, Suzie returned from the counseling office, and with tears in her eyes, headed straight into my arms for a hug that I, perhaps even more than she, needed.

It was then that I realized that no matter how angry she was at me, she would still need her best friend to help her get through what was going to be a very difficult journey. I had just learned one of my first lessons of growing up and being a true friend—that it can be hard, and even terrifying, to do what you know is the right thing.

A year later, Suzie handed me my copy of her school picture. In it, she had color in her cheeks again, and the smile that I had missed for so long spread across her face. And on the back, this message:

> Kel,
>
> You were always there for me, whether I wanted you to be or not. Thank you. There's no getting rid of me now—you're stuck with me!
> I love you,
> Suzie

Kelly Garnett

Donna and Claudia

Donna is my sister, and I always thought of her as beautiful. Our father called her his princess. When Donna entered high school, with her long blond hair and incredible blue eyes, she caught the attention of the boys. There were the usual crushes and school dances, phone calls and giggles, and hours of combing and brushing her hair to make it glow. She had eye shadow to match the perfect blue of her eyes. Our parents were protective of us, and my father in particular kept close watch over the boys she dated.

One Saturday in April, three weeks before Donna's sixteenth birthday, a boy called and asked her to go to an amusement park. It was in the next state, about twenty miles away. They would be going with four other friends. Our parents' first answer was a firm no, but Donna eventually wore them down. On her way out the door, they told her to be home by eleven, no later.

It was a great night! The roller coasters were fast, the games were fun and the food was good. Time flew by. Finally one of them realized it was already 10:45 P.M. Being young and slightly afraid of our father, the boy who was driving decided he could make it home in fifteen minutes. It never occurred to any of them to call and ask if they could be late.

Speeding down the highway, the driver noticed the exit too late. He tried to make it anyway. The car ripped out nine metal guardrails and flipped over three times before it came to a stop on its roof. Someone pulled Donna from the car, and she crawled over to check on her friends. There was blood everywhere. As she pulled her hair back from her eyes so she could see better, her hand slipped underneath her scalp.

The blood was coming from her. Practically the entire top of Donna's head had been cut off, held on by just a few inches of scalp.

When the police cruiser arrived to rush Donna to a nearby hospital, an officer sat with her, holding her scalp in place. Donna asked him if she was going to die. He told her he didn't know.

At home, I was watching television when a creepy feeling went through me, and I thought about Donna. A few minutes went by, and the telephone rang. Mom answered it. She made a groaning noise and fell to the floor, calling for my father. They rushed out the door, telling my sister Teri and me that Donna had been in a car accident, and that they had to go to the hospital to get her. Teri and I stayed up for hours waiting for them. We changed the sheets on Donna's bed and waited. Somewhere around four o'clock in the morning, we pulled the sofa bed out and fell asleep together.

Mom and Dad were not prepared for what they saw at the hospital. The doctors had to wait until our parents arrived to stitch up Donna's head. They didn't expect her to survive the night.

At 7:00 A.M., my parents returned home. Teri was still sleeping. Mom went straight to her bedroom and Dad went into the kitchen and sat at the table. He had a white plastic garbage bag between his legs and was opening it up when I sat down at the table with him. I asked him how Donna was and he told me that the doctors didn't think she was going to make it. As I struggled to think about that, he started pulling her clothes out of the bag. They were soaked with blood and blond hair.

Some of the hair had Donna's scalp attached to it. Every piece of clothing she had worn that night was soaked with blood. I can't remember thinking anything. All I did was stare at the clothes. When Teri woke up, I showed them to her. I'm sure it was an awful thing to do, but I was in such shock that it was all I could think of.

At the hospital later that morning, Teri and I had to wait outside for a long time before we could see Donna. It was an old hospital and it smelled old, and Teri and I were afraid of it. Finally we were allowed in to see our sister. Her head was wrapped in white gauze that was stained with blood. Her face was swollen, which I couldn't understand because she had lost so much blood. I thought she would look smaller. She reached up and touched my long brown hair and started to cry.

The next day, I called a neighbor who was a hairdresser and asked her to cut my hair. It's a funny thing—I loved my long brown hair and it curled just right, but I never, ever missed it or wanted it back. All I wanted was for Donna to come home and sleep in the clean sheets that Teri and I had put on her bed.

Donna was in the hospital for two weeks. Many of her friends went to see her, especially Claudia, who was there a lot. Mom and Dad never liked Claudia—maybe because she seemed "fast," maybe because she spoke her mind; I don't really know. They just didn't like her being around.

Donna came home with the entire top half of her head shaved. She had hundreds of stitches, some of which came across her forehead and between her left eye and eyebrow. For a while she wore a gauze cap. Eventually she had our hairdresser neighbor cut the rest of her hair. It had been so soaked and matted with blood that she couldn't get it out. The hairdresser was such a kind person. She found Donna a human hair wig that perfectly matched her hair.

Donna celebrated her sixteenth birthday and went back to school. I don't know where rotten people come from, and I don't know why they exist, but they do. There was a very loud-mouthed, self-centered girl in some of Donna's classes who took great pleasure in tormenting my sister. She would sit behind her and pull slightly on Donna's wig. She'd say very quietly, "Hey, Wiggy, let's see your scars." Then she'd laugh.

Donna never said anything to anybody about her tormentor until the day she finally told Claudia. Claudia was in most of Donna's classes, and from then on kept a close eye on my sister. Whenever that girl got close to Donna, Claudia would try and be there. There was something about Claudia that was intimidating, even to the worst kids in school. No one messed with her. Unfortunately, though, Claudia wasn't always around, and the teasing and name-calling continued.

One Friday night, Claudia called and asked Donna to come spend the night at her house. My parents didn't want Donna to go—not just because they didn't like Claudia, but because they had become so protective of Donna. In the end, they knew they had to let her go, even though they probably spent the whole night worrying.

Claudia had something special waiting for my sister. She knew how awful Donna felt about her hair, so Claudia had shaved off her own beautiful long brown hair. The next day, she took Donna wig shopping for identical blond and brown wigs. When they went to school that Monday, Claudia was ready for the teasers. In a vocabulary not allowed inside school walls, she set them straight so that anyone ready to tease my sister knew they would have to mess with Claudia. It didn't take long for the message to get through.

Donna and Claudia wore their wigs for over a year, until they felt their hair had grown out enough to take them off. Only when Donna was ready did they go to school without them. By then, she had developed a stronger self-confidence and acceptance.

My sister graduated from high school. She is married and has two great kids. Twenty-eight years later, she is still friends with Claudia.

Carol Gallivan

I Need You Now

My friend, I need you now—
Please take me by the hand.
Stand by me in my hour of need,
Take time to understand.

Take my hand, dear friend,
And lead me from this place.
Chase away my doubts and fears,
Wipe the tears from off my face.

Friend, I cannot stand alone.
I need your hand to hold,
The warmth of your gentle touch
In my world that's grown so cold.

Please be a friend to me
And hold me day by day.
Because with your loving hand in mine,
I know we'll find the way.

Becky Tucker

Choices

Hold a friend's hand through times of trial,
Let her find love through a hug and a smile;
But also know when it is time to let go—
For each and every one of us must learn to grow.

Sharon A. Heilbrunn

When I first met Molly, she instantly became my best friend. We enjoyed the same things, laughed at the same jokes and even had the same love for sunflowers.

It seemed like we had found each other at the right time. Both of us had been in different groups of friends that didn't get along or we didn't feel comfortable in. We were thrilled to find each other.

Our friendship grew very strong. Our families became friends, and everyone knew that wherever you found Molly, you found me, and vice versa. In fifth grade, we were not in the same class, but at lunch we both sat in nearby assigned seats and turned around to talk to each other. The lunch ladies did not like this. We were always blocking the aisle, talking too loudly and not eating our lunches, but we didn't care. The teachers

knew we were best friends, but we were also a distur-
bance. Our big mouths got us into trouble, and we were
warned that we would never be in the same classes
again if we kept this up.

That summer, Molly and her brother were at my house
quite often. My mom took care of them while their mom
worked. We went swimming, played outside and practiced playing our flutes. We bought best-friend charms
and made sure to wear them as often as possible.

Summer went by very quickly, and middle school
began. As the teachers had warned us, we were not in the
same classes. We still talked on the phone, went over to
each other's houses, sang in choir and practiced our flutes
together in band. Nothing could destroy this friendship.

Seventh grade started and, again, we were not in the
same classes and could not sit near each other at lunch. It
seemed as if we were being put to a test. We both made
new friends. Molly started to hang out with a new group
of people and was growing very popular.

We spent less time together, and we rarely talked on the
phone. At school, I would try to talk to her, but she would
just ignore me. When we did take a minute to talk, one of
her more popular friends would come up and Molly would
just walk away with her, leaving me in the dust. It hurt.

I was so confused. I'm sure she didn't know at the
time how badly I felt, but how could I talk to her if she
wouldn't listen? I began to hang around with my new
friends, but it just wasn't the same. I met Erin, who was
also a friend of Molly's. She was in the same situation I was
with Molly. She and Molly had been close friends, and
lately Molly had been treating Erin the same way as me.
We decided to talk to her.

The phone call was not easy. Talking and saying how I
felt was difficult. I was so afraid that I would hurt her feelings and make her angry. It was funny, though—when it

was just the two of us talking on the phone, we were friends again. It was the old Molly.

I explained how I was feeling, and she did, too. I realized I was not the only one hurting. She was alone without me to talk to. What was she supposed to do, not make new friends? I didn't think about this before, but she was feeling left out by me and my new friends. There were times when I didn't even notice I was ignoring her. We must have talked for a long time, because once we were finished I had used a handful of tissues for my tears, and felt as if I had lifted a heavy weight off my heart. We both decided that we wanted to be with our new friends, but we would never forget the fun and friendship we had shared with each other.

Today, I look back on all of this and smile. Molly and I are finally in the same classes, and you know what? We still get in trouble for talking too loudly. Molly is not my best friend anymore, but more like my sister. We still enjoy the same things, laugh at the same jokes and share the same love for sunflowers. I will never forget her. Molly taught me something very important. She taught me that things change, people change, and it doesn't mean you forget the past or try to cover it up. It simply means that you move on, and treasure all the memories.

Alicia M. Boxler

"You're my friend, Katie, but we just don't
fight enough to be *best* friends."

Reprinted by permission of Randy Glasbergen.

Friends Forever

It seemed as if Chrissy and I had been friends forever. Ever since we'd met on the first day of fourth grade, we had been inseparable. We did almost everything together. We were so close that when it came time to pick partners, it was just assumed that we'd pick each other.

In ninth grade, however, things changed. We had been in the same classes for the last five years, but now we were going to different schools. At first we were as good friends as ever, but eventually we found we had no time for each other. Slowly but surely, we were drifting apart. Promises were broken and important get-togethers postponed. I think both of us knew we were breaking apart, but neither of us wanted to admit it.

Then one day, I finally faced the fact that Chrissy and I weren't close anymore. We'd both grown up, and didn't have much in common any longer. I still missed her, though. We had shared five incredible years together—years I will never forget. Years I don't *want* to forget.

One day, as I was thinking of our great times together, I wrote a poem about our friendship. It was about letting go and growing up, but never forgetting friends.

I still talk to Chrissy sometimes, though now it's hard because we both have such busy schedules.

To this day, I still think of Chrissy as one of my best friends . . . even though by some definitions we aren't. But when I'm asked to list my friends, I never hesitate to add her name. Because as she would always say: "Real friends are forever." When I gave her this poem we both cried, for it's changes like these that make growing up so difficult.

Changes

"Friends forever," you promised.
"Together till the end."
We did everything with each other.
You were my best friend.

When I was sad, you were by my side.
When I was scared, you felt my fear.
You were my best support—
If I needed you, you were there.

You were the greatest friend,
You always knew what to say:
You made everything seem better.
As long as we had each other,
Everything would be okay.

But somewhere along the line,
We slowly came apart.
I was here, you were there,
It tore a hole in my heart.

Things were changing,
Our cheerful music reversed its tune.
It was like having salt without pepper,
A sun without its moon.

Suddenly we were miles apart,
Two different people, with nothing the same.
It was as if we hadn't been friends;
Although we knew deep in our hearts
Neither one of us was to blame.

You had made many new friends
And luckily, so had I
But that didn't change the hurt—
The loss of our friendship made me cry.

As we grow older, things must change
But they don't always have to end.
Even though it is different, now,
You will always be my friend.

Phyllis Lin

I Remember Gilbert

It's been seven months since I last saw the light in Gil's room. Mrs. Blithe waved at me from his bedroom window next door. I smiled, but inside I was numb.

I will never forget the first day I met Gil and his mom. I was seven, and Mom and Dad were taking me to our new house in the suburbs. My mother's employer transferred her, so we'd had to move and leave everything behind.

I missed my room and my best friends back home. I could not believe how my parents were torturing me. The idea of going to a new school was frightening. I didn't have any friends to talk to, and I did not want to make new friends either.

My grandparents were at the new two-story house to welcome us, and I noticed a lady hugging my mother. It turned out that Mrs. Blithe was Mom's best friend from high school and our new next-door neighbor.

Mom took me to my room upstairs, and I let myself fall onto the bed. I must have fallen asleep because the next thing I knew, it was getting dark. The huge window in my room was open, and I could hear loud music coming from outside. I looked out the window, and across from me was another window. A boy in dark clothes was looking through his telescope and into the glittering night sky. Right away, I noticed the white Christmas lights on his ceiling.

"Hi, I'm Gilbert Jim Jonathan Blithe. Call me Gil." He startled me.

"I'm Katharine Kennedy—Katie for short," I shouted back.

It was our beautiful beginning. I realized then and there that I liked this weird neighbor of mine. Gil was like a brother to me. We spent countless hours just talking and telling stories to each other. My dad put a fire escape ladder on my window. After that, Gil used it as an entrance to my room. Funny, he never used the front door. And he had lights on his ceiling because the stars and planets fascinated him.

When school started, we biked there together. He kept me safe and held me back from hurting myself. Sometimes, *I* had to keep *him* out of trouble. Afterwards, we would go to the park and play on the monkey bars. Most of the time my family's backyard was our playground, and the big acacia tree, which had boards nailed to its trunk, held our tree house. It was home, and nobody was allowed in there except us.

Summers passed and I turned thirteen. Gil gave me April blossoms. Then Mrs. Blithe told Mom and me that Gil was sick and needed a heart transplant. When I heard that, I was so distressed, I felt I needed one, too.

The hospital was gloomy. A white-walled prison that had disgusting food. Every day, Gil had to eat mushy-looking meals. I promised him I'd bring chocolate-covered peanuts the next day, and I knew I made him happier.

Whenever Gil sensed I was anxious or about to cry, he would tell me to look out my bedroom window. "Let the light in my room tell you I'm always there," he said softly.

He always found a way to make me smile.

After a month in the hospital, Gil came home. It was the first time I had ever been in his room, and it felt peculiar. It was unexpectedly neat. After jumping onto his bed and throwing me a pillow, he said he missed his room. I said I missed him more. It troubled me that things might never be the same, but Gil was up and about after a couple of weeks. I knew he was all right when he climbed up to my room and ate pizza with me.

Before we knew it, Gil and I were in high school. School and girls kept him occupied, but he was always there. Despite our jobs, we spent sunny summers together. As usual, the days hanging out with him passed quickly. But then he got sick again.

During the first semester of our senior year, Gil was taken to the hospital for the second time. At first I thought it was a false alarm, but it was worse than I could imagine. All I could do was hope and pray that he would get better. The unlit room across from mine was the constant reminder of his being away. I visited him in the hospital as often as I could, even though I never knew what to say. To tell him that everything would be all right was a fallacy, yet it comforted us both.

Christmas was spent in a cold hospital room. He was determined that we would go to our graduation together. I assured him we would. I held his hand and looked into his eyes until they stopped looking into mine. No words were uttered; we both knew what we were feeling. He looked peaceful when he said his last good-bye.

I locked his face at that moment in my thoughts, but it wounded my soul. He went away even though I tried my best to keep time from slipping.

How could a friend, someone who was with me and kept me happy, be the one person who would leave me now, forever? There was no one now to console me.

Now, as I stood looking at his bedroom window and the stars and planets on his ceiling, I knew he would always be there—in my room, in my heart and in my memories. I wiped away the tears on my cheek, and I saw a little boy waving at me. Until this day, I cannot figure why I could not say "I love you" to Gil, even at the last second. Maybe because I knew he felt the same way.

I'm leaving for college soon, and I am sad he won't be there to laugh at my jokes or comfort me when I'm blue. But because of a little boy looking through a telescope into the infinite night sky, I now know that friendship goes beyond time. I will always remember Gilbert, and the light of his love tells me he's always there.

April Joy Gazmen

The Tragic Reunion

I almost dropped the phone when I heard the words. "Julia's father died today." After I hung up, I walked to my room in a daze and fumbled with my CD player, hoping that the sound of my favorite songs would provide some comfort.

Although I had known this day was coming, I still felt as if the wind had been knocked out of me. As I sat on my bed, the tears came. My mother came quietly into the room and held me in a gentle embrace.

As I sat cradled in my mother's arms, I thought about last summer. I had gone with Julia and her parents on a trip to an island off the coast of South Carolina. We'd had a great time together, sharing breathtaking sunsets on the beach, eating at posh restaurants and biking along the rugged coastline. Julia's dad had taken it upon himself to fulfill our every desire.

Now I knew that beneath all the laughter and fun, Mr. Yolanda must have been suffering. One night, as Julia and I were getting ready to go out, Mrs. Yolanda came into our room looking upset. She told us that Mr. Yolanda was sick and was not up to coming with us. Julia didn't seem alarmed, and we went out as we had planned without her father.

The next day Mr. Yolanda appeared to be his usual self: soft-spoken, generous and on the go. Since his illness was not mentioned again, I didn't think about it any more for the rest of that wonderful trip.

When school started, my friendship with Julia began to change. I watched as she became caught up in making new friends. She didn't include me in her new plans, and I felt left in the dust. Pretty soon, we were no longer best friends. In fact, we were barely friends at all.

One day, my mother sat me down and told me that Mr. Yolanda had terminal pancreatic cancer. Shocked, my thoughts turned to Julia. At school she seemed a happy-go-lucky teen. Her sunny exterior displayed no sign of any turmoil, but now I knew it had to be present somewhere within her. Not wanting to upset Julia in school, and still feeling separate from her, I didn't say anything to her about her father. But inside, I wanted to run up to her in the hallway, give her a hug, and let her know that I was there and that I cared.

Now I wondered, as I walked nervously into the funeral home, if it was too late. Wakes make me uncomfortable, probably because they make death so real. And the thought of seeing Julia in this setting, knowing what a very private person she was, also made me uneasy. As my friends and I got in line to pay our respects to Mr. Yolanda, I noticed pictures of the Yolandas surrounding the casket. One photograph in particular jumped out at me. It was of Mr. Yolanda and Julia on our vacation in South Carolina.

The photograph triggered an overwhelming sadness in me, and I began to weep. I simply could not understand why God would take a parent away from his child. Julia found me then and seeing me in tears, she too began to cry.

Even though I told her how sorry I was about her father, I realized I could never fully understand what she was going through. What was it like to come home every day to a house where someone you loved was dying, or to head off to school each morning not knowing if your father would be alive when you got home? I couldn't imagine. But I did know how to express support and compassion. It wasn't too late.

Julia apologized for her neglect of our friendship, and we vowed to be friends again. A funeral is a strange place to make up with a friend, but I guess a tragic reunion is better than none at all.

Amy Muscato
Submitted by Olive O'Sullivan

My Fairy Tale

The road to a friend's house is never long.

Danish Proverb

He was the stuff fairy tales are made of—not unrealistically suave, but definitely charming. Tall and handsome, he was a prince by all conventional definitions and had the ability to steal unsuspecting young girls' hearts.

Our first kiss was perfect, and from that moment on, our relationship soared. Some days, he picked me up early for school so that we could eat breakfast together, and other days we sneaked away for snowball fights during study hall. On weekends, I watched him play soccer, and he came to all of my softball games. And then we'd end our week with the ritual of a Saturday night movie at his house. Without fail, we talked on the phone every night until we fell asleep. A few months into our relationship, I had no time for anyone but him. But at the time, I liked it that way. I was perfectly content to be with him every second, because I was, without a doubt, in love.

But sometime during our nine-month walk in the

clouds, the honeymoon stage ended, and our relationship lost its spontaneity and sparkle. Saturday nights spent together became routine, and phone calls and kisses became as natural and expected as breathing.

On one particularly cold June day, Chris broke up with me. He said that he woke up that morning and realized he didn't love me. He said our relationship consisted of nothing but the memories of our past. It was two days before our nine-month anniversary. I felt empty inside, and the thought of being alone was uncomfortable and scary. Moreover, the person on whom I depended to pull me through hard times was the cause of my pain. My heart literally hurt.

Not knowing what else to do, I ran to a familiar place, Ashley's house. It was a place I hadn't visited often in the nine months before this afternoon. I stood at the door, and Ashley, seeing my tears, immediately understood what had happened. Within an hour, my three closest friends, the girls I had once spent so much time with, all arrived at Ashley's house. For the next two days, we camped out at Ashley's and analyzed every aspect of Chris's and my relationship, attempting to pinpoint where it went wrong.

Unable to form any meaningful conclusions, we agreed that we would never understand the male population, and so we moved on to bashing Prince Charming until he was reduced to a creature with the appeal of a toad. It felt good, and I even caught myself laughing for brief moments. Slowly, I began to reclaim my pre-boys, pre-broken-heart days with a little more wisdom and experience than I had before. I realized that life would go on, and I loved and appreciated my girlfriends for that invaluable realization.

Toward the end of our healing party, while we were laughing over ice cream sundaes, Erica looked at me and said, "We've missed you." The truth was, I had really missed them, too. I had unfairly neglected them in the midst of love's wake, and the past two days had shown me just how precious my friends were.

When love had removed its blindfold and all was said and done, I realized that maybe I hadn't had such a fairy-tale boyfriend after all. What I had were fairy-tale friendships. It took a heartbreak to realize the special gift I possessed all along: my girlfriends.

Kathryn Vacca

Colorful Shades of Gray

Moths are very ugly creatures. At least that is what I always thought until a reliable source told me otherwise. When I was about five or six years old, my brother Joseph and I stayed overnight at our Aunt Linda's house, our favorite relative. She spoke to us like adults, and she always had the best stories.

Joseph was only four years old and still afraid of the dark, so Aunt Linda left the door open and the hall light on when she tucked us into bed. Joe couldn't sleep, so he just lay there staring at the ceiling. Just as I dozed off to sleep, he woke me up and asked, "Jennie, what are those ugly things near the light?" (I had always liked that he asked me questions because I was older and supposed to know the answers. I didn't always know the answers, of course, but I could always pretend I did.) He was pointing to the moths fluttering around the hall light. "They're just moths. Go to sleep," I told him.

He wasn't content with that answer or the moths near his night light, so the next time my Aunt walked by the door he asked her to make the ugly moths go away. When she asked why, he said simply, "Because they're ugly and scary, and I don't like them!" She just laughed, rubbed his head, and said, "Joe, just because something is ugly outside doesn't mean it's not beautiful inside. Do you know why moths are brown?" Joe just shook his head.

"Moths were the most beautiful insects in the animal kingdom. At one time they were more colorful than the butterflies. They have always been helpful, kind and generous creatures. One day the angels up in heaven were crying. They were sad because it was cloudy and they couldn't look down upon the people on earth. Their tears fell down to the earth as rain. The sweet little moths hated to see everyone so sad; they decided to make a rainbow. The moths figured that if they asked their cousins, the butterflies, to help, they could all give up just a little bit of their colors, and they could make a beautiful rainbow.

"One of the littlest moths flew to ask the queen of the butterflies for help. The butterflies were too vain and selfish to give up any of their colors for either the people or the angels. So, the moths decided to try to make the rainbow themselves. They beat their wings very hard and the powder on them formed little clouds that the winds smoothed over like glass. Unfortunately, the rainbow wasn't big enough so the moths kept giving a little more and a little more until the rainbow stretched all the way across the sky. They had given away all their color except brown, which didn't fit into their beautiful rainbow.

"Now, the once-colorful moths were plain and brown. The angels up in heaven saw the rainbow and became joyous. They smiled, and the warmth of their smiles shone down on the earth as sunshine. The warm sunshine made the people on earth happy, and they smiled, too. Now every time it rains the baby moths, who still have their colors, spread them across the sky to make more rainbows."

My brother sank off to sleep with that story and hasn't

feared moths since. The story my aunt told us had been gathering dust in the back corners of my brain for years, but recently came back to me.

I have a friend named Abigail who always wears gray clothes. She is also one of the most kind and generous people I've ever met. When people ask her why she doesn't wear more colors, she just smiles that smile and says, "Gray is my color." She knows herself, and she doesn't compromise that to appease other people. Some may see her as plain like a moth, but I know that underneath the gray, Abigail is every color of the rainbow.

Jennie Gratton

My Best Friend Mike

A friend is one who knows you and loves you just the same.

Elbert Hubbard

"Hi. It's Mike . . ."

"Hi, Mike, what's the matter?" Mike had been going through a lot lately, and it was not unusual for him to sound upset.

"I need to tell you something, but I'm not sure if I should," he said. Curiosity got the best of me, and I convinced him to let me in on his big secret. "I can't tell you on the phone. Come over." I walked for five minutes around the block, rang his doorbell and followed his mother's instructions to go up to his room.

Mike had been my best friend for the past two years. At first I thought he was weird. We met during our freshman year of high school and soon became inseparable. The summer after that year was the highlight of our friendship. I never had more fun with any other person. We spent every night and every day together. Time flies when you are having fun, however, and we soon found ourselves back in school. I began to notice a change in Mike. The fun ceased, and I felt a strain in our friendship.

Mike was suffering from depression, and I could not understand why. He seemed to have everything going for him. He was doing well in school, there were no problems at home, and he had many friends who loved him. I soon found myself spending every weekend in his bedroom, trying to convince him to cheer up. Nothing seemed to work. His parents became worried and decided to seek professional help.

Mike began to take medication to counteract his depression, and things seemed a little better, but they were not what they used to be. I was still clueless as to what had been causing this change in his behavior. I did not want to give up on my true best friend, so I continued spending painful hours trying to drag him out of his house.

It was one of those weekends, and there I was, sitting on his bed, waiting to hear what he had to say. I had a sense that he was about to tell me something serious. There was a strange look in his eyes, and he would not focus them on me. The silence was overbearing. He finally looked up at me.

"I'm gay." It hit me like a bolt of lightning. I was shocked. "Okay" was all I managed to utter. Silence followed for minutes afterward.

It took some getting used to, but I decided right then and there that I was not going to lose my best friend over it. Mike seems to be back to his normal self these days. We're seniors now, and I still spend a large portion of my time with him and his friends.

A smile comes to my face every time I think back to the first day we met, and the first thought that came to my mind as I approached the bus stop that day: *Who is that weird kid?* That weird kid is my true best friend, Mike, and there is nothing weird about him.

Brian Leykum

Kim

Friends are treasures.

Horace Bruns

We both lie sideways on her bed, the screen door slapping open and shut with the California breeze. We thumb through fashion magazines, laughing at the hairstyles and smelling the perfume samples. It seems like any other Sunday between girlfriends; laughter filling the room, a half-eaten carton of cookies between the two of us. This was my Sunday afternoon ritual, the two of us and our magazines, and from the time I was twelve, I lived for these afternoons. She was my friend, but more than that, she was a safe place, an unconditional love, and she was an adult.

I had known Kim most of my life. For the first ten years of my life, Kim wasn't one of the closest adults in my life, but her husband John doted on me and was one of the only "grown-ups" to understand my fearless and abundant energy.

When I was twelve, I moved to Los Angeles to live with

my father. Kim and John also lived nearby, and soon after my move, I began spending time at their home. Kim was fun; she liked to laugh and talk about boys. She listened to me while I talked about my crushes and fights with my family. She spoke to me as an equal, as a friend, not a child.

As I grew older, these visits became more important. I would cry over heartbreaks and whine about the latest rejection. The gap in age between us stayed the same, but the space between us grew closer. I called her with secrets, which she kept, and went to her when I couldn't handle my world for a while.

I think my parents went through periods of jealousy and hurt regarding Kim and our friendship, because they wished they could be the ones to whom I came with my stories. I had reached an age where it was harder to relate to my parents, but I still needed guidance. Kim offered that guidance; she didn't force-feed it.

Soon I was sixteen, and things began to change. I sunk into sadness, and I was slipping away from everyone, including Kim. I was taken to the hospital after swallowing a bottle of pain medication, and there, without question, was Kim. She was two hours away when the call came, and she showed up at the hospital with hair things and, of course, magazines. We didn't talk about the incident, but when she pulled my hair up for me, I saw in her eyes true fear and heartache. She used to say to me, "You wouldn't want to spend so much time with me if I really was your mom." I didn't understand those words until that day when she offered me the feeling of love without obligation. She wasn't my mom; she wasn't obligated to love me, she just did.

After my suicide attempt, things between us, though unspoken, began to change. I stopped spending Sunday afternoons at her house. I called, but not as often. I didn't feel good about myself, so I couldn't feel good about our friendship. I figured I had grown up and that we had just grown apart. Like any normal friendship, it had transformed, and I believed that I no longer needed Kim or the friendship.

The summer before I left for college, I went to say goodbye to Kim. Though we hadn't been as close for the last two years, we both cried when I left. I walked down the walkway from her house, and she called out from the kitchen window, "Call me if you need anything." I knew she meant that.

My first semester was hard. I was far from home, a little lonely, and things began to swing back down for me. With pure instinct, I picked up the phone. It was late. Kim picked up the phone, and I asked, "Were you sleeping?" She replied, "Yes, but it's okay. What's wrong? What do you need?" What I needed was Kim. I needed to hear her voice, and feel that California breeze in her back bedroom. I needed to tell her that our friendship had finally surpassed the age gap.

We talked about once a week after that, every Sunday afternoon. I called with the stress of my finals and with my newest boy problem. When I returned home for the summer, I went to Kim's, and we read magazines and ate cookies. I had become an adult, what she had always been. When I was younger, she had related to me on a level that I needed at that time, and now she relates to me as an equal. She was right; things would have been different if she were my mom. I didn't need another mom. I had one. I needed exactly what she gave: love, unconditional. And because she wanted me in her life, not because she had to have me.

Lia Gay

When Forever Ends

An insincere and evil friend is more to be feared than a wild beast; a wild beast may wound your body, but an evil friend will wound your mind.

Buddha

I look back on it now with only sorrow; the passing of time has worn down the sharp edges of bitterness that plagued me for so long. I switch the bracelet from hand to hand, first yanking at it, then soothingly stroking the well-formed stitches, and admiring the skill and precision of the intricately woven strands. Each tightly pulled knot lends the bracelet a nice shape, but does not destroy its delicate softness. I finger the cheap plastic beads, but I don't think scornfully of the inferior material anymore; I can only cherish the way the beads catch the light, reflecting a deep aquamarine, like the shimmering sea before me. In the imitation crystal surface of each little bead I see myself, I see a precious friendship lost, and I wonder for the thousandth time how it could possibly be that I didn't see it coming.

The sunlight streamed in the French windows of the colonial cottage, an odd location to house ninety middle-schoolers during the daytime hours. I knelt on the rough, maroon carpeting and spun the dial of my combination lock. Clockwise to sixteen, opposite to twenty-four, around and back again to eight. I tossed my American history test into my neat and tidy locker, smiling again in satisfaction at the scarlet "A" scrawled on top. I hastily removed the books that I would need over the weekend and stuffed them into my backpack. As I slammed my locker door shut, I caught a glimpse of the pictures and magazine clippings adorning the inside, and, for a split-second, thought of nothing but the happy times shared with friends and captured for posterity in those photographs. Just then, I noticed a small, white envelope flutter to the ground. Stooping, I picked it up. My name was printed on the front in plain block letters, but the generic envelope and handwriting gave no indication of its author. Consumed with curiosity, I tore it open.

"Dear Molly," it began, "I'm sorry, but we can't be friends anymore."

It went on, but my eyes cut quickly to the bottom, searching for a signature. Katie. Katie wrote it? My best friend wrote me a hate letter? Why in the world . . . ? I took a deep breath and started again from the beginning.

"Look, it's nothing you did, I just don't want to be friends anymore, okay?"

Nothing I did?! Why couldn't we be friends if it's nothing I did?!

The letter continued nebulously, a lot of wishy-washy garbage that skirted around any real issues that should have been addressed (not that I could think of any). Nowhere did she state any reason for writing such a thing to me. We hadn't fought in a long time, not really fought, anyway, just the kind of teasing and bantering that are part of healthy friendship. Out of the blue, my best friend hated me? How could she have put up such a casual veneer if all the while her mind was filled with hatred toward me?

A honk from outside jarred me out of my trance. My ride had arrived. Still contemplating the bizarre and unsettling occurrence, I picked up my bag (which suddenly felt like it was filled with bricks) and, with an even heavier heart, headed outside.

Someone was entering as I was leaving, and I started to brush past until I lifted my eyes from the floor and saw who it was. The crumpled note fell from my dangling palm and tumbled down the gray staircase. The tall, gangly blond started to apologize for running into me, but stopped short when she saw the open confusion and horror that creased my dramatic features. Her mouth opened and closed a few times, but she was lost for words, much like I was at the moment. She knew that I had read it. The anxiety was apparent on her ghostly pale face.

She broke the stare first as her eyes looked to the bottom of the staircase, where her note lay in a wrinkled ball. I heard a cough, and at once realized that we were not alone to do battle. Two piercing orbs behind wire-rim glasses and boy-cut bangs approached when Bev stepped forward, as if to shield Katie from the tongue-lashing she mistakenly thought I was prepared to give.

"Look, Molly, Katie doesn't want to be friends with you anymore, okay? She's my friend now."

If I were good at giving retorts on the spur of the moment, I would have unleashed every bit of antipathy within my petite body towards the controlling witch standing before me. If I had, maybe it would have given my former friend the courage she needed to stand up against her new "leader." However, my mind was unable to process what was happening that quickly, and the hundreds of verbally abusive comments that would flash before me in neon lights five minutes later did me no good. I stood, empty inside, as Bev grabbed Katie's sleeve and pulled her up the stairs. My ex-friend shot me one last helpless look, then straightened her mouth into a grim line and marched up the stairs behind her new friend, leaving her old one lost and powerless at the bottom, left to toy with a simple bracelet of beads and string. I had worn her handiwork from the emergence of our friendship through to its demise at that very moment.

Years later, I fiddle with the very same bracelet as I did on that very afternoon. I ask myself the same questions that tormented me then, and I wonder if fighting back would have saved a friendship that was worth fighting for. Katie was weak; she followed Bev as a sheep follows a herder, without question, without fail. I knew that the two of them had grown dependent on each other over the previous couple of years, widening the swiftly growing chasm between Katie and me, but I never dreamt of such a sudden end to our friendship. It shook me to learn that Bev's jealousy of my relationship with "her" friend would surface so spontaneously and drive her to such cruel and desperate measures. I later learned that she had given Katie an ultimatum: Break off her friendship with me or Bev would stop being friends with her. Bev was clever and conniving; she knew whom Katie would choose. I ask myself for the last time why I didn't see it coming. Then I lift the unwieldy and troublesome burden off my shoulders, and heave it into the ocean in the form of a small, string bracelet. Friendships rise and fall like the tide. I cannot stop the tide; I cannot stop what is beyond my control. We swore to be friends forever, but was it right for us to make that promise?

As the beaded trinket sails through the air, another question for the first time enters my thoughts: *Does she still have the bracelet that I made for her?*

Molly Karlin

Falling Out

Dear Travis,

What's happened to us? I used to feel so close to you, but now it's as if there are miles between us. I have always believed that friends come before everything else—girlfriends and boyfriends—everything. I guess I was wrong. Thanks for the push back to reality. I am sorry that we have had a falling out, but I want you to know that I will still be here when (and if) you need me. I will miss you.

Melissa

No "love you," no "yours sincerely" . . . as I noticed how plain my name looked on the paper all by itself, Travis walked into the hallway where I stood waiting by his locker. I glanced around quickly, looking for a way to escape, but before I could leave without being seen, I heard his all-too-familiar "Hey," as he spotted me.

I put my head down as he approached, hoping that he wouldn't see the pain in my eyes. I handed over the letter, which he took with a small smile. "Thanks, Melissa."

"Can you call me tonight?" I replied, "After you read the letter?" My voice was shaking, and my words were unsure, but if he noticed, he didn't let on. I gave him a quick hug and left the hall, though turning from him was one of the hardest things I've ever done.

An hour later, as I talked with my friend Caitlan on the phone, I explained that I couldn't believe what I had actually given to him. What was he going to think?

"He's your *friend*, Melissa. It's going to be okay," Caitlan reassured me. As I listened to her words, I thought of just how important a friend he was. I had always found it easier to confide in guys, because somehow they seem to judge you a little less, while understanding you a little more. That was definitely what I had with Travis. He could understand me when the rest of the world couldn't. He trusted me, let me grow and listened to what I had to say without judgment—whether it was something he wanted to hear or not.

When I had realized that Travis had a thing for my other best friend Janette, I never thought that his asking her out would affect as many things as it did. Suddenly, it was as if he and I had no chance to talk on the phone or write letters, no freedom to hug or be ourselves. Suddenly Janette, whom I had known since the second grade, didn't trust me enough to be with her new boyfriend. She felt jealous . . . but she didn't realize that I, too, had my own feelings of jealousy. I was jealous of the time she got to spend with Travis, and resentful of the time I could not.

The click of call waiting brought my thoughts back to the present, and I answered the other line knowing that it was Travis.

"Hey, so um . . . yeah, that was the saddest letter I have ever read," he began. "I never knew you felt that way."

"Yeah, well, you weren't exactly around to ask, either," I replied harshly.

"Yeah Missa, I know, I know . . . I am sorry that we haven't had much time together, but all I can say is that it will get better. I mean, it can't get any worse. But we can beat this—you and I will always be friends."

"Trav, everybody says that, but you and I both know that it is not going to happen." My voice trembled, and tears welled up in my eyes, threatening to spill over.

"It's different with us, remember? Nothing can tear us apart. We will be friends forever." I hung up the phone that night feeling a little bit better, yet at the same time, wondering if the promise would last.

Time went on, and nothing seemed to change. We seemed to grow farther and farther apart, and the thought that we would ever be friends again slowly faded. We talked once in a while, usually a polite "hi" in the hallway, but our "friendship," as it was, was making me crazy. The night before winter break, I made the decision to bring closure to the situation. I put everything that reminded me of Travis into a box, and put the box in my closet. There was one thing I could not put away: a stuffed lobster named Allen that I had won on a trip to Las Vegas. It was a trip I had spent with Travis. I knew what I had to do.

I saw him at school the next day, and handed him the stuffed animal.

"What's this?" he asked.

"Allen—you do remember him, don't you?"

"Yeah, but . . . " he started to say.

"It's so he can be with you . . . while I can't." My last few words trickled out, and big tears started rolling down my face as I realized this was the last time I could call him a friend. Travis looked at me, motionless and silent, as if only realizing then that we had grown apart, too far beyond repair.

"Are you sure you want to do this?" he asked me. I nodded my head as more tears streamed down my face. He pulled me into his arms, Allen and all. It was one of those hugs that reassures you that someday everything will be all right. And now, I do not regret what happened between us. It was an experience that will make me stronger and help me grow. I had never paid attention to the saying about how boyfriends and girlfriends will come and go, while your friends will last forever. But now, I see it as the most important advice I had ever been given. One day, I know it will be better. Sometimes I see him with Janette, and before he passes, he always gives me that famous smile. . . .

Melissa Lew

My Best Friend

Mmm. Look at those eyes, crystal-blue with just a touch of green. Those long eyelashes are just reaching for me. I can feel it. Oh, my God! Is he looking over here? No, that's silly. I'm looking at him; therefore, there is no way that he'd be looking at me. I mean, that doesn't happen in my life. Or maybe he actually is! No, no, that's just my imagination playing tricks on me. Well, you never know, crazy things do . . .

"What's up, Katie?"

"Oh, hey," I replied as my best friend, Michelle, abruptly interrupted my ongoing battle of mind versus heart.

"So who have you got your eye on tonight? I see those thoughts circling around in that mind of yours. Maybe tonight you'll actually act upon them!"

"What are you talking about? I don't have any of *those* thoughts in my head, as you like to put it. I'm perfectly content to be by myself right now."

I could feel the obviousness of the lie throughout my entire body as I tried to look Michelle straight in the eyes. I'd never lied to her before, and I'm not exactly sure why I did right then. I couldn't believe that I pulled it off. I mean, that's what best friends are for, to obsess over our crushes with. But something inside me prevented me from telling her about this one. I really liked this guy and, as horrible as this sounds, I didn't want any of my friends to mess it up. Every time I even mention that I think a guy is cute, Michelle goes into full matchmaker mode and won't snap out of it until she feels she has accomplished something. Needless to say, that never happens. She makes my crush into such a big deal that I become completely nervous around the guy, and then he thinks I am a complete idiot. I wasn't about to let that happen this time.

"Well, whatever you say. Let's go talk to Tommy, he's hot!"

What did she say? Tommy?!! How did she know? I didn't even tell her this time. No! Now she's going to become little miss matchmaker again and screw things up. Maybe I'm overreacting. Maybe she just thinks Tommy is cute. No, that's terrible! We can't go after the same guy. Michelle would never be interested in Tommy. He's too short for her. Okay, nothing to worry about.

"Come on, Katie! He's walking away!" Michelle screamed as she forcefully tugged on my cute new suede jacket.

"Okay, okay, I'm comin'."

All right, so now we are approaching him. My right foot just got closer. Now my left, right, left, right. STOP THIS! I'm not in the army! It's okay. I can do this. What is the big deal about talking to a guy anyway? He's just a human like me. Oh, but he's such a beautiful human! Look at that body! I can't do this. I can't do . . .

"Hi, Tommy. How's it goin'?" *Oh, my God, I must have sounded like the biggest nerd!*

"What's up, Katie? Hey, Michelle. You girls are looking good tonight. Having fun?"

His voice is so sexy. And he said I looked good!! But he said girlssss. He can't flirt with both of us. That's not allowed.

"Oh, Tommy, stop it. You're so silly. Ha ha. You're tickling me."

Michelle's giggling was loud enough to interrupt all of the conversations at that party. I couldn't believe how much she was flirting with him. Even worse, he was flirting back! Here is my best friend with the guy of my dreams—even though she doesn't know that—and the guy of my dreams was rejecting me more and more by the second. I couldn't exactly pull Michelle aside and ask her to stop. That would only make things worse. She would either be mad at me for not telling her before or she wouldn't even believe me. The only thing I could do was sit there and be quiet.

The whole drive home from the party I had to listen to Michelle go on and on about how amazing Tommy is. She was completely "in love" with him.

"Did you see the way he was flirting with me? I think he likes me. We were talking for an hour and he didn't seem to be paying attention to anyone else! Aren't you happy for me?"

I had always admired Michelle for the amount of confidence she had when it came to guys. If she wanted one, she went for him. Now she just sounded arrogant, as if any guy would be stupid not to like her. I just clenched my teeth, nodded my head and kept on driving.

After what seemed like the longest car ride in human history, we finally reached Michelle's house. I dropped her off, and the second I heard the door shut I started bawling.

Why was this making me so mad? She is my best friend. I should be happy for her. But I thought this was going to be my turn. I was really going to go for Tommy and make something happen with him. Michelle doesn't like him the way I do. But it's too late to say anything. We always promised each other never to let a guy come between us. I guess this is the tester.

I was awakened the next morning with a phone call, which I thought would be Michelle calling to obsess more about Tommy.

"Hello," I said in that groggy, don't-want-to-answer-it-but-feel-I have-to kind of tone.

"Hi, Katie?" A thick male voice replied through the phone, and I knew in an instant it was Tommy!

Why is he calling me? If this is to ask for Michelle's number, then I'm gonna hang up right now. No, I have to be mature about this. I should be nice. Yeah, right, man, I don't have to be nice to anybody.

"Katie, are you there?"

"Yeah, yeah, I'm here."

"Well, how are you?"

He wants to know how I am! I'll tell him how I am! I'm a depressed teenage girl who thought she had a chance with a guy who she thought had some class. But now she finds out that this guy is in love with her best friend when he has no clue what he'd be missing by going out with her. I've been bawling and tossing all night as if I was trying to quit an addiction, and hearing his voice right now drives me even crazier because it reminds me how much I still like him.

"Oh, I'm fine, just catching up on some sleep." It's amazing how the lie seemed to shoot right out of my mouth.

"I'm sorry if I woke you. I was just calling . . . well . . . I feel kind of weird doing this . . ."

Just get it out already! I'll give you her number!

"Okay, here goes. Do you want to see a movie or something tonight? You probably think I'm really weird since we haven't even spoken that much. But you seemed really cool, and I thought I would take a chance. If you really don't want to it's okay, I'll understand. I just thought . . ."

Oh, my God! Oh, my God! What's happening here? He's asking me out! What happened to Michelle? This can't be right.

But it is. It is! It is! It is! I have to say something now. Breathe. Calm. Act like a sane person.

"That sounds great, Tommy. Which movie were you thinking?"

Which movie?! Why did I say that? It doesn't matter which movie we see!

"I don't know. Why don't I pick you up at seven and we'll go and see which ones are playing?"

He sounds so calm. I wonder if I sound that calm.

"Okay, great, I'll see you at seven. Bye."

"Bye."

I am going on a date with TOMMY!!! I can't believe this. This is amazing, it's incredible, it's . . . terrible! What about Michelle? She's going to kill me. I have to call her.

"Michelle, I really need to talk to you." My voice was as shaky as my body, she had to know something was up.

"What's wrong? Are you okay?" She was worried about me. Great, I'm about to hurt my best friend.

"Yeah, I'm fine. I just wanted to tell you that Tommy called me. He wanted . . ."

"He wanted my phone number, huh? I knew it!"

"Well, not exactly. He seemed kind of, well, I don't know . . . he asked me to go see a movie tonight." The words came out slower than imaginable. I thought I was about to be attacked by Michelle's raging hormones any second now. "Before you get mad, I want to explain myself, and you have to believe me."

I was completely honest with Michelle. I explained how I liked Tommy for a long time and apologized profusely for not telling her sooner. I told her about her matchmaker disease and how I had cried the whole night before. I recited my conversation with Tommy word for word and poured out a million more apologies. The weight had been lifted off my shoulders, but I felt I had just passed it on to her. The long period of silence that followed assured me that Michelle was not going to accept my apology that quickly.

After not being able to take the silence any more, I broke in and asked, "Are you all right? What are you thinking? Do you hate me? Do you want me to break my date? What? At least give me an idea of how you feel."

The heavy breathing on the other side of the phone was about to become a whimper when I heard the *click*. She didn't even say a word, just hung up. I called her back fifty times that day only to hear an answering machine that demanded that I never call her again. I have never felt so torn before in my life. The first time that something exciting actually happens to me, it has to break up the only solid relationship that I have in my life. Michelle and I always thought we were above this type of situation. Our friendship was too strong to let a boy break it up. We refused to be like those other cliques of girls that back-stabbed each other all the time.

I called Tommy and explained the whole situation. He felt terrible and agreed that we could cancel our date for the night. He was disappointed but he understood. Every day for the following three weeks, I felt like I was in some never-ending chase. I would track Michelle down when-ever I could and try to convince her to talk to me. I would fail each time. She would either snicker some rude com-ment or just shoot me down or she wouldn't say anything at all. I never realized she had the ability to be so cruel. After the countless number of rejections, I slowly began to give up. I couldn't keep chasing after something that she seemed to have given up on a long time ago. It was too frustrating and disappointing.

Tommy was great throughout the whole ordeal. We continued to see each other and became extremely close. I could safely say he was my best friend. As for Michelle, her hostility toward me slowly began to wear down but we still weren't friends. We had one of those say-hi-to-each-other-in-the-hallway relationships. The pain of losing her friendship never diminished either. I would find myself suddenly crying sometimes when I would think of what happened to our relationship. I wondered if she ever even missed me.

About a week ago, eight months after everything had happened, I built up the courage to ask Michelle if she wanted to go out to lunch with me. To my ultimate surprise, she agreed. We spent most of the lunch having little chit-chat conversations about the things happening in our lives. The whole time I wanted to scream at her about how much I missed her. I wanted to go back to my house, change into our pajamas, and gossip about every little detail about every little thing that could possibly be gossiped about! I wanted to laugh with her and feel comfortable around her. I wanted to curl up and eat five scoops of Häagen-Dazs coffee chip ice cream while we watched our favorite movies that we've both seen 50 million times. Most of all, I wanted the security of knowing that I had my best friend back.

The meaningless chit-chat continued until I reached Michelle's house to drop her off. The last time I had dropped Michelle off I had wanted to strangle her for obsessing over Tommy so much. Now all I wanted to do was hug her so tight so that she could never leave me again. Fortunately, I didn't have to. As I pulled the car over to the curb, Michelle looked at me with her welcoming warm eyes and said the four words that brought my whole eight months of misery to an end, "I've really missed you!"

Tears began to fall down my face but no words would come out. I looked into her eyes, leaned forward and gave my best friend a big hug.

Lisa Rothbard

My Perfect Friend

Sometimes people look at me like I'm strange. I catch them staring out of the corner of my eye and shudder. Their sideways glances pass through me, and I feel judged, unaccepted. My best friend, Mariah, never looks at me that way, though. Even though we are opposites— I spend my time in the world of books, escaping into other stories, while she spends hers in the world of boys and crushes—we have always gotten along perfectly. Somehow, our differences just seem to work well to create a relationship of comfort and acceptance.

On our first day of high school, Mariah and I walked into school together. It was intimidating, so I was glad that I had Mariah at my side. As we turned the corner toward our first class, we both saw him. He was beautiful. We giggled like little girls and followed him. When we lost sight of him, we both sighed with regret, wishing he had passed our way.

After school, Mariah and I waited at the bus stop together, discussing the day's events, eating whatever snack was left over from our lunch that day, and laughing. In mid-sentence, I looked over, and there he was, standing right next to us! I threw my half-eaten banana to the side and fiddled nervously.

Although I'm painfully shy, Mariah doesn't have that problem. As I stood petrified by his looks, she walked boldly up to him and asked him his name. "Jonathan," he said, while he ran a hand through his hair, brushing it out of his pale blue eyes. That is when my infatuation began, even though I knew nothing about him. And for the first time in our whole lives, Mariah and I had the same crush.

"So, where are you from . . . Jonathan?" Mariah asked, emphasizing his name. As the bus pulled up and we boarded, I caught Mariah's eye. She winked, and I giggled. Jonathan sat across from me on the bus, and as he sat, he smiled. I awkwardly attempted to smile back.

That began the routine that I followed for about a week: seeing him in the hall, nervously sitting near him on the bus, and calling Mariah each night to reconstruct every detail. Our school had a dance planned, and the date was approaching. Mariah was determined to go with Jonathan, but she had a list of guys, just in case he didn't work out. I laughed, the chances of Jonathan asking me were slim to none, but it was fun to fantasize.

Then, one afternoon, we boarded the bus in the same fashion, hoping to sit as close to Jonathan as possible. But this afternoon was different. I didn't have to try to sit near him, for he sat right down beside me. I caught Mariah's eye and shot her a quizzical look. I thought to myself, *No one has liked me before, what is this guy doing?*

Then, my question was answered. He leaned over to me and whispered, "Hey, how about you let me take you to the dance on Friday?" It was more a statement than a question. I nearly choked on my gum.

I barely squeaked out my reply, "Yeah, sure, I guess . . . I mean, if you want to."

He smiled and said, "Cool."

Without words, Mariah motioned for me to get off at her stop. I quickly took inventory of the situation: the same guy who had been plaguing my thoughts just asked me out. I was on cloud nine. We remained calm until the bus was out of sight, and then, as the coast became clear, we grabbed onto each other and started jumping up and down. For once, I didn't feel so different. Mariah screeched, "Danielle, this is s-o-o-o-o-o cool!"

"I know. Was I shaking?" I replied.

She gave me a hug. "No. You were so calm, you did great." We split at the road and left it at that. I had done great.

The night of the dance, I was frantic. Desperately trying to apply my makeup in a hurry while talking to Mariah on the phone at the same time, I heard my mother yell that I was going to be late. Soon Mariah's parents dropped her off.

On our way to the dance, we met up with Mariah's date, Ben. When we reached the school, Jonathan wasn't there yet, so I waited outside and motioned for Mariah and Ben to go on ahead while I waited. I looked up and saw him. There he stood, with those pale blue eyes, that soft hair, that smooth skin and that sweet smile. There he stood, but . . . with another girl! He wasn't alone, and he definitely wasn't waiting for me.

I hid myself behind a tree. *How could I have been so stupid?* I should have known it was too good to be true. He was popular, and I wasn't. I let myself feel ugly and undesirable. But worst of all, worse than the embarrassment and the shame, I felt heartbroken.

I made my way out from behind the tree, just in time to see their backs as they entered the dance together. I walked home and into my room, ignoring my mother's questions of why I had returned so early. Sitting alone on my bed, I was plagued by a voice in my head, the voice that told me I was ugly and unloved.

Later, my phone rang. It was Mariah. I knew she wasn't calling to torture me with the dance details, but, rather, to comfort me. This was my first time playing in her world, and I had been hurt. She knew that, and her soothing words helped mend my aching heart and silence that voice in my head that told me I wasn't good enough. Maybe Jonathan didn't think I was good enough, but who cared? Mariah reminded me that there would always be other guys. She told me I was beautiful, and most of all, that I was loved. The self-deprecating voice quickly faded. Mariah and I may be different, even worlds apart, but she accepts me for who I am, and she is my perfect friend.

Danielle Eberschlag

Sometimes Things Are Never the Same

I wish they would only take me as I am.

Vincent van Gogh

Michelle and I had been best friends since the fourth grade. She was a beautiful person inside and out, one of the kindest I'd ever met. We were like paper and glue—completely inseparable.

When we began junior high, the new social life was a tough adjustment. But our friendship endured, and we were there for each other. I took comfort in the fact that I could tell her anything and always trust her.

Sixth grade passed, as did seventh, and soon eighth grade was upon us. It was that year that things slowly started to change between Michelle and me. I became a social butterfly, fluttering around to different cliques of friends, discussing the hottest gossip and relishing my new categorization as "popular." Although I made many new friends that year, I still loved Michelle and wanted her to hang out with my new, fairly large social group. I attempted to drag her along to my social gatherings, but

I soon noticed the disapproving looks and whispers about Michelle—a clear message that she was not "cool enough" to hang out with us.

My new, so-called friends made up lies and rumors about Michelle in order to ruin our friendship. And somewhere along the way, I fell into their trap. I started to believe that I shouldn't be friends with Michelle just because my other friends didn't like her.

One night, one of my new friends, Jamie, came over after school. I was thrilled that she wanted to come over to my house and spend time with me. After a couple of hours of laughing and having a great time, Michelle's name came up in our conversation. Slowly, a mischievous grin formed on Jamie's face. Remembering that Michelle was madly in love with a boy named Zach, Jamie ordered that I tell Michelle that Jamie was going out with Zach, and then rub it in her face. Afraid that my new friends would dislike me if I refused, just like they did Michelle, I picked up the phone, dialed Michelle's number and blurted it out to her. She was more sad, heartbroken and furious than I'd expected, and as I listened to her hysterically cry over the phone, I remembered how close we used to be. At that moment, I realized how much I treasured her friendship, and the cruelty of my actions sunk in. Needing to think about what I had just done, I got off the phone.

I soon called Michelle back and told her the truth. Zach was not going out with Jamie, and I was deeply sorry that I decided to betray her. I was sorry for not being there for her in the last few months, and I was sorry for letting my friends pressure me into situations like these. I wanted to be her best friend again. But she was not as forgiving as I had hoped. "It's not that easy," she said solemnly.

For the next couple of weeks, I did everything I could to win back Michelle's friendship. I sent her a thousand apology notes, I gave her pictures of the two of us, and I called her every night. I even stopped hanging out with my new group of friends who had been so cruel to Michelle. They weren't true friends anyway.

One night, I was sitting on my bed doing homework when I heard the doorbell ring. Unsure of who was at the door, I opened it tentatively, and there stood Michelle. I was shocked. "I forgive you," she said. "I wanted to let you know."

"Really?" I responded excitedly. "So, do you want to come in? Maybe you could sleep over, and we can talk."

"No, I can't. I don't want to," she said.

"Well, maybe we can catch a movie this weekend," I said with a hint of desperation.

"No," she answered.

"I thought you forgave me, Michelle," I said, unable to hide the disappointment in my voice.

"I do forgive you, but what you did changed what we used to be and what we are now. There is still a hole in my heart from what you did; it will never be the same."

She turned away. "I'll see ya around," she said, without looking back.

Every once in a while, Michelle and I run into each other at school, and she waves without saying a word. I always held out hope that our friendship would rekindle. But it hasn't, and things between us will never be the same. I lost my best friend, and it changed my heart forever. I wish I could undo the damage and take back what I have done. Never again will I let the influences of others get in the way of genuine friendships. I owe that to Michelle.

Celine Geday

My Star

My head plopped down right in the middle of my open calculus book.

Maybe the information will just work its way into my brain through osmosis. I was beginning to think that was my only hope for learning this material. I felt like I was on a different planet. *How could this seem so foreign to me?* Of all the classes that I had taken so far in college, I could not make this one work. I couldn't even lay out a logical study plan. *What now?* I pondered, with my head down on my desk in the middle of class.

When I lifted my head off the page, unbeknownst to me, a Post-it Note had stuck to my bangs. There was a pretty picture. I turned to face the guy next to me; he laughed and reached over to pull the note off my bangs in hopes of retrieving some of my dignity.

That was the beginning of a great friendship. The guy who was willing to pull a sticky note off my hair would soon become my calculus savior. I didn't know it at the time, but Matt Starr was the literal "star" of the class. I was convinced he could teach it. And, as luck would have it, he was willing to help me.

He lived in an apartment just off campus, and I would

go over there for tutoring. In exchange for his help, I cleaned his apartment and brought over bribe treats. Cookies, snacks, even dinner sometimes. He was so smart and would get so involved in the material. He would say, "Don't you realize that this is the stuff that the universe is made of?" Not *my* universe. I told him that my universe was made up of child development and psychology classes and an occasional shopping mall, not equations like this. He would just laugh and persevere. He was convinced that he could get me to understand this material, and in a way he was right. He was so crystal clear in his understanding that I began to see it through his eyes.

Matt and I started spending more time together. We would take long walks, go to movies—when he wasn't forcing me to study. I helped him put together a very hip wardrobe, and he taught me how to change the oil in my car—something every girl should know. When I brought home a B in calculus, we celebrated for three days.

Throughout college we stayed as close as a guy and a girl who are friends can be. We dated, only briefly, but the chemistry we shared was more like that of a brother and sister. We did, however, help each other through our other various and odd relationships; and when it looked hopeless, like neither one of us would ever find a mate, we took the next logical step—we got a puppy. Having rescued it from the pound, we called this little shepherd mix Tucker. We had been spending so much time together that when I moved out of my dorm, Tucker, Matt and I became roommates.

The day he came home and told me he was sick, it was raining. It rained that entire week, almost as if the world was mirroring our tears. Matt had AIDS.

Two weeks later, he was in the hospital with pneumocystis. The hows and the whys didn't matter when we were both spending every moment trying to get him

better. Between taking final exams, figuring out medications, visiting healers and making Matt drink wheatgrass
juice, I was exhausted—but he was getting better.

Matt and I decided that we were going to make the
time either one of us had left on this planet count. By the
time we arrived at our senior year, I had lived life more
fully than I had in all my twenty previous years. When we
graduated, we all proudly wore our caps and gowns,
Tucker included. Two months later, Matt went home to
Minneapolis to live with his family.

Life continued; we e-mailed each other voraciously. I
sent him tons of JPEG images of Tucker and his antics, and
we went back and forth recounting stories of our lives.

Matt lived only two years more. When I got the news
that he had been taken to the hospital, I flew out to be
with him. By then, he had fallen into a coma from which
he would never awaken. At the funeral, I artfully arranged
a yellow Post-it Note in my hair and put one of Tucker's
favorite chew toys in the casket.

One night, about a year after Matt's funeral, Tucker and
I were driving in the hills of Mulholland. Suddenly, I
smelled something so very familiar to me, and yet
I couldn't place it. It was a lovely cologne-like fragrance.
Then Tucker began acting peculiar.

"What's the matter, boy, did you smell it, too? What is
that smell? I just can't place it."

Stopped at a red light, I looked up at the night sky and
Tucker barked. What I saw next amazed me. It was a
shooting star. A star! Of course, Matt Starr! It was his
cologne I smelled.

"Is our friend trying to say hello and tell us he's okay?"
Tucker started wagging his tail furiously. Whether it was
a sign or not, I felt the warmest and most secure feeling
I've felt while thinking about Matt since his death. The
giant gaping void that was created when he left was

suddenly filled with that warm love the two of us always shared. He wasn't gone, he was right here with me, as he always would be.

Suddenly and quite clearly, I understood how it all fit together. The universe, my friend and his beloved calculus.

Zan Gaudioso

Have a Seat upon a Cloud

Have a seat upon a cloud and make yourself at home
You are now inside my dreams, inside a book, inside a
   poem.

Where anything can happen if you only make it real
Plunge into my waters if you're not afraid to feel.

Take off your shoes and close your eyes, relax upon my
   sand
Join me in my land of dreams, reach out and take my
   hand.

Let me share my dreams with you until you find your
   own
I'll take you there if you believe, take mine out on loan.

Where birds are words so gracefully they glide across
   the sky
Leave behind your worries, here the rules do not apply.

Pick my flowers if you like and plant a seed or two
Paint the sky in polka dots if you do not like it blue.

Climb my trees, face your fears; erase them one by one
See the world from up above and don't stop at the sun.

When the world starts raining down and the sun is out
of sight
Let your dreams control your mind and help you
through the night.

There's a place inside my dreams for all who care to
roam
So have a seat upon a cloud and make yourself at
home.

Danielle Rosenblatt

The Birth of an Adult

The ultimate measure of a man is not where he stands in moments of comfort and convenience, but where he stands at times of challenge and controversy.

Martin Luther King, Jr.

The doctors started to rush into the room. The delivery was going smoothly, but to me it felt like hysteria. The walls were a chalky gray like the wall of a jail cell. It wasn't the best setting for Jamie's labor, but it would have to do. Jamie was only a seventeen-year-old junior in high school. And now she was giving birth. She lay back in pain. Her only movements consisted of shaking her head from side to side, in an effort to escape the pain.

I took Jamie's hand, comforting her and trying to soothe her agony. Her eyes opened, and she looked at me. Our eyes met, and suddenly I felt every emotion I have ever known. I always knew Jamie would challenge me to better myself; however, I didn't think it would entail being her sidekick during her pregnancy.

All this began on the afternoon of New Year's Eve, 1997.

I sat in Jamie's basement awaiting the urgent news she had to tell me. She collapsed onto the couch and told me how she had broken up with her boyfriend, Eric, who had left the country to study abroad. This came as something of a relief, although I did my best not to show it. I didn't think Eric, or any other guy she had dated, was good enough for her. Okay, I'll admit it, I was—how should I put it—a little jealous. But I'd convinced myself we were better off as friends, anyway. And now she needed one.

Then the real news came: She was six weeks pregnant. Tears rolled down her face as she told me. I sat in shock and disbelief. The words were not registering in my head. She reached out and gave me a hug, which must have lasted only a few seconds but seemed like hours. My arms were still at my sides. We talked for a little while, and then I left her house and drove around in my car. I was in shock. I was upset about her lack of birth control because this whole ordeal could have been prevented. I was too young to deal with her pregnancy. Being a seventeen-year-old and a junior in high school was confusing enough without dealing with my own real-life afterschool special.

That evening I arrived at a party to drink my worries away. The air was filled with smoke and the partygoers reeked of alcohol. I could not take the atmosphere for long, so I left. I went to Jamie's house and stood on her front porch staring at the front door. *What should I do?* I asked myself. My foot started to turn from the door, but my hand reached out and pushed the doorbell. I wanted to run and go back to the party. I wanted to have fun this New Year's Eve. Suddenly, the door opened and Jamie stood in the doorway with her head down. "You can't spend New Year's Eve by yourself," I blurted out. She smiled, and we hugged in the doorway. This symbolized the beginning of the new journey that lay ahead for us. That night, we sat and laughed like usual while watching

Dick Clark ring in the New Year. After that night, my life would change. I wouldn't be a crazy teenager anymore. I would become a young adult.

Weeks passed and Jamie told her parents about the pregnancy. She and her parents made the decision to go through with the pregnancy, but to give the baby up for adoption. My parents talked with her parents and offered their support, almost like they were discussing our marriage; Jamie and I were growing and maturing together.

During her first trimester, I found myself at Jamie's house every day after school giving her a foot massage while she relaxed and watched her soap opera. She wasn't able to walk very much. I made snacks for her and enough food runs to Taco Bell to last us both a lifetime. My friends were not considerate about what I was going through. While I was busy helping a friend, they were busy making fun of me. They would call Jamie's house wondering what I was doing. They already knew, but they just wanted to poke fun. At school, the jokes surfaced like, "Gonna be a good daddy?" and "What are you doing this weekend . . . Lamaze class?" I shrugged them off and ignored them. I went on with my daily chores and focused on Jamie. I tried to make her life as easy as possible.

Later, one Saturday afternoon as I was catching up on sleep, Jamie called.

"Did you want to do something today?" she asked.

"What did you have in mind?" I replied.

"I want you to help me choose the baby's family," she said.

My ears turned hot, and I felt uneasy. But I told her I would pick her up. As I drove to her house, I thought about how much I had changed. I was more responsible, but I still considered myself a child. I felt I had no business choosing a path for an unborn baby. I groaned and doubted myself. I arrived at her house and helped her into the car.

As we were driving to the adoption agency, Jamie pointed out to me, "You're not speeding."

It occurred to me that I was no longer a crazy driver, thinking about how quickly I could get from one place to the other. I was now responsible for making sure we got there safely.

"I'm driving for three people now," I told her.

We arrived at the agency and were seated in a conference room. Fifty manila folders lay on the table, each containing a couple. One of these folders would be the lucky one. One of these couples would be the parents of Jamie's baby. The counselor and Jamie and I went through each folder discussing their spiritual, psychological, financial, genealogical and emotional backgrounds. I began browsing through one folder, which read "Jennifer and Ben." The folder was more like a booklet chronicling their life with pictures of where they'd been, who they are and who they wanted to become. Their explanation of why they wanted a baby caught my attention. This couple intrigued me. We kept narrowing down the couples, until we were down to two couples: Jennifer and Ben and Jamie's pick. We discussed both couples, finally agreeing on Jennifer and Ben.

As we were getting ready to leave, I took a picture of Jennifer and Ben out of the folder and slipped it into my jacket pocket without Jamie noticing. I wanted to have a record of them before their life was to be changed forever. I put on my jacket, and we left the agency.

It was a miserably cold spring day. After helping Jamie into the car, I walked around the car and a warm breeze struck me. I stood by the trunk of my car feeling the summer draft. I couldn't understand it. It was a cold day, but the wind was warmer than an August breeze. It felt like a sign, an anonymous thank you. We drove away and I thought about the decision we made. I thought about the families we didn't pick. How much longer would it take for them to receive the gift of a child?

A few weeks later we met Jennifer and Ben for the first time. They impressed me. They were a close couple, and I knew they would apply the love they had for each other to their child. Jamie told them that I urged her to pick them, which made this meeting even more overwhelming for me. I tried not to show it, though, as we bonded almost immediately. They urged Jamie to take a childbirth class so she would be ready for all of the upcoming events. She needed a partner for the class, so I agreed. She signed up for a class, and every Tuesday night Jamie and I attended together.

The first class was awkward. I had never felt so out of place in my entire life. Jamie and I sat down together, trying to ignore the seven married couples staring at us. We were too young and too ignorant to be going through a pregnancy and a birthing class. Nevertheless, Jamie had to do it, and I would not let her be alone. After time, we all began to bond and develop a tremendous amount of respect for each other. Everyone realized what a struggle it was for us to get this far.

During the "Mom Time," the dads and I sat outside talking about the babies' futures. The dads talked about pee-wee football, mutual funds and insurance. I talked about Shakespeare and geometry. I was out of place, for sure, but I realized there is more to giving birth than nine months and a doctor. So much freedom was sacrificed, replaced with a huge amount of responsibility. The dads respected me and praised me for my humanity towards a friend, not to mention my maturity. I still just couldn't believe I was sitting around talking about babies. I wanted to be innocent again. I wanted to drive my car fast and go to parties, but more important responsibilities called me. I was maturing.

I was getting ready for school one morning when Jamie called me from the hospital. "Um, do you want to get over here?" she asked.

"It's only another sonogram. Besides, I can't miss class," I said.

"Well, I think you might want to get over here, 'cause I'm having the baby!" she shouted.

I ran out of the house and darted to the hospital. At the hospital, the nurse handed me scrubs and I entered her room. She lay there as I sat next to her.

"Well this is it," she said. "Nine months, and it's finally here." She grimaced with pain and moved her head back and forth. Doctors were in and out of her room every two seconds with medication. She was about to give birth. After a few hours of getting Jamie settled, she was fully dilated.

"Okay, here we go. When I say 'push,' you push," the doctor said.

She acknowledged him while grabbing my hands and nodding her head quickly several times. Jamie gave three pushes of strength and, with one final push, she breathed life into a new baby. The doctors cut the umbilical cord and cleaned the baby off. I sat in awe. Every possible human emotion struck me like a freight train.

"It's a boy," they exclaimed.

I smiled, and tears of joy ran down my cheek. No more fear, no more chores, just pure happiness. The baby was handed to Jamie, and she spent the first moments of the baby's life holding him in her arms. She looked up at me, and I looked at her.

"You did it, kiddo," I whispered in her ear.

The doctors left with the baby to run tests and weigh him. Jennifer and Ben came in with the birth certificate. "What's his name?" Ben asked. Jamie motioned for him to come closer, and she whispered in his ear. Ben smiled and went into a different room. I walked outside to get a drink.

I came back in a few minutes and saw the completed birth certificate. It read Blake Jonathan.

I smiled and cried. The doctors brought Blake back in. They passed Blake to me, and I held new life in my hands. I thought about the dads in birth class. Then I thought about Blake's future. His first steps, peewee football games, the first day of school and his first broken heart. All the dads' talk finally caught up with me. Jennifer and Ben looked at me and smiled. Tears rolled down their cheeks. I gave Blake to Ben and received a gracious hug from Jennifer. They were his parents now. They were his keepers. Jamie still lay there, crying but filled with delight. I went over to her and gave her a big hug.

"Everything okay?" she asked.

"Fine. Absolutely fine," I whispered, and kissed her softly on her forehead. I would never be the same.

Jonathan Krasnoff

3

ON LOVE AND KINDNESS

Kindness in words creates confidence.
Kindness in thinking creates profoundness.
Kindness in giving creates love.

Lao-tzu

Bright Heart

The greatest gift is a portion of thyself.

Ralph Waldo Emerson

Last year around Halloween, I was invited to participate in a carnival for Tuesday's Child, an organization that helps children with the AIDS virus. I was asked to attend because I'm on a television show; I went because I care. I don't think that most of the kids recognized me as a celebrity. They just thought of me as a big kid who came to play with them for the day. I think I liked it better that way.

At the carnival they had all kinds of booths. I was drawn to one in particular because of all the children that had gathered there. At this booth, anyone who wanted to could paint a square. Later that square was going to be sewn together with the others, to make a quilt. The quilt would be presented to a man who had dedicated much of his life to this organization and would soon be retiring.

They gave everyone fabric paints in bright, beautiful colors and asked the kids to paint something that would make the quilt beautiful. As I looked around at all the squares, I saw pink hearts and bright blue clouds, beautiful orange sunrises and green and purple flowers. The pictures were all bright, positive and uplifting. All except for one.

The boy sitting next to me was painting a heart, but it was dark, empty, lifeless. It lacked the bright, vibrant colors that his fellow artists had used.

At first I thought maybe he took the only paint that was left and it just happened to be dark. But when I asked him about it, he said his heart was that color because his own heart felt dark. I asked him why and he told me that he was very sick. Not only was he very sick, but his mom was very sick also. He said that his sickness was not ever going to get better and neither was his mom's. He looked straight into my eyes and said, "There is nothing anyone can do that will help."

I told him I was sorry that he was sick and I could certainly understand why he was so sad. I could even understand why he had made his heart a dark color. But . . . I told him that it isn't true that there is nothing anyone can do to help. Other people may not be able to make him or his mom better . . . but we can do things like give bear hugs, which in my experience can really help when you are feeling sad. I told him that if he would like, I would be happy to give him one so he could see what I meant. He instantly crawled into my lap and I thought my own heart would burst with the love I felt for this sweet little boy.

He sat there for a long time and when he had had enough, he jumped down to finish his coloring. I asked him if he felt any better and he said that he did, but he was still sick and nothing would change that. I told him I understood. I walked away feeling sad, but recommitted to this cause. I would do whatever I could to help.

As the day was coming to an end and I was getting ready to head home, I felt a tug on my jacket. I turned around and standing there with a smile on his face was the little boy. He said, "My heart is changing colors. It is getting brighter . . . I think those bear hugs really do work."

On my way home I felt my own heart and realized it, too, had changed to a brighter color.

Jennifer Love Hewitt
actress, Party of Five

The Secret of Happiness

If you would be loved, love and be lovable.

Benjamin Franklin

There is a wonderful fable about a young orphan girl who had no family and no one to love her. One day, feeling exceptionally sad and lonely, she was walking through a meadow when she noticed a small butterfly caught unmercifully in a thornbush. The more the butterfly struggled to free itself, the deeper the thorns cut into its fragile body. The young orphan girl carefully released the butterfly from its captivity. Instead of flying away, the little butterfly changed into a beautiful fairy. The young girl rubbed her eyes in disbelief.

"For your wonderful kindness," the good fairy said to the girl, "I will grant you any wish you would like."

The little girl thought for a moment and then replied, "I want to be happy!"

The fairy said, "Very well," and leaned toward her and whispered in her ear. Then the good fairy vanished.

As the little girl grew up, there was no one in the land

as happy as she. Everyone asked her the secret of her happiness. She would only smile and answer, "The secret of my happiness is that I listened to a good fairy when I was a little girl."

When she was very old and on her deathbed, the neighbors all rallied around her, afraid that her fabulous secret of happiness would die with her. "Tell us, please," they begged. "Tell us what the good fairy said."

The lovely old woman simply smiled and said, "She told me that everyone, no matter how secure they seemed, no matter how old or young, how rich or poor, had need of me."

The Speaker's Sourcebook

Smile

She smiled at a sorrowful stranger.
The smile seemed to make him feel better.
He remembered past kindnesses of a friend
and wrote him a thank-you letter.
The friend was so pleased with the thank-you
that he left a large tip after lunch.
The waitress, surprised by the size of the tip,
bet the whole thing on a hunch.
The next day she picked up her winnings,
and gave part to a man on the street.
The man on the street was grateful;
for two days he'd had nothing to eat.
After he finished his dinner,
he left for his small dingy room.
(He didn't know at that moment
that he might be facing his doom.)
On the way he picked up a shivering puppy
and took him home to get warm.
The puppy was very grateful
to be in out of the storm.
That night the house caught on fire.

The puppy barked the alarm.
He barked 'til he woke the whole household
and saved everybody from harm.
One of the boys that he rescued
grew up to be President.
All this because of a simple smile
that hadn't cost a cent.

Barbara Hauck

Mrs. Link

I was eighteen, about to start college and broke. To make some money, I plodded down a quiet street of older homes, selling books door-to-door. As I approached one gate, a tall, handsome woman in her eighties came to the gate in her bath robe. "There you are darling! I've been waiting for you! God told me you'd be coming today." Mrs. Link needed help around her yard and house, and, apparently, I was the one for the job. Who was I to argue with God?

The next day I worked for six hours, harder than I had ever worked before. Mrs. Link showed me how to plant bulbs, what flowers and weeds to pull up, and where to haul the wilted plants. I finished off the day by mowing the lawn with a mower that looked like an antique. When I had finished, Mrs. Link complimented me on my work and looked under the mower at the blade. "Looks like you hit a stone. I'll get the file." I soon learned why everything Mrs. Link owned looked like an antique, but worked like brand-new. For six hours of work she gave me a check for three dollars. It was 1978. God's funny sometimes, isn't he?

The next week I cleaned Mrs. Link's house. She showed

me exactly how to vacuum her antique Persian rug with her antique-looking vacuum. As I dusted her beautiful treasures, she told me where she had acquired them while she traveled the world. For lunch she sautéed fresh vegetables from her garden. We shared a delicious meal and a lovely day.

Some weeks I got to be a chauffeur. The last gift to Mrs. Link from Mr. Link was a glorious new car. By the time I met Mrs. Link, the car was thirty years old, but still glorious. Mrs. Link was never able to have children, but her sister, nieces and nephews lived nearby. Her neighbors also were fond of her, and she was active in civic affairs.

A year and a half passed since I met Mrs. Link. School, work and church were taking up more of my time, and I saw Mrs. Link less and less. I found another girl to help her around the house.

Valentine's Day was coming, and being very undemonstrative and very broke, I was compiling a very short list of my valentines. Mom glanced at my list and said, "You need to get Mrs. Link a valentine."

I incredulously asked, "Why? Mrs. Link has a lot of family, friends and neighbors. She's active in the community. I don't even spend a lot of time with her anymore. Why would Mrs. Link want a valentine from me?"

Mom was unimpressed. "Get Mrs. Link a valentine," she insisted.

On Valentine's Day I self-consciously presented Mrs. Link a small bouquet, which she graciously accepted.

A couple of months later, I visited Mrs. Link again. Centered on her mantle, in her living room full of beautiful things, stood my wilted and faded Valentine's Day bouquet—the only valentine Mrs. Link received that year.

Susan Daniels Adams

A Gift for Two

You never know what happiness a simple act of kindness will bring about.

Bree Abel

It was a beautiful day for sightseeing around downtown Portland. We were a bunch of counselors on our day off, away from the campers, just out for some fun. The weather was perfect for a picnic, so when lunch time came, we set our sights on a small park in town. Since we all had different cravings, we decided to split up, get what each of us wanted, and meet back on the grass in a few minutes.

When my friend Robby headed for a hot dog stand, I decided to keep her company. We watched the vendor put together the perfect hot dog, just the way Robby wanted it. But when she took out her money to pay him, the man surprised us.

"It looks a little on the cool side," he said, "so never mind paying me. This will be my freebie of the day."

We said our thanks, joined our friends in the park, and dug into our food. But as we talked and ate, I was distracted by a man sitting alone nearby, looking at us. I could tell that he hadn't showered for days. Another homeless person, I thought, like all the others you see in cities. I didn't pay much more attention than that.

We finished eating and decided to head off for more sightseeing. But when Robby and I went to the garbage can to throw away my lunch bag, I heard a strong voice ask, "There isn't any food in that bag, is there?"

It was the man who had been watching us. I didn't know what to say. "No, I ate it already."

"Oh," was his only answer, with no shame in his voice at all. He was obviously hungry, couldn't bear to see anything thrown away, and was used to asking this question.

I felt bad for the man, but I didn't know what I could do. That's when Robby said, "I'll be right back. Please wait for me a minute," and ran off. I watched curiously as she went across to the hot dog stand. Then I realized what she was doing. She bought a hot dog, crossed back to the trash can, and gave the hungry man the food.

When she came back to us, Robby said simply, "I was just passing on the kindness that someone gave to me."

That day I learned how generosity can go farther than the person you give to. By giving, you teach others how to give also.

Andrea Hensley

Tell the World for Me

Some fourteen years ago, I stood watching my university students file into the classroom for our opening session in the theology of faith. That was the day I first saw Tommy. He was combing his hair, which hung six inches below his shoulders. My quick judgment wrote him off as strange—very strange.

Tommy turned out to be my biggest challenge. He constantly objected to or smirked at the possibility of an unconditionally loving God. When he turned in his final exam at the end of the course, he asked in a slightly cynical tone, "Do you think I'll ever find God?"

"No," I said emphatically.

"Oh," he responded. "I thought that was the product you were pushing."

I let him get five steps from the door and then called out. "I don't think you'll ever find him, but I am certain he will find you." Tommy shrugged and left. I felt slightly disappointed that he had missed my clever line.

Later I heard that Tommy had graduated, and I was grateful for that. Then came a sad report: Tommy had terminal cancer. Before I could search him out, he came to me. When he walked into my office, his body was badly wasted, and his long hair had fallen out because of chemotherapy. But his eyes were bright and his voice, for the first time, was firm.

"Tommy! I've thought about you so often. I heard you were very sick," I blurted out.

"Oh, yes, very sick. I have cancer. It's a matter of weeks."

"Can you talk about it?"

"Sure. What would you like to know?"

"What's it like to be only twenty-four and know that you're dying?"

"It could be worse," he told me, "like being fifty and thinking that drinking booze, seducing women and making money are the real 'biggies' in life." Then he told me why he had come.

"It was something you said to me on the last day of class. I asked if you thought I would ever find God and you said no, which surprised me. Then you said, 'But he will find you.' I thought about that a lot, even though my search for God was hardly intense at that time.

"But when the doctors removed a lump from my groin and told me that it was malignant, I got serious about locating God. And when the malignancy spread into my vital organs, I really began banging against the bronze doors of heaven. But nothing happened. Well, one day I woke up, and instead of my desperate attempts to get some kind of message, I just quit. I decided I didn't really care about God, an afterlife, or anything like that.

"I decided to spend what time I had left doing something more important. I thought about you and something else you had said: 'The essential sadness is to go through life without loving. But it would be almost equally sad to leave this world without ever telling those you loved that you loved them.' So I began with the hardest one: my dad."

Tommy's father had been reading the newspaper when his son approached him.

"Dad, I would like to talk with you."

"Well, talk."

"I mean, it's really important."

The newspaper came down three slow inches. "What is it?"

"Dad, I love you. I just wanted you to know that."

Tommy smiled at me as he recounted the moment. "The newspaper fluttered to the floor. Then my father did two things I couldn't remember him doing before. He cried and he hugged me. And we talked all night, even though he had to go to work the next morning.

"It was easier with my mother and little brother," Tommy continued. "They cried with me, and we hugged one another, and shared the things we had been keeping secret for so many years. I was only sorry that I had waited so long. Here I was, in the shadow of death, and I was just beginning to open up to all the people I had actually been close to.

"Then one day I turned around and God was there. He didn't come to me when I pleaded with him. Apparently he does things in his own way and at his own hour. The important thing is that you were right. He found me even after I stopped looking for him."

"Tommy," I practically gasped, "I think you are saying something much more universal than you realize. You are saying that the surest way to find God is not by making him a private possession or an instant consolation in time of need, but rather by opening to love.

"Tommy," I added, "could I ask you a favor? Would you come to my theology-of-faith course and tell my students what you just told me?"

Though we scheduled a date, he never made it. Of course, his life was not really ended by his death, only changed. He made the great step from faith into vision. He found a life far more beautiful than the eye of humanity has ever seen or the mind ever imagined.

Before he died, we talked one last time. "I'm not going to make it to your class," he said.

"I know, Tommy."

"Will you tell them for me? Will you . . . tell the whole world for me?"

"I will, Tommy. I'll tell them."

John Powell, S.J.

Like People First

The more we know the better we forgive.
Whoever feels deeply, feels for all who live.

Madame de Staël

Craig, a close friend of mine in graduate school, brought energy and life into any room he entered. He focused his entire attention on you while you were talking, and you felt incredibly important. People loved him.

One sunny autumn day, Craig and I were sitting in our usual study area. I was staring out the window when I noticed one of my professors crossing the parking lot.

"I don't want to run into him," I said.

"Why not?" Craig asked.

I explained that the previous spring semester, the professor and I had parted on bad terms. I had taken offense at some suggestion he had made and had, in turn, given offense in my answer. "Besides," I added, "the guy just doesn't like me."

Craig looked down at the passing figure. "Maybe you've got it wrong," he said. "Maybe you're the one who's turning away—and you're just doing that because you're afraid. He probably thinks you don't like him, so he's not friendly. People like people who like them. If you show an interest in him, he'll be interested in you. Go talk to him."

Craig's words smarted. I walked tentatively down the stairs into the parking lot. I greeted my professor warmly and asked how his summer had been. He looked at me, genuinely surprised. We walked off together talking, and I could imagine Craig watching from the window, smiling broadly.

Craig had explained to me a simple concept, so simple I couldn't believe I'd never known it. Like most young people, I felt unsure of myself and came to all my encounters fearing that others would judge me—when, in fact, they were worrying about how I would judge *them*. From that day on, instead of seeing judgment in the eyes of others, I recognized the need people have to make a connection and to share something about themselves. I discovered a world of people I never would have known otherwise.

Once, for example, on a train going across Canada, I began talking to a man everyone was avoiding because he was weaving and slurring his speech as if drunk. It turned out that he was recovering from a stroke. He had been an engineer on the same line we were riding, and long into the night he revealed to me the history beneath every mile of track: Pile O'Bones Creek, named for the thousands of buffalo skeletons left there by Indian hunters; the legend of Big Jack, a Swedish track-layer who could lift 500-pound steel rails; a conductor named McDonald who kept a rabbit as his traveling companion.

As the morning sun began to tint the horizon, he grabbed my hand and looked into my eyes. "Thanks for listening. Most people wouldn't bother." He didn't have to thank me. The pleasure had been all mine.

On a noisy street corner in Oakland, California, a family

who stopped me for directions turned out to be visiting from Australia's isolated northwest coast. I asked them about their life back home. Soon, over coffee, they regaled me with stories of huge saltwater crocodiles "with backs as wide as car hoods."

Each encounter became an adventure, each person a lesson in life. The wealthy, the poor, the powerful and the lonely; all were as full of dreams and doubts as I. And each had a unique story to tell, if only I were willing to hear.

An old, stubble-bearded hobo told me how he'd fed his family during the Depression by firing his shotgun into a pond and gathering up the stunned fish that floated to the surface. A traffic patrolman confided how he'd learned his hand gestures by watching bullfighters and symphony conductors. And a young beautician shared the joy of watching residents in a nursing home smile after receiving a new hairstyle.

How often we allow such opportunities to pass us by. The girl who everyone thinks is homely, the boy with the odd clothes—those people have stories to tell, as surely as you do. And like you, they dream that someone is willing to hear.

This is what Craig knew. Like people first, ask questions later. See if the light you shine on others isn't reflected back on you a hundredfold.

Kent Nerburn

Bobby, I'm Smiling

Little deeds of kindness, little words of love, help to make Earth happy.

Julia Carney

When I was ten years old, my grade school closed, and I was transferred to a school in a nearby town. In each classroom, the teachers would seat my classmates and me alphabetically, thus seating me beside the same boy, time and time again. His name was Bobby, and he was as outgoing as I was shy. I didn't make friends easily, but Bobby managed to reach beyond my shyness, and eventually, we became friends.

As the years passed, Bobby and I shared all the normal school experiences—first loves, double dating, Friday night football games, parties and dances. He was my friend. My confidant. My devil's advocate. It didn't matter that we were so different—he the popular, handsome, self-assured football star who had a beautiful girlfriend; me the overweight, inhibited and insecure teenage girl. We were friends, regardless.

One morning during the spring of our senior year, I

opened my locker and, to my surprise, there was a beautiful flower. I looked around to see who might have left it for me, but no one stood by waiting to take credit.

I knew that Gerry, a guy in my history class, had a crush on me. *Had he left it?* As I stood wondering, my friend Tami walked by.

"Nice flower," she said.

"Yes, it is. It was left in my locker without a note, but I think I know who gave it to me," I said. "I'm just not interested in dating him, but how do I tell him without hurting his feelings?"

Tami said, "Well, if you're not interested in going out with him, tell him *I* will. He's awesome!"

"But Tami," I said, "you know that Gerry and I aren't anything alike. It would never work out."

At that, Tami laughed and said, "Gerry didn't give you that flower. Bobby did."

"Bobby? Bobby Matthews?"

Then Tami explained.

Earlier that morning, she had passed Bobby in the school's parking lot. Noticing the flower and unable to resist, she had asked him who it was for. His only reply had been that it was for someone special and meant to brighten their day.

I was touched by Tami's story but was certain that the flower had been intended to be given anonymously.

Later that morning, I carried the flower to class and set it on my desk. Bobby noticed it and said nonchalantly, "Nice flower."

I smiled and said, "Yes, it's beautiful."

Minutes later, while we stood to recite the Pledge of Allegiance, I leaned over to Bobby and whispered "Thank you," then proceeded to finish the pledge.

As we were retaking our seats, Bobby said, "For what?"

I smiled. "The flower."

At first, Bobby feigned ignorance, but then he realized I had discovered his secret. "But how did you know?"

I simply smiled and asked why he had given it to me.

He hesitated only briefly before answering. "I gave it to you, because I wanted you to know you're special."

In retrospect, as I look back over seventeen years of friendship, I don't believe that I ever loved Bobby more than I did at that moment. The flower itself paled in comparison with his unexpected and purely giving act of kindness. That kindness meant the world to me then— and still does.

As Bobby had hoped, I did feel special—not only on that day, but for many days to follow. To paraphrase Mark Twain, a person can live a month off a compliment. It's true. I've done it.

When my lovely flower finally wilted and died, I pressed it in a book.

In the years that followed, Bobby and I remained good friends, and although our lives took different paths, we kept in touch.

When Bobby was twenty-five, he was diagnosed with terminal cancer. Shortly before his twenty-seventh birthday, he died.

Since then, I've lost track of the times I have recalled that spring day so long ago. I still treasure my pretty pressed flower, and when I hear the old cliché, "Remember with a smile," I'm certain that it was coined by someone who understood the meaning of a friend's love, and the lasting impression of a kind gesture.

Bobby, I'm smiling.

E. Keenan

An A for Mrs. B

I was sitting next to Missy in my ninth-grade world history class when Mrs. Bartlett announced a new project. In groups, we were to create a newspaper around the culture we were studying.

On a piece of paper, we wrote the names of three friends we wanted in our group. After collecting all the requests, Mrs. B. informed us that she would take into consideration the names we chose and would let us know the results the next day. I had no doubt I would get the group of my choice. There were only a handful of sociably decent people in the class, and Missy was one of them. I knew we had chosen each other.

The next day, I anxiously awaited the class. After the bell rang, Missy and I stopped talking as Mrs. B called for our attention. She started to call out names. When she reached group three, Missy's name was called. *So I'm in group three*, I thought. The second, third and fourth members of the group were called. My name was not included. There had to be some mistake!

Then I heard it. The last group: "Mauro, Juliette, Rachel, Karina." I could feel the tears well in my eyes. How could

I face being in that group—the boy who barely spoke English, the one girl who was always covered by skirts that went down to her ankles, and the other girl who wore weird clothes. Oh, how badly I wanted to be with my friends.

I fought back tears as I walked up to Mrs. B. She looked at me and knew what I was there for. I was determined to convince her I should be in the "good" group. "Why. . . ?" I started.

She gently placed a hand on my shoulder. "I know what you want, Karina," she said, "but your group needs you. I need you to help them get a passing grade on this assignment. Only you can help them."

I was stunned. I was humbled. I was amazed. She had seen something in me I hadn't seen.

"Will you help them?" she asked.

I stood straighter. "Yes," I replied. I couldn't believe it came out of my mouth, but it did. I had committed.

As I bravely walked to where the others in my group sat, I could hear the laughter from my friends. I sat down and we started. Different newspaper columns were assigned according to interests. We did research. Halfway through the week, I felt myself enjoying the company of these three misfits. There was no need for pretending—I grew sincerely interested in learning something about them.

Mauro, I found out, was struggling with the English language and his lack of friends. Juliette was also alone, because people didn't understand that she was only allowed to wear long skirts or dresses because of her religion. Rachel, who had requested to do the fashion column, wanted to be a fashion designer. She had a whole barrel of unique ideas. What a walk in another person's shoes did for me! They weren't misfits, just people that no one cared enough about to try to understand—except

Mrs. B. Her insight, vision and thoughtfulness brought out the potential in four of her students.

I don't recall what the newspaper's headline was or even the culture we wrote about, but I did learn something that week. I was given a chance to see other people in a new light. I was given the opportunity to see in myself a potential that inspired my actions in later years. I learned that who we are is more important than what we are or seem to be.

After that semester ended, I always received a friendly hello from my group. And I was always genuinely happy to see them.

Mrs. B gave us an A on that assignment. We should have handed it right back, for she was the one who truly deserved it.

Karina Snow

Kids Who Are Different

Here's to kids who are different,
Kids who don't always get As,
Kids who have ears
Twice the size of their peers,
And noses that go on for days.

Here's to the kids who are different,
Kids they call crazy or dumb,
Kids who don't fit,
With the guts and the grit,
Who dance to a different drum.

Here's to the kids who are different,
Kids with a mischievous streak.
For when they have grown,
As history has shown,
It's their difference that makes them unique.

Digby Wolfe
Submitted by Vania Macias

McDonald's

Most of my friends are what society would call "punks." We are the teenagers who hang out at the coffee shops or the movies for lack of anything better to do. But being punks doesn't mean much.

One evening, after a day of not doing much, we were sitting in McDonald's when a guy in our group whom I had just met that day walked in. Brian was the typical punk teenager, dressed in black with the dyed hair. Right before he stepped inside, he yelled something outside to a man walking down the street. I just hoped he wasn't trying to start trouble. He sat down and a minute later, a burly homeless man stuck his head in and looked at Brian.

"Did you say something to me?" the man demanded, and I thought I saw a mean glint in his eyes. I shrank back, thinking that if Brian had tried to pick a fight, this was the wrong guy to do it with. I had seen too many people and places kick teenagers like us out for pulling stuff.

While the rest of us were looking for a place to back into, Brian got up and walked up to him. "Yeah . . . would you like something to eat?"

The relief was almost audible, and the man smiled and walked in.

After a large meal of hamburgers, fries and dessert, the man left, and even the staff waved good-bye to him. When we asked Brian about it, he explained how he had money that he didn't need and the man had none, so it was only right.

Shelly Miller

A Valentine for Laura

Ann, a friend of mine, disliked Valentine's Day as a girl. She was plain—not ugly, but not beautiful. Valentine's Day is not kind to plain girls. It wasn't so bad in elementary school, when the obligatory thirty valentines arrived: one from each classmate. She overlooked the fact that her cards were not oversized like those of the popular girls, and did not contain the love notes like those of the pretty girls. But later, in middle school, the valentine exchange was no longer mandatory. Just when the yearning for romance budded, when the desire for admiration and flirtation became imperative, and a valentine was needed most, no card arrived. Not for Ann. Not for plain girls anywhere. Only for the pretty and the popular. At such a time, stories of ugly ducklings that will one day turn into beautiful swans do not assuage the hurt and rejection.

As fate would have it (and often does), in subsequent years Ann did become pretty and turned many a boy's head. As she received more attention and flirtations, she came to feel—and therefore to be—very beautiful. But even years later, grown and with a family of her own, she did not forget those long-ago days of rejection and dejection.

Today, Ann's family includes two boys in middle school. For a dollar, their Student Council will deliver a Valentine's Day carnation. Ann gives a dollar to each of her boys to buy flowers for their girlfriends. Then she adds another dollar apiece with this instruction: "Pick another girl, one who is nice, but plain—someone who probably won't get a flower. Send her a flower anonymously. That way she will know that someone cares, and she will feel special."

Ann has done this for several years, spreading Valentine's Day a little beyond her own world.

One year, Laura, who was plain to behold but beautiful to know, received one of these gifts. Ann's son reported that Laura was so happy and surprised, she cried. All day long, she carried the flower on her books and chattered with the other girls about who her admirer could be. As Ann heard the account, she too had to dry her eyes—for she remembered.

Don Caskey

A Simple Hello

I have always felt sympathy and compassion for the kids I see at school walking all alone, for the ones that sit in the back of the room while everyone snickers and makes fun of them. But I never did anything about it. I guess I figured that someone else would. I did not take the time to really think about the depth of their pain. Then one day I thought, what if I did take a moment out of my busy schedule to simply say hello to someone without a friend or stop and chat with someone eating by herself? And I did. It felt good to brighten up someone else's life. How did I know I did? Because I remembered the day a simple kind hello changed my life forever.

Katie E. Houston

Change for a Dollar

Make yourself a blessing to someone. Your kind smile or pat on the back just might pull someone back from the edge.

Carmelia Elliot

All he wanted was some juice. As tables full of high school students sat in Cafeteria B2 on that cloudy afternoon, he was thirsty. We sat near yet away from him, fixing our hair and worrying about the test next period we hadn't studied for. He was far away from our world, yet forced to be a part of it.

He stood at the drink machine with purpose, fumbling through his fake leather wallet for some change. He came up with a wrinkled dollar bill, and nervously glanced back at his table where other students in his special needs class were sitting. With the coordination of a six-year-old, he tried to make the machine accept his money. After a few unsuccessful attempts, the snickers and comments began. People were laughing. Some were even throwing things at him. He began to quiver, and his eyes misted with tears. I saw him turn to sit down, defeated. But for some reason, he decided against it. He wasn't leaving until he got a drink.

With a determined expression, he continued to aimlessly thrust the dollar bill in the machine. Then something terrific happened. A popular senior rose from her seat, and with a look of genuine compassion, went over to the boy. She explained how the machine had a hard time accepting dollars, then gave him some change and showed him where to place it. The boy gave her his dollar and chose a flavor of fruit juice. Then the two walked off in different directions.

Although it was clear that they were from very different worlds, for one moment, they'd shared a real understanding. As I walked away from my lunch table that day, I looked at the boy. I remember thinking how he and the dollar were very much alike. They both weren't accepted where the world said they were supposed to be. But just as the dollar had found a place in a caring girl's pocket, I was sure the boy would eventually find his, too.

Bonnie Maloney

My Friend Charley

As an insecure and scared freshman in college, my first year was filled with many new and strange experiences. I quickly learned the difficult lesson that things aren't always what they seem and love can be found in the most unexpected places.

My first introduction to the "real world" began at Camp Virginia Jaycee, a camp for people who are mentally retarded or handicapped. Twice a year, my college offered a volunteer opportunity to students who wished to donate a weekend of their time. At the last minute and after much deliberation, I made a decision that would soon change my life. I volunteered for camp.

I had no idea what to expect, and it was the complete and utter unknown that scared me the most. As the campers slowly arrived, the noises and sounds of the unfamiliar filled the air. I looked around the room at faces that expressed no clue just how different they really were.

Each student volunteer was assigned one camper for the weekend. As a counselor, I was expected to help "my" camper eat, bathe and walk. I was expected to be his friend.

My camper's name was Charley. He was forty years old, with a severe case of autism and no visible means of communication. I was scared. My hands shook with fear as I tried to introduce myself. His attention roamed everywhere except to me. He seemed completely uninterested in anything I had to say. We stood outside waiting to get into our cabin, when suddenly he went to the bathroom, right in front of everyone. I discovered that he was just as scared as I was; we just had very different ways of showing it.

Charley couldn't speak, but he could eat and walk. That night I showed him how to take a shower. As I stood in front of the shower and told him what to do, he did everything I said. I guess he did understand me, in some strange new way. By the next night when it was time for Charley to take his shower, he laughed and smiled like a young schoolboy. I proudly tucked him in that night, but as I started to walk away from his cot, he grabbed my arm. He placed my hand on his head wanting only comfort. It was so overwhelming that this complete stranger could need me to love him. For that instant, Charley made the world seem so simple.

As the weekend came to a close and the time to leave approached, Charley reached out to hold my hand. We were two scared human beings experiencing something so new that it was frightening. I forgot about facades and fake smiles, and instead felt a genuine love for another human being from the depths of my soul.

Robin Hyatt

So How Do You Boost an Ego?

If you treat an individual as he is, he will remain as he is. But if you treat him as if he were what he ought to be and could be, he will become what he ought to be and could be.

Goethe

Mr. Rickman, our psych teacher, doesn't give the kind of assignments other teachers do, such as read a thousand pages; answer the questions at the end of the chapter; work problems 47 through 856. He's more creative than that.

Mr. Rickman led up to last Thursday's assignment by saying that behavior is a means of communicating. "'Actions speak louder than words' isn't just an empty phrase," he told us. "What people do tells you something about what they are feeling."

He paused a minute for that to sink in before he gave the assignment. "Now see if you can build up somebody, boost his or her ego enough that you notice a change in the way the person acts. We'll report the results in class next week."

When I got home from school that afternoon, my mom was really feeling sorry for herself. I could tell the minute I came in. Her hair was straggling around her face, her voice was whiny and she kept sighing while she got dinner. She didn't even speak to me when I came in. Since she didn't speak, I didn't either.

Dinner was pretty dreary. Dad wasn't any more talkative than Mom and I were. I decided to try out my assignment. "Hey, Mom, you know that play the university drama club is putting on? Why don't you and Dad go tonight? I've heard it's really good."

"Can't make it tonight," Dad said. "Important meeting."

"Naturally," Mom said. Then I knew what was bugging her.

"Well then, how about going with me?" I asked. Right away, I wished I could take back the invitation. Imagine a high school kid being seen out in the evening with his mother!

Anyway, the invitation was hanging there in the air, and Mom said in an excited voice, "Really, Kirk?"

I swallowed a couple of times. "Sure. Why not?"

"But guys don't take their mothers out." Her voice was getting more pleasant all the time, and she pushed the straggles of hair up on top of her head.

"There's no law that says they can't," I told her. "You just go get ready. We're going out."

Mom started toward the sink with some dishes. Her steps were perky now instead of draggy.

"Kirk and I will take care of the dishes," Dad offered, and Mom even smiled at him.

"That was a nice thing for you to do," my dad said, after Mom left the kitchen. "You're a thoughtful son."

Thanks to psychology class, I thought gloomily.

Mom came back to the kitchen looking about five years younger than she had an hour earlier. "You're sure you don't have a date?" she asked, as if she still couldn't believe what was happening.

"I do now," I said. "C'mon, let's go."

That evening didn't turn out so badly after all. Most of my friends had more exciting things to do than watch a play. The ones who were there weren't at all startled to see me with my mom. By the end of the evening, she was genuinely happy, and I was feeling pretty good myself. Not only had I aced a psych assignment, I had also learned a lot about boosting an ego.

Kirk Hill

Losing an Enemy

If your enemy is hungry, feed him; if he is thirsty, give him something to drink.

Romans 12:20

Last year, my brothers were enrolled in Pioneer Clubs, a weekly kids program at our church. Daniel was nine, and Timothy was seven. My sister, my dad and I were all teachers at the same church program. At one point during the year, my brothers began to complain that a boy named John was picking on them.

John, an eleven-year-old foster boy, was in my dad's class. He was the type of kid who always seemed to be in trouble. Worse, he didn't consider that it was his behavior that was the problem, but instead decided my dad was picking on him. He often took it out on my brothers by knocking off their hats, calling them names, kicking them and running away. Even I received the occasional rude remark from John. We all thought he was a real pain.

When my mom heard about the problem, she came home from town a few days later with a bag of wrapped butterscotch candies.

"These are for John," she told Daniel and Timothy.

"For *who?*"

"For John." Mom went on to explain how an enemy could be conquered by kindness.

It was hard for any of us to imagine being kind to John; he was so annoying. But the next week the boys went to Pioneer Clubs with butterscotch candies in their pockets—one for themselves and one for John.

As I was heading to my class, I overheard Timothy saying, "Here John, this is for you." When we got home, I asked Timothy what John's response had been.

Timothy shrugged. "He just looked surprised, then he said thank you and ate it."

The next week when John came running over, Tim held on to his hat and braced himself for an attack. But John didn't touch him. He only asked, "Hey, Tim, do you have any more candy?"

"Yep." A relieved Timothy reached into his pocket and handed John a candy. After that, John found him every week and asked for a candy, and most times Timothy remembered to bring them—one for himself, and one for John.

Meanwhile, I "conquered my enemy" in another way. One time as I passed John in the hall, I saw a sneer come over his face. He started to open his mouth, but I said, "Hi, John!" and gave him a big smile before he had a chance to speak.

Surprised, he shut his mouth, and I walked on. From then on, whenever I saw him I would greet him with a smile and say, "Hi, John!" before he had a chance to say anything rude. Instead, he started to simply return the greeting.

It's been a while since John picked on my brothers, and he's not rude to me anymore, either. Even my dad is impressed with the change in him. He's a nicer John now than he was a year ago—I guess because someone finally gave him a chance.

He wasn't the only one to change. My whole family learned what it meant to love an enemy. What's strange is that in the process, we lost that enemy—he was "conquered" by love.

Love: It never fails.

Patty Anne Sluys

Coffee-Shop Kindness

If you can't return a favor, pass it on.

Louise Brown

My senior year of high school was an extremely hectic one, to say the least. If I wasn't studying and worrying about my grades, I was juggling multiple extracurricular activities or attempting to make sense of my plans for college. It seemed as if my life had turned into one crazy cloud of confusion, and I was stumbling around blindly, hoping to find some sort of direction.

Finally, as senior year began to wind down, I got a part-time job working at the local coffee shop. I had figured that the job would be easy and, for the most part, stress-free. I pictured myself pouring the best gourmet coffees, making delicious doughnuts and becoming close friends with the regular customers.

What I hadn't counted on were the people with enormous orders who chose to use the drive-thru window, or the women who felt that the coffee was much too creamy, or the men who wanted their iced coffees remade again and again until they reached a certain level of perfection. There were moments when I was exasperated with the human race as a whole, simply because I couldn't seem to please anyone. There was always too much sugar, too little ice and not enough skim milk. Nevertheless, I kept at it.

One miserable rainy day, one of my regular customers came in looking depressed and defeated. My coworker and I asked what the problem was and if we could help, but the customer wouldn't reveal any details. He just said he felt like crawling into bed, pulling the sheets up over his head and staying there for a few years. I knew exactly how he felt.

Before he left, I handed him a bag along with his iced coffee. He looked at me questioningly because he hadn't ordered anything but the coffee. He opened the bag and saw that I had given him his favorite type of doughnut.

"It's on me," I told him. "Have a nice day."

He smiled and thanked me before turning around and heading back out into the rain.

The next day was miserable as well, rain spilling from the sky. Everyone in town seemed to be using the drive-thru window because no one wanted to brave the black skies or the thunder and lightning.

I spent my afternoon hanging out the window, handing people their orders and waiting as they slowly counted their pennies. I tried to smile as the customers complained about the weather, but it was difficult to smile as they sat in their temperature-controlled cars with the windows rolled up, while I dealt with huge droplets of water hanging from my visor, a shirt that was thoroughly soaked around the collar and an air conditioner that blasted out cold air despite sixty-seven-degree weather. On top of that, no one was tipping. Every time I looked into our nearly empty tip jar, I grew more depressed.

Around seven o'clock that evening, I was in the middle of making another pot of vanilla hazelnut decaf when the customer from the day before drove up to the window. But instead of ordering anything, he handed me a single pink rose and a little note. He said that not too many people take the time to care about others, and he was glad there were still people like me in the world. I was speechless and very touched; I nearly forgot yesterday's deed. After a moment, I happily thanked him. He told me I was welcome and, with a friendly wave, drove away.

I waited until I saw his Jeep exit the parking lot, then I ran to the back of the shop and read the note. It read:

Christine,

Thanks for being so sweet, kind and thoughtful yesterday. I was sincerely touched by you. It is so nice to meet someone who's genuinely nice, warm, and sensitive and unselfish. Please don't change your ways because I truly believe that you will excel. Have a great day!

Hank

As the day passed, I had plenty of complaining customers, but anytime I felt depressed or frustrated, I thought of Hank and his kindness. I would smile, hold my head up high, clear my throat and politely ask, "How can I help you?"

Christine Walsh

Mary Lou

It was my first day as newcomer to Miss Hargrove's seventh-grade class. Past "newcomer" experiences had been difficult, so I was very anxious to fit in. After being introduced to the class, I bravely put on a smile and took my seat, expecting to be shunned.

Lunchtime was a pleasant surprise when the girls all crowded around my table. Their chatter was friendly, so I began to relax. My new classmates filled me in on the school, the teachers and the other kids. It wasn't long before the class nerd was pointed out to me: Mary Lou English. Actually she called herself Mary Louise. A prim, prissy young girl with a stern visage and old-fashioned clothes. She wasn't ugly—not even funny looking. I thought she was quite pretty, but I had sense enough not to say so. Dark-eyed and olive-skinned, she had long, silky black hair, but—she had pipe curls! Practical shoes, long wool skirt and a starched, frilly blouse completed the image of a total dork. The girls' whispers and giggles got louder and louder. Mary Lou made eye contact with no one as she strode past our table, chin held high with iron determination. She ate alone.

After school, the girls invited me to join them in front of the school. I was thrilled to be a member of the club, however tentative. We waited. For what, I didn't yet know. Oh, how I wish I had gone home, but I had a lesson to learn.

Arms wrapped around her backpack, Mary Lou came down the school steps. The taunting began—rude, biting comments and jeering from the girls. I paused, then joined right in. My momentum began to pick up as I approached her. Nasty, mean remarks fell unabated from my lips. No one could tell I'd never done this before. The other girls stepped back and became my cheerleaders. Emboldened, I yanked the strap of her backpack and then pushed her. The strap broke, Mary Lou fell, and I backed off. Everyone was laughing and patting me. I fit in. I was a leader.

I was not proud. Something inside me hurt. If you've ever picked a wing off a butterfly, you know how I felt.

Mary Lou got up, gathered her books and—without a tear shed or retort given—off she went. She held her head high as a small trickle of blood ran down from her bruised knee. I watched her limp away down the street.

I turned to leave with my laughing friends and noticed a man standing beside his car. His olive skin, dark hair and handsome features told me this was her father. Respectful of Mary Lou's proud spirit, he remained still and watched the lonely girl walk toward him. Only his eyes—shining with both grief and pride—followed. As I passed, he looked at me in silence with burning tears that spoke to my shame and scalded my heart. He didn't speak a word.

No scolding from a teacher or preaching from a parent could linger as much as that hurt in my heart from the day a father's eyes taught me kindness and strength and dignity. I never again joined the cruel herds. I never again hurt someone for my own gain.

Lynne Zielinski

Healing with Love

On a bitterly cold and cloudy winter's day in upstate New York, I saw my brother again for the first time in a year. As my father and I pulled up to the reform school after four hours of driving, his attempts at cheerful commentary did nothing to ameliorate the dismal apprehension that I felt. I had little hope that my brother would be changed and, furthermore, I had convinced myself that any appearance of change would not necessarily be genuine.

Being with my brother after so long was like getting to know him all over again. Over the next couple of days, I felt a kind of peace developing between us, and, for the first time, I wasn't tense around him, nor was I scared of what he would do or say next. It seemed as though I would finally find a friend in my brother, and, more than that, I would find a true brother in my brother. While part of me rejoiced in his transformation, another part of me thought it was too good to be true, and so I remained skeptical of his seeming progress. Two days was surely not enough time to erase the hostility that had built up between us over the years. I showed this cynical front to my father and brother, while the hopeful voice remained hidden deep inside of my heart, afraid to appear, lest it should be trampled upon. My brother himself commented several times on my depressed disposition, but I knew he would never understand the complexity of my feelings, so I remained elusive.

I wrapped myself in this same protective silence during, what was for me, the most emotionally trying part of the visit. Meals at the school were more than just meals. They were chaperoned with two teachers at each table, and provided a forum for judging the students' progress and/or continued delinquency. My father had told me that these meals often lasted for an hour or two, as each student was treated separately and with the full attention of the table. As we sat down for lunch, I knew I wouldn't be able to make it through the meal without crying.

Several boys and girls were "brought up" in front of the table for transgressions they had committed, but a boy named Brian touched me the most. A fairly new arrival at the school, he hadn't yet lost the initial anger and bitterness at having been brought there against his will. He was an attractive boy, about sixteen years old and was, my father whispered to me, an exceptional soccer player with a promising future in the sport. As the head teacher at our table conducted a heavy interrogation of him, Brian shifted his weight nervously every two seconds, and I saw in his eyes what I had become so good at reading in my brother's. They darted anxiously about the room, resting upon everything except the man addressing him, and I knew that he was searching for someone or something to blame. He wasn't yet aware that only when he stopped looking for excuses could he truly hear and learn from those trying to help him.

Suddenly, out of the corner of my eye, I became aware of a bearded man standing at the closed door and peering in apprehensively at our solemn gathering, which must have looked more like an AA meeting than a meal. The realization that it was Brian's father trying to catch a glimpse of his son precipitated the first tear I had shed all weekend.

"Why is Brian here?" I whispered softly to my father.

"Oh, you know, the usual, drugs, violence . . . I think the last straw was when he hit his father in the head with one of his soccer trophies. . . . He was chosen for the National All-Star team, you know. . . . Must be quite a player."

As the tears flowed more freely down my face, Brian looked straight ahead at the wall and told us that he had refused to see his father who had driven for many hours to see him.

Then the teacher spoke, "Brian, I talked to your dad, and he says he brought you your puppy because he knows how much you must miss him. He's willing to accept the fact that you don't want to see him, but he wants you to know that you can see your puppy."

I was screaming inside. I wanted to stand up and tell Brian how lucky he was to have a father who obviously loved him so much, and who loved him enough to do the hardest thing a parent ever has to do: send his child away. I was bursting to enlighten him, but I knew it was something he would have to learn on his own, so I remained still and just let the overwhelming sadness spread over me like a dark cloud.

That afternoon, I saw my brother waving good-bye as we pulled up the dirt drive and out of the gates of the school. I couldn't look back, as I was too busy trying to suppress the emotion that I felt creeping up on me with the force of a tidal wave. I was filled with hopelessness and empathy for these kids who had somehow gotten lost along the way. I knew there was a fine line between them and me, a line I had walked like a tightrope at several times in my life. Indeed, part of my sadness lay in the guilt I felt for not having such a heavy load to bear and for never being able to fully comprehend the nature and sheer weight of this load my brother carried.

Several months later I returned to the school, this time in early spring and accompanied by my whole family, including my mother and two sisters. Everything looked brighter and more colorful in the sun. Wildflowers bloomed on the hillside looking out over the valley, and the water in the pond sparkled like jewels. I closed my eyes, held my face up to the sun and smiled. It was my family's first reunion in over a year. As it was family weekend, everywhere I looked I saw proud, attentive parents and beaming kids. This is when the full force of what I was experiencing hit me. For the first time in a while, I didn't feel the despair and hopelessness of these kids' lives, but the tremendous amount of love and support that surrounded each one of them. After a whole year spent doubting that my brother would ever be able to function normally in society, I allowed the seeds of hope to germinate in my mind, as well as in my heart.

Moments later, my new outlook was strengthened and forever cemented by the most beautiful sight I think I have ever seen. At first I couldn't believe my eyes. Brian and his father were walking arm in arm across the grass towards the pond and seemed to be in quiet discussion about one of those everyday, mundane things that is the business of fathers and their sons. A golden retriever, now fully grown, wagged its tail in delight as he trotted after them.

Cecile Wood

Forgive

Forgive the sun who didn't shine
The sky had asked her in to dine

Forgive the stars that heard your wish
The moon prepared their favorite dish

Forgive the rain for its attack
The clouds have tears they can't hold back

Don't hate the birds 'cause they are free
Don't envy all the things they see

Don't block the wind, but hear its cry
Or else that wind may pass you by

Forgive the storm it means no harm
Could not resist to show its charm

Forgive the earth that never turns
Don't hate the sun, because too much burns

Life intends to not cause pain
The flowers bloom from all the rain

The storm will come and it will pass
The sun that shines, it grows the grass

The wind it cannot help but cry
The stars at night light up the sky

Forgive the world in which we live
We'll all find peace if we forgive

Danielle Rosenblatt

The Gift of Time

What we do for ourselves dies with us. What we do for others and the world remains and is immortal.

Albert Pine

His name was Bryce. I inherited him when I was nine years old. Actually, he became part of our family when my mother married his uncle.

It was a second marriage for my mother, and while it might have been less than desirable for my two older brothers, for me it was a slice of heaven. We moved to a beautiful neighborhood, into a house three times the size of the one in which I had been born and raised. Not only did this marriage come with a big house, a pool and huge yard, it also came with Bryce. He lived in Northern California with his brother and parents, but he visited frequently, sometimes spending entire summers with us.

Bryce became my good friend. He was six years older than I, but we had an instant rapport that belied the gap in our ages. He taught me how to dive and do flips off the diving board, he helped my stepfather build a tree house for me, and he helped me learn how to expertly negotiate my new bicycle built for two that I had won in a contest. By the time I was thirteen, we had become best friends.

Bryce and I spent many summers together, and as the years passed we still remained close. The activities changed—tennis, hiking, beach trips and computers—but our bond didn't. He was handsome, smart and funny, and even though I was only fourteen years old, I fantasized about marrying him someday. I couldn't conceive of my life without him.

Bryce was the eldest of two boys, and he was his parents' pride and joy. He lived nearly a picture-perfect life. Achieving in school, becoming an award-winning athlete, and having this incredibly huge, compassionate heart, he was a parent's dream. When his mother's brother decided to marry my widowed mother, Bryce helped create a bridge that served to unite the two families. He was charismatic, funny and a great mitigating influence for two teenage boys who didn't want their mother to marry this man. But, his family came with Bryce, and at the very least, Bryce was cool.

One summer, Bryce and I went swimming at a friend's house. They had a pool to envy. Complete with diving boards, a slide, waterfalls and a small island in the center, it was by far the coolest pool in the San Fernando Valley. I was fifteen, Bryce was twenty-one. It was one of those perfect days, and we were having so much fun. At one point, I decided to slide down the slide on my belly. Apparently, given the location of the slide, this was not a good idea. I smacked down hard on the bottom of the pool and was knocked out. By the time anyone figured out that I wasn't just playing around (the blood that began to tint the water was probably a good clue) I was starting to drown. Bryce saved my life. He jumped into the pool, pulled me to safety and helped to clear the water out of my lungs so that I could breathe. When I finally regained consciousness, Bryce was kneeling beside me, with tears in his eyes.

He was now my friend and my savior. I grew up with him; he became the first boy that I really loved. He treated me like I was the only person in his life who really mattered, even though I'm sure he had girlfriends.

By the time I turned sixteen, I was already fairly proficient behind the wheel of a car, thanks to Bryce. He made it very clear to me that it was my turn to drive the seven hours it required for us to visit each other. I was more than happy to oblige.

I would drive up to Redding, and we would go to the river and live in the water. We would jet ski, swim, snorkel and sun on the dock until those long summer days finally claimed the sun. Then we'd go back to his parents' house and barbecue, laugh and hang out.

By the end of my senior year in high school, there was only one person I wanted to take me to my prom, so I was thrilled when he finally asked me. I accepted without reservation. Even though there were other boys who had asked, it was Bryce I wanted to share the occasion with. Besides, grad night at Disneyland required someone with the guts to ride all the coasters several times, and I knew he was up for the task.

During that next year, our lives became busy, and we didn't see each other that often. I was starting college, and he was working. We wrote and talked to each other on the phone, but it seemed that our lives were taking us in two different directions. I missed him dearly, so I was overjoyed when I found out he would be coming down for his birthday. My stepfather had a special gift that he wanted to give him.

We had a little party for Bryce, and my stepfather gave him his gift. It was a gold Hamilton tank-style watch that

was given to my stepfather by his mother, Bryce's grandmother, when he was younger. Engraved on the back
were my stepfather's initials and the date, 11/30/48. It was
a special memento that my stepfather held very dear, so
the gesture of giving it to his nephew meant a great deal
to Bryce. He cherished it. He wore it all the time. And
when the band broke, he just put it in his pocket and carried it around that way. He was never without it.

One winter night, Bryce and I were on the phone on
one of those two-hour-long telephone conversations. It
was around eleven o'clock at night, he was at his parents'
house having dinner with them and some guests who
were visiting from out of town. Bryce said that he had to
go. His mother had asked him to take these friends back
to the hotel where they were staying. It was at least an
hour out of town and he was already tired. We made some
vague plans to meet on the dock in the summer.
Sometimes it was the only thing that would get me
through a tough school year. Then before he hung up he
said something that made me smile. He said, "Just remember, no matter what you do in this life, I will always be
there for you if you bump your head." I told him that he
would always be my hero, and then we hung up.

Bryce's car was found the next day. He had driven off
the road when he fell asleep at the wheel. My sweet Bryce
was killed instantly. He was twenty-five years old. The
pain and upset that spread through our family was profound. I was left with a huge hole in my heart, a hole I was
afraid would never mend.

That summer, as agreed, I went to the dock. I sat on the
dock, knowing that Bryce would never come. I sat down
and started to weep, my tears falling into the river. I found
myself getting angry. How could he have done this to
me? Why did he have to die? I was questioning God,
Bryce and whomever else was listening.

Then, remembering our conversation the night before he died, I started to hit my head.

"I'm hitting my head ... I'm bumping it, where are you? You lied to me! Do I really need to hurt myself?"

In a moment of emotional frenzy, I picked up an oar that was lying on the pier. Suddenly, underneath where the oar had just been, something shiny caught my eye. There was something wedged between the boards. I set the oar down and bent down to retrieve the shiny object. When I finally pried it free, I immediately recognized it. It was the watch my stepfather had given Bryce on his birthday. I sat down and cried. With the object still cradled in my hand, I held it up close to my heart. I soon realized that this little 1948 old-fashioned watch that needed to be wound every twenty-four hours was still ticking. Goose bumps covered my skin, and the warmest, most loving feeling came over me. I felt as if I were being hugged from the inside out. There he was, still with me.

I'll never know exactly how that little watch happened upon that pier. But I think that Bryce left it behind for me. I bought a new band for the watch, and to this very day I still wear it. It will always be a symbol of unconditional love, something time could never stop.

Zan Gaudioso

The Boy Under the Tree

In the summer recess between freshman and sopho-more years in college, I was invited to be an instructor at a high-school leadership camp hosted by a college in Michigan. I was already highly involved in most campus activities, and I jumped at the opportunity.

About an hour into the first day of camp, amid the frenzy of icebreakers and forced interactions, I first noticed the boy under the tree. He was small and skinny, and his obvi-ous discomfort and shyness made him appear frail and fragile. Only fifty feet away, two hundred eager campers were bumping bodies, playing, joking and meeting each other, but the boy under the tree seemed to want to be anywhere other than where he was. The desperate loneli-ness he radiated almost stopped me from approaching him, but I remembered the instructions from the senior staff to stay alert for campers who might feel left out.

As I walked toward him, I said, "Hi, my name is Kevin, and I'm one of the counselors. It's nice to meet you. How are you?" In a shaky, sheepish voice he reluctantly answered, "Okay, I guess." I calmly asked him if he wanted to join the activities and meet some new people. He quietly replied, "No, this is not really my thing."

I could sense that he was in a new world, that this whole experience was foreign to him. But I somehow knew it wouldn't be right to push him, either. He didn't need a pep talk; he needed a friend. After several silent moments, my first interaction with the boy under the tree was over.

At lunch the next day, I found myself leading camp songs at the top of my lungs for two hundred of my new friends. The campers eagerly participated. My gaze wandered over the mass of noise and movement and was caught by the image of the boy from under the tree, sitting alone, staring out the window. I nearly forgot the words to the song I was supposed to be leading. At my first opportunity, I tried again, with the same questions as before: "How are you doing? Are you okay?" To which he again replied, "Yeah, I'm all right. I just don't really get into this stuff." As I left the cafeteria, I realized this was going to take more time and effort than I had thought—if it was even possible to get through to him at all.

That evening at our nightly staff meeting, I made my concerns about him known. I explained to my fellow staff members my impression of him and asked them to pay special attention and spend time with him when they could.

The days I spend at camp each year fly by faster than any others I have known. Thus, before I knew it, mid-week had dissolved into the final night of camp, and I was chaperoning the "last dance." The students were doing all they could to savor every last moment with their new "best friends"—friends they would probably never see again.

As I watched the campers share their parting moments, I suddenly saw what would be one of the most vivid memories of my life. The boy from under the tree, who had stared blankly out the kitchen window, was now a shirtless dancing wonder. He owned the dance floor as he and two girls proceeded to cut a rug. I watched as he shared meaningful, intimate time with people at whom he couldn't even look just days earlier. I couldn't believe it was the same person.

In October of my sophomore year, a late-night phone call pulled me away from my chemistry book. A soft-spoken, unfamiliar voice asked politely, "Is Kevin there?"

"You're talking to him. Who's this?"

"This is Tom Johnson's mom. Do you remember Tommy from leadership camp?"

The boy under the tree. How could I not remember?

"Yes, I do," I said. "He's a very nice young man. How is he?"

An abnormally long pause followed, then Mrs. Johnson said, "My Tommy was walking home from school this week when he was hit by a car and killed." Shocked, I offered my condolences.

"I just wanted to call you," she said, "because Tommy mentioned you so many times. I wanted you to know that he went back to school this fall with confidence. He made new friends. His grades went up. And he even went out on a few dates. I just wanted to thank you for making a difference for Tom. The last few months were the best few months of his life."

In that instant, I realized how easy it is to give a bit of yourself every day. You may never know how much each gesture may mean to someone else. I tell this story as often as I can, and when I do, I urge others to look out for their own "boy under the tree."

David Coleman and Kevin Randall

Someday When I'm Older

I am only seven and a lot of things are confusing to me. Grown-ups tell me that someday I'll understand, but I wish that "someday" were now. Life is really complicated. I always have to say "please," be nice, clean up—and sometimes I just don't want to. Then there is something grown-ups call death. I know it's not a good thing, but I don't know quite what it is. I think I am supposed to understand, but no one wants to help me; maybe some-day when I'm older.

* * * *

I don't usually wait with Grace for her bus before school in the morning, but today we are sitting on the steps together. Christmas is just two weeks away, and there is fresh snow outside from last night. I can't wait until recess so I can go out and play in it. The bus has just stopped outside our house. Grace is eleven and she doesn't like to hug me too often, but this morning, she hugs me good-bye. I don't know why.

In art class today, I drew a picture for Grace's teacher: baby Jesus in the manger with an angel above him. But now school is over, and I don't know where my picture is. I never gave it to her. One of the teachers tells me that she has to drive me home. She says that Grace was in an accident. I wonder if she'll have to wear a cast in the Christmas pictures.

Now I'm walking into my house. Mommy's crying. She never cries, even when I'm really, really bad. Two policemen are in our living room. No one is telling me why they are there. All the grown-ups are talking, but I can't understand what they are saying; maybe someday I will. Daddy is the only one who says anything to me.

"You have to go to Mrs. Riffs's house for awhile." I like Mrs. Riffs, but I really want to stay with Mommy and Daddy. No one is listening to me, so I will just keep that inside. Mommy is really sad. I think Grace has more than a broken arm. All I can do is pat Mommy on the shoulder and whisper like she does when I'm sad.

"Grace is going to be okay," I say. I'm not quite sure though. No one will tell me how bad things are, and seeing Mommy crying scares me most of all. But Grace *has* to be okay. I already made her Christmas present, and we are supposed to make snow angels together on the front lawn.

Mommy and Daddy are always telling people that I have a short "tensions pan." I think that means I don't like to watch movies that are too long. Tonight seems to be taking a lot longer than the longest movie I have ever seen. It is past my bedtime, and I just want to go home. I think I hear a car in the driveway. Mommy and Daddy are coming inside now. Daddy wants to talk to me, but I don't want to hear what he is going to say.

"Grace has gone up to heaven."

I'm crying now. I don't really want to, but Mommy is, and I think it's the right thing to do. I am so confused. Mommy and Daddy told me that heaven is where we go when we die, but Grace can't be dead. I want to ask questions, but I know I'm supposed to just be sad now. This is really complicated. I want someone to explain, but as usual, I'm too young to understand anyway. I feel bad for not feeling like crying, so I am trying my best.

It is past Christmas now, but I still have a lot of questions. I try to keep them inside because I don't want Mommy to cry again. Sometimes they tell me more about "the accident": Grace was waiting for the bus after school with some other kids. A car was driving too fast on the icy road, went out of control and hit her. They tell me she didn't feel any pain. That's good, because I don't want Grace to be hurting.

I am trying very hard to understand death. I read the books that people give me about Joe and what happened when his dog died. I still feel too young to get it. I feel sad and angry and frustrated. I love Grace, and I miss playing with her. Mommy is crying less now. I think it's okay to ask her a question.

"Mommy, why did it have to be Grace that was hit? Why couldn't it have been someone else who was standing there?" Mommy has started crying again and I wish I didn't ask her the question, but now she is smiling and hugging me. She says, "Because then another family would have to go through all the pain and sadness that we feel." I am not sure why she said that, but it's not the time for any more questions.

Now it is a few weeks later. Mommy and Daddy tell me that the man who hit Grace found out that he killed her, so he killed himself. I think I am old enough to understand what this means.

"That's good, right, Mom? Now he has paid for what he did." Mommy speaks very quietly when she answers. She tells me, "No, it's not good. Now his family has to go through everything that we felt. They shouldn't have to do that."

* * * *

I am sixteen now and I know a lot more than I did then. I know that seven years is a short time to learn about forgiveness. Back then, I didn't quite understand why Mom didn't want the man to be punished, but I trusted that she was right. Now Mom's words echo in my heart as clearly as they did when I first heard them nine years ago. Since that time, there have been so many instances when I have found it difficult, almost impossible to forgive someone. Then I hear Mom again. I realize that if Mom could forgive the man who killed her daughter, surely I can forgive my best friend for forgetting our Saturday afternoon plans.

It took me a long time to understand exactly what that horrific day and my sister's death meant. I have gradually accepted that I will not see Grace for a long time, but I know I will see her again in heaven. I also know that Grace is happy and that she is still with me. With time, my wounds have healed. I have learned that it's okay to be sad, and it's also okay not to be sad. As I have learned more about life, I have also come to understand death better. More important than all this, though, I will never forget Mom's lesson of the ultimate forgiveness.

Andrea Gonsalves

Dear Child—A Sister's Message

Today I look into your tender young face, you're all of eleven years old, and I shudder at that thought. Perhaps I am trying to relive my adolescence through you and I recall how tough that age was for me. It was about the time Mom and Dad divorced, the year I had my first real crush and the beginning of junior high—three hard-hitting blows to a confused, awkward kid. That is possibly why I want to write a letter that could somehow condense all my experiences and all my sufferings in one neat page, for you to look at and say, "my mistakes—never!" You see, my experiences weren't unusual or extraordinary, but at the time they took place I felt as if the world would sooner swallow me whole, than allow me to overcome it with some sense of self intact.

So, somehow, I want to call upon that girl I once was and ask her to help me find the words that will give you the armor, that will make all the cruel insults you will surely encounter simply roll off your back. I want to find the potion that will make you see how extraordinary you are so that when that first heartbreak comes along, although you may doubt the love of others, you will never once doubt the love you hold for yourself. I want to make you aware of the beauty that is woman, so that you will always be proud and bold, never flinching in the eye of a man, or most likely a boy, who will try with all his might to convince you that you have a lesser place in the world. I want to show you how to adore this temple in which you house your mind and soul, always respect it and treat it as the jewel that is you. Remember, dear child, that whomever you allow near this temple, this possession that is solely yours, is completely your choice. No amount of convincing or begging could ever change that. Your heart—the treasure box that holds dreams and secret wishes—don't allow it to become a house for fear. Fear will consume you; it will beckon you to keep from shining, to step down for the light on the horizon. Don't hesitate, not even for a moment, because in that moment you may be draining the life of your spirit. Instead, walk with firm, steady steps into the glare of failure and humiliation, two of your greatest foes—believe me, they are no match.

Friends will test your best judgment. You will ask yourself if you chose wisely, or perhaps you will not choose carefully enough and in desperation of walking alone, you will allow yourself to be surrounded by meaningless acquaintances, who have little interest in your true self. These friendships could at times prove to be soul-killing and exhausting, and, although this may seem out of touch right now, I want you to know that at times there is more dignity in marching alone. Loneliness is what you will feel if you build your friendships on longings of being mirrored by visions of your self.

There will always be those that are different from you, in aspects ranging from ethnic background to physical challenges. I wonder, "will she be gracious and kind, an angel cloaked in a child's disguise, or will she be cruel and sharp with a tongue solely shaped to stab at the heart?" Who will you be, sister? Will those around you regard you as boring and snotty for not wanting to partake in the spirit-bashing of those unaccepted souls? Or will you be leader of such tragic slander? Although you may be cast out for any goodness you exhibit, will you have the commanding strength to remain true to what you've been taught? True to yourself?

Dear child, I know this is huge and unsettling, and perhaps too much to digest at this place and time, but will you tuck this away in a safe, unrelenting place so that its presence will always peer into your conscience? Perhaps you will have a question someday and you will remember these words, my words, which today seem unfitting, uncompromising. I don't think I've covered every possible adolescent terror that you will be struck with, but I can't possibly anticipate all the life that will come your way. What I can say is that you will survive, but not without scars in the most unimaginable place—your heart. Wear them like a badge of courage once you have survived this battle referred to as "growing up." You will be all the wiser, dear child—I know I am.

Danette Julene Gomez

Finger Paints and Crayons

With chalk in hand she wrote her name across a board
    once bare
And then she sat behind her desk without a single care
And for fifteen minutes, she did not make a sound
Until the final student, had finally settled down
Then she stood before them, and told them all her name
And then politely asked, each student to do the same
Then without hesitation, she took papers from a sack
And placed them in two piles, one white, the other
    black
And deliberately quite slowly, with a slight, mis-
    chievous smile
She began handing out the papers, up and down each
    aisle
And once each student had a piece; she continued
    within their sights
To gather two piles of crayons, one black, the other
    white
And then she took a painting, from behind her walnut
    desk
Then placed a painter's smock, overtop her navy dress

And to no one in particular, she spoke in peaceful tones
"I've been working on this painting, for years in my
own home."
She stood staring at the painting, its brilliant colors
mixed as one
Upon a vast horizon, the presence of a sun
It indeed was not a Rembrandt, a Picasso, or Michelangelo
to say the least
But it nonetheless was beautiful; its presence spoke of
peace
And no doubt that lovely painting, had taken so much
time
For every color known to man, seemed to intertwine
And so it came with wonder, what they witnessed with
surprise
The act that took them all off guard, done right before
their eyes
With finger paints now gathered, and opened on her
desk
She smeared the colors upon her hands, in an en-
tangled awful mess
And then as though she'd lost her mind, she smeared
her hands across
The painting once so beautiful . . . now a total loss
It did not make a bit of sense, they did not understand
As they sat and watched their teacher, wipe the paints
from off her hands
And then she took the crayons, and went up and down
the rows
And handed to each student, the colors that she chose
"Now," she told her students, "I want you to create
A picture filled with beauty, devoid of any hate."
Mouths dropped open widely; mumbles filled the room
And students looked to one another, as unasked ques-
tions seemed to loom

For the students with white paper, were given crayons
the same shade
And the students with black crayons, had been given a
raven-colored page
And how could one create splendor, with no colors to
mix and match
The students were quite certain, their teacher had left
out most the facts
"Teacher," a student's voice was heard, "I'm not so sure
I can"
Staring at the white crayon, and white paper in her hand
Silence overtook the room; it eerily crept about
Causing the teacher's gentle voice, to erupt into a shout
"You each share the same problem, you each possess
the power to resolve
But only the students with open minds, will have the
ability to solve."
Minutes ticked away, class was nearing to an end
And not one single student, knew quite how to begin
And when the bell rang out, and they hurried to their feet
Their teacher told them commandingly, to return back
to their seat
"Before you leave this classroom, I think you each
should know
For this assignment you receive a failing grade, for you
have no work to show
And tomorrow and the next day, your assignment shall
be the same
And those who fail my class, will have only themselves
to blame."
The next day and the following, students weren't quite
sure what to do
Until at last, a solution, began to surface through
When one student with his crayon, and paper both in
black

Turned to the student behind him and asked, "May I
    borrow that?"
The student hesitated, but then gave up his crayon
    made of white
And ultimately the assignment, no longer seemed a
    plight
For students all throughout the class, switched crayons
    up and down the aisles
And certain that they'd found the solution, their faces
    lit with smiles
And just as every student began to draw, across an
    empty page
The teacher whom they'd all began, to see as certainly
    quite strange
Collected all the pages and crayons, without a single
    mark
And then spoke aloud, "Thank you, for bringing hope
    into my heart
You see, I wanted you to realize, that in order to create
A picture filled with beauty, devoid of any hate
You needed first to recognize, that a problem did exist
And that a practical solution, could be found within
    your midst
And that racism is a problem, each of us must face
Working all as one, before it's much too late
And with open eyes and open hearts, we must see the
    person, not the color of their skin
And come to the understanding, that racism has to end
For together we are family, we cry tears, we all feel pain
And though we may not look the part, that's exactly
    what we do
For crayons are just colors, that's all our skin is, too."

Students looked about the room, a variety of colors on
their skin
As the point she was trying to make, began to settle in
The looks upon their faces, readily explained
That they each were trying to contemplate: that indeed
they were the same
A nervous shuffling of papers, and coughs throughout
the room
Portraying the vital image, that fighting over crayons
was a stupid thing to do
It was then each student realized, the purpose of
crayons and papers the same shade
Was to prove they each needed the other color, to help
fill their empty page

Silence seized the moment, as one student raised his
open hand
And then spoke in hesitation, "I just don't understand . . .
Why you took your painting, the one you seemed to
enjoy so very much
Gathered up your finger paints, to destroy it in a
touch."

Sadness filled her face, as a tear trailed upon her cheek
And in slow and heartfelt words, she began to speak
"To show you each that colors can be beautiful, but they
also can destroy
Everything we love and work for, everything we each
enjoy
And the destruction of something that I loved, was to
make a point to you
That racism destroys the beauty in us all,
And that fighting over colors, is a destructive thing to
do."

Cheryl Costello-Forshey

A Message for Ben

Coming of age in this dangerous world is a dauntingly,
   difficult thing.
How will you live up to the promise of what the future
   will bring?
You've shown by example that God has a plan
for helping this old boy become a young man.

We encourage you, Ben, to accept every challenge
with strength and conviction, with patience and balance.
Be truthful, be gentle and always forgive.
Through compassion you learn how to live and let live.

Take to adventure with your eyes open wide.
To steady the journey, travel often inside.
Seek poetry, passion, beauty and art.
Keep magic and wonder tucked close to your heart.

Celebrate failure with just one more try.
Be mindful of the riches that money can't buy.
Be grateful for wealth, but know what's at stake.
And give back to the earth, always, more than you take.

Plant gardens, feed pigeons, walk softly through snow.
When you nurture all life, you help yourself grow.
Be childlike, laugh often, and share every joy.
Honor the man, remember the boy.

Cry at sad movies and when you feel grief.
Tears are the heart's way of bringing relief.
Learn from your pain, it will help make you wise.
Above all, remember that love never dies.

Then, at the end, as you walk your last mile,
Looking back on your life with a well-deserved smile,
Recall all the faces that helped light the way.
Give thanks for their love and remember this day.

Tom Witte

[EDITORS' NOTE: *Ben's uncle, Tom Witte, wrote this poem for Ben for his thirteenth birthday. Tom passed away from complications from AIDS, shortly after he gave him the poem.*]

4

ON FAMILY

Other things may change us, but we start and end with family.

Anthony Brandt

Reprinted by permission of Dave Carpenter.

What My Father Wore

What my father wore embarrassed me as a young man. I wanted him to dress like a doctor or lawyer, but on those muggy mornings when he rose before dawn to fry eggs for my mother and me, he always dressed like my father.

We lived in south Texas, and my father wore tattered jeans with the imprint of his pocketknife on the seat. He liked shirts that snapped more than those that buttoned, and kept his pencils, cigars, glasses, wrenches and screwdrivers in his breast pocket. My father's boots were government-issues with steel toes that made them difficult to pull off his feet, which I sometimes did when he returned from repairing air conditioners, his job that also shamed me.

But, as a child, I'd crept into his closet and modeled his wardrobe in front of the mirror. My imagination transformed his shirts into the robes of kings and his belts into soldiers' holsters. I slept in his undershirts and relied on the scent of his collars to calm my fear of the dark. Within a few years, though, I started wishing my father would trade his denim for khaki and retire his boots for loafers. I stopped sleeping in his clothes and eventually began dreaming of another father.

I blamed the way he dressed for my social failures. When boys bullied me, I thought they'd seen my father wearing his cowboy hat but no shirt while walking our dog. I felt that girls snickered at me because they'd glimpsed him mowing the grass in cut-offs and black boots. The girls' families paid men (and I believed better-dressed ones) to landscape their lawns, while their fathers yachted in the bay wearing lemon-yellow sweaters and expensive sandals.

My father only bought two suits in his life. He preferred clothes that allowed him the freedom to shimmy under cars and squeeze behind broken Maytags, where he felt most content. But the day before my parents' twentieth anniversary, he and I went to Sears, and he tried on suits all afternoon. With each one, he stepped to the mirror, smiled and nodded, then asked about the price and reached for another. He probably tried ten suits before we drove to a discount store and bought one without so much as approaching a fitting room. That night my mother said she'd never seen a more handsome man.

Later, though, he donned the same suit for my eighth-grade awards banquet, and I wished he'd stayed home. After the ceremony (I'd been voted Mr. Citizenship, of all things), he lauded my award and my character while changing into a faded red sweatsuit. He was stepping into the garage to wash a load of laundry when I asked what even at age fourteen struck me as cruel and wrong. "Why," I asked, "don't you dress 'nice,' like my friends' fathers?"

He held me with his sad, shocked eyes and searched for an answer. Then before he disappeared into the garage and closed the door between us, my father said, "I like my clothes." An hour later my mother stormed into my room, slapped me hard across the face and called me an "ungrateful little twerp," a phrase that echoed in my head until they resumed speaking to me.

In time they forgave me, and as I matured I realized that girls avoided me not because of my father but because of his son. I realized that my mother had slapped me because my father could not, and it soon became clear that what he had really said that night was that there are things more important than clothes. He'd said he couldn't spend a nickel on himself because there were things I wanted. That night, without another word, my father had said, "You're my son, and I sacrifice so your life will be better than mine."

For my high-school graduation, my father arrived in a suit he and my mother had purchased earlier that day. Somehow he seemed taller, more handsome and imposing, and when he passed the other fathers they stepped out of his way. It wasn't the suit, of course, but the man. The doctors and lawyers recognized the confidence in his swagger, the pride in his eyes, and when they approached him, they did so with courtesy and respect. After we returned home, my father replaced the suit in the flimsy Sears garment bag, and I didn't see it again until his funeral.

I don't know what he was wearing when he died, but he was working, so he was in clothes he liked, and that comforts me. My mother thought of burying him in the suit from Sears, but I convinced her otherwise and soon delivered a pair of old jeans, a flannel shirt and his boots to the funeral home.

On the morning of the services, I used his pocketknife to carve another hole in his belt so it wouldn't droop around my waist. Then I took the suit from Sears out of his closet and changed into it. Eventually, I mustered the courage to study myself in his mirror where, with the exception of the suit, I appeared small and insignificant. Again, as in childhood, the clothes draped over my scrawny frame. My father's scent wafted up and caressed my face, but it failed to console me. I was uncertain: not about my father's stature—I'd stopped being an ungrateful little twerp years before. No, I was uncertain about myself, my own stature. And I stood there for some time, facing myself in my father's mirror, weeping and trying to imagine—as I will for the rest of my life—the day I'll grow into my father's clothes.

Bret Anthony Johnston

She Didn't Give Up on Me

She never once gave up. My mom is my hero.

Kimberly Anne Brand

I lay on the floor, furiously kicking my legs and screaming until my throat felt raw—all because my foster mother had asked me to put my toys away.

"I hate you," I shrieked. I was six years old and didn't understand why I felt so angry all the time.

I'd been living in foster care since I was two. My real mom couldn't give my five sisters and me the care we needed. Since we didn't have a dad or anyone else to care for us, we were put in different foster homes. I felt lonely and confused. I didn't know how to tell people that I hurt inside. Throwing a tantrum was the only way I knew to express my feelings.

Because I acted up, eventually my current foster mom sent me back to the adoption agency, just as the mom before had. I thought I was the most unlovable girl in the world.

Then I met Kate McCann. I was seven by that time and living with my third foster family when she came to visit. When my foster mother told me that Kate was single and wanted to adopt a child, I didn't think she'd choose me. I couldn't imagine anyone would want me to live with them forever.

That day, Kate took me to a pumpkin farm. We had fun, but I didn't think I'd see her again.

A few days later, a social worker came to the house to say that Kate wanted to adopt me. Then she asked me if I'd mind living with one parent instead of two.

"All I want is someone who loves me," I said.

Kate visited the next day. She explained that it would take a year for the adoption to be finalized, but I could move in with her soon. I was excited but afraid, too. Kate and I were total strangers. I wondered if she'd change her mind once she got to know me.

Kate sensed my fear. "I know you've been hurt," she said, hugging me. "I know you're scared. But I promise I'll never send you away. We're a family now."

To my surprise, her eyes were filled with tears. Suddenly I realized that she was as lonely as I was!

"Okay . . . Mom, " I said.

The following week I met my new grandparents, aunt, uncle and cousins. It felt funny—but good—to be with strangers who hugged me as though they already loved me.

When I moved in with Mom, I had my own room for the first time. It had wallpaper and a matching bedspread, an antique dresser and a big closet. I had only a few clothes I'd brought with me in a brown paper bag. "Don't worry," Mom said. "I'll buy you lots of pretty new things."

I went to sleep that night feeling safe. I prayed I wouldn't have to leave.

Mom did lots of nice things for me. She took me to church. She let me have pets and gave me horseback riding and piano lessons. Every day, she told me she loved me. But love wasn't enough to heal the hurt inside me. I kept waiting for her to change her mind. I thought, "If I act bad enough, she'll leave me like the others."

So I tried to hurt her before she could hurt me. I picked fights over little things and threw tantrums when I didn't get my way. I slammed doors. If Mom tried to stop me, I'd hit her. But she never lost patience. She'd hug me and say she loved me anyway. When I got mad, she made me jump on a trampoline.

Because I was failing in school when I came to live with her, Mom was very strict about my homework. One day when I was watching TV, she came in and turned it off. "You can watch it after you finish your homework," she said. I blew up. I picked up my books and threw them across the room. "I hate you and I don't want to live here anymore!" I screamed.

I waited for her to tell me to start packing. When she didn't, I asked, "Aren't you going to send me back?"

"I don't like the way you're behaving," she said, "but I'll never send you back. We're a family, and families don't give up on each other."

Then it hit me. This mom was different; she wasn't going to get rid of me. She really did love me. And I realized I loved her, too. I cried and hugged her.

In 1985, when Mom formally adopted me, our whole family celebrated at a restaurant. It felt good belonging to someone. But I was still scared. Could a mom really love me forever? My tantrums didn't disappear immediately, but as months passed, they happened less often.

Today I'm sixteen. I have a 3.4 grade point average, a horse named Dagger's Point, four cats, a dog, six doves and a bullfrog that lives in our backyard pond. And I have a dream: I want to be a veterinarian.

Mom and I like to do things together, like shopping and horseback riding. We smile when people say how much we look alike. They don't believe she's not my real mom.

I'm happier now than I ever imagined I could be. When

I'm older, I'd like to get married and have kids, but if that doesn't work out, I'll adopt like Mom did. I'll pick a scared and lonely kid and then never, ever give up on her. I'm so glad Mom didn't give up on me.

Sharon Whitley
excerpted from Woman's World Magazine

Unconditional Mom

*My mother had a great deal of trouble with
me, but I think she enjoyed it.*

Mark Twain

I was a rotten teenager. Not your average spoiled, know-
it-all, not-going-to-clean-my-room, getting-an-attitude-
because-I'm-fifteen teenager. No, I was a manipulative,
lying, acid-tongued monster, who realized early on that I
could make things go my way with just a few minor adjust-
ments. The writers for today's hottest soap opera could not
have created a worse "villainess." A few nasty comments
here, a lie or two there, maybe an evil glare for a finishing
touch, and things would be grand. Or so I thought.

For the most part, and on the outside, I was a good kid.
A giggly, pug-nose tomboy who liked to play sports and
who thrived on competition (a nice way of saying: somewhat pushy and demanding). Which is probably why
most people allowed me to squeak by using what I now
call "bulldozer behavior tactics," with no regard for anyone I felt to be of value. For a while, anyway.

Since I was perceptive enough to get some people to

bend my way, it amazes me how long it took to realize how I was hurting so many others. Not only did I succeed in pushing away many of my closest friends by trying to control them; I also managed to sabotage, time and time again, the most precious relationship in my life: my relationship with my mother.

Even today, almost ten years since the birth of the new me, my former behavior astonishes me each time I reach into my memories. Hurtful comments that cut and stung the people I cared most about. Acts of confusion and anger that seemed to rule my every move—all to make sure that things went my way.

My mother, who gave birth to me at age thirty-eight against her doctor's wishes, would cry to me, "I waited so long for you, please don't push me away. I want to help you!"

I would reply with my best face of stone, "I didn't ask for you! I never wanted you to care about me! Leave me alone and forget I ever lived!"

My mother began to believe I really meant it. My actions proved nothing less.

I was mean and manipulative, trying to get my way at any cost. Like many young girls in high school, the boys whom I knew were off limits were always the first ones I had to date. Sneaking out of the house at all hours of the night just to prove I could do it. Juggling complex lies that were always on the verge of blowing up in my face. Finding any way to draw attention to myself while simultaneously trying to be invisible.

Ironically, I wish I could say I had been heavy into drugs during that period of my life, swallowing mind-altering pills and smoking things that changed my personality, thus accounting for the terrible, razor-sharp words that came flying from my mouth. However, that was not the case. My only addiction was hatred; my only high was inflicting pain.

But then I asked myself why. Why the need to hurt? And why the people I cared about the most? Why the need for all the lies? Why the attacks on my mother? I would drive myself mad with all the why's until one day, it all exploded in a suicidal rage.

Lying awake the following night at the "resort" (my pet name for the hospital), after an unsuccessful, gutless attempt to jump from a vehicle moving at eighty miles per hour, one thing stood out more than my Keds with no shoe laces. I didn't want to die.

And I did not want to inflict any more pain on people to cover up what I was truly trying to hide myself: self-hatred. Self-hatred unleashed on everyone else.

I saw my mother's pained face for the first time in years—warm, tired brown eyes filled with nothing but thanks for her daughter's new lease on life and love for the child she waited thirty-eight years to bear.

My first encounter with unconditional love. What a powerful feeling.

Despite all the lies I had told her, she still loved me. I cried on her lap for hours one afternoon and asked why she still loved me after all the horrible things I did to her. She just looked down at me, brushed the hair out of my face and said frankly, "I don't know."

A kind of smile penetrated her tears as the lines in her tested face told me all that I needed to know. I was her daughter, but more important, she was my mother. Not every rotten child is so lucky. Not every mother can be pushed to the limits I explored time and time again, and venture back with feelings of love.

Unconditional love is the most precious gift we can give. Being forgiven for the past is the most precious gift we can receive. I dare not say we could experience this pure love twice in one lifetime.

I was one of the lucky ones. I know that. I want to extend the gift my mother gave me to all the "rotten teenagers" in the world who are confused.

It's okay to feel pain, to need help, to feel love—just feel it without hiding. Come out from under the protective covers, from behind the rigid walls and the suffocating personas, and take a breath of life.

Sarah J. Vogt

The Home Run

On June 18th, I went to my little brother's baseball game as I always did. Cory was twelve years old at the time and had been playing baseball for a couple of years. When I saw that he was warming up to be next at bat, I decided to head over to the dugout to give him a few pointers. But when I got there, I simply said, "I love you."

In return, he asked, "Does this mean you want me to hit a home run?"

I smiled and said, "Do your best."

As he walked up to the plate, there was a certain aura about him. He looked so confident and so sure about what he was going to do. One swing was all he took and, wouldn't you know, he hit his first home run! He ran around those bases with such pride—his eyes sparkled and his face was lit up. But what touched my heart the most was when he walked back over to the dugout. He looked over at me with the biggest smile I've ever seen and said, "I love you too, Ter."

I don't remember if his team won or lost that game. On that special summer day in June, it simply didn't matter.

Terri Vandermark

My Big Brother

First say to yourself what you would be; and then do what you have to do.

Epictetus

I never thought that the absence of smelly socks and loud music would make my heart ache. But my brother is off at college, and at age fourteen, I miss him terribly. We share a rare kind of closeness for siblings, but then, my brother is a rare kind of guy. Of course he's smart and kind, plus my friends say he is gorgeous and all that. But it's more how he handles things, how he treats his friends and his family, how he cares about people that makes me so proud. That's the stuff that I aspire to be. If it's okay with you, I would like to show you what I mean. . . .

He applied to fourteen colleges. He was accepted to all but one, the one he wanted, Brown University. So he opted for his second choice, and off he went to a fine though uneventful first year. When he came home for summer vacation, he informed us that he had come up with a plan. He was going to do whatever it took to get into Brown. Would we support him?

His plan was to move to Rhode Island near Brown, find a job, and do whatever he could to become known in the area. He'd work his heart out, he said, and do the very best at everything. Someone, he was sure, would notice. This was a big deal for my parents because it meant agreeing to a year without college, a scary thing for them. But they trusted him and encouraged him to do whatever he thought it would take to achieve his dream.

It wasn't long before he was hired to produce the plays at—yes, you guessed it—Brown. Now was his chance to shine, and shine he did. No task was too big or too small. He put every bit of himself into the job. He met teachers and administrators, talked to everyone about his dream and never hesitated to tell them what he was after.

And sure enough, at the end of the year, when he reapplied to Brown, he was accepted.

We were all really happy, but for me the happiness went very deep. I had learned an important lesson—a lesson no one could have taught me with words, a lesson I had to see with my own eyes. If I work hard for what I want, if I keep trying after I've been turned away, my dreams also can come true. This is a gift I still hold in my heart. Because of my brother, I trust life.

Recently, I flew to Rhode Island all by myself to visit him, and I had a blast hanging out for a week in an apartment without parents. The night before I left, we were talking about all kinds of stuff like boyfriends, girlfriends, peer pressure and school. At one point, my brother looked me right in the eye and said he loved me. He told me to remember to never do anything that I feel isn't right, no matter what, and never to forget that I can always trust my heart.

I cried all the way home, knowing that my brother and

I will always be close, and realizing how lucky I am to have him. Something was different: I didn't feel like a little girl anymore. Part of me had grown up on this trip, and for the first time I thought about the important job that I had waiting for me at home. You see, I have a ten-year-old little sister. It looks as though I've got my work cut out for me. But you know, I had a great teacher.

Lisa Gumenick

A Brother's Voice

Most people have an inspiration in their life. Maybe it's a talk with someone you respect or an experience. Whatever the inspiration, it tends to make you look at life from a different perspective. My inspiration came from my sister Vicki, a kind and caring person. She didn't care about accolades or being written about in newspapers. All she wanted was to share her love with the people she cared about, her family and friends.

The summer before my junior year of college, I received a phone call from my father saying that Vicki was rushed to the hospital. She had collapsed and the right side of her body was paralyzed. The preliminary indications were that she suffered a stroke. However, test results confirmed it was much more serious. There was a malignant brain tumor causing her paralysis. Her doctors didn't give her more than three months to live. I remember wondering how this could happen? The day before Vicki was perfectly fine. Now, her life was coming to an end at such a young age.

After overcoming the initial shock and feeling of emptiness, I decided that Vicki needed hope and encouragement. She needed someone to make her believe that she would overcome this obstacle. I became Vicki's coach. Everyday we would visualize the tumor shrinking and everything that we talked about was positive. I even posted a sign on her hospital room door that read, "If you have any negative thoughts, leave them at the door." I was determined to help Vicki beat the tumor. She and I made a deal that was called 50-50. I would do 50 percent of the fighting and Vicki would do the other 50 percent.

The month of August arrived and it was time to begin my junior year of college three thousand miles away. I was unsure whether I should leave or stay with Vicki. I made the mistake of telling her that I might not leave for school. She became angry and said not to worry because she would be fine. There was Vicki lying ill in a hospital bed telling me not to worry. I realized that if I stayed it might send a message that she was dying and I didn't want her believing that. Vicki needed to believe that she could win against the tumor.

Leaving that night feeling it might be the last time I would ever see Vicki alive was the most difficult thing I have ever done. While at school, I never stopped fighting my 50 percent for her. Every night before falling asleep I would talk to Vicki, hoping that there was some way she could hear me. I would say, "Vicki I'm fighting for you and I will never quit. As long as you never quit fighting we will beat this."

A few months had passed and she was still holding on. I was talking with an elderly friend and she asked about Vicki's situation. I told her that she was getting worse but that she wasn't quitting. My friend asked a question that really made me think. She said, "Do you think the reason she hasn't let go is because she doesn't want to let you down?"

Maybe she was right? Maybe I was selfish for encouraging Vicki to keep fighting? That night before falling asleep, I said to her, "Vicki, I understand that you're in a lot of pain and that you might like to let go. If you do, then I want you to. We didn't lose because you never quit fighting. If you want to go on to a better place then I understand. We will be together again. I love you and I'll always be with you wherever you are."

Early the next morning, my mother called to tell me that Vicki had passed away.

James Malinchak

The Champ

He had a featherweight build, but what this fifteen-year-old lacked in strength and speed, he made up for in attitude. Jason never missed a practice, even though he rarely got playing time, and then only in the fourth quarter when our team outdistanced the opponent by at least three touchdowns. Even so, number thirty-seven never so much as frowned, let alone complained, and always put forth his best effort—even if it amounted to very little.

One day he didn't come to practice. When he didn't show up on the second day, as his concerned coach, I telephoned his home to check on him. The out-of-town relative I spoke with informed me that Jason's father had passed away and the family was making funeral arrangements.

Two weeks later, my faithful number thirty-seven was again in the lineup, ready for practice. Only three days of practice remained before our next game. This was an important game because it was against our most fierce opponent and late in the season, and we only had a one-game lead over them. This was a critical game at a pivotal point in the season.

When the big day rolled around, my top players were ready to bolt onto the field. All the familiar faces were there but one—Jason. But suddenly, Jason appeared at my side and with a totally uncharacteristic look and manner said, "I'm going to be a starter today. I'm ready now." He left no room for refusal or argument. When the game began, he was in position on the field. The regular starter whom he replaced sat awestruck on the bench.

Jason played like a first-stringer that day. He was in every respect equal if not better than the best player on the team. He ran fast, found every open hole in the line, and jumped up after every tackle as if he had never been hit. By the third quarter he had run for three touchdowns. As a grand finale, as if to remove even the slightest doubt in anyone's mind, he scored another touchdown in the last seconds of the fourth quarter.

As he ran off the field with his teammates, Jason received a volley of body slaps and body slams against the backdrop of thunderous applause from the crowd. Despite all the adulation, Jason managed to maintain his characteristic humble, low-key manner. Puzzled by Jason's sudden transformation, I approached him and said, "Jason, you played an extraordinary game today. By the second touchdown, I had to wipe my eyes and pinch myself. But by the time the clock ran out in the fourth quarter, my curiosity got the best of me. What happened to you?"

Jason, hesitating at first, said, "Well, Coach Williams, as you know, my father recently died. When my dad was alive he was blind, so he couldn't see me play. But now that he has gone to heaven, this is the first time he has been able to see me play. I wanted to make him proud."

As told by Nailah Malik, the "Vela Storyteller"

I Love You, Dad

If God can work through me, he can work through anyone.

St. Francis of Assisi

I met a man who came to Tampa for his father's funeral. Father and son hadn't seen each other in years. In fact, according to the son, his father had left when he was a boy, and they had had little contact until about a year ago, when his father had sent him a birthday card with a note saying he'd like to see his son again.

After discussing a trip to Florida with his wife and children and consulting his busy schedule at his office, the son tentatively set a date to visit his father two months later. He would drive his family down when school was out for vacation. He scribbled a note and with mixed emotions, dropped it in the mail.

He heard back immediately. Written on lined paper torn from a spiral notebook, such as a schoolboy would use, were words of excitement penned in a barely legible scrawl. Misspelled words, poor grammar and incorrect punctuation bounced off the page. The man was embarrassed for his father. He thought twice about the upcoming visit.

It just so happened that the man's daughter made the cheerleading squad at her school and had to go to a camp conducted for cheering techniques. Coincidentally, it started the week after school was out. The trip to Florida would have to be postponed.

His father said he understood, but the son didn't hear from him again for some time. A note here or there, an occasional call. They didn't say much—muttered sentences, comments about "your mother," a couple of clouded stories about the man's childhood—but it was enough to put together a few of the missing pieces.

In November the son received a call from his father's neighbor. His father had been taken to the hospital with heart problems. The son spoke with the charge nurse, who assured him his father was doing well following a heart attack. The doctor could provide details.

His father said, "I'm fine. You don't have to make a trip out here. The doctor says there was minor damage, and I can go home day after tomorrow."

He called his father every few days after that. They chatted and laughed and talked about getting together "soon." He sent money for Christmas. His father sent small gifts for his children and a pen and pencil set for his son. It was a cheap set, probably purchased at a discount pharmacy or variety-type store, and the kids tossed their tokens from Grandpa aside without much notice. But his wife received a precious music box made of crystal. Overwhelmed, she expressed her gratitude to the old man when they called him on Christmas Day. "It was my mother's," the old man explained. "I wanted you to have it."

The man's wife told her husband that they should have invited the old man for the holidays. As an excuse for not having done so, she added, "But it probably would be too cold for him here, anyway."

In February, the man decided to visit his father. As luck would have it, however, his boss's wife had to have an operation, and the man had to fill in and work a few extra hours. He called his father to tell him he'd probably get to Florida in March or April.

I met the man on Friday. He had finally come to Tampa. He was here to bury his father.

He was waiting when I arrived to open the door that morning. He sat in the chapel next to his father's body, which had been dressed in a handsome, new, navy blue pinstriped suit and laid out in a dark blue metal casket. "Going Home" was scripted inside the lid.

I offered the man a glass of water. He cried. I put my arm around his shoulder and he collapsed in my arms, sobbing. "I should have come sooner. He shouldn't have had to die alone." We sat together until late afternoon. He asked if I had something else to do that day. I told him no.

I didn't choose the act, but I knew it was kind. No one else came to honor the life of the man's father, not even the neighbor he spoke of. It cost nothing but a few hours of my time. I told him I was a student, that I wanted to be a professional golfer, and that my parents owned the funeral home. He was an attorney and lived in Denver. He plays golf whenever he can. He told me about his father.

That night, I asked my dad to play golf with me the next day. And before I went to bed, I told him, "I love you, Dad."

Nick Curry III

Beautiful, She Said

I never thought that I understood her. She always seemed so far away from me. I loved her, of course. We shared mutual love from the day I was born.

I came into this world with a bashed head and deformed features because of the hard labor my mother had gone through. Family members and friends wrinkled their noses at the disfigured baby I was. They all commented on how much I looked like a beat-up football player. But no, not her. Nana thought I was beautiful. Her eyes twinkled with splendor and happiness at the ugly baby in her arms. Her first granddaughter. Beautiful, she said.

Before final exams in my junior year of high school, she died.

Seven years earlier, her doctors had diagnosed Nana with Alzheimer's disease. Our family became experts on this disease as, slowly, we lost her.

She always spoke in fragmented sentences. As the years passed, the words she spoke became fewer and fewer, until finally she said nothing at all. We were lucky to get one occasional word out of her. It was then that our family knew she was near the end.

About a week or so before she died, her body lost the ability to function at all, and the doctors decided to move her to a hospice. A hospice: where those who enter never come out.

I told my parents I wanted to see her. I had to see her. My uncontrollable curiosity had taken a step above my gut-wrenching fear.

My mother brought me to the hospice two days later. My grandfather and two of my aunts were there as well, but they hung back in the hallway as I entered Nana's room. She was sitting in a big, fluffy chair next to her bed, slouched over, eyes shut, mouth numbly hanging open. The morphine was keeping her asleep. My eyes darted around the room at the windows, the flowers and the way Nana looked. I was struggling very hard to take it all in, knowing that this would be the last time I ever saw her alive.

I slowly sat down across from her. I took her left hand and held it in mine, brushing a stray lock of golden hair away from her face. I just sat and stared, motionless, in front of her, unable to feel anything. I opened my mouth to speak but nothing came out. I could not get over how awful she looked, sitting there helpless.

Then it happened. Her little hand wrapped around mine tighter and tighter. Her voice began what sounded like a soft howl. She seemed to be crying in pain. And then she spoke.

"Jessica." Plain as day. My name. Mine. Out of four children, two sons-in-law, one daughter-in-law and six grandchildren, she knew it was me.

At that moment, it was as though someone were showing a family filmstrip in my head. I saw Nana at my baptizing. I saw her at my fourteen dance recitals. I saw her bringing me roses and beaming with pride. I saw her tap-dancing on our kitchen floor. I saw her pointing at her own wrinkled cheeks and telling me that it was from her that I inherited my big dimples. I saw her playing games with us grandkids while the other adults ate Thanksgiving dinner. I saw her sitting with me in my living room at Christmas time, admiring our brightly decorated tree.

I then looked at her as she was . . . and I cried.

I knew she would never see my final senior dance recital or watch me cheer for another football game. She would never sit with me and admire our Christmas tree again. I knew she would never see me go off to my senior prom, graduate from high school and college, or get married. And I knew she would never be there the day my first child was born. Tear after tear rolled down my face.

But above all, I cried because I finally knew how she had felt the day I had been born. She had looked through what she saw on the outside and looked instead to the inside, and she had seen a life.

I slowly released her hand from mine and brushed away the tears staining her cheeks, and mine. I stood, leaned over, and kissed her and said, *"You look beautiful."*

And with one long last look, I turned and left the hospice.

Jessica Gardner

Steeped with Meaning

My mom and I sat in the small college café with our large mugs of something that smelled like lemon and tasted like home. We were catching up on the past four months of our lives and the hours just weren't long enough. Sure, we had talked on the phone and occasionally written. But the calls were long distance, and it was rare to find a moment when my roommate wasn't waiting for the phone, or my younger brother or sister wasn't waiting for my mom. So while we knew of each other's experiences, we had not yet dissected them. As we discussed her new job, my latest paper, my new love and her latest interview, I leaned back into my cushion and thought: *I always knew when she became my mother, but when had she become my friend?*

As far back as I can remember my mom was always the first person that I came to with every tear and every laugh. When I lost a tooth and when I found a friend, when I fell from my bike and when I got back on it, she was there. She never judged me; she let me set my own expectations. She was proud when I succeeded and supportive when I didn't. She always listened; she seemed to know when I was asking for advice and when I just needed a good cry. She multiplied my excitement with her own and divided my frustrations with her empathy and understanding. When she picked me up from school, she always asked about my day. I remember that one day when I asked about hers. I think I was a little surprised that she had so much to say. We rarely had late-night talks (because she was already asleep), nor early-morning ones (because I was not yet up), but in between the busy hours of our filled days, we found the time to fill each other's ears with stories and hearts with love. She slowly shared more and more of her own life with me, and that made me feel more open with her. We shared experiences and hopes, frustrations and fears. Learning that she still had blocks to build and to tumble made me more comfortable with my own. She made me feel that my opinions were never immature and my thoughts never silly. What surprises me now is not that she always remembered to tell me "sweet dreams," but that she never forgot to tell me that she believed in me. When she started going through some changes in her life, I had the opportunity to tell her that I believed in her, too.

My mother had always been a friend. She had given me her heart in its entirety; but her soul, she divulged in pieces, when she knew that I was ready.

I sat across from the woman who had given me my life and then shared hers with me. Our mugs were empty, but our hearts were full. We both knew that tomorrow she'd return to the bustle of Los Angeles and I'd remain in the hustle of New Haven. I know that we are both growing and learning. Yet, we continue to learn about each other and grow closer. Our relationship was like the tea that we had sipped: the longer it steeped, the better it tasted.

Daphna Renan

"I already know about sex, but could you explain
where Beanie Babies come from?"

Reprinted by permission of Harley Schwadron.

A Father's Wish

It's a wonderful feeling when your father becomes not a god but a man to you—when he comes down from the mountain and you see he's this man with weaknesses. And you love him as this whole being, not as a figurehead.

Robin Williams

I write this . . . as a father. Until you have a son of your own, you will never know what that means. You will never know the joy beyond joy, the love beyond feeling that resonates in the heart of a father as he looks upon his son. You will never know the sense of honor that makes a man want to be more than he is and to pass on something good and hopeful into the hands of his son. And you will never know the heartbreak of the fathers who are haunted by the personal demons that keep them from being the men they want their sons to see.

You will only see the man that stands before you, or who has left your life, who exerts a power over you—for good or for ill—that will never let go.

It is a great privilege and a great burden to be that man.

There is something that must be passed from father to son, or it is never passed as clearly. It is a sense of manhood, of self-worth, of responsibility to the world around us.

And yet, how to put it in words? We live in a time when it is hard to speak from the heart. Our lives are smothered by a thousand trivialities, and the poetry of our spirits is silenced by the thoughts and cares of daily affairs. The song that lives in our hearts, the song that we have waited to share, the song of being a man, is silent. We find ourselves full of advice but devoid of belief.

And so, I want to speak to you honestly. I do not have answers. But I do understand the questions. I see you struggling and discovering and striving upward, and I see myself reflected in your eyes and in your days. In some deep and fundamental way, I have been there and I want to share.

I, too, have learned to walk, to run, to fall. I have had a first love. I have known fear and anger and sadness. My heart has been broken and I have known moments when the hand of God seemed to be on my shoulder. I have wept tears of sorrow and tears of joy.

There have been times of darkness when I thought I would never again see light, and there have been times when I wanted to dance and sing and hug every person I met.

I have felt myself emptied into the mystery of the universe, and I have had moments when the smallest slight threw me into a rage.

I have carried others when I barely had the strength to walk myself, and I have left others standing by the side of the road with their hands outstretched for help.

Sometimes I feel I have done more than anyone can ask; other times I feel I am a charlatan and a failure. I carry within me the spark of greatness and the darkness of heartless crimes.

In short, I am a man, as are you.

Although you will walk your own earth and move through your own time, the same sun will rise on you that rose on me, and the same seasons will course across your life as moved across mine. We will always be different, but we will always be the same.

This is my attempt to give you the lessons of my life, so that you can use them in yours. They are not meant to make you into me. It is my greatest joy to watch you become yourself. But time reveals truths, and these truths are greater than either of us. If I can give them a voice in a way that allows me to walk beside you during your days, then I will have done well.

To be your father is the greatest honor I have ever received. It allowed me to touch mystery for a moment, and to see my love made flesh. If I could have but one wish, it would be for you to pass that love along. After all, there is not much more to life than that.

Kent Nerburn

"Someday, son, you'll finally be
old enough to do anything you want to do . . .
but your son will have the car, so you'll have
to stay home and watch television."

Reprinted by permission of Randy Glasbergen.

The Bridge Between Verses

Things do not change. We change.

Henry David Thoreau

My brother is the boy with the big black eyes. He has an aura about him that feels strange and nervous. My brother is different. He doesn't understand when jokes are made. He takes a long time to learn basic things. He often laughs for no reason.

He was pretty average until the first grade. That year, his teacher complained of him laughing in class. As a punishment, she made him sit in the hall. He spent all his time on the fake mosaic tile outside the room. The next year, he took a test that showed he needed to be placed in a special-education class.

As I grew older, I began to resent my brother. When I walked with him, people stared. Not that anything was physically wrong with him; it's just something that radiated from him that attracted attention. I would clench my teeth in anger sometimes, wishing he were like other people, wishing he were normal.

I would glare at him to make him uncomfortable. Every time my eyes met his, stark and too-bright, I would say loudly, "What?" He'd turn his head quickly and mutter, "Nothing." I rarely called him by his name.

My friends would tell me I was being mean to him. I brushed it off, thinking that they were also horrible to their siblings. I did not consider the fact that their brothers and sisters could retaliate. Sometimes I would be nice to my brother just because they were around, but return to being mean the minute they left.

My cruelty and embarrassment continued until one day last summer. It was a holiday, but both my parents were working. I had an orthodontist appointment and was supposed to take my brother with me. The weather was warm, being a July afternoon. As spring was over, there was no fresh scent or taste of moisture in the air, only the empty feeling of summer. As we walked down the sidewalk, on impulse I began to talk to him.

I asked him how his summer was going, what his favorite kind of car was, what he planned to do in the future. His answers were rather boring, but I wasn't bored. It turns out I have a brother who loves Cadillacs, wants to be an engineer or a business person, and loves listening to what he calls "rap" music (the example he gave was Aerosmith). I also have a brother with an innocent grin that can light up a room or an already sunny day. I have a brother who is ambitious, kind, friendly, open and talkative.

The conversation we had that day was special. It was a new beginning for me.

A week later, we were on a family trip to Boston, and I was in the back seat of our van. I was reading a Stephen King novel, *Rage*, while my dad and my brother sat up front talking. A few of their words caught my attention, and I found myself listening to their conversation while pretending to be engrossed in my book. My brother said, "Last week, we were walking to the bus stop. We had a good conversation and she was nice to me."

That's all he said. As simple as his words were, they were heartfelt. He held no dislike toward me. He just accepted that I'd finally become the sister I should have been from the beginning. I closed the book and stared at the back cover. The author's face blurred as I realized I was crying.

I will not pretend everything is fine and dandy now. Like changes in a *Wonder Years* episode, nothing's perfect, and nothing's permanent. What I will say is that I do not glare at my brother any more. I walk with him in public. I help him use the computer. I call him by his name. Best of all, I continue to have conversations with him. Conversations that are boring in the nicest possible way.

Shashi Bhat

The Ones in Front of Me

At some point in my childhood, I realized that my parents were never going to get along; the lines had been drawn and the die had been cast. So when my parents announced that they were filing for a divorce, it wasn't a huge shock. I never thought it was my fault. I also never had the illusion that they would miraculously fall back in love. So, I guess I accepted their decision.

For most of my childhood it didn't bother me that they weren't together. In fact, I had the best of both worlds. I got to live in Hawaii with my mom and travel to Los Angeles to see my dad. Somewhere during the process, however, I began to feel the effects of our "broken home." Although they tried not to make it too obvious, my parents' disdain for each other was becoming apparent.

When I was twelve, I wanted to live with my dad, so I moved to Los Angeles. It's not that I didn't love my mom; it's that I had spent most of my childhood with her and started to feel as if I didn't know much about my dad.

After the move, I started to realize how much my parents' divorce really affected me. My dad would tell me to tell my mom to send me money, and my mom would tell me to tell my dad that she shouldn't have to. I felt caught in the middle. My mom would try to pull information out of me about how it "really" was at my dad's. It was a constant struggle to duck out of the line of fire.

My parents tried to respect each other, for my sake I guess, but it was obvious that a lot of hurt lay underneath their actions. It had been ten years since they divorced, but it felt as if the struggle had just begun. They constantly argued over money and parenting styles. As much as they both promised that it didn't involve me, it always did. I felt they were fighting over me, and that it was somehow my fault—feelings I didn't have when I was five.

Growing up with divorced parents today seems to be a regular occurrence. It's actually rare to find two parents who are still together, but that doesn't make going through it hurt any less. Although I may not have felt it at the time, eventually, it was something that I had to work through—whether I was five or fifteen.

I wish I could say that my parents have worked out all their problems, and that we now work as a perfect team. It is never that simple. But, they try. They love me, and while it took all of us a while to realize it, now we know that their love for me will always keep them together in some way—they have learned to work together in order to raise me.

The other day, the three of us got together to talk about my upcoming trip to visit colleges. I think they are both sad about the idea of me leaving—and that is what keeps them together: the joy and sadness of watching me grow.

As we sat there the thought crossed my mind, *What if my family were still together?* Then, as I watched my parents intently looking through my college brochures, I smiled to myself, *This is my family, and we are "together."*

Lia Gay

"You mean Dad started out as a date?"

Role Reversal

It was a Friday night, and I had just returned from climbing one of the Red Rocks of Sedona. The night was chilly, the moon was high and I was looking forward to crawling into my warm bed. My faculty adviser, Bunny, approached me as I walked through the arches to my dorm room. She took me to her home where she told me that my mother had been in a terrible car crash and had been taken to the intensive care unit of a nearby hospital in critical condition.

When I got to the hospital my grandmother pulled me aside and said whatever I did, I mustn't cry in front of my mother.

A nurse unlocked the door that led down a wide hallway with machines all around. A strong smell of medicine brought a nauseous feeling to my already turning stomach. My mother's room was right next to the nurses' station. As I turned into the room, I saw her lying on her side, with her tiny back to me and a fluffed pillow between her bandaged legs. She struggled to turn around but couldn't. I slowly crept to the other side of the bed and said "hi" in a calm voice, stifling my urge to cry out.

The cadaverous condition of her body stunned me. Her

swollen face looked like it had been inflated and kicked around like a soccer ball, her eyes had huge dark bruised rings around them, and she had tubes down her throat and in her arms.

Gently holding my mother's cold swollen hands, I tried to keep my composure. She kept looking at me and rolling her eyes into the back of her head as she pounded her hand against the bed. She was trying to tell me how much pain she was in. I turned my face away from her, trying to hide the tears that were rolling down my face. Eventually I had to leave her for a moment because I couldn't hold my anguish in any longer. That was when it struck me that I really might lose my mother.

I kept her company all day long; in time the doctors took the respirator out of her throat for a short while. She was able to whisper a few words, but I didn't know what to say in return. I felt like screaming but knew I mustn't. I went home and cried myself to sleep.

From that night on, my life completely changed. Up to that point, I'd had the luxury of just being a kid, having to deal with only the exaggerated melodramas of teenage life. My concept of crisis was now forever altered. As my mother struggled first to stay alive and then to relearn to walk, my sense of priorities in life changed drastically. My mother needed me. The trials and tribulations of my daily life at school, which had seemed so important before, now appeared insignificant. My mother and I had faced death together, and life took on new meaning for both of us.

After a week of clinging to life in intensive care, my mother's condition improved enough to be taken off the respirator and moved to a regular hospital room. She was finally out of danger but, because her legs had been crushed, there was doubt that she would be able to walk again. I was just grateful that she was alive. I visited my mother in the hospital as often as I could for the next two months. Finally, a sort-of hospital suite was set up in our family room, and to my relief and joy, she was allowed to come home.

My mother's return home was a blessing for us all, but it meant some unaccustomed responsibilities for me. She had a visiting nurse, but much of the time I took care of her. I would feed her, bathe her, and when she was eventually able to use a toilet, would help her to the bathroom. It struck me that I was pretty much playing the role of mother to my own mother. It wasn't always much fun, but it felt good to be there when my mother really needed me. The difficult part for me was trying to always be upbeat, and to keep my mother's spirits up when she became frustrated with the pain and her inability to do simple things for herself. I always had a smile on my face when, really, I was suppressing tears in my heart.

My mother's reliance on me changed our relationship. In the past, we had more than our share of the strains of mother-daughter relationships. The accident threw us into a relationship of interdependence. To get my mother back, I had to help her regain her strength and ability to resume an independent life. She had to learn to accept my help as well as the fact that I was no longer a child. We have become the closest of friends. We genuinely listen to one another, and truly enjoy each other's company.

It has been over two years since my mother's crash. Although it was devastating to see my mother go through the physical pain and emotions that she still continues to experience, I have grown more in that time than in all the years before. Being a mother figure to my own mother taught me a lot about parenthood: the worries, the protectiveness and, most of all, the sweetness of unconditional devotion and love.

Adi Amar

Snowdrops

"Are they up yet?" Grandmother asks hopefully.

"No, not yet," Mother answers patiently, as if addressing an eager child. From her position on the edge of my
grandmother's bed, I see her smile silently as she continues knitting. She is smiling because of the familiarity of
the question. For the last few weeks of her illness, my
grandmother has been living to see the snowdrops bloom
in her garden. Sometimes I think the only reason she
doesn't succumb to her cancer is so she will live to see the
tiny, white flowers she so adores, one last time. I don't
understand her strong feelings for the snowdrops, as they
are, by far, not the most beautiful flowers growing in
Grandmother's garden. I wish to ask why she is so drawn
to them but Mother's presence stops me. For some reason, I feel the need to ask the question in private. I realize
then that Grandmother's eagerness for such a simple
thing is almost childlike, and this causes me to reflect. We
come into this world as children, and exit in almost the
same way.

"Grandmother, why do you like snowdrops so much?" I
ask during a visit one day, once Mother has gone downstairs.

She looks so fragile lying in her bed, I almost regret asking the question. Answering may prove to be too much exertion for her weak lungs to handle. However, she takes a breath and begins to talk, slowly and quietly.

"When your grandfather and I were married, around this time of year, the snowdrops were in bloom. I wore them in my hair at our wedding. Your grandfather adored them. Every year we planted them in our garden, and through some bizarre miracle, they always bloomed on our anniversary.

"After your grandfather died, I missed him terribly. All I had to do, though, was look at the snowdrops, and I felt close to him, as if he were with me again. Our snowdrops were what saved me on days I missed him so much I wanted to die." Grandmother finishes her story and stares silently into space, thinking. I don't want to interrupt her thoughts, so when she closes her eyes and drifts off to sleep, I still don't speak.

We visit Grandmother again, but on this day Mother asks me to stay downstairs. Grandmother's condition is worsening and she can't cope with any visitors except Mother. She no longer has the strength to talk, and I remember my most recent talk with Mother. She was in need of someone to confide in, and I was the only ear available; otherwise, I'm sure she wouldn't have burdened me with her pain. She told me of her visits alone with Grandmother, and how she wished Grandmother would just give up and allow herself to go, to end her own suffering. I could see Mother's pain, and how much she longed to cry; but for my sake, she would not. I imagine what my mother is doing upstairs right now—sitting on Grandmother's bed, holding her hand and encouraging her not to fight anymore.

My thoughts are interrupted as I notice a glossy, white album on a shelf across from where I am seated. On the binding there is a date printed in gold ink: April 13, 1937. I pull the large book from the shelf and gingerly open it. I am mesmerized by the black-and-white photo that greets my eyes. I recognize Grandmother and Grandfather, posing together happily, and I know this must be their wedding album. Grandmother's beautiful white gown draws my attention. Then my eye is attracted by the tiny white flowers perched in Grandmother's hair. They are her snowdrops, and for the first time, I can see just how beautiful they really are.

The telephone rings on the most gorgeous day of spring so far. When Mother answers it, I know right away what has happened. My first question is, "What day is it?" Through her tears, Mother answers, confirming my suspicions. She doesn't want me to come with her today, but I insist. There is something I need to see.

When we arrive at Grandmother's house I immediately run to the backyard. While the image of the snowdrops is blurred by my tears, they have bloomed just the same. I am upset that Grandmother didn't get to see them, but then I realize that this year she didn't need to. For the first time in many years, she won't miss Grandfather on their anniversary. Despite my sadness I smile, for I know they are celebrating together in heaven.

Sarah McCann

My Most
Memorable Christmas

The fall of 1978, our daughter Carol, age thirteen, was thrown from a motorcycle on which she had been a passenger. She sailed eighty-nine feet through the air and landed in a ditch, where she almost died. My wife and I were on a mission in Korea when we got the news that the doctors were in the process of amputating her left leg.

Our flight home took twenty-two hours. I suppose I did more crying on that flight than I ever have in my entire life. When my wife and I arrived at our daughter's side, unable to think of adequate words of comfort, surprisingly enough, Carol began the conversation.

"Dad," she said, "I think God has a special ministry for my life to help people who have been hurt as I have." She saw possibilities—positive ones—in tragedy! What a lift those words gave me. But we were just beginning what would prove to be a long, exhausting battle.

Carol's femur had broken in four places and plunged through the thigh bone into the ditch of an Iowa farm, next to a slaughterhouse. There it picked up a form of bacteria that had previously been resistant to any known antibiotics.

In November, Carol went back into the hospital for surgery that would, hopefully, release muscles in her knee that might make her leg more usable. The doctor was delighted when he opened her thigh and knee and discovered no pus pockets. But the hidden bacteria, which until that time had remained dormant, erupted like a prairie fire when exposed to the open air. Three days after surgery, she was the sickest little girl I've ever seen.

Each passing day, the bacteria multiplied with increasing impatience. Carol's fever soared to 104 degrees and lingered there day after day, night after night. Her leg continued to swell and the infection raged out of control.

About that time, we were blessed with a minor miracle. With no knowledge of my daughter's need, the Federal Drug Administration released, for the first time, an antibiotic that was declared significantly effective against the specific strain of bacteria that Carol contracted while lying in that Iowa ditch. She was the first human being in Children's Hospital, Orange County, California, to receive it. In a matter of hours after the first dosage, her temperature went down. Each successive culture reading showed fewer and fewer bacteria. Finally, about three weeks before Christmas, a culture came back that showed no bacteria growth.

Lying in her hospital bed with the intravenous tubes still in her hands, Carol asked the visiting doctor, who was standing in for her own surgeon, when she would be released. "Will I be home for Christmas, Doctor?" she asked.

"I don't know," he replied cautiously.

"Will I be able to get my new prosthesis?" she asked.

"Well," the doctor cautioned, "I don't believe you can get it yet."

But when her own doctor returned, he checked her over. That same day Carol called me at my office. "Daddy,

I have good news," she announced.

"What is it?" I asked.

"Doctor Masters is an angel," she exclaimed. "He said I can come home for Christmas!"

On December 16, a Saturday night, Carol was released from the hospital. I was told to stay home and await a surprise. My wife went to pick her up. I saw the lights of the car as it rolled up the driveway, and I ran to the front door. My wife barred my way and said, "Bob, you have to go back in and wait. Carol wants you to wait by the Christmas tree."

So I waited nervously by the Christmas tree, counting the seemingly interminable seconds. Then I heard the front door open and the squeak of rubber on the wooden floor. I knew the sound came from the rubber tips of Carol's crutches. She stepped into the open door, ten feet away from my seat by the Christmas tree. She had gone straight from the hospital to the beauty parlor, where her hair stylist gave her a beautiful permanent. There she stood with lovely curls framing her face. Then I looked down and saw two shoes, two ankles, two legs and a beautiful girl.

She had come home and, because of it, made that Christmas my most memorable.

Reverend Robert Schuller

There Is an Oz

They arrive exactly at 8:00 A.M. to take her home, but she has been ready since before seven. She has taken a shower—not an easy task lying down on a shower stretcher. She isn't allowed to sit up yet without her body brace, but regardless, here she is, clean and freshly scrubbed and ever so anxious to go home. It has been two-and-a-half months since she has seen her home—two-and-a-half months since the car accident. It doesn't matter that she is going home in a wheelchair or that her legs don't work. All she knows is that she is going home, and home will make everything okay. Even Dorothy says so: "Oh, Auntie Em, there's no place like home!" It's her favorite movie.

As they put her in the car, she thinks now of how much her father reminds her of the scarecrow in *The Wizard of Oz*. Like the scarecrow, he is built in pieces of many different things—strength, courage and love. Especially love.

He isn't an elegant man. Her father is tall and lanky and has dirt under his fingernails from working outside. He is strictly blue collar—a laborer. He never went to college, didn't even go to high school. By the world's standards he isn't "educated." An awful lot like the scarecrow—but she knows differently. He doesn't speak much, but when he does, she knows it is worth remembering. Even worth writing down. But she never has to write down anything that her father says because she knows she'll never forget.

It is hard for her to sit comfortably while wearing the body brace and so she sits, stiff and unnatural, staring out the window. Her face is tense and tired and older somehow, much older than her seventeen years. She doesn't even remember the world of a seventeen-year-old girl—it's as if that world never was. And she thinks she knows what Dorothy must have meant when she said, "Oh, Toto, I don't think we're in Kansas anymore." It is more than an issue of geography, she is quite certain.

They pull out onto the road to begin their journey and approach the stop sign at the corner. The stop sign is just a formality; no one ever stops here. Today, however, is different. As he goes to coast through the intersection, she is instantly alert, the face alive and the eyes flashing. She grips the sides of the seat. "Stop! That's a stop sign! You could get us killed! Don't you know that?" And then, more quietly and with even more intensity, "You don't know what it's like—you have never been there." He looks at her and says nothing. The scarecrow and Dorothy journey onward.

As they continue to drive, her mind is constantly at work. She still hasn't loosened her grip on the seat. She thinks of the eyes, the eyes that once belonged to her—big, brown, soulful eyes that would sparkle with laughter at the slightest thought of happiness. Only the happiness is gone now and she doesn't know where she left it or how to get it back. She only knows that it is gone and, in its absence, the sparkle has gone as well.

The eyes are not the same. They no longer reflect the soul of the person because that person no longer exists. The eyes now are deep and cold and empty—pools of color that have been filled with something reaching far beyond the happiness that once was there. Like the yellow brick road it stretches endlessly, maddeningly, winding through valleys and woodlands, obscuring her vision until she has somehow lost sight of the Emerald City.

She lightly touches the tiny gold bracelet that she wears. It was a present from her mother and father, and she refuses to remove it from her wrist. It is engraved with her name on the side that is visible to others, but as in everything there are two sides, and only she knows the other is there. It is a single word engraved on the side of the bracelet that touches her skin and touches her heart: "Hope." One small word that says so much about her life and what is now missing from it. She vaguely remembers hope—what it felt like to hope for a college basketball scholarship or maybe a chance to dance professionally. Only now, she's not sure she remembers hope as it was then—a driving force, a fundamental part of her life. Now, hope is something that haunts her.

The dreams come nightly. Dreams of turning cartwheels in the yard or hitting a tennis ball against a brick wall. But there is one, the most vivid and recurring, and the most haunting of all. . . . There is a lake and trees, a soft breeze and a perfect sky. It is a scene so beautiful it is almost beyond imagining. And in the midst of it all, she is walking. She has never felt more at peace.

But then she awakens and remembers. And remembering, she knows. She instinctively fingers the bracelet, the word. And the fear is almost overwhelming—the fear of not knowing how to hope.

She thinks of her father's God and how she now feels that God abandoned her. All at once, a single tear makes a trail down her thin, drawn face. Then another and another, and she is crying. "Oh Daddy, they say I'll never walk again! They're the best and they say I'll never walk. Daddy, what will I do?"

He looks at her now and he stops the car. This is the man

who has been with her down every road, every trail and every path—so very like the scarecrow. And he speaks. "I know that they can put you back together. They can put steel rods in your back and sew you up. But look around you. Not one of your doctors can make a blade of grass."

Suddenly she knows. He has taught her the most valuable lesson in her life and in all her journey: that she is never alone. There is an Oz; there is a wizard; there is a God. And there . . . is . . . hope. She releases her grip on the seat, looks out the window and smiles. And in that instant she loves her father more than she has ever loved him before.

Terri Cecil

The Perfect Family

Divorce. That's a word I dreaded more than any other word in the English dictionary.

All my life, I thought I had the perfect family. Perfect parents, two great sisters and a younger brother. We all got along well. But during the last several years, my parents had started to fight more and more.

My dad came home less and less, working more hours than ever in Vermont. And now here we all were, sitting in the television room as a family, with my parents saying they had an announcement to make. I began to cringe.

There it was: that nightmare word, the one that made me sick to my stomach. They were, they announced, getting a divorce. The big D word. My sisters and brother and I gaped at each other. How many times had I asked my mom and dad: "Are you getting a divorce?" How many times had they assured me that would never happen and given me hugs and kisses?

"This is some sort of April Fool's joke, right?" I said.

My mom's eyes welled with tears and she held me in her arms.

"No, Marc, I'm sorry," she whispered.

I felt betrayed. How could they do this to us? Most of all, I wanted to know what we had done wrong. What had *I* done wrong?

My mother could see the dread in my eyes, the fear, the hurt and the pain. It all welled within my belly and I felt sick. She promised she would take care of me, of us. All of us.

But how could I believe her now? My family had collapsed before my eyes. We were splintered. Shattered. There would be no more perfect family. And of course, things would get worse rather than better. They'd get a lot worse.

My mom told me that we would have to leave our home. The home I'd lived in all my life.

I felt like I was losing everything. My family. My home. My dad. The good news: My mother would have custody of all of us and my father wouldn't dispute it.

We moved into a tiny home with my mom's parents. At first, I wasn't very happy. The house was small. We were all squished in together. Sometimes I felt there wasn't enough room to breathe. There was one thing, however: We loved each other. My grandparents, Mom, sisters, brother and visiting aunts and uncles tried to do everything to fill the house with warmth and caring. My grandparents paid special attention to all us kids. I'd never felt so close to them in my life.

They asked me about school and were actually interested. They asked me about my friends, my grades. We sat at the kitchen table and talked often. They could never replace my father, but they spread their warmth to all of us.

Still, I carried a lot of guilt. I couldn't understand what bad thing happened to split up my parents. At times, I agonized over it, lying in bed, wondering in a cloud-like state what possibly could have been the reason that my parents quit loving each other. Was it something I had done?

And then more unexpected news: We learned my father was gay.

I was sure as word got around that the other kids would laugh and make fun of me. Some did. But, there were a lot of kids, however, who didn't say a word. They still hung around me and could care less what my dad did. They liked me before and they liked me still. I had learned who my real friends were, and the ones I lost were not the kind of people I wanted in my life anyway.

I also learned that I was really loved by my family. They supported me. They cared about me. My grandparents adored me. Eventually, we were able to move out from their home and get a condominium. I started junior high school and started doing well.

I have since learned to redefine that funny concept I had about a perfect family.

Maybe a perfect family really means a lot of love and a lot of support. Maybe it really means giving, sharing and caring. Maybe I still have a perfect family after all.

Marc St. Pierre

Kicki

Throughout my childhood, I constantly dreamed of being an only child—having no one around to fight with, to share with, to grab the remote away from me in the middle of a "big game." I would have the biggest bedroom in the house and be able to talk on the phone as long as I wanted, without being asked a million times, "Are you off yet?" But I was not born an only child; I was born with an older sister. I have always called my sister "Kicki," instead of her real name, Christie, because, when I was younger, I had trouble pronouncing the *r* and *s*. To this day, she is still "Kicki."

I started playing basketball when I was eight years old. My dad was the coach of my team, and my mom kept score. So my sister, not old enough to stay home alone, was forced to come to all of my games. I remember looking into the stands for my mother's approval during games and seeing my sister's face, confused. It was obvious that she wasn't thrilled to be there, but she cheered along with the crowd anyway. Her hair was cut short, almost as short as mine, and her teeth stuck out. I teased her often, calling her "bucky beaver." She wasn't a very attractive little girl, and she looked more like my older brother than my sister.

After the games, on the car rides home, my parents and I relived every move I had made on the court. My sister sat in the backseat with me in silence, not knowing how or when to enter the conversation. Most nights she came into my room and said, "Good night, Brad. Good game." I would smile and thank her. I never really took her compliment seriously. I mean, she hardly understood what was going on in the games; she couldn't possibly know whether I had played well or not.

It wasn't until I reached high school that I realized what a truly beautiful person my sister was. Everybody knew her and thought highly of her, and I was referred to as "Christie's little brother." Kicki was on the Homecoming Court her senior year, and she stood tall and beautiful. I was astonished at the person she had become: smart, sweet and beautiful. To me, she was still the ten-year-old little girl with the boyish looks and buckteeth.

I played basketball in high school, and although Christie wasn't forced to attend my games anymore, she still came every week, cheering me on from the stands. I remember one game in particular, the last game of the season. My sister sat in the bleachers with her boyfriend and a large group of friends. Printed on her shirt, in big bright red letters, were the words "BRAD'S SISTER." Suddenly I was embarrassed. But it wasn't her presence that embarrassed me, rather, it was the fact that I had never appreciated her support before. She was never embarrassed to be my sister, even though I had been embarrassed to call her that so many years ago. She didn't care what anyone thought, and she never had.

I am an only child now; my sister left for college a few months after that last game. I finally have the biggest room in the house and the remote control all to myself.

But now that she's gone, I kind of miss having someone to fight with for the phone, and the big bedroom isn't all that great anyway.

I went to visit her at college for a weekend, and as I stood outside her dorm, waiting for her to come out, a friend of hers walked past me and questioned, "Hey, aren't you Christie's brother?" I beamed and said proudly, "Yeah, I am. I'm Christie's brother."

Brad Dixon

Rikki's Hug

I'm walking up the sidewalk to our brown, three-bedroom condo. I've lived here for so many years that I can't even remember the day we moved in. I know that sidewalk, steps and porch so well that I could easily walk them blind. As I pause at the door to search for my key in my purse, I get a whiff of the familiar dryer sheet smell that is flowing from the vent near the porch. It's a comforting smell, one that most people would overlook. But I've always noticed it. I gaze up at the same old gray Connecticut sky. The cool breeze that frequents early spring in the Northeast whips my windbreaker around my shoulders and leaks through the sleeves, causing me to shiver. My day at school was pretty typical, although I didn't do as well in all of my classes as I wanted to. I'm behind in my outlining for history, which is usually the most lacking area of my schoolwork because I dread it so much.

Tonight I am supposed to go out for a mid-week dinner and then to the gym, but play rehearsal ran over. It's getting late, and I have so much work ahead of me this evening. What began as an ordinary day is now anything

but ordinary. The breeze feels like a fierce, wintry gust.
My head hurts, my liveliness faded to a shade of tired. It's
too much. I can't do it anymore. I struggle to turn the key
in the door when it swings wide open.

There she stands, her little body clad in Osh-Koshes
that have Pooh on them, her long brown curls free and
flowing down her back to her waist. She lets me put her
hair up very rarely; she prefers it to be let alone to do
what it wants. She's wise beyond her years. Her eyes
remind me of milk chocolate with a fleck of summer sunshine in them. They retain the gentle radiance of summer
long after the leaves have fallen off the trees and have
been replaced with frigid snow. But it's her smile that I
notice. Her smile never ceases to amaze me. It lights up
her face with an innocent and happy luminescence. It's a
contagious smile. "Gaga is home!" She's called me that
name since she first started talking. She's put behind her
all of the other baby names for friends and family, but
mine sticks. That's because I'm her favorite sister, her
favorite person. Well, that's what she tells me and I choose
not to acknowledge that she's only four and doesn't
understand yet what the depths of the word "favorite"
are. I understand what it means, so I can legitimately say
that she's my favorite. Though she may not understand
the extremity in this word, she sure understands me.

Her little arms wrap around me as I hug the little girl
whom I still call, "Baby." Only when she misbehaves do I
use her real name. Though she's at that age when babies
no longer are babies and want to be "big girls," she never
corrects me. And only when she's upset with me does she
ever use my actual name. With that one gesture, everything's okay again. She puts a butterfly kiss on my cheek.
Then come the sweetest words you could ever hear,
which could easily be mistaken for the sound of an angel:

"I missed you." *Isn't it funny how with one simple display of affection, everything turns around?* The world suddenly seems okay and I can no longer find a reason to be tired. And even though when that moment is over, the toils and troubles of life return, it's always waiting for me at my front door. All I have to do is turn the key.

Kathryn Litzenberger

What Siblings Know

When I was twelve and my brother David was seventeen, we were home one Halloween night watching a horror movie we'd rented. It was an entertaining but silly movie about a woman who becomes a witch. The woman who played the witch was young and looked like a model. Every time she cast a spell, her long red hair whipped around her face and her eyes got bright green. Once when this happened, my brother said, "Wow, she looks really hot."

I stared at him. I was astonished at what he'd said. I hadn't noticed it before, but until that night I'd never, ever heard my brother voice an attraction to women, even though he was a teenager and supposedly in the prime of his life.

This is what I remember when people ask me when I first knew my brother was gay. I didn't realize he was different until I heard him saying something that most guys his age would say without a second thought.

My brother tried to like girls. The thought of him trying— even by saying something as trivial as "She looks hot" about an actress on a television screen—breaks my heart. All that time he was trying, through middle school and high school and into college, he couldn't tell me or my parents how hard it was for him. He was all alone.

When I was twelve, David went out of state for college. He came home for holidays and a few weeks in the summer, and he called every week, but every year he seemed to pull farther away from me and my parents. When he was home, he was quiet and distant, and on the phone he was polite but tense, the way people get when they are hiding really big secrets.

My parents were slow, but they weren't stupid. A couple of years after David left for college, when they still hadn't heard mention of any girlfriends or even dates, they became suspicious. My mother started asking me questions, thinking that I must know something she didn't know, because siblings tell each other things they don't tell their parents. But David hadn't told me anything. He never had, not even before he left for college. I always knew he loved me, but he was more independent than the rest of us, and I never felt he needed me.

The next time David came home, I did a terrible thing. I wanted to borrow his leather backpack and I knew he wouldn't let me if I asked him, so I just took it. But before I filled it with my things, I had to take out his things to make room. There were some schoolbooks and a fancy notebook bound with a rubber band. I was curious. I pulled off the rubber band and started reading.

Immediately, I found myself immersed in a world of suppressed anger, self-loathing and tentative romances. I learned more about my brother in those pages than I ever could from him, at least back then. I learned that he'd known he was gay his entire life, but that not until he escaped to college did he admit it to another human being. That human being was his roommate, Rob. I remembered him mentioning how Rob had transferred dorm rooms in the middle of the semester, and when I read my brother's journal I learned that Rob changed rooms because he didn't want to live with someone who was gay.

It was a little while—a few pages into the journal—before my brother told anyone else. He joined a campus group and made some gay friends, and slowly his life forked into two lives. There was the life my parents and I saw—a life with lies and friends who didn't know him, and no one to love—and there was a second life, a life with friends and crushes and dates. A life where he was happy.

I put the backpack—and the little notebook—back in my brother's room, and I never told him what I'd learned. But my parents continued to badger me about David and his lack of love life—they knew he was gay, I'm sure, but denied it even to themselves—and eventually I called him up. "David," I said, "you have to tell them."

He didn't ask me how I knew, and I didn't tell him. But looking back, I understand that reading my brother's journal—a horrible crime I would never commit again—only filled in some of the details. Somehow, I already knew the story. Maybe it is true that siblings know each other better than their parents know them. I like to think so.

The next Thanksgiving, after a pretty typical family meal, my brother suggested we all take a walk. We walked past the end of our street and onto the grounds of the high school, then onto the track. Then my brother stopped. "I have something to tell you," he said. I felt my parents' hearts skip a beat—they wanted so badly, back then, for it not to be true. "I wanted to tell you that I'm gay."

My parents were pretty rational, considering. They told David that he was just experimenting, that eventually he'd find a woman he wanted to marry. He listened to them, then politely but firmly said that this was something that wasn't going to change. They argued but never raised their voices, and eventually we went home and took naps in separate rooms. The following days were very quiet. Then David went back to school, to his happy life.

It was five years before my parents came to truly accept my brother. My brother was fortunate to be out of the house during that time, but I was not so lucky. My parents fought more than ever, my father drank a lot, and I spent time out of the house. But slowly—*very* slowly—my parents got used to the idea. After a year, my mother told one of her friends about David, then my father told one of his. They received love and support—David was a great kid, said my parents' friends. That hadn't changed. Secretly, I'm sure they were relieved that it wasn't their kid who was gay. After my parents learned not to hide it, there was still the matter of being proud of David, of not only tolerating hearing about his romantic life, but wanting to hear about it.

About a week before Christmas one year, my brother called home to ask my parents if he could bring a friend home for the holiday. A boyfriend. My parents told David they'd think about it, then called him back and said absolutely not. My brother felt hurt and rejected, and when he came home, relations between him and my parents were strained. Then he and my father got into a fight on Christmas Eve, and David took an early flight back to school. Christmas Day was sadder and lonelier than it had ever been.

I called David a few days later. "You can't rush them," I said, feeling guilty for defending them.

"It's been three years," said David. He was frustrated, which I understood. So was I. I didn't understand why my parents couldn't just get over it. It seemed simple. Every time my mother asked me how a date had gone or said she liked a boy I'd introduced to her, I thought, *What's so different between me and David? Don't you want him to be happy, too?*

But David's patience paid off. My mother joined a support group for parents of gays and lesbians, and soon she was succeeding in dragging my father with her to the meetings. She was even asked to speak at a conference for high-school teachers about being unbiased toward homosexuality in the classroom. Time passed. My parents eased into not only accepting the fact that David wasn't ever going to be straight, but also that it wasn't a bad thing at all. That for David, it was a very good thing.

Then they did the craziest and most wonderful thing. I still laugh when I think about it. They made a list of all the people they hadn't told about David, including old friends, siblings and their own parents, and they planned a three-week road trip across the country. They had news to deliver, and they wanted to deliver it in person and do some sightseeing in the meantime. They'd gotten this idea in their heads that it wasn't enough for David to come out of the closet. He would never feel they'd truly accepted him until they came out of the closet, too, as the loving parents of a gay son.

David's apartment was the last stop on their journey, and I took an airplane up to meet them when they arrived. We took another family walk, and David told us about his new boyfriend and I told them about mine. Finally, after so much pain and hard work, my brother's two lives started to merge.

Danielle Collier

Relief

I'm not quite sure when the turning point came. But I know that it came after a fight I had with my mother. It was a typical fight for that rebellious summer. You know how it is, you lie once, and then they all start to pile up. And nothing happens evenly—it's always all at once. That summer I drifted apart from my mother, and my two best friends, whom I needed to turn to, were angry with me. That's where I learned my second lesson (the first being not to lie)—never keep your feelings hidden. That's what my friends did, and when I found out, it was too late.

Anyway, my house was a battle zone. I'd sleep till I had to go to work and then sleep after work. In between, I'd cry and feel sorry for myself, well, when I wasn't fighting with my mom. That day it all changed.

She was screaming at me about how I wasn't a part of the family anymore—that no one liked being around me because I was always so hostile. I yelled back, as most sixteen-year-olds would. But my mom doesn't ground me (well, I was already grounded) or take away the phone; she assigns essays. My assignment was to apologize for my behavior.

I cried tears of rage in my room, yelling about what I could possibly write. But then I started to write. And the apology turned into an explanation. I poured out every pain and emotion, ones that I had hidden behind my rage, the ones I cried about at night. I didn't know how to get back to being me, and I hated what I had become. I felt so lost. And, most of all, I felt like everyone that I had depended on had left me. Alone.

I left the letter on her bed and went to sleep, exhausted from sobbing. I wrapped myself up in my warm, flannel blankets to ease the cold. Although it was a warm and humid summer night, I shivered. The next morning I woke up early enough to go to work so that no one was awake yet. I crept into the bathroom and noticed a card with my name written on it in my mother's handwriting taped to the mirror. I opened it. It said that she understood. She understood that I was lost and scared. And she promised that she would help me.

I got into the hot shower, silently sobbing. My salty tears mixed with the water on my face. Except that this time, the tears were of relief, not of despair.

Kathryn Litzenberger

Don't Cry, Dad

During my years in junior high, I developed an after-school routine. Every day I walked in the back door of my home and proceeded up the three flights of stairs to my bedroom. I closed the door, turned my music up loud and lay on my bed for two hours until someone came to get me for dinner. I ate dinner in silence; I tried desperately to avoid talking to my family and even harder not to make eye contact with them. I hurriedly finished my dinner and rushed back to my room for more music. I locked myself in my room until it was time for school the next day.

Once in a while, my parents would ask me if there was anything wrong. I would snap at them, saying that I was just fine and to stop asking so many questions. The truth was, I couldn't answer them because I didn't know what was wrong. Looking back, I was very unhappy. I cried for no reason, and little things made me explode. I didn't eat well, either. It wasn't "cool" at that time to be seen actually eating lunch during school. I wasn't much of a breakfast eater, and if I weren't required to eat dinner with my family every night, I probably wouldn't have eaten at all.

The summer before my freshman year, my dad told me

that he wanted to talk. I was *not* thrilled. In fact, I resented him. I did not want to talk to anyone, especially my dad.

We sat down, and he started the conversation by asking the usual questions: "Are you okay? Is everything all right?" I didn't answer; I refused to make eye contact.

"Every day I come home from work, and you're locked in your room, cut off from the rest of us." He paused a moment, his voice was a little shaky as he began again. "I feel like you're shutting me out of your life." Having said that, my father, a man who I thought was stronger than steel, began to cry. And I don't mean just a few tears rolling down his cheeks. Months of hidden pain flooded from his eyes. I felt like I had been slapped. Never in my fourteen years had I seen my dad cry. Through his tears he went on to tell me that he wanted to be a part of my life and how he ached to be my friend. I loved my dad more than anything in the world, and it killed me to think I had hurt him so deeply. His eyes shifted towards me. They looked tired and full of pain—pain that I had never seen, or maybe that I had ignored. I felt a lump forming in my throat as he continued to cry. Slowly, that lump turned to tears, and they started pouring from my eyes.

"Don't cry, Dad," I said, putting my hand on his shoulder.

"I hope I didn't embarrass you with my tears," he replied.

"Of course not."

We cried together a little more before he left. In the days that followed, I had a hard time breaking the pattern I had become so accustomed to over the last two years. I tried sitting in the living room with my parents while they drank their coffee. I felt lost in their world, while I was desperately trying to adjust to new habits. Still, I made an effort. It took almost another full year before I felt completely comfortable around my family again and included them in my personal life.

Now I'm a sophomore in high school, and almost every day when I come home from school, I sit down and tell my dad about my day while we have our coffee. We talk about my life, and he offers advice sometimes, but mostly, he just listens.

Looking back, I am so glad my father and I had that talk. Not only have I gained a better relationship with my father, I've gained a friend.

Laura Loken

"Thanks anyway, Dad, but I'll walk.
I wouldn't be caught dead driving around
with your bumper stickers."

Reprinted by permission of Dave Carpenter.

Ghost Mother

Six months before my thirteenth birthday, my parents gave my brother and me "the talk." The one about their loving us, but not each other and how much happier everyone would be if they separated. Yet, my parents rewrote the ending: "We think it would be best if you lived with your father." My mother was the one who said this, running her red nails through my hair. That moment has stayed in the center of my stomach since then, like a jagged stone rolling around.

Mothers are supposed to be that one person who represents home, who somehow makes everything okay when your world is shaking. A mother should be there for you no matter how many times you change your Halloween costume, how messy your room gets or what happens to her marriage. But mine saw motherhood as an optional endeavor, something she could easily discard like a sweater that no longer fit.

She quickly settled into her own life and her new apartment. Having married at twenty-one, this was the first time she was on her own. Her decorating business was growing, and she was more interested in catering to her clients than to two kids and a husband of fifteen years.

A few weeks after she moved out, she called on a Friday night. "Tomorrow, let's have lunch and then go shopping. Okay?" she asked. I was so excited that I could hardly answer. That night I dreamed of riding beside my mom in the car. Saturday, I woke early, put on my favorite overalls and finished my homework in case she wanted to spend Sunday together, too. My friend Jennifer called. "Aren't you coming to the movies?" she asked. "Everyone's going."

"My mom and I have stuff to do. Shopping or something," I said, forcing my tone to be matter-of-fact. But morning turned into afternoon, and she didn't call. I spent the day by the phone pretending to read, playing solitaire and braiding my hair. I wouldn't eat anything because I thought at any minute she'd be there and want to take me out for lunch. And I didn't want my mom to have to eat alone. But she didn't call until after six o'clock. "Sorry, honey, I was working all day and not near a phone," she said quickly. "And now I'm so tired, I just need to take a nap. You understand, don't you?" No Mom, I didn't understand.

This same scenario happened many weekends for several years after she left. The rare times I did see her, she'd rent me four-hour movies like *Tess* and leave me alone to watch them. Or I'd go on her errands or to her office, never really with her, more like a balloon trailing after her. I'd sit alone at a desk in her office eating Chinese food out of a paper carton while she worked or talked on the phone. But I never complained or stopped going. How could I when this was all I had of her?

Almost a year after she moved out, the clothes she didn't want remained in her walk-in closet. My father said he was too busy to pack them, but I think that—just as I did—he hoped it meant she wasn't gone for good. I used to sit in that closet, breathing in the lingering smell of her Ralph Lauren perfume. I'd wrap myself in her ivory cashmere cardigan and run my fingers along the beaded surface of a pink bag, remembering when she'd carried it with a chiffon dress. She had looked just like a princess. I'd rock the bag gently, feeling sorry for it that she had left it behind, too.

Living with my father and brother in their masculine world of boxer shorts and hockey games wasn't easy. Just when I should have been stepping out of my tomboy stage of wearing my brother's worn Levi's and buttondowns and starting to become a young woman, I was screaming at the basketball players on TV and munching on Doritos. Each of my friends watched her mother apply eyeliner and blush and practiced with her makeup while she was out. The only makeup I knew about was the black smudges under football players' eyes.

Growing up without my mother, I always had to carry myself to each new stage of life or get left behind. I wore the same clothes that my friends did, bought my first bra by myself and started shaving my legs when they did. But to me I was just following clumsily behind them, self-conscious that my motherlessness was showing. When I got my period, I huddled in my pink bathroom, feeling like a little girl at this sign of being a woman. Having to say, "I got my period, Dad," was mortifying. But the truth was, I felt more comfortable telling him than my mother. When she called the following week, she said, "Dad told me what happened, but he took care of it." This was a statement, not a question.

My mother became like a distant relative whom I saw several times a year, who sent a birthday card if she remembered and to whom I was stiffly polite and didn't curse in front of. The word "mom" was foreign to me. She never asked about my friends or school or seemed to notice that I was struggling to grow up without her. Each time I said good-bye, I knew it would be months before I saw her again.

Why didn't my mother want me? I wondered. Teachers and friends' parents always wore a look of pity when my father picked me up from parties, came alone to plays and parent-conference day and talked to them to arrange car pools. Hating their pity, I'd mix the few minutes my mother did give me with my imagination. Then I'd casually talk about her at lunch or at friends' houses so they wouldn't see that all I had was a ghost mother who touched my life only in memories.

Although it was tough at first, my father tried to do everything he could to fill the gaps my mother left. He put my brother and me first, at times sacrificing his own happiness for ours. Despite losing his wife and marriage, my father wore a smile on his face. After all, he was the person we looked toward to tell us everything was going to be okay, so we couldn't see him sad. He had no spouse to pick up where he left off or to help him with daily issues and unexpected situations. He took us to the doctor, listened to our problems and helped us with homework. He was there with treats when my friends slept over and told the kind of dumb fatherly jokes that made us laugh and roll our eyes. He was always at all my school plays and softball games. He never missed a gymnastics meet or recital. Most fathers never took off work to come to even one of these things; my father was at all of them. Most of all, he was always conscious of my disappointments and tried to make a bad situation better. After a while, all the people who pitied me noticed my father's intense interest in my well-being and realized, as I did, that though my life was different, there was nothing wrong with it or me. In time, I adjusted to this. And though I never stopped wishing my mother were a more central part of my life, I saw the fact that she wasn't; she was just a part of who I am.

In recent years, I have become closer with her. I accept her for who she is, regardless of the fact that she wasn't always the mother I wanted her to be. As I have gotten older, I can look at what she did from a different perspective. And I think I've reached this point because my father taught me to be understanding of and sensitive to others. I've realized it's okay not to have a storybook home with a mom, dad, two kids and a dog. Who said that is the definition of family? My home may have been unique, but it had in it the same love and loyalty as other families.

Michele Bender

Dear Diary . . .

The greatest happiness of life is the conviction that we are loved—loved for ourselves or rather, loved in spite of ourselves.

Victor Hugo

Dear Diary,

Drip. Drip. Drip. For three hours I've waited in this train station and for three hours I've heard the faint splash of water fall from an old water fountain onto the cold, hardwood floor. The wood is old and worn but somehow doesn't allow any of the water drops to seep through. Funny, how something . . . Suddenly a horn whistles from a departing train, interrupting my thoughts and allowing them to come crashing back to reality.

I glance at my watch and realize I've missed my train, and the next one isn't going to leave this town for the next four hours. What am I going to do now? It's a quarter past midnight, and I'm cold and hungry. I have a meeting with the admissions officer in a college at 8:00 A.M., and by the look of things, I'm not going to make it on time. What a way to make a first impression, huh?

I begin to feel the tears burn the back of my eyes, and soon they are dancing upon my cheek. I am here alone. There isn't a familiar face around to comfort me. My mother was supposed to be here with me, to say one final good-bye before I enter adulthood. But with the many fights and unkept promises we've shared I didn't expect her to want to come here with me. Maybe I shouldn't have left the house this evening without saying I'm sorry. Sorry for the many disagreements and disappointments. Sorry for my hurtful words and actions. But we've passed the point where "sorry" heals things and makes them better again. Still, what I wouldn't give to have her here with me. Maybe she's right. Maybe I'm not the know-it-all mature adult I think I am. Maybe I am still just a scared kid who needs the protection of a mother's love.

It's almost 4:00 now, and the morning sun should be rising soon. I am able to grab a cup of coffee and change my clothes during the wait. I figure if I catch a 7:00 bus in Boston I can still make my appointment. . . .

Until next time,
Me

Putting away my journal I reach into my bag to get out my ticket, but instead a plain white envelope emerges in my hand. I don't need to read the name on the front to know who it's from. She wants us to have a better relationship and put the past behind us. Have a fresh start. My mother even admitted she was sorry for all the arguments we've had over the course of the years. The note also said she would be waiting for me at the train station in Boston and we would walk into college together. Enclosed was an upgraded ticket and a "P.S." telling me to look in the bottom of my bag. There I would find money for a bite to eat and a sweater in case I got cold in the station. As I make my way to the train I pass the broken water fountain, which no longer drips, and I realize, for the first time in this life, I'm about to see a woman for who she truly is. My mother.

Liz Correale

A Birthday Gift

She lived a life of solitude.
She lived a life in vain.
She lived a life in which there was
A strong, ongoing pain.

She had no friends on which to lean
And cry her problems to.
She had no friends to give her love
And hope and kindness, too.

She thought about it day and night;
She lay upon her bed.
Her mind made up, she grabbed a gun
And put it to her head.

Just then a ring came from the phone.
She pulled the gun away.
Her mom was on the other end
And wanted just to say,

"Happy Birthday, my dear girl.
Today is just for you.
I care for you with all my heart,
I hope you know that's true."

These words ran through her mind so much.
The gun was down for good.
She changed her mind about her life
And then she changed her mood.

She thought about this special day
And what her mom had said.
The gift her mom gave her that day
Was the gift of life, *again*.

Thad Langenberg

My Real Father

I came across a quotation the other day: "He who raises a child is to be called its father, not the man who only gave it birth." How true this is! I only wish I had realized it sooner, for my failure to do so caused every person in my family a lot of unnecessary grief, including me.

My mom married the man I knew as Dad when I was four years old, and even then I felt this animosity toward him that was incredible, especially for a child so young. My dad tried so hard to be a good father to me, and I responded with spite and anger. He showered me with love, and I spit in his eye. Oh, he legally adopted me, and I called him Dad, but in my heart, I was a fatherless child. This incredible anger only grew when we moved from Ohio, where I had relatives on every street corner, to South Dakota, where I knew nobody. When I reflect now on my terrible behavior, I feel such shame. Just because he loved my mother, he was stuck with a little brat whose every move was calculated to bring him grief. But he didn't give up on me as a lesser man might have.

The strange thing is, I had come to love this man, but I didn't know how to stop my hateful behavior. I can only be glad that eventually, I grew out of it.

When people find out I'm adopted, their first question is always, "Who's your real father? Do you know him?" My answer is, "Yes, I know him. I live with him."

My dad is the man who refused to spank me, even though I deserved it. He's fed me and clothed me and loved me for thirteen years. He's there when I cry, and when I feel sick. Dad can always fix it with something out of his magical medicine collection. He worries about me if I'm out late. He bought me my first car, my first prom dress. He's the one who is proud of me when I get a good report card or win an honor or just handle a difficult situation in a mature way. He's my father, my dad and my daddy in every way except the one that doesn't count.

And as soon as my daddy gets home, I'm going to tell him, for the first time, how much I love him and how much I appreciate that he didn't give up on me . . . even when I had given up on myself.

Anonymous

The Mother Who Matters

I have eyes that are said to be "cow brown," and my long blond hair is my best feature. My nose is a little too big; my face is oval shaped. I am not overweight, but I'm not skinny either. The only way to describe my height is "vertically challenged."

I'm relatively happy with my appearance, but where did I get it? Do I share the same features as some unknown stranger? Oftentimes, while walking down the street, I try to pick out that stranger, imagining that one of the women I pass could possibly be my biological mother.

I never met my birth mother. I was adopted the moment I was born, and I was taken into a wonderful family. For a long time I wondered what life would be like with my birth mother. Would I still be the same? Where would I live? Would I be happier? Who would my friends be?

I was never dissatisfied with my life; I just never stopped wondering what it would be like to have been raised by my biological mother. And then one day, I was baby-sitting with a friend, and I came across a poem on the nursery wall. It compared adoption to a seed that was planted by one person and then taken care of by another.

The second person had watered the seed and made it grow to be tall and beautiful. I found that it compared perfectly to my situation.

I realized that my mom had made me who I am today, no matter what either of us looks like. And I started to notice that we had the same silly personality, the same outlook on life, and the same way of treating people, along with some other things. She curled my hair for my first dance. She was there for my first heartbreak. She held my hand every time I got a shot at the doctors. She'd been smiling in the crowd for my first school play. She'd been there for everything that ever mattered, and what could compare to that? She's my mom.

Sometimes when we're out somewhere, people comment on how much we look alike, and we turn to each other and laugh, forgetting until that moment that it wasn't she who carried me in her womb for nine months.

Though I may not know why I look the way I do, I know why I am who I am. The mom I have now is the best one I ever could have hoped for, not only because she holds a tremendous amount of unconditional love, but because she has shaped who I am today, my qualities and characteristics. She is the one who made me beautiful!

Kristy White

Never Enough

Sometimes I know the words to say,
Give thanks for all you've done,
But then they fly up and away,
As quickly as they come.

How could I possibly thank you enough,
The one who makes me whole,
The one to whom I owe my life,
The forming of my soul.

The one who tucked me in at night,
The one who stopped my crying,
The one who was the expert,
At picking up when I was lying.

The one who saw me off to school,
And spent sad days alone,
Yet magically produced a smile,
As soon as I came home.

The one who makes such sacrifices,
To always put me first,

Who lets me test my broken wings,
In spite of how it hurts.

Who paints the world a rainbow,
When it's filled with broken dreams,
Who explains it all so clearly,
When nothing's what it seems.

Are there really any words for this?
I find this question tough . . .
Anything I want to say,
Just doesn't seem enough.

What way is there to thank you,
For your heart, your sweat, your tears,
For ten thousand little things you've done,
For oh-so-many years.

For changing with me as I changed,
Accepting all my flaws,
Not loving 'cause you had to,
But loving "just because."

For never giving up on me,
When your wits had reached their end,
For always being proud of me,
For being my best friend.

And so I come to realize,
The only way to say,
The only thank you that's enough,
Is clear in just one way.

Look at me before you,
See what I've become,
Do you see yourself in me?
The job that you have done?

All your hopes and all your dreams,
The strength that no one sees,
A transfer over many years,
Your best was passed to me.

Thank you for the gifts you give,
For everything you do,
But thank you, Mommy, most of all,
For making dreams come true.

Love,
Your Daughter

Laurie Kalb

Angel

I just sit here, watching the funny looking bird through the window. It is washing itself in the driveway, which is full of rain from last night's shower. I think, *What if I were a bird? Where would I go? What would I do?* Of course, I know that is not possible, especially now. I'm just sitting here, watching my life pass by, second by second, minute by minute. I know I should do something productive, like homework, but I just feel like it's my job to watch the funny looking bird. Then the bird flies away, and I turn on the TV and watch a show about buffalo.

School's almost out, but I'm not there. I have to be sick, stuck inside with the flu, stuck inside underneath this blanket.

It's such a beautiful day outside, and I feel so sick. I feel like I am falling up (which just isn't possible, but I still feel like it). My head is spinning, almost as if I am in a daze. My brain starts pounding, like someone is hitting my skull with a hammer. The sun is shining, which doesn't help; it just makes it worse. I hide under the covers. This is the one time I feel like the sun is a bad thing.

Now my stomach starts to ache, so I move from the

couch to my room to lie on my bed. Even though my brain hurts, I start to think. I let my imagination go.

I think about how much easier it is to tap your foot to a country song than to a rock song. I think about how long a day seems when you're bored, but when you do something fun the time flies by. I think about how they make us go to school for seven hours, then expect us to do three hours of homework every night and endure a big test in science or history the next day.

I start to dream, daydream that is, even more. I wander even further into my imagination. Somehow the thought of an angel comes into my head. *What do they look like? Do they have golden wings? Do they live in the moment, rather than the past or the future? Are they light?*

For some reason I can't stop wondering about them. *Can a human being become an angel after life?* My friends tell me no, but I think my grandpa is my grandma's guardian angel. I take out a piece of paper and start drawing what I think an angel looks like. In the finished drawing, the angel has golden hair as rich as the sun and gold wings that stretch from her body so that she can touch everyone's heart. She is wearing a smile and a pure white robe. A golden halo of stars floats atop her head.

The drawing makes me smile, and I feel a little better. *Tomorrow will be a better day,* I think. At that, I fall asleep.

"Anyone home?" greets me as I awaken.

"Hi, Mom," I reply.

"How are you feeling?" she asks.

"Better."

She insists on making me some chicken noodle soup anyway. Moms sure know how to make me feel better when I'm sick. Seems like she would take my sickness away from me in a second and give it to herself if she could. That's what moms are for, always there for you. Mothers hate to see their children suffer, even if it's just a little flu bug.

I don't need to know what an angel looks like, I think, *I already know.* An angel is a mom, my Mom. Her smile is that light that fills the room when it's dark. And her thoughtfulness touches my heart. My mom is an angel, watching over me. Thanks, Mom.

Nathen Cantwell

5

ON LEARNING AND LESSONS

I am always ready to learn, but I do not always like being taught.

Winston Churchill

Egg Lessons

We should be careful to get out of an experience only the wisdom that is in it.

Mark Twain

Robby Rogers . . . my first love. What a great guy, too. He was kind, honest and smart. In fact, the more I think about him, the more reasons I find for loving him as much as I did. We had been going out for a whole year. As you know, in high school that's a very long time.

I don't remember why I was not at Nancy's party that Saturday night, but Robby and I had agreed we would see each other afterward. He would come over around 10:30. Robby always showed up when he said he would, so at 11:00 I started feeling sick. I knew something wasn't right.

On Sunday morning he woke me with a phone call. "We need to talk. Can I come over?"

I wanted to say, "No, you cannot come over here and tell me something is wrong." Instead, I said, "Sure," and hung up with a knot in my stomach.

I had been right. "I got together with Sue Roth last

night," Robby informed me, "and we're going out now." He followed with the usual, "I'm so confused. I would never do anything to hurt you, Kim. I'll always love you."

I must have turned white because I felt the blood leave my face. This wasn't what I expected; my reaction surprised me. I felt such anger that I was unable to complete a sentence. I was so hurt that everything but the pain in my heart seemed to be moving in slow motion.

"Come on, Kim, don't be like this. We can be friends, can't we?"

Those are the cruelest words to utter to someone you're dumping. I had loved him deeply, shared every little weakness and vulnerability with him—not to mention the four hours a day I had spent with him for the last year (not counting the phone time). I wanted to hit him really hard, over and over, until he felt as horrible as I did. Instead, I asked him to leave. I think I said something sarcastic like, "I hear Sue calling you."

As I sat on my bed and cried for hours, I hurt so bad that nothing could make it stop. I even tried eating an entire gallon of ice cream. I played all of our favorite songs again and again, torturing myself with memories of good times and kind words. After making myself ill with shameless self-indulgence, I made a decision.

I would turn to revenge.

My thinking went like this: Sue Roth is—was—one of my closest friends. Good friends do not throw themselves at your boyfriend when you're not around. Obviously, she should pay.

That weekend, I bought a few dozen eggs and headed for Sue's house with a couple of friends. I started out just venting a little anger, but it got worse. So when someone found an open basement window, we threw the remaining eggs inside. But that's not the worst part. The Roths were out of town for three days!

As I lay in my bed that night, I started to think about what we had done. *This is bad, Kim . . . this is really bad.*

Soon it was all over school. Robby and Sue were going out *and* someone had egged her house while she was out of town, *and* it was so bad that her parents had to hire a professional to get rid of the smell.

As soon as I got home from school, my mom was waiting to talk. "Kim, my phone has been ringing all day, and I don't know what to say. Please—you have to tell me. Did you do it?"

"No, Mom, I didn't." It felt really bad to lie to my mom.

My mother was furious when she got on the phone to call Mrs. Roth. "This is Ellen. I want you to stop accusing my daughter of throwing eggs at your house." She was yelling at Sue's mother now, her voice getting louder and louder. "Kim would *never* do such a thing, and I want you to stop telling people that she did!" She was really going now. "And what's more, *I want you to apologize to me and to my daughter!*"

I felt good about the way my mom was sticking up for me, but awful about the reality. The feelings were all sort of twisted inside of me, and I knew that I had to tell her the truth. I signaled for my mom to get off the phone.

She hung up, reached for the table and sat down. She knew. I cried and told her how sorry I was. Then she cried, too. I would have preferred anger, but she'd used all of that up on Mrs. Roth.

I called Mrs. Roth and told her I'd give her every penny of my baby-sitting savings to help pay for the damages. She accepted, but told me not to come over until she was ready to forgive me.

Mom and I stayed up late that night, talking and crying. She told me about the time her boyfriend left her for her sister. I asked her if she'd egged her own house, and she actually laughed. She told me that although I'd done a terrible thing, it made her furious to think about the things Mrs. Roth had said on the phone. "After all," Mom said, "what about the fact that her daughter steals boyfriends?"

Then she told me how hard it is sometimes being a parent because you want to yell at everyone who causes your child pain, but you can't. You have to stand back and watch while your children learn hard lessons on their own.

I told my mom how incredible it had felt to hear her defend me like that. And at the end of the night, I told her how special it was to spend this kind of time with her. She gave me a hug and said, "Good. We can spend next Saturday night together, and the one after that. I did tell you, didn't I, that you're grounded for two weeks?"

Kimberly Kirberger

A Long Walk Home

*Experience: that most brutal of teachers.
But you learn, my God do you learn.*

C. S. Lewis

I grew up in the south of Spain in a little community called Estepona. I was sixteen when one morning, my father told me I could drive him into a remote village called Mijas, about eighteen miles away, on the condition that I take the car in to be serviced at a nearby garage. Having just learned to drive, and hardly ever having the opportunity to use the car, I readily accepted. I drove Dad into Mijas and promised to pick him up at 4:00 P.M., then drove to a nearby garage and dropped off the car. Because I had a few hours to spare, I decided to catch a couple of movies at a theater near the garage. However, I became so immersed in the films that I completely lost track of time. When the last movie had finished, I looked down at my watch. It was six o'clock. I was two hours late!

I knew Dad would be angry if he found out I'd been watching movies. He'd never let me drive again. I decided to tell him that the car needed some repairs and that they had taken longer than had been expected. I drove up to the place where we had planned to meet and saw Dad waiting patiently on the corner. I apologized for being late and told him that I'd come as quickly as I could, but the car had needed some major repairs. I'll never forget the look he gave me.

"I'm disappointed that you feel you have to lie to me, Jason."

"What do you mean? I'm telling the truth."

Dad looked at me again. "When you did not show up, I called the garage to ask if there were any problems, and they told me that you had not yet picked up the car. So you see, I know there were no problems with the car." A rush of guilt ran through me as I feebly confessed to my trip to the movie theater and the real reason for my tardiness. Dad listened intently as a sadness passed through him.

"I'm angry, not with you but with myself. You see, I realize that I have failed as a father if after all these years you feel that you have to lie to me. I have failed because I have brought up a son who cannot even tell the truth to his own father. I'm going to walk home now and contemplate where I have gone wrong all these years."

"But Dad, it's eighteen miles to home. It's dark. You can't walk home."

My protests, my apologies and the rest of my utterances were useless. I had let my father down, and I was about to learn one of the most painful lessons of my life. Dad began walking along the dusty roads. I quickly jumped in the car and followed behind, hoping he would relent. I pleaded all the way, telling him how sorry I was, but he simply ignored me, continuing on silently, thoughtfully and painfully. For eighteen miles I drove behind him, averaging about five miles per hour.

Seeing my father in so much physical and emotional pain was the most distressing and painful experience that

I have ever faced. However, it was also the most successful lesson. I have never lied to him since.

Jason Bocarro

The Purse

My mother always has the Purse with her. The Purse contains a receipt for everything she has purchased that cost more than twenty-five cents since around 1980. The Purse also contains at least one dose of every conceivable over-the-counter medication, all expired.

If you need something, more likely than not, it can be found in the Purse. Tissues? In the Purse. Breath mint? But, of course. Tweezers, nail polish remover, nail clippers, needle and thread, pens, pencils, calendar, calculator, paper clips, tiny stapler—all in the Purse.

The Purse started out a relatively normal size, but over the years it has expanded to what seems like two feet in width. It is hopelessly, permanently open and overflowing. If you need something, virtually everything in the Purse has to be removed and examined in order to locate it, usually onto the nearest park bench or desktop. Many great discoveries are often found during such expeditions into the Purse, like pieces of paper containing long-forgotten locker combinations or telephone messages that should have been returned three or four weeks ago.

My mom just can't bear to not know what I am up to at any given moment. For example, when I get home from school, I have to download everything that happened during the day. Over the years, she has developed expert interrogation techniques that enable her to remove every tiny detail of a day's events from my brain. No detail is too small or too insignificant or too boring for her. And the same applies when she is telling you a story about something that happened to her.

I think my mother's mind is kind of like the Purse inside—all jumbled up with tiny artifacts and useless items. Most of them have to come out and be spread around before you get to something good or what you were looking for, but when she does get to that one valuable thing, it is as if you have just won the lottery.

When I first started hanging out with Heather, it was mostly at school or on the weekends. I don't know why I didn't tell my mom about her. I guess I just wanted to keep something private, or maybe I didn't want her to make a big deal about it, or maybe I was afraid my mom, with the Purse, would want to meet Heather. I think it was mostly that.

And so, every day I would come home from school and proceed to tell my mom what happened in each class, between each class, at lunch and after school. I would be urged to disclose what happened on the way to school and on the way home from school and up until the very second that I walked into the house. But every day I would conveniently leave out all details about Heather.

This went on for a few months and I knew my mom was starting to get suspicious, but I just couldn't tell her about Heather. I didn't want to admit it to myself, but I was ashamed of my mother. It made it worse that she prided herself on the honesty we shared, telling her friends that I could tell her anything and it would be okay.

Since I mostly saw Heather in groups, I would tell my mom that I was going to the movies with Katrina and

Steve and Trevor and Julian, but conveniently leaving out Heather. But one Saturday night I decided I wanted to see Heather alone. I wanted to go out on a real date with her. I had two choices: Either come clean and tell my mom about Heather, or lie. So I told my mom I was going to the movies with "some friends." I don't know why I thought this would work. She wanted to know which friends, what movie, what theater, who was driving, what time, if it was an R-rated movie, where I was going afterward, what time I would be home and whether or not I planned on buying popcorn. She left me no choice. I lied to her, and once I got started, I couldn't stop. I lied about things that didn't matter. I told her I was going to buy Red Vines when I knew I wanted Raisinettes, and I told her the wrong movie at the wrong theater. I told her I was going with Katrina and Trevor. I told her Katrina's mom was driving.

And so I left the house with a pit in my stomach. I wasn't good at this lying thing, and I felt guilty. I walked to Heather's house, and we caught the bus to the movies. I don't even remember what movie we saw, but the whole time I could only think about the fact that I had lied to my mom. We came out of the movie holding hands and, to my complete horror, my mom was standing there with the Purse. She had decided to take my sister to a movie and since she didn't want to intrude on me with my friends, she had chosen a different theater than the one I had told her, which of course was the wrong one because I had lied.

She didn't say anything, but if I had been paying attention, I would have been able to read the look of disappointment on her face. I was too busy worrying about her embarrassing me in front of Heather. All I could see was the Purse. I couldn't lie anymore, so I introduced my mom to Heather. My mom just stood there. She was in shock. I was in shock. And then I saw the look.

I guess I should have been relieved when she smiled at me, and then Heather, and invited us to dinner. It seems she had a coupon for Sizzler, they were having some sort of family dinner special for four, and my mom thought it was just perfect that we had run into each other. A coupon? What were we, homeless? I couldn't believe she suggested a coupon in front of Heather. And just when I thought things couldn't get worse, she started looking for the coupon. Oh no! Not the Purse!

At first I tried to stop her as she started to open the Purse. Then I realized there was no stopping her, so I tried to help. The Purse had to be completely unloaded onto a bench outside the theater. I was shuffling through the papers, trying to find the prized coupon, and I guess I was moving my hands too fast and I knocked the Purse. It flipped up in the air and as it did, I saw my life flash before my eyes, as if in slow motion, each one of those million receipts representing an important event. They ended up on the ground, spread about the theater, just as the movie next door was letting out. Crowds of people were stepping on all those papers.

That's when I lost it. The words came out in torrents, and I was powerless to stop them. "I can't believe you!" I yelled. "You are totally embarrassing me! Why do you have to carry all this crap with you all the time? Who cares about all these stupid receipts?" I picked up a Target receipt from the early 1990s. "Look at this," I said. "You bought T-shirts for Dad, and you got them on sale. Isn't that special?"

Heather looked on in shock. She grabbed me by the arm and pulled me to the side. "It's no big deal," she said.

"Yes, it is. I can't believe she's embarrassing me like that. She's so lame."

"Calm down," Heather replied. "It's okay. She was just trying to take us out to a nice dinner. I like Sizzler."

I couldn't calm down. Heather and I just stared at each other.

My mom and my sister were on their hands and knees picking up all those little pieces of paper and bits of string and lint-covered pills. I got down there and helped them. We left the theater and drove Heather home in silence. Other than hello and good-bye, my mom didn't speak to me for the rest of the weekend. I went to school on Monday, and Heather acted weird. I came home from school and walked in as usual. My mom was there, but she didn't say anything to me. Not even, "How was your day?" She just had that look of disappointment on her face. As long as I live, I will never forget that look.

I went up to my room to do some homework and play around on the computer. It was eerily silent. *Hey, this isn't so bad,* I thought. *I have a lot more time to myself.* But after a few hours, I began thinking about my day. I had gotten an A on an algebra test. It didn't seem to have any value until I could tell my mom about it. And I wanted to go down there and tell her about Heather. I wanted her to know how bad I felt. Worst of all, I had disappointed her. We had a good relationship and an honest one until I blew it. I lied. I was so disappointed in myself.

I finally got up the courage to go down there. She was sitting at the kitchen table with the Purse, sorting through all those receipts. Next to her was a *new* purse. A nice, flat, closable purse. She was transferring things into the new one. Just a few things. I sat there silently for a few minutes watching her sort. I noticed a restaurant receipt from Pizza Hut. I picked it up from the discard pile and noticed the date: August 26. My birthday.

"Hey, remember my birthday party last year?" My mom just looked at me. "You know, when I got the new skateboard?" Silence. More sorting. "I got an A on my algebra test." Silence. It was unbearable. I couldn't take it.

"I'm sorry. I'm really sorry. I didn't mean any of the stuff I said. I . . . I . . . miss you." She looked up from the sorting. There was a long pause. I was waiting for her to yell at me. I expected her to tell me how mad she was. I was ready for the worst, but all she said was, "How was your day?"

It's a few months later now, and that new purse, the one my mom was sorting, has become *the* Purse. And the next time Heather and I run into my mom and the Purse, I hope she has dinner plans in there somewhere.

Tal Vigderson

The Cost of Gratefulness

I was about thirteen. My father frequently took me on short outings on Saturdays. Sometimes we went to a park, or to a marina to look at boats. My favorites were trips to junk stores, where we could admire old electronic stuff. Once in a while we would buy something for fifty cents just to take it apart.

On the way home from these trips, Dad frequently stopped at the Dairy Queen for ten-cent ice cream cones. Not every single time; just often enough. I couldn't expect it, but I could hope and pray from the time we started heading home to that critical corner where we would either go straight for the ice cream or turn and go home empty-handed. That corner meant either mouth-watering excitement or disappointment.

A few times my father teased me by going home the long way. "I'm just going this way for variety," he would say, as we drove by the Dairy Queen without stopping. It was a game, and I was well fed, so we're not talking torture here.

On the best days he would ask, in a tone that made it sound novel and spontaneous, "Would you like an ice cream cone?" and I would say, "That sounds great, Dad!" I'd always have chocolate and he'd have vanilla. He would hand me twenty cents and I would run in to buy the usual. We'd eat them in the car. I loved my dad and I loved ice cream—so that was heaven.

On one fateful day, we were heading home, and I was hoping and praying for the beautiful sound of his offer. It came. "Would you like an ice cream cone today?"

"That sounds great, Dad!"

But then he said, "It sounds good to me too, Son. How would you like to treat today?"

Twenty cents! Twenty cents! My mind reeled. I could afford it. I got twenty-five cents a week allowance, plus some extra for odd jobs. But saving money was important. Dad told me that. And when it was my money, ice cream just wasn't a good use of it.

Why didn't it occur to me that this was a golden opportunity to give something back to my very generous father? Why didn't I think that he had bought me fifty ice cream cones, and I had never bought him one? But all I could think was "twenty cents!"

In a fit of selfish, miserly ingratitude, I said the awful words that have rung in my ears ever since. "Well, in that case, I guess I'll pass."

My father just said, "Okay, Son."

But as we turned to head home, I realized how wrong I was and begged him to turn back. "I'll pay," I pleaded.

But he just said, "That's okay, we don't really need one," and wouldn't hear my pleading. We drove home.

I felt awful for my selfishness and ungratefulness. He didn't rub it in, or even act disappointed. But I don't think he could have done anything to make a deeper impression on me.

I learned that generosity goes two ways and gratefulness sometimes costs a little more than "thank you." On that day gratefulness would have cost twenty cents, and it would have been the best ice cream I'd ever had.

I'll tell you one more thing. We went on another trip the next week, and as we approached the crucial corner, I said, "Dad, would you like an ice cream cone today? My treat."

Randal Jones

Mrs. Virginia DeView, Where Are You?

There are high spots in all of our lives, and most of them come about through encouragement from someone else.

George Adams

We were sitting in her classroom, giggling, jabbing each other and talking about the latest information of the day, like the peculiar purple-colored mascara Cindy was wearing. Mrs. Virginia DeView cleared her throat and asked us to hush.

"Now," she said smiling, "we are going to discover our professions." The class seemed to gasp in unison. Our professions? We stared at each other. We were only thirteen and fourteen years old. This teacher was nuts.

That was pretty much how the kids looked at Virginia DeView, her hair swirled back in a bun and her large, buck teeth gaping out of her mouth. Because of her physical appearance, she was always an easy target for snickers and cruel jokes among students.

She also made her students angry because she was demanding. Most of us just overlooked her brilliance.

"Yes; you will all be searching for your future professions," she said with a glow on her face—as though this was the best thing she did in her classroom every year. "You will have to do a research paper on your upcoming career. Each of you will have to interview someone in your field, plus give an oral report."

All of us went home confused. Who knows what they want to do at thirteen? I had narrowed it down, however. I liked art, singing and writing. But I was terrible in art, and when I sang my sisters screamed: "Oh, please shut up." The only thing left was writing.

Every day in her class, Virginia DeView monitored us. Where were we? Who had picked their careers? Finally, most of us had selected something; I picked print journalism. This meant I had to go interview a true-blue newspaper reporter in the flesh, and I was terrified.

I sat down in front of him barely able to speak. He looked at me and said: "Did you bring a pencil or pen?"

I shook my head.

"How about some paper?"

I shook my head again.

Finally, I think he realized I was terrified, and I got my first big tip as a journalist. "Never, never go anywhere without a pen and paper. You never know what you'll run into."

For the next ninety minutes, he filled me with stories of robberies, crime sprees and fires. He would never forget the tragic fire where four family members were killed in the blaze. He could still smell their burning flesh, he said, and he would never forget that horrid story.

A few days later, I gave my oral report totally from memory, I had been so mesmerized. I got an A on the entire project.

As we neared the end of the school year, some very resentful students decided to get Virginia DeView back for the hard work she put us through. As she rounded a corner, they shoved a pie into her face as hard as they could. She was slightly injured physically, but it was emotionally that she was really hurt. She didn't return to school for days. When I heard the story, I felt a deep, ugly pit fill my stomach. I felt shame for myself and my fellow students who had nothing better to do than pick on a woman because of how she looked, rather than appreciate her amazing teaching skills.

Years later, I forgot all about Virginia DeView and the careers we selected. I was in college scouting around for a new career. My father wanted me in business, which seemed to be sound advice at the time, except that I had no sense of business skills whatsoever. Then I remembered Virginia DeView and my desire at thirteen to be a journalist. I called my parents.

"I'm changing my major," I announced.

There was a stunned silence on the end of the phone.

"What to?" my father finally asked.

"Journalism."

I could tell in their voices that my parents were very unhappy, but they didn't stop me. They just reminded me how competitive the field was and how all my life I had shied away from competition.

This was true. But journalism did something to me; it was in my blood. It gave me the freedom to go up to total strangers and ask what was going on. It trained me to ask questions and get answers in both my professional and personal life. It gave me confidence.

For the past twelve years, I've had the most incredible and satisfying reporting career, covering stories from murders to airplane crashes and finally settling in on my forté. I loved to write about the tender and tragic moments of people's lives because somehow I felt it helped them in some way.

When I went to pick up my phone one day, an incredible wave of memories hit me and I realized that had it not been for Virginia DeView, I would not be sitting at that desk.

She'll probably never know that without her help, I would not have become a journalist and a writer. I suspect I would have been floundering in the business world somewhere, with great unhappiness shadowing me each day. I wonder now how many other students in her class benefited from that career project.

I get asked all the time: "How did you pick journalism?"

"Well, you see, there was this teacher . . ." I always start out. I just wish I could thank her.

I believe that when people reflect back over their school days, there will be this faded image of a single teacher— their very own Virginia DeView. Perhaps you can thank her before it's too late.

Diana L. Chapman

"I imagine you'll be interested in one of the
more highly visible occupations?"

Challenge Days

Shared joy is double joy.
Shared sorrow is half sorrow.

Swedish Proverb

My name is Tony. I always looked out for myself because I thought no one else would, and I thought it would always be that way. That changed the day I got out of class for something called Challenge Day.

The people running it had big hopes of helping us join together and making us leaders. I just wanted to get out of class. I figured that after signing in I would sneak out.

In the school gym, I found myself sitting in a big circle, face to face with a hundred students that no one could have paid me to spend the day with. I was keeping up my front, my cool, but I was kind of nervous. I'm used to either sitting hidden in the back of a classroom waiting for a break, or skipping school and hanging with the guys. I wasn't used to not knowing what was going to happen.

I made fun of how a bunch of kids were dressed and of a girl who was fat. Some of the girls had worn pajamas and brought stuffed animals. Pretty stupid, I thought.

The day started with each of us standing up and saying our names into a microphone "loud and proud." A bunch of kids were really shy, but since I rap sometimes, I acted really cool when it was my turn. No one knew there was a lump in my throat. You see, I'm from a tough neighborhood, and showing your weakness only makes you a target. I was a target when I was real young, both for my brothers and for the people who called themselves my friends. We sure didn't know how to be friends, though. Fighting and putting each other down were a normal way of life.

Anyway, we started playing these games I thought were really childish. I hung back a little with my buddies, acting cool and not wanting to play like a little kid. After a couple of games, though, it didn't seem like anyone else was hanging back, and they were all having a good time. I thought, "Why not me?" I have to admit that I was playing a little rough, but it beat sitting on the edge.

What happened next was almost unbelievable. Carl, one of the only guys who is more feared and respected than me at school, was helping one of the leaders demonstrate how to give hugs. Everyone was laughing at first, but it was getting harder and harder to put anyone down that day. The leaders kept teaching us to open our hearts and minds, to share our true feelings and to give put-ups instead of put-downs. It wasn't what I was used to.

Then we did an exercise called "the power shuffle." Before the game started, the leaders talked about oppression. "Yeah," I thought, "like they really know what it's like to be oppressed. Here I am, a young Latino growing up in a white society. I get harassed and pushed around every day by store owners, teachers and all these adults who think I'm a gangster just because of the color of my skin. Yeah, I act hard, but what am I supposed to do when I have to watch my friends drop from drive-bys?"

The leaders said we had to be silent, to make it safe for everyone. They called out broad categories and asked us to cross over the line if we fit into the category. I was still snickering in my buddy's ear as the first few were called out.

But the leaders meant it about being quiet. One of the adults softly put his hand on me and said, "You'll want them to respect you; please respect them."

Category after category was called out. In silence, group after group, people crossed the line. Then a topic was called that I fit into, and I figured I would be the only one who experienced this kind of pain. "Cross the line if you've ever been hit, beaten or abused, in any way." I walked heavy in my shoes. Looking straight down as I walked, I turned around, having a hard time not laughing to cover what was going on inside me.

But as I looked up, half the group was walking with me. We stood together in silence, looked into each other's eyes, and for the first time in my life, I felt like I wasn't alone.

One by one we dropped our masks. I saw that these people, whom I had judged before, were in reality very much like me. Like me, they, too, knew how it felt to be hurt.

I walked back across the line. My friend tried to joke with me but it didn't seem right any more. Another topic was called, one where all the women and girls crossed. I had never seen before how much men and boys disrespect and hurt women. I became more uncomfortable as I noticed tears appearing in many of my friends' eyes.

We crossed the line next for having lost someone close to us in gang violence. So many of us crossed that line. It just wasn't right! I started feeling really angry inside, and tears were coming to my eyes. The leaders kept saying, "When the tears are on the outside, the inside is healing," and, "It takes a strong man to cry."

I had to make the choice of whether or not to have the courage to show my tears. I was still scared of being called names, but the tears came out. I cried, and with my tears I proved that I was a strong man.

Before we left that day, each of us stood up and shared our experiences. I stood up, again not sure if I should fight the tears or not. The leader encouraged me to look out at the group and ask if it was okay for a man to cry. So I did.

Then each person stood up in front of their chairs to show they respected me for showing my tears. Amazed, I started talking. I said I was sorry to a few of those people I had judged and pushed around in the halls because I thought they had it so much better than me. With tears in their eyes, they came up to me, one by one, and gave me a hug. Now I know what it is really like to share love with someone. I hope I can do this with my dad some day.

Here was a day I thought I was cutting from school, but instead I found myself telling the people I hurt that I was sorry, and people were saying the same thing to me. It was like we were all one family and we never knew it until that day. It wasn't magic—we just looked at each other in a different light.

Now it is up to us. Do we look through these eyes for just one day, or do we have the courage to remember that most people are just like us, and help others learn that it is safe to be themselves?

As told to Andrew Tertes

If I Knew

You know how you always hear people say, "If I knew then what I know now . . ."?

Have you ever wanted to say . . . yeah . . . well . . . go on . . .

So here we go . . .

I would listen more carefully to what my heart says.

I would enjoy more . . . worry less.

I would know that school would end soon enough . . . and work would . . . well, never mind.

I wouldn't worry so much about what other people were thinking.

I would appreciate all my vitality and tight skin.

I would play more, fret less.

I would know that my beauty/handsomeness is in my love of life.

I would know how much my parents love me and I would believe that they are doing the best they can.

I would enjoy the feeling of "being in love" and not worry so much about how it works out.

I would know that it probably won't . . . but that something better will come along.

I wouldn't be afraid of acting like a kid.
I would be braver.
I would look for the good qualities in everyone and enjoy them for those.
I would not hang out with people just because they're "popular."
I would take dance lessons.
I would enjoy my body just the way it is.
I would trust my girlfriends.
I would be a trustworthy girlfriend.
I wouldn't trust my boyfriends. (Just kidding.)
I would enjoy kissing. Really enjoy it.
I would be more appreciative and grateful, for sure.

Kimberly Kirberger

The Bat

The best part about running, for me, is the finish. The moment when, flushed and out of breath, I reach my destination: my backyard. Ironically, I have run full circle, ending up where I began. Yet, I have also taken a positive step forward in my life, determined and acted out by no one other than myself. My decision, my action.

As I sit and wait for my breathing to slow and the rush to subside, I wish upon a star. "Star light, star bright . . ." A bat flits across my path of vision and my eyes follow it. Without any warning, the bat suddenly swerves and changes direction. It has changed its path forever.

And now, having been interrupted, my wish seems futile and absurd. I am filled with a rushing understanding of the part I play in my own life.

I am not just a bystander. My life is not to be controlled by the stars, but by me, and me alone. Like the bat, I am free to choose my own path, however haphazard and illogical it might appear to be.

Bryony Blackwood

Making Sarah Cry

He stood among his friends from school,
He joined their childhood games
Laughing as they played kickball
And when they called poor Sarah names.
Sarah was unlike the rest;
She was slow and not as smart,
And it would seem to all his friends
She was born without a heart.
And so he gladly joined their fun
Of making Sarah cry.
But somewhere deep within his heart,
He never knew just why.
For he could hear his mother's voice,
Her lessons of right and wrong
Playing over and over inside his head
Just like a favorite song.
"Treat others with respect, son,
The way you'd want them treating you.
And remember, when you hurt others,
Someday, someone might hurt you."
He knew his mother wouldn't understand
The purpose of their game

Of teasing Sarah, who made them laugh
As her own tears fell like rain.
The funny faces that she made
And the way she'd stomp her feet
Whenever they mocked the way she walked
Or the stutter when she'd speak.
To him she must deserve it
Because she never tried to hide.
And if she truly wanted to be left alone,
Then she should stay inside.
But every day she'd do the same:
She'd come outside to play,
And stand there, tears upon her face,
Too upset to run away.
The game would soon be over
As tears dropped from her eyes,
For the purpose of their fun
Was making Sarah cry.
It was nearly two whole months
He hadn't seen his friends.
He was certain they all must wonder
What happened and where he'd been
So he felt a little nervous
As he limped his way to class.
He hoped no one would notice,
He prayed no one would ask
About that awful day:
The day his bike met with a car,
Leaving him with a dreadful limp
And a jagged-looking scar.
So he held his breath a little
As he hobbled into the room,
Where inside he saw a "Welcome Back" banner
And lots of red balloons.

He felt a smile cross his face
As his friends all smiled, too
And he couldn't wait to play outside—
His favorite thing to do.
So the second that he stepped outdoors
And saw his friends all waiting there,
He expected a few pats on the back—
Instead, they all stood back and stared.
He felt his face grow hotter
As he limped to join their side
To play a game of kickball
And of making Sarah cry.
An awkward smile crossed his face
When he heard somebody laugh
And heard the words, "Hey freak,
Where'd you get the ugly mask?"
He turned, expecting Sarah,
But Sarah could not be seen.
It was the scar upon his own face
That caused such words so mean.
He joined in their growing laughter,
Trying hard to not give in
To the awful urge inside to cry
Or the quivering of his chin.
They are only teasing,
He made himself believe.
They are still my friends;
They'd never think of hurting me.
But the cruel remarks continued
About the scar and then his limp.
And he knew if he shed a single tear
They'd label him a wimp.
And so the hurtful words went on,
And in his heart he wondered why.
But he knew without a doubt

The game would never end, until they made him cry.
And just when a tear had formed,
He heard a voice speak out from behind.
"Leave him alone you bullies,
Because he's a friend of mine."
He turned to see poor Sarah,
Determination on her face,
Sticking up for one of her own tormentors
And willing to take his place.
And when his friends did just that,
Trying their best to make poor Sarah cry,
This time he didn't join in,
And at last understood exactly why.
"Treat others with respect, son,
The way you'd want them treating you.
And remember, when you hurt others,
Someday, someone might hurt you."
It took a lot of courage
But he knew he must be strong,
For at last he saw the difference
Between what's right and wrong.
And Sarah didn't seem so weird
Through his understanding eyes.
Now he knew he'd never play again
The game of making Sarah cry.
It took several days of teasing
And razzing from his friends,
But when they saw his strength,
They chose to be like him.
And now out on the playground,
A group of kids meets every day
For a game of kickball and laughter
And teaching their new friend, Sarah, how to play.

Cheryl Costello-Forshey

Lessons in Baseball

There are always two choices, two paths to take. One is easy. And its only reward is that it's easy.

Unknown

As an eleven-year-old, I was addicted to baseball. I listened to baseball games on the radio. I watched them on TV. The books I read were about baseball. I took baseball cards to church in hopes of trading with other baseball card junkies. My fantasies? All about baseball.

I played baseball whenever and wherever I could. I played organized or sandlot. I played catch with my brother, with my father, with friends. If all else failed, I bounced a rubber ball off the porch stairs, imagining all kinds of wonderful things happening to me and my team.

It was with this attitude that I entered the 1956 Little League season. I was a shortstop. Not good, not bad. Just addicted.

Gordon was not addicted. Nor was he good. He moved into our neighborhood that year and signed up to play baseball. The kindest way of describing Gordon's baseball skills is to say that he didn't have any. He couldn't catch. He couldn't hit. He couldn't throw. He couldn't run.

In fact, Gordon was afraid of the ball.

I was relieved when the final selections were made and Gordon was assigned to another team. Everyone had to play at least half of each game, and I couldn't see Gordon improving my team's chances in any way. Too bad for the other team.

After two weeks of practice, Gordon dropped out. My friends on his team laughed when they told me how their coach directed two of the team's better players to walk Gordon into the woods and have a chat with him. "Get lost" was the message that was delivered, and "get lost" was the one that was heard.

Gordon got lost.

That scenario violated my eleven-year-old sense of justice, so I did what any indignant shortstop would do. I tattled. I told my coach the whole story. I shared the episode in full detail, figuring my coach would complain to the League office and have Gordon returned to his original team. Justice and my team's chances of winning would both be served.

I was wrong. My coach decided that Gordon needed to be on a team that wanted him—one that treated him with respect, one that gave everyone a fair chance to contribute according to their own ability.

Gordon became my team member.

I wish I could say Gordon got the big hit in the big game with two outs in the final inning, but it didn't happen. I don't think Gordon even hit a foul ball the entire season. Baseballs hit in his direction (right field) went over him, by him, through him, or off him.

It wasn't that Gordon didn't get help. The coach gave him extra batting practice and worked with him on his fielding, all without much improvement.

I'm not sure if Gordon learned anything from my coach that year. I know I did. I learned to bunt without tipping off my intention. I learned to tag up on a fly if there were less than two outs. I learned to make a smoother pivot around second base on a double play.

I learned a lot from my coach that summer, but my most important lessons weren't about baseball. They were about character and integrity. I learned that everyone has worth, whether they can hit .300 or .030. I learned that we all have value, whether we can stop the ball or have to turn and chase it. I learned that doing what is right, fair and honorable is more important than winning or losing.

It felt good to be on that team that year. I'm grateful that man was my coach. I was proud to be his shortstop and his son.

Chick Moorman

A Lesson for Life

The turning point in the process of growing up is when you discover the core strength within you that survives all hurt.

Max Lerner

"Look at fatso!"

Freshmen in high school can be cruel and we certainly were to a young man named Matt who was in my class. We mimicked him, teased him and taunted him about his size. He was at least fifty pounds overweight. He felt the pain of being the last one picked to play basketball, baseball or football. Matt will always remember the endless pranks that were played on him—trashing his hall locker, piling library books on his desk at lunchtime and spraying him with icy streams of water in the shower after gym class.

One day he sat near me in gym class. Someone pushed him and he fell on me and banged my foot quite badly. The kid who pushed him said Matt did it. With the whole class watching, I was put on the spot to either shrug it off or pick a fight with Matt. I chose to fight in order to keep my image intact.

I shouted, "C'mon, Matt, let's fight!" He said he didn't want to. But peer pressure forced him into the conflict whether he liked it or not. He came toward me with his fists in the air. He was no George Foreman. With one punch I bloodied his nose and the class went wild. Just then the gym teacher walked into the room. He saw that we were fighting and he sent us out to the oval running track.

He followed us with a smile on his face and said, "I want you two guys to go out there and run that mile holding each other's hands." The room erupted into a roar of laughter. The two of us were embarrassed beyond belief, but Matt and I went out to the track and ran our mile— hand-in-hand.

At some point during the course of our run, I remember looking over at him, with blood still trickling from his nose and his weight slowing him down. It struck me that here was a person, not all that different from myself. We both looked at each other and began to laugh. In time we became good friends.

Going around that track, hand-in-hand, I no longer saw Matt as fat or dumb. He was a human being who had intrinsic value and worth far beyond any externals. It was amazing what I learned when I was forced to go hand-in-hand with someone for only one mile.

For the rest of my life I have never so much as raised a hand against another person.

Medard Laz

Terri Jackson

On the first day of sixth grade, I sat in my quiet home-room class and observed all the people who I would eventually befriend and possibly graduate with. I glanced around the room and noticed that the majority of the middle-class kids were dressed in their nicest first-day outfits. My glance stopped on a shy-looking girl in the back of the room. She wore a stained, yellow plaid shirt with a pair of frayed jeans that had obviously had several owners before her. Her hair was unusually short and unwashed. She wore dress shoes that were once white, and frilly pink socks that had lost their frill with too many wearings. I caught myself thinking, "That's disgusting. Doesn't she know what a bathtub is?" As I looked around, I figured others were probably thinking the same thing.

The teacher began checking the attendance, each person casually lifting his or her hand as names were called in turn.

"Terri Jackson?" the teacher asked, following the roll with her finger. Silence. "Um, Terri Jackson?"

Finally we heard a meek answer from the back of the room, followed by the sound of ripping cloth. We all shifted in our seats to see what had happened.

"Scary Terri ripped the armpit of her shirt!" one boy joked.

"Eww, I bet it's a hundred years old!" another girl commented. One comment after another brought a roar of laugher.

I was probably laughing the loudest. Sadly, making Terri feel insecure made me feel secure and confident. It was a good break from the awkward silence and uncomfortable first-day jitters.

Terri Jackson was the joke of the whole sixth grade that year. If we had nothing to talk about, Terri's trip through the lunchroom was an entertaining conversation starter. Her grandma-looking dress, missing front tooth and stained gym clothes kept us mocking and imitating her for hours.

At my twelfth birthday party, ten giggly, gossipy girls were playing Truth or Dare, a favorite party game. We had just finished a Terri Jackson discussion. It was my turn at the game.

"Umm . . . Sydney! Truth or Dare?" one of my friends asked.

"How about a dare? Bring it on. I'll do anything." Oh, if only I'd known what she was about to say.

"Okay, I dare you to invite Terri Jackson over to your house next Friday for two whole hours!"

"Two whole hours?! Please ask something else, *please!*" I begged. "How could anybody do that?" But my question was drowned out by a sea of giggly girls slapping their hands over their mouths and rolling on the floor, trying to contain their laughter.

The next day, I cautiously walked up to Terri as if her body odor was going to make me fall over dead. My friends huddled and watched from a corner to see if I would follow through with the brave dare.

I managed to choke out, "Hey Scary—I mean Terri—you want to come over for two hours Friday?" I didn't see her face light up because I had turned to my friends and made a gagging expression. When I was satisfied with their laughter of approval, I turned back to Terri. Terri's face was buried in her filthy hands; she was crying. I couldn't stand it. Half of me felt the strongest compassion for her, but the other half wanted to slap her for making me look so cruel and heartless. That was exactly what I was being.

"What's got you all upset? All I did was invite you over," I whispered, trying not to show my concern.

She looked up and watched my eyes for what seemed like forever. "Really?" That was all she could say. Her seldom-heard voice almost startled me.

"I guess so, if you're up to it." My voice sounded surprisingly sincere. I'd never seen her flash her toothless smile so brightly. The rest of the day I had a good feeling, and I was not dreading the two-hour visit as I had before. I was almost looking forward to it.

Friday rolled around quickly. My time with Terri passed by in a flash as the two hours slipped into four hours, and I found myself actually enjoying her company. We chatted about her family and her battles with poverty. We discovered that we both played violin, and my favorite part of the afternoon occurred when she played the violin for me. I was amazed by how beautifully she played.

I would love to tell you that Terri and I became best friends and that from then on I ignored all my other friends' comments. But that's not how it happened. While I no longer participated in the Terri bashings and even tried to defend her at times, I didn't want to lose everyone else's acceptance just to gain Terri's.

Terri disappeared after the sixth grade. No one is sure

what happened to her. We think that she may have transferred to a different school because of how cruelly the kids treated her. I still think about her sometimes and wonder what she's doing. I guess all I can do is hope that she is being accepted and loved wherever she is.

I realize now how insecure and weak I was during that sixth-grade year. I participated in the cruel, heartless Terri-bashing sessions because they seemed kind of funny in a distorted way. But they were only funny because they falsely boosted my own self-confidence; I felt bigger by making someone else feel smaller. I know now that true confidence is not proven by destroying another's self-esteem, but rather, by having the strength to stand up for the Terri Jacksons of the world.

Sydney Fox

Courage

Darkness cannot drive out darkness; only light can do that. Hate cannot drive out hate, only love can do that.

Martin Luther King Jr.

The excited sound of seventh-grade laughter and voices tumbled down the hallway as the students filed into the gym. I scanned the room, searching for my friends, and soon spotted them near the door to the restroom. I weaved my way through the mass of people and sat down next to my best friend, Lauren.

"So, what exactly are we doing here?" she questioned.

"Well, according to Mrs. Marks, we're supposed to be listening to a speaker about bullying, peer pressure and put-downs." I said this somewhat sarcastically, because the entire year our grade had been lectured over and over again on these topics. We were earning the reputation as the worst class in the school, which was not a reputation that my friends nor I were particularly proud of. As our science teacher stood in front of the entire grade level, attempting to get our attention, my friends and I sat back, prepared to sit through another monotonous speech full of harsh remarks about "Kids these days . . ." and "Your maturity level when you put someone down is no greater than that of an eight-year-old."

But as soon as she started talking, I snapped to attention. She had this way about her, as if she knew how to reach into our minds and souls and make us think. And for once, I actually began to think about what it was she was preaching about. I thought about all the kids who came to school every day, despite knowing that they would have to face cruel comments and sneering faces all day long.

One boy, in particular, came to mind. Every day, this boy came to first hour late, and I suspected it was because he needed to get medicine from the nurse. But this didn't stop the kids in the class from making fun of him. They punched him in the shoulder and said, "Hey, man! Where have you been?" And then another would add, "How's that girlfriend of yours? Oh sorry, we forgot. You don't *have* a girlfriend. You only have *boyfriends*." This harassment would continue until the teacher cut in, forcing the boys to stop. But it was too late—it always was. The boy would put his head down on his desk in shame. The worst, though, was when he tried to retaliate. His attackers only laughed and continued the cruelty until the entire room was laughing at his expense.

As I sat in the auditorium, absorbing everything the speaker had to say, thoughts of this poor boy crept into my head. I sighed, thinking how sorry I felt for him, not that there was anything I could do. I tuned back into the speaker and listened intently to her words of wisdom.

"Now, before I leave today, I would like to give everyone here an opportunity to say *anything* he or she wants to on the subject of bullying or peer pressure. You may apologize to a friend, thank someone for his or her kindness, *anything*. And this is the one time I can promise that *no one,* but *no one,* will laugh at you."

The stillness in the room made me believe her. Slowly, I saw a few hands raise tentatively in the air behind me. One girl wanted to apologize to a friend she had been ignoring recently. Another thanked a boy for his kindness when she slipped on the steps the other day. It was then that my moment of courage happened. The speaker called on me, and with shaking hands and clammy palms, I began to talk.

"What you said today really made sense. I know that it's true, because I see it every day in class. There is one person who is always made fun of. It doesn't matter why—it could be the way he looks, talks or even takes notes." My voice shook. "I think that everyone here has made fun of him at one time or another. I know I have. And now I really regret it. To us, it may just be a game, but to him, it must hurt. And I think . . . well, I think we need to stop."

Scared of my classmates' reaction, I felt like the silence that followed lasted forever. But then, soft clapping started in the front of the room, quickly spreading through the entire crowd. By the time I looked up, the soft pitter-patter had turned into a thunderous roar of applause. I had voiced something that everyone was feeling.

Later on that day, the boy whom I had been talking about came up to me privately and said thank you.

I noticed that from that day on, people began to treat him a little better. The teasing stopped, and people greeted him in the halls with a friendly, "Hi!" It was those little, everyday things that I noticed, and I'm sure he noticed them, too.

Ruth Ann Supica

My Most
Embarrassing Moment

[AUTHOR'S NOTE TO HER MOM AND DAD: *I'm sorry you have to find out about this at the same time all of America does. I never told anyone.*]

Honor student, tennis team player, Spanish Club president. Sunday school teacher assistant, Swing Choir piano accompanist. Although these publicly recognized accomplishments of my teenage years went on to influence my life in many ways, there was one particular group activity I participated in that had an even greater impact on me: Mustard Gang Member.

The fall of 1977 found me enrolled as a freshman in the school system I had attended since kindergarten. My student file over the last ten years could be summed up with positive comments such as "consistently above average," "enjoys extracurricular activities" and "cooperates with teachers and fellow classmates." No suspensions. No detentions. Basically, a model student. However, within a total time period of approximately one hour, this trademark behavior would fly right out the window (at the speed of sound).

Three of my lifelong girlfriends—who would fall under a fairly close ditto description of that above—caught up to me after school on a Friday afternoon. One of them had just received her driver's license and was going cruising in a nearby town to celebrate. She asked if I would like to come along. (Rhetorical question.) The final bell was sounding as we piled into an older model Dodge Charger on its last leg of life. Regardless of its condition, it had a full tank of gas and the ability to get us from Point A to Point B.

Within minutes of leaving the school parking lot, we were on the open highway. As I look back now, that highway was pretty significant. It not only separated two towns, it separated those of us in the car from the people who knew us and the people who didn't. We became daring.

When the novelty of just driving around wore off, someone suggested it might be fun to squirt mustard on parked cars as we drove past them. *(Author's sensible reaction twenty years later: WHAT?!)* A unanimous agreement must have followed, because all four of us stood beside each other in the checkout line where the bottle of mustard was ultimately purchased.

Loading back into the car, each of our faces looked as though we couldn't believe what we were doing. We couldn't. Four kids, four clean records. *Lost time was about to be made up for.*

We decided that the person sitting by the passenger's side window would be the Designated Squirter, while the others in the car would be responsible for choosing the target ahead. Since I was cowardly, trying to hide in a corner of the backseat, I thought this sounded swell. Feeling my guilt would be somewhat lessened if I didn't actually *touch* the mustard bottle, I thought. I was off the hook. A nervous sigh of relief was escaping me until the words "and we'll pull over every other block and switch seats so it will be fair." Hook re-inserted.

The "talk" in the car proved to be more productive than the "action" as the first and second girls took their turn in the passenger seat, both chickening out at the last second, squealing, "I can't!" Before I knew it, the car had stalled and it was me who was climbing in beside the driver. Sliding my sweaty palms up and down the bottle's sides, the target was being pointed out to me, loudly and with demanding encouragement. The attack was to be launched on a little red Volkswagen up ahead, fast approaching. "Do it! Do it! Do it!" my friends chanted. . . . *And I almost did.* But, as was the case with the girls before, feathers grew from within me and we soon sped past the car, leaving it as solid red as it had been when first spotted.

Since the driver couldn't take a respective turn as the shooter, we headed for home, the mischief supposedly ended. Just when we were nearing the highway, we passed two girls jogging, their hands moving up and down in front of them. Still looking for trouble, we interpreted their innocent actions. "Hey! They just gave us the finger!" And of course, if we had been needlessly insulted, they certainly would have to pay. Simple as that.

Within seconds, they were jogging into a Kmart parking lot. . . . And we were right behind them. Jumping out of the car, we ran toward our unsuspecting prey yelling, "Get 'em!" We did. Well, *I* did. After all, there was only one bottle, and it was my turn. Silently, they just stood there.

My hearing must have been the last of my senses to fail, for the car door did not slam shut behind me without the words from one of these mustard-covered strangers ringing in my ears: "That wasn't very funny, Rochelle." Clear words. Echoing words. Rochelle. Rochelle. Rochelle. Not only had I just left two people covered with mustard back in a parking lot, but at least one of them wasn't a stranger.

Although no one in the car physically recognized either victim, there was no doubt among any of us that the voice that just spoke was a familiar one. But whose? The longest minute of my life followed until I figured it out: *Miss Greatens, MY TYPING TEACHER!*

Miss Greatens, fresh out of college, was committed to making a strong professional impression on the business class students she taught. Her hair was always gathered on top of her head, large glasses covered her eyes and crisp business suits were her chosen attire. And yet outside of her work environment, she suddenly changed. Drastically. Her hair looked as though it grew a foot or so (since just this afternoon), she shrank a solid two inches (heels removed), contact lenses replaced glasses and her business suit was traded in for a sweatsuit. She no longer looked like Miss Greatens; she looked more like . . . well, *us!*

Situation assessment: WE HAD A PROBLEM. The Dodge Charger immediately went chasing back to the parking lot, but the joggers were nowhere in sight. Plan B was implemented. A telephone booth directory could provide her home address. Success. She lived right across from Kmart in an apartment complex.

Little did we know that Miss Greatens was doing some of her own phone referencing while we were trying to find her. First she called the school principal at home, then she called my parents. *(My life, as I knew it, was about to end.)* However, she hung up after the first two rings before anyone answered either call. She had decided to speak to us first.

And here we were.

Miss Greatens answered the door graciously, standing before us with mustard-stained clothes and tear-stained cheeks, wanting to hear what possible explanation warranted her pain. There was none. Absolutely none. What we had done was uncalled for. Our consciences made that perfectly clear as we poured out a flood of genuine remorse and tears to equal her own.

Then something extraordinary happened: *She forgave us.* Fully. Right there on the spot. She could have spoken to all of our parents about what happened, but didn't. She could have contacted school officials and sought stern reprimands for each of us, but didn't. And she could have held the incident over our heads for a very long time and reminded us of what we had done at will, but didn't.

Will we ever do anything like that again? NO WAY. You see, that is the power of forgiveness.

Rochelle M. Pennington

Call Me

"I know it's here somewhere." Cheryl drops her book bag at her feet so she can dig through her coat pockets. When she dumps her purse out onto the table, everyone waiting in line behind her groans.

Cheryl glances up at the lunch room clock. Only three minutes until the bell and this is the last day to order a yearbook, if you want your name imprinted in gold on the front. And Cheryl did, if only she could find her wallet. The line begins to move around her.

"Come on, Cheryl." Darcy might as well stamp her foot, she sounds so impatient. "We'll be late for class."

"Darcy, please!" Cheryl snaps back. Best friends or not, Darcy and Cheryl often frustrate each other. They are just so different. Today is a good example. Darcy had "budgeted" for her yearbook and ordered it the first day of school while Cheryl had almost forgotten . . . again.

"Darcy, my wallet's gone." Cheryl throws her things back into her purse. "My yearbook money was in it." The bell interrupts her search.

"Someone took it!" Darcy, as usual, is quick to point away from the bright side of things.

"Oh, I'm sure I just misplaced it," Cheryl hopes.

They rush into class just before the second bell rings. Darcy takes center stage to Cheryl's problem and happily spreads the news about the theft.

By gym the last hour, Cheryl is tired of being stopped and having to say over and over again, "I'm sure I just left it at home." Rushing into the locker room, she changes quickly and checks the list posted by the field door to see where her group is playing soccer, then hurries out to catch up with them.

The game was a close one, and Cheryl's team is the last one back to the locker room.

Darcy stands waiting for Cheryl by her locker. Cheryl brushes passed Juanita, the new girl. It's the shocked look on Darcy's face and the startled gasps of those around her that stop Cheryl.

There, at her feet, is her wallet.

"It fell out of her locker!" Darcy points at Juanita. "She stole it."

Everyone speaks at once.

"The new girl stole it."

"Darcy caught her red-handed."

"I knew there was something about her."

"Report her."

Cheryl turns and looks at Juanita. She's never really noticed her before, beyond her "new girl" label.

Juanita picks up the wallet and holds it out to Cheryl. Her hands are trembling. "I found it in the parking lot. I was going to give it to you before gym, but you were late."

Darcy's words spit anger. "I'm so sure!"

"Really. It's true." Juanita's voice is high and pleading.

Cheryl hesitates. Juanita's eyes begin to fill with tears.

Cheryl reaches for her wallet.

"I'm so glad you found it." Cheryl smiles. "Thanks, Juanita."

The tension around them breaks. "Good thing she found it." Everyone but Darcy agrees.

Cheryl does another quick change and then bangs her locker closed. "Hurry, Darcy. There's just enough time to order a yearbook."

"*If* there is any money left in your wallet."

"Not now, Darcy!"

"You are so naive!"

It isn't until they are standing in line that Cheryl opens her wallet.

"It's all here." Cheryl can't help feeling relieved. A small piece of paper flutters down from her wallet.

"She just didn't have time to empty it yet." Darcy bends down to pick up the note. "I know her type. I had her pegged the first day she came." She hands the note to Cheryl.

Cheryl reads it and then looks up at Darcy. "You had her pegged, all right. Maybe that's the problem. Maybe you spend too much time pegging people."

Darcy grabs the note, reads it and throws it back at Cheryl. "Whatever!" she says and stomps off.

Cheryl reads the note again.

Cheryl,

I found your wallet in the parking lot. Hope nothing is missing.

Juanita

P.S. My number is 555-3218. Maybe you could call me.

And Cheryl did.

Cynthia Hamond

The Player

It was his attitude that got me. That self-assured smile and those cocky mannerisms gave me the irresistible urge to challenge such conceit. I had never met a person so sure of himself. He assumed that when you first met him, you had no choice but to like him. It made me want to prove him wrong. I would show him that I could not only resist his charms, but that I could beat him at his own game.

So our relationship began as a battle, each trying to gain a foothold, trying to pull ahead of the other and prove our dominance. We waged an unrelenting war of mind games, insults and tests.

But somewhere in the middle of our warfare, the teasing became playful and we became friends. We found in each other not just a challenge, but someone to turn to when we didn't feel like fighting anymore. Josh loved to "communicate." He often talked for hours as I listened, covering every topic that affected him and his life. I soon realized that he was more concerned about himself than anything else. But because I didn't always have a lot to say, it didn't seem that it would be a conflict in our relationship.

It was several months after our friendship started that

Josh began a discussion about love. "It takes a lot for me to love someone," he told me, in a tone more serious than I had ever heard from him. "What I need is trust. I could never fall in love with someone who I didn't feel I could tell everything to. Like you. You're my favorite person in the entire world. I could tell you anything," he said, looking straight at me.

I blushed, unsure of what response I should give in return, afraid that whatever I said would betray the new emotions I had begun to feel for Josh over the past few weeks. The look in my eyes must have given me away, because from that moment on, it seemed that he began to do everything in his power to make me fall deeper and deeper into the way I felt about him. Was it love? He seemed to glow in the attention that I paid him. And I enjoyed adoring him. Yet it didn't take me very long to figure out that Josh had no intention of returning my devotion.

When we were alone, he would kiss me and hold me and tell me how special our relationship was to him, and that he didn't know anyone else who made him so happy. But a few weeks into our relationship, I found out that he was involved with another girl and had been for some time. The pain I felt at his betrayal was overwhelming, but I found I couldn't be angry with him. I felt sure inside that he really did care, and that it was his friendship that was important to me.

At school one day, I saw him standing with a group of girls, and by the flirtatious smile on his face, I could tell he had again been working his magic. "Josh!" I yelled down the hallway to him. He looked up at me, then back at the girls, and with a groupie under each arm, he turned and made his way in the opposite direction. I stood completely deflated, not wanting to acknowledge what had just happened. But I couldn't avoid the truth any longer. My "best friend" had ignored me so I wouldn't hurt the reputation he was working on.

After that, I began to watch Josh, not as someone who had a crush on him, but as an outside observer. I began to see the darker side of his personality. It was only when I moved away from him that my cloudy vision cleared. It was as if the shadow my adoration had thrown over the situation grew smaller, and I finally saw what I had not been able to see before.

Josh spent day after day making new acquaintances that he thought might adore him. He flirted with girls, knowing how to make them feel pretty. He knew how to play the game just right—to make sure that everyone felt they had his complete attention. When you were with him, you felt he was interested only in you. He hung out, telling jokes and acting cool, giving off an aura that made people want to be around him. But now I could see that he did it all for himself because he needed to be surrounded by people who thought he was great.

And while he acted as though he really cared about these people, I heard him belittle them behind their backs, saw him ignore them in the process of making new friends. I saw the pain on their faces that I understood only too well.

I talked to Josh once more after that day. Even though I understood his nature and was opposed to everything he stood for, there was still a part of me that wanted him to care, and still wanted things the way they used to be.

"What happened?" I asked him. I cringe when I think how pitiful I must have sounded. "I mean, I thought we were best friends. How can you just give up all the time we spent together? All the things we talked about? The . . . the love that you always told me was there?"

He shrugged and replied coldly, "Hey, these things happen," before he turned and walked away.

I stood, watching him go, with tears running down my face. I cried not for him, but for the friendship I thought we had, for the love I thought we had felt. I had lost the game in a big way.

Now, even though it was one of the most painful experiences I've ever endured, I am grateful for my "friendship" with Josh because it made me stronger. Now I know the kind of person and the kind of friend I never want to be.

Perhaps I won the game after all.

Kelly Garnett

"I want the prime rib with a baked potato.
My boyfriend isn't sure what he wants.
He can't commit to anything."

Kissing the Bully

I looked down at my skinny body and turned to the side. I was awkward; my knobby knees led down to thin, bony legs. I looked around, enviously watching as the other girls pulled on their bras and hooked the back. I pulled on the bra I barely fit into, the one I had forced my mom to take me to buy, just so you could see the outline through the back of my shirt. I was a late-bloomer; there was no questioning that.

I walked home from school with my equally skinny best friend Laura at my side; she had hidden her embarrassment of her not-yet-developed body with a larger-than-life attitude. It was the normal walk home: She and I were taunted by Ben and a few other boys our age who inevitably found a way to make me cry.

I reached my house, knowing that the phone would ring later that night with some crank call and muffled sounds of prepubescent boy's laughter. I knew that the same pattern would be repeated the next day: They would walk behind us on the way to school, laughing about the "wall," Ben's less-than-endearing reference to my chest.

To ease my despair, I was told, "They only do that because they like you." My dad reassured me that once I blossomed, they'd be begging to go out with me. I hadn't had a boyfriend yet, and it seemed like everyone else was well on his or her way to awkward handholding and spin-the-bottle games. I pined for some sort of attention from the opposite sex. I didn't realize at the time that the torture from Ben and his friends was actually attention.

By the ninth grade, Laura and I were no longer walking to school; we caught the number-three bus on our corner to the local high school. Ben, by this point, had moved on to hitting us with spitballs. So every morning, I had to clean the wads of gross spit-covered paper out of my hair, making sure the evidence was gone. I would yell at him to stop, which only provoked more torture. I had known him for four years at this point, and the funny thing was we considered each other friends. He would talk to me, if the other boys weren't around, and I knew, despite his tough exterior, that he actually enjoyed my company.

Throughout middle school, Ben maintained the ritual of Rollerblading to my house after school, but I'm sure he never told his friends that in the seventh grade he had held my hand down the street, teaching me to use the Rollerblades I had just received for my birthday. It seemed that the nicer he was to me in private, the meaner he had to be to me in public.

I vowed that once I "blossomed," he would want to be my boyfriend, that the group of boys who tortured me in middle school would long for me in high school. I had a cruel fantasy of one of them asking me out and my rejecting him coldly, in front of everyone. I wanted to make them feel the embarrassment I had felt during all those walks home, and on all the bus rides with spitwad-filled hair.

High school finally came along and, better late than

never, I did blossom. I grew out of my awkward, bony body. My wavy red hair grew longer and straightened itself out. Although I didn't transform, I grew up, more in mind than in body. I started to accept the freckles and felt blessed to be naturally thin. I even wore a little makeup. And my dad was right, it did happen. I finally had a boyfriend. He was from a different middle school than I had attended, and he was unaware of my uncomfortable beginnings.

I still saw Ben; we attended the same high school parties and shared the same group of friends. He teased me a bit, but it didn't really bother me as much. I went through a few boyfriends in high school, and it seemed that the awkward years were finally over.

This summer I returned home from my first year of college. Ben and I ran into each other. He stood about a foot taller than I did, and I realized how much he had grown up throughout our eight years of friendship. He lives on his own now and invited me over to see his new apartment. The walls were sparse; it looked like a college boy's room, which struck me as odd. I knew so many college boys, but it was hard for me to picture Ben as one. I still saw the skinny blond boy who sat behind me in eighth grade snapping my bra straps.

We started talking about those years, and we both laughed. A few other old friends filled the apartment, and one of Ben's old partners-in-crime leaned over and said, "You have gotten so pretty." I thanked him, smirking at the same time. It seemed like I had waited eight years for this, for my revenge.

I found myself sitting outside with Ben, and then, it happened. He leaned over, and he kissed me, something that had never happened between us before. For a second, I thought, *This is it, I can finally tell him off and embarrass him for all the times he belittled me.* But I didn't. I no longer needed revenge. I continued to look at him, and I asked, "Did you ever have a crush on me?"

And he responded, "I had a crush on you the whole time. I was just too embarrassed to tell you."

Lia Gay

A Difficult Lesson

Of all the words of tongue or pen, the saddest
are those . . . it might have been.
John Greenleaf Whittier

It was August 1984, Kalamazoo, Michigan, Western Michigan University. The temperature was in the mid-eighties, the sun was shining and it was my first day of college. And, as if all this weren't enough, it was also the day I met Cindy.

She was stunningly beautiful. The type of beauty that turned heads. Casual attire and sparse amounts of makeup reflected her confident and self-assured persona. No need to flaunt her beauty.

Cindy and I met under precarious terms on this special day. While riding up in the elevator, she gave me a smile, which I returned. We got off on the same floor, which shocked me into insinuating that she must have been mistaken. Boys and girls on the same floor? In college? I shrugged it off, still not believing. As I stood outside my room, waiting for my brother's arrival with a load of my stuff, Cindy walked down the hall directly toward me. As she approached me, the butterflies began to stir in my stomach. Outwardly I tried to be cool, confident and funny. I calmly said with a wide grin, "I am not waiting for you." Cindy shot back with "You're a jerk" and entered her dorm room key into the very next door. I could not believe the most beautiful girl in the whole dorm lived on the other side of my wall. So much for me having a clue.

I was able to overcome my less-than-desirable first impression and we began to date. By mid-November we were an inseparable pair. We were in love. For me, this type of love was a first. We had many things in common. We were both outgoing, fun seeking and shared the same musical tastes. We shared close to a year-and-a-half of wonderful but tumultuous times. Being in love brought forth many different emotions from within me, the majority of which were positive. Some however were negative. Negative emotions I had never dealt with, like jealousy, the most powerful of those emotions.

Cindy and I broke up, for good, in February of 1986. I had allowed jealousy to consume, smother and destroy my first love. When I last saw Cindy, the only emotion I shared with her was anger. My anger compelled me to present to her a full envelope of pictures of good times we shared together. Pictures that, in anger, I had torn into thousands of little pieces. I did not keep one single picture. Cindy opened the envelope and saw the pictures. The last words she spoke to me were the same as the first: "You're a jerk." This time she was right. The last words I spoke to her I will live with forever. I looked her in the eyes, with passion no longer of the loving kind, and said, "I don't care if I ever see you or hear from you again." And I walked away.

Unfortunately for me the story doesn't end with just another jealous young man messing up. Within that year, I began to grow up. I regretted the way I dealt with my jealousy and anger. I regretted the things I said and did that stemmed from those emotions. I wanted desperately to apologize, to make things right and tell her I didn't mean those hurtful things. I wanted to let her know that she was right, that I was a jerk and if she didn't forgive me I would understand. I wanted to tell her she was really special to me and I would always love her.

I finally got the nerve to call her one night in December however there was no answer. I found out two weeks later that my first love had died. She died the very night I had attempted to say I'm sorry, in a car accident involving a drunk driver. She died not knowing that I was sorry for my actions. She died too soon.

Rick Reed

Myself

A human being's first responsibility is to shake hands with himself.

Henry Winkler

I have to live with myself, and so
I want to be fit for myself to know
I want to be able as days go by
Always to look myself straight in the eye;
I don't want to stand, with the setting sun,
And hate myself for things I have done.
I don't want to keep on a closet shelf
A lot of secrets about myself,
And fool myself, as I come and go,
Into thinking that nobody else will know
The kind of man I really am;
I don't want to dress myself up in sham.
I want to go out with my head erect,
I want to deserve all man's respect;
And here in the struggle for fame and wealth,
I want to be able to like myself.
I don't want to look at myself and know

That I am a bluffer, an empty show.
I can never hide myself from me:
I see what others may never see,
I know what others may never know;
I never can fool myself, and so,
Whatever happens, I want to be
Self-respecting and guilt-free.

Peer Counsellor Workbook

Firmer Ground

I'd had a crush on him for as long as I could remember. His sandy blond hair was to his shoulders. His eyes were brown, his skin pale. He was quiet, mild-mannered. Most of all, I was drawn to his smile—when I could coax it out of him. I was in junior high. He was in high school.

He was my friend's brother and, for some reason, I believed he was taboo. Maybe because I knew instinctively my friend would be angry if I ever started to see him. Or maybe I knew the age gap of three years would not sit well with my parents. Or maybe, more than anything, I was terrified he'd reject me.

So I kept my feelings as quiet as a cat hiding from a pack of dogs. But every time I saw him at my friend Tina's house, my heart beat hard and I could barely breathe. When I saw him walking up the street alone, I'd rush over to him and glow in his warmth. He'd wave, smile a weak hello and ask me how I was doing.

He was an artist and a good one, and the day he gave me a pen drawing of a seagull soaring through the sky, I was in my glory. I saw it as a symbol, a sign perhaps, of affection shown by an older boy who felt it wise to keep his love for me inside. Of course, it was more likely that he just felt sorry for such a gangly kid.

It didn't matter. I cherished his artwork and truly believed that he would be a great artist someday. If only I had such talent, I'd moan. He'd always tell me that I probably did have a lot of talent. I just hadn't found it yet.

Somewhere as we were growing older and suffering the pangs of adolescence, Mike lost his ground. I'm not sure if he knew where to put his feet anymore. His family life was a disaster: a mentally ill mother, a father with a wicked second wife (at least that's how the children saw her) and a new baby who took all the interest away from three other kids.

Whenever I walked by his home, there was always a man—often a different man—parked in a car across the street from Mike's house. It happened so often that I began to wonder what was going on. I began to ask questions of my friends. I learned that my sweet, reserved Mike had turned into a high school drug dealer. Not the small kind of drug dealer. He was a big fish and according to my friends, he was in trouble. Someone was closing in on him—the police or the creeps who got him involved in the first place.

I knew that a lot of kids dabbled in drugs—mostly marijuana. But no one, and I mean no one, took the risk of dealing. The odds of getting hurt or busted were far too great in this middle-class neighborhood. I often wondered what led Mike there. Did he hate his parents? Did he feel lost? Did he want payback time for his dad remarrying and leaving his mom? Who knows what went on in his brain. I just wished he had talked to me because I really cared about him. The problem was that he didn't care. And I was too afraid to go to Mike and confront him about whether he was selling drugs.

When the knock on the door came, I looked out the

balcony of my house and saw one of my neighbors standing there. "I thought you and your family should know I
found Mike in the canyon this morning. My sons and I
were walking there and I saw Mike bowing as though he
were praying. It didn't look too good."

Our neighbor had held his young boys back as he
investigated. Mike was dead. He had hung himself from a
tree, and had died in a kneeling position on the ground,
his head slumped forward. The news pounded my face as
if a block of cement had struck. I thought I would pass
out, but instead, I was sobbing. Within the hour, I raced
up to Mike's to see how Tina was.

She was sitting on her bed, just staring out at empty
space. I would learn later that she was in shock. In a dull
voice, she explained that she and her older brother, Gary,
had known that Mike was dealing drugs. After Mike's body
was discovered, Gary went into Mike's room and cleaned
out Mike's top drawer before the police came. There,
tucked underneath a few shirts, was every drug imaginable: LSD, cocaine, pot and an abundance of colorful pills.
Soon after, Tina ran away. It took us hours to find her.

My parents tried to explain why Mike died. But they
couldn't. They didn't even know he was a dealer. They
didn't know the ugly things we kids faced going to school
every day. It was a trying time not only because Mike
died, but because I was shocked to peel away the layers
and find a Mike I had never known. Or maybe he was that
kind, sweet boy who let his difficult life suck him into a
world of deceit, fast bucks and danger.

To this day, I always wonder if he really killed himself
or if some other drug dealers helped him along the way.
It was just too odd that he had supposedly hung himself
from a thin tree limb but was kneeling, his weight
supported by the earth.

I will never know the answer. But I do know this: He

was a good artist. I kept that drawing he gave me for years after, always looking at it with wonder and admiration, wishing I could sketch that way.

I also know that along the way Mike lost his ground, but he gave me a lot to think about, and what I thought about gave me strength. My family moved to the East Coast my first year of high school. My new friends were just beginning to experiment with drugs, and there was tremendous peer pressure for me to go along.

But by now, I felt old and weary when it came to drugs. Been there, done that, seen what they can do. I decided I wanted the chance to know what I was going to be in the future. Mike had given me some firm ground to stand on.

Diana L. Chapman

Love and Belonging

Walking down the steps of the psychology building, I spot my buddy Walter and his girlfriend, Anna. Walt and I have known each other almost all our lives. We grew up next door to each other, and fought and played our way through elementary school, adolescence, junior high and high school. Our parents had been best friends, and life even as recently as a year ago seemed so simple, so secure.

But now, while I'm struggling with my parents' divorce, Walter's world is intact—his parents are still together and living in the same house where he grew up. My mom is alone now in our house, while Dad is living the life of a newlywed with his second wife, in an apartment across town. I feel my stomach churn as I think of that, and mild irritation as Walter puts his arm around Anna.

"Hey, Jesse," he says as he sees me. I notice a sudden, self-conscious grin wash over his face. "How was the exam?"

"Oh, okay, I guess." I wish Anna would disappear. Walter's apparent happiness irritates me, and I suddenly feel very tired. "What are you up to?" I don't care if I seem rude in ignoring Anna.

"Well," Walter begins, and his grip around Anna's shoulder tightens, "we're on our way to check out some CDs at that new sound shop down the street. Want to come along?"

"Nah, I think I'll take a nap before my next class."

Anna speaks up. "How are you doing these days, Jesse?" I can see the sympathy in her eyes, and I hate her.

"I'm fine—just great. Life couldn't be better."

"Well . . ." she struggles with what to say next. I find myself enjoying her obvious discomfort. "Sorry you can't go with us." But I hear relief in her voice even as she says it. Walter takes Anna's hand, and together they cross the street.

Why should they seem so happy and look so secure? They don't have a clue as to what's going on in the real world.

I turn and walk down the sidewalk and across the Commons. Maybe it's true, what my Coach Carter said, that I have my antennae out these days. It seems as if every couple reminds me of the failure in my family.

"How can this have happened to my family, Carter? Why didn't I realize what was happening? Maybe I could have done something!"

Just then Carter picked up a crystal paperweight from his desk and tossed it to me. I caught it purely from reflex.

"Why did you do that?" I asked, half mad–half serious.

Looking around the room, he said, "You knew you had to be careful with that paperweight, didn't you, Jesse?"

"Sure. It might break." I put it back on his desk.

"People take care of things that seem obviously fragile. Think about it. When you buy a house, you don't expect it to maintain itself. Or a car; you make sure you do things like change the oil every few thousand miles and buy tires when they are worn.

"With so many things in life, Jesse, you expect to have to care for them, keep a close eye on them, nurture them.

We're more careful with an insignificant paperweight than we are with our closest relationships."

"You're telling me that my mom and dad were careless with their marriage?" I heard my voice rise unnaturally, my fingers clenched in my palms.

"Not necessarily careless, Jesse. Perhaps they just expected it to flourish on its own. But marriage, like anything else, won't flourish in an environment of neglect. No one should take a good relationship for granted."

"But what do I do? You're telling me to accept all this— Mom and Dad splitting up; Dad marrying someone I don't even know. She can't take Mom's place. No way!"

"I'm suggesting that you try to accept it," Carter said gently, "because for you, that's all you can do. You can't change your parents, and you can't change what happened. You don't have to love your stepmother as you do your mother, and probably no one expects you to. But to get beyond this and to be able to handle your parents' new, more complex relationships—and your future relationships with women—then you do need to learn to accept what has happened."

"Well, I just don't see how you can ask me to do that. I can't stand seeing them apart!"

As I stood up to leave his study he said, "I know you're feeling pretty alone right now. But believe me, you'd be surprised at how many young people have sat in this office and asked me why divorce had to happen in their family. Maybe it will help if you remember that there are a lot of people who are hurting just like you. And remember—this divorce is not your fault. Don't ever forget that."

Walking down the street, I see a city bus slow down and then stop at the corner. On impulse, I get on.

I pay the driver and begin to look for a seat.

An elderly couple is seated at the back of the bus. I sit beside them.

We ride in silence toward town. I glance over at the couple and notice that they are holding hands. The wedding ring on the old woman's finger is a dull gold, and there is a tiny diamond in the center of the band.

I watch as the old man rests his left hand on top of hers, and I see that his wedding ring matches hers. His, too, is scratched and dull with age.

As they sit in companionable silence, I notice the resemblance of their features. Both wear glasses, and both have short, pure white, wiry hair. They even wear the same style of shirt—simple white cotton, short-sleeved.

Occasionally the woman points at something as we pass by, and the man nods in agreement. I am mystified, and yet I feel a sense of peace sitting next to them.

Before too long we reach their stop. A row of neat, white frame houses lines the quiet side street.

The old man gets up slowly and pulls his walking stick from the seat next to him. He waits patiently for his wife to get up before he starts to walk to the front of the bus. The woman rises just as slowly and pulls a blue cardigan over her thin arms. He takes her hand, and as they turn to walk to the front of the bus, I catch his eye. I can't let them leave without asking, "How long have you two been married?"

He looks inquisitively at her. She smiles and gently shrugs her shoulders. It doesn't matter. It hasn't mattered for some time.

Finally he says in a raspy voice, "I don't know exactly— many years." Then he adds, "Most of our lives."

They walk down the aisle of the bus and are gone.

I lean back in my seat. It takes me a few moments to realize that the cold, hard knot in my stomach doesn't seem so tight now. And the face reflected back at me from the glass of the bus window looks a little less tense.

Watching the colors of the trees slide by, my mind wanders back to the old couple and finally comes to rest on my parents. The realization quietly dawns on me that I have been looking for answers when maybe I don't have to know at all. I don't have to hurt for them and me, too. I don't have to have all the answers about love and life and why things work out the way they do sometimes. Maybe no one has the answers.

"Hey, buddy," the bus driver says to me. I look up and realize I'm alone on the bus. We're downtown at the square. "This is the end of the line. You can get off here or go back."

I think for a minute. "Do you go by that new sound shop close to campus?"

"Yeah, sure."

"Well, drop me off there," I say. "There's someone there. A friend. And I need to talk to him."

T. J. Lacey

What I Wish I'd Known Sooner

For the past year or two, I have devoted a section of my home page on the Internet to a list entitled "What I Wish I'd Known Sooner." Since I am seventeen, there are a lot of stupid things I do that make me wish I had already known not to do them! Anyone can add to this list—I have received additions from all over the world, by people of all ages. I often add to it myself (after the fact)!

Some are lighthearted, some are serious, all are very true. Here are a few of the gems:

- Don't drink grape juice while wearing a white shirt and driving to school.
- Don't let your life wait for other people.
- Dropping a cellular phone into a bathtub of water kinda kills the phone.
- Your mother will find out if you dye your hair purple.
- You haven't really lived until you've gotten a 48 on an Advanced Placement U.S. History test.
- Don't ever fall in love with someone who is more than one thousand miles away from you. It usually doesn't work.
- Milk crates make boring pets.

- If it hurts, DON'T DO IT AGAIN!
- That which does not kill you will ultimately make you stronger.
- Speaking in public gets easier with practice.
- Don't sprint around a pool if you're trying to impersonate Jim from Huck Finn.
- Ten years from now most of what we freak out about won't make any difference.
- All that's gold doesn't glisten.
- Zits always pop up when you really can't afford for them to pop up.
- Always stay after class because that's where connections are made.
- When in doubt, duck. When certain, don't bother, 'cause you're already screwed.
- While driving a car through a gate, always, ALWAYS make sure the gate is open! The consequences might be fatal to your car.
- If you're not living (I mean really living), you're dead already.
- Never pierce your belly button in the dark.
- Just because someone flirts with you incessantly doesn't necessarily mean he or she likes you.
- If your calculus teacher tells you to quit talking after a test or he'll give you a zero for your test grade, he means it. Really.
- Sometimes smart people can do very, very stupid things.
- Being nice to people will get you far.
- The one person you can truly love is often right in front of you.
- Never, ever, EVER let a member of the opposite sex make you compromise your standards. Never.
- Nothing is ever too good to be true (said by Michael Faraday).
- If you start to like a girl, her roommate will immediately start liking you.

- Parents aren't around forever, and you need to treasure them while they are.
- Don't take the SAT twice if you already have a good score in the first place.
- Never do something if the risk is greater than the reward.
- Think carefully before you act.
- Dreaming and doing go hand in hand.
- Life moves fast, but not so fast that you can't slow down to enjoy it.
- Instead of waiting for life to get better, do something about it.
- You REALLY should do what needs to be done NOW, and not later. Procrastination is the easiest way, but not the most profitable.
- If your intuition is telling you not to do something, then don't. Your intuition is not stupid!
- Cereal is a vital staple food for all college students. Who cares how ridiculous you look eating it at 7:30 P.M.?
- If he doesn't respect you, then he's not worth any of your time.
- Learn to play an electric guitar: young women really dig it.
- Don't juggle knives unless you're really, really good at it.
- If at first you don't succeed, try again. Then give up. No sense being ridiculous about it.
- Sticking things up your nose isn't the smartest idea in the world.
- You can't light fireworks in the basement and not get caught.
- Hair is flammable. *Very* flammable.
- Never ever trust your friend with a pair of scissors against your hair.
- Dyeing hair strawberry blond that is already strawberry blond makes it turn strawberry pink.
- White dogs and black pants don't mix.

- God doesn't make junk!
- Someday you will look back on this and it will all seem funny.
- You never know when you're making a memory.
- The heart does heal and you will love like this again— except that when you do, you'll deny that you ever loved like this before.
- Nothing matters if you don't have loved ones to share it with. Your siblings are incredibly precious. If you don't know this now, you will—trust me!
- If you can laugh at yourself, you are going to be fine.
- If you allow others to laugh with you, you'll be great!
- Kissing is the most fun thing. Dancing is almost as fun.

Meredith Rowe

A Wider Classroom

Our white van meandered its way through the broken West Virginia landscape and pulled up alongside Jim's avocado-colored house. As the doors opened, we poured out with hammers in hand. We were eight teenagers on a week-long service project to repair the homes of the less fortunate residing in the Appalachian mountains. The area seemed to contradict itself, for it held so much beauty yet housed so much poverty. Maybe we hailed ourselves as being able to serve those people in need; I do not think we ever imagined that what they could give us would perhaps be more valuable then any services we could render.

We rotated jobs as we basked in the southern sun; some of us scraped and painted windows, while others stained the deck or worked on the roof. All the while Jim sat in a lawn chair observing us: the kindest of old men, only too sorry that he could not labor alongside us on the ladders. We passed the time with inside jokes and songs, truly enjoying ourselves regardless of the tedium of treating window after window as Jim just silently observed.

As the clock neared noon, we took our lunch break

in the shade of a small tree in Jim's front yard. Sam, our moderator, planted Jim's chair beside us and announced that since he was eager to help in any way possible, Jim would lead us in a before-meal prayer. He kept it succinct and we all began to eat.

"Let me tell you a story. . . ." he then began. And from the pit of his humble heart he began to unravel his eighty-some-odd years for us. He was a school teacher and a baseball coach who had a loyal dog named Pretty-Face. He told of old hunting expeditions in the mountains where his life was almost lost to a bear, and he talked of conquering a rattlesnake, even showing us the rattles.

Then his cavernous eyes just wandered off as if he was no longer talking solely for our benefit, but more for his own. He described that day his dog died, as fat tears rolled down his weathered cheeks and he gripped the end of his cane. He recalled her loyalty to the end as with one last thump of the tail, looking up at him, Pretty-Face passed on. He remembered his wife gazing up at him much the same way seconds before her death.

He always affectionately called his wife "Mama," and he told of how she'd always stayed up until the small hours of the morning to bake the bread for the next day, while he, often tired from a long day of teaching or hunting, would retire to bed.

"Why didn't I just stay up with her?" he said in a distant voice as his eyes gazed beyond us. "Why couldn't I have just taken that extra time? Why?"

I remember how profoundly those words rang inside of me. Here was a man brimming with wisdom and reflections on his life, telling me to make the most of mine, to take that extra time with those I love. I was inspired; I was mesmerized by this extraordinary old man that I had thought I was helping. Jim's house was not a job at all, it was a classroom.

Kate McMahon
Submitted by Olive O'Sullivan

Forever Changed

The great use of life is to spend it for something that will outlast it.

William James

Every morning when I wake up, I peel back the blankets that keep my body warmth hostage and look around my room. I see cherished family photos, my favorite mahogany dresser and of course my love beads that hang from the windows. I can't imagine my life without a loving family surrounding me or a roof shielding me from the night.

This past July, I went on a mission trip to Monterrey, Mexico, with my youth group. I sat on a bus for two days, not knowing what to expect. My friends on the bus described all the bugs that had infested the orphanages we were to work at for the next week. They told me how dirty everything would be and how dangerous the streets were. Secretly, I was hoping the bus would turn around somehow. But it did not. The first night we arrived, a man said, "We have come here to change Mexico, but instead, Mexico will change us."

Each morning during the hour-and-a-half bus ride to the orphanage, I would think of how little I had slept the night before, how tired I was, and how there was no air conditioning on the bus. But, as soon as the orphanage came into view, all those feelings melted away. The children would run up to the gates, scream, and jump up and down because we had finally arrived. The first day I walked cautiously inside the metal gates. I saw one girl with a huge smile on her face. When I walked over to her, she gave me a hug. I looked around at all the other children. All were smiling. All were laughing. They were not upset, nor complaining about their lives and living conditions.

I met a little girl at the orphanage named Erica. She had short black hair and a big scar beneath her nose. I picked her up and swung her around. She squealed with laughter. Every day when we arrived, she always ran up to me, gave me a hug and kissed my cheeks. I began looking forward to this.

The whole time, I was thinking, *Who would give such a wonderful child up?* I saw other children in the orphanage. They did not fight over the toys we brought them. Instead, they shared them because they wanted everyone to experience the joy of the new toys.

On the last day, the kids were singing songs to us. Rose, the lady in charge, told us that one of the children wanted to share her story with us. To my amazement, Erica went up to speak. She smiled at me and began her story: "I am so happy to be here in the orphanage." *Happy*, I thought. *Who would be happy to be in an orphanage?* "When I was in my house," she continued, "my parents used to beat me. They threw me against the wall and hurt me."

When she was done, I ran over to tell her how proud I was of her. I looked down and saw the scar near her nose. Now I knew how she got it.

The day we left is a day I'll never forget. Everyone was crying. I held Erica for fifteen minutes, too scared to put her down. I kissed her scar, hoping, once more, to erase her memories. I told her I loved her. She stopped crying and smiled. When our time with the children was done, they waved once again through the gates. This time it was good-bye.

When I came home, I looked in my room while unpacking. I looked at all my clothes hanging in my closet on multicolored hangers. The visions of Erica's closet with two shirts in it flashed before my eyes. She tried to give me one of her stuffed animals in return for my friendship. I told her I did not need one. She said she didn't either because she had two. Erica is only seven. It will take me a long time to learn what she already knows.

JoLynn Shopteese

Children's Eyes

What kind of world is it my friend
   that little children see?
I wonder if they see God first
   because they just believe?

Do they see strength in caring eyes
   who watch them as they play—
or maybe love through gentle hands
   that guide them on their way?

Do you think they dream of future times
   when they would be a king—
or just enjoy their present life
   while with their friends they sing?

Do they see the acts of kindness
   done for people who are poor?
Is the very best in everyone
   what they are looking for?

And when the day is over,
   as they close their eyes to sleep,

do they look forward to tomorrow
with its promises to keep?

If this is what the children see,
then it should be no surprise,
the world would be a better place
if we all had children's eyes.

Tom Krause

China's Story

China was fourteen, she gave what she got
She had many friends, who loved her a lot.
She loved them back, too, and would always be
    there,
But at prettier girls, she could not help but stare.

You must understand, that this group was a sight,
With their Cover Girl masks, and their shirts way
    too tight.
The guys hung around them, as though in a trance,
They were always the first ones who were asked to
    dance.

They seemed so secure, knowing just what to say.
And they said what they said in *the* coolest of ways
They never were seen without smiles on their
    faces.
Their clothes were real tight in all the right places.

You can see what I mean, when I say they were
    cool.
They were by far the sexiest girls in the school.

So China dreamed on, by day and by night,
Wishing her shirts would fit her as tight.
She wondered what contest she would have to win.
For, she'd give up the world, and her life to fit in.

She kept it a secret, hoping nobody knew,
But her friends caught on fast, and they found it
    was true.
They tried to warn her of their pretentious way.
But China grew more and more stubborn each day.

As cool as they were, and as hot as their show,
They struggled in school and their grades were
    quite low.
The groups of girls smoked, and were known to
    drink beer,
But this was not stuff China wanted to hear.

So China tried hard to fit in with the clique,
She giggled at jokes that she knew were just sick.
She gave her attention to these cool girls alone,
She dressed just like them, in a style not her own.

China's old friends feared her drifting away,
They were losing her slowly, and didn't know what
    to say.
They told China the truth, that the group was all fake,
But their words of advice, China just wouldn't take.

Why aren't they happy for me? China thought,
I don't act like myself, but now look where I've got.
She thought her old friends were jealous and tart,
She was truthfully happy, deep down in her heart.

China laughed at her old friends, along with her
new,
They made fun of so many and smiled at so few.
China's new friends were cool, she was in with the
clan,
She was treated like they were, she was happy
again.

China's old group of friends sadly melted away,
They left China alone, but watched close every
day.
They longed for her friendship, the warmth in her
smile.
And hoped she'd miss them, and come back in a
while.

But the jokes kept on coming, so the group with a
sigh,
Turned their backs on harsh China, and walked
silently by.
The pain was too deep and the torture too hard,
Her old friend's poor hearts had been torn out and
scarred.

As all this did happen, the cool did their thing,
They giggled and gossiped and made actions sting.
They mutated China, the best that they could,
And taught her to be like a glamour girl should.

China went to parties, she got into fights,
She became really cool, but during the night,
She tried to discover just what was the scoop,
Why she wasn't content in her newly found group.

Then one day it hit her, came into her head,
That the answer was one that she truly did dread.
She had run ahead quickly and back round the bends,
She had left her companions, she had ditched her
true friends.

China realized her error, "This group's not a sight,
With their makeup done perfect and hair fixed just
right.
That's not what they look like, it's a lie what you
see,
It's the Maybelline models they wish they could
be."

Then early one night, around seven o'clock,
A girl opened her door to the sound of a knock.
Out in the cold, standing there in the rain,
Stood teary-eyed China, her old self again.

Neither one spoke, as she ushered her in,
The girl knew from experience, where China had
been.
She had also once felt that those girls were the best,
But those long-ago thoughts, she had put down to
rest.

The girls sat up talking for a good length of time,
China knew in her heart that she would be just fine.
She couldn't believe just how much she'd been
blessed,
That her loving dear friends would forgive her like
this.

This tale ends happy, but not all stories will,
Some friends aren't so forgiving, they go in for the
kill.

China was lucky, but you may not be,
So choose your friends wisely, and help others see.

The moral is not to have one group of friends,
From a particular table, with particular trends.
It's to teach of the truth, that those girls tried to
   hide,
You will always be cool if it comes from inside.

Libby Barnes

Accentuating Difference

Julia and I met in math class—right before lunch. We soon realized that we both hated word problems, both loved egg salad sandwiches and both thought Bobby Bisbee was the only boy we could ever kiss. During recesses, we were inseparable. One Friday, Julia had an idea. "Hey, let's make plans for the weekend," she said. "We could have a sleep-over or something."

We were both so excited we couldn't sit still during math, or any other class. But when the bell sounded the end of school, I suddenly got very nervous.

"Hi, Talia. How was school today?" my mom asked with a smile. Today, her warm and caring hello did not sound comforting. Instead, all I heard in the loving syllables was her thick foreign accent.

I was so embarrassed. Julia and I were no longer the same. The sound of my mom's voice made me feel like an outsider. What would Julia think?

I didn't have to wait long to find out. From across the schoolyard, I saw Julia pulling her mother towards us.

"Hello, I'm Julia's mother. I hear the girls want to get together this weekend."

"Oh, that sounds wonderful," my mom replied.

But all I heard was the *v* replacing the *w* and the roll of the *r*: *vonderrrful*.

I was mortified. Were they staring? Had Julia changed her mind? Did I dare look into her eyes? I did. She answered my unspoken fears with an excited smile while our moms exchanged phone numbers. That Sunday we went to the movies.

Years later, Julia and I sit on my bed talking. Graduation is only days away. Julia has plans of becoming a math and physics major and I no longer like egg salad sandwiches. Neither of us has ever kissed Bobby Bisbee. (There are others who have left much more permanent marks on our hearts and our lips.) My mom comes into my room to see what we're up to. We tell her of our plans to spend the afternoon with friends at the beach, and maybe see a movie after dinner. "That sounds wonderful," she replies.

I no longer hear the *v* replacing a *w* in her speech. But I think it still does. Somewhere in the passing of math classes and lunch recesses, I realized that it is my mom's cheerful, compassionate nature that people hear, and love. She shares my excitements and frustrations with overflowing compassion, tender words and rolling *r*s. Sometimes, she still reminds me that I am different. But I think that differences between people are as valuable as similarities. As my mom closes the door, I look at Julia and smile. Our friendship has been strengthened not only by our shared interests but also by our distinctly differing ones.

Daphna Renan

6

TOUGH
STUFF

The soul would have no rainbow had the eyes no tears.

John Vance Cheney

I'll Always Be with You

On a quiet September night our seventeen-year-old son, Mike, got into his cherished yellow '68 Mustang, his heart broken after the sudden ending of his first romance. His girlfriend had told him she was going to get engaged to someone else. Sitting in the car he had so lovingly restored and treasured, Mike shot and killed himself. In the note he left, he wrote: "I wish I could have learned how to hate. . . . Don't blame yourselves, Mom and Dad. I love you." His note ended "Love, Mike, 11:45 P.M." At 11:52 P.M. that night, we and Mike's older brother, Vic, pulled into the driveway alongside Mike's car—seven minutes too late!

It wasn't long before stories about Mike started coming in from all sides. We heard many of them for the first time. His oldest friend, Danny, told us about the time he was frightened to have his picture taken in kindergarten. "It's easy. Just go like this," Mike assured him as he grinned from ear to ear, displaying the bright smile that became his trademark. Years later, when a classmate became a single parent, Mike helped her care for her baby. One of Mike's friends was shot in a drive-by shooting but recovered, with Mike's support. When his high school band went to Florida to march in the Orange Bowl parade, Mike assisted a fellow band member who was blind.

A young mother phoned to tell the story of how Mike had helped her when her car broke down. She and her children were stranded on the roadside when Mike came by. He stopped, showed her his driver's license to assure her he wouldn't hurt her and her children, and got her car started. He followed them home to make sure they arrived safely.

One of Mike's friends revealed the truth about why Mike never got the new transmission we thought he planned to install in his Mustang in preparation for the local drag race. Mike canceled his order for the transmission and instead bought two transmissions from a salvage yard—so his friend could get his car running, too. Mike had told us the reason he didn't buy the brand-new transmission was that it just wasn't right for the way he wanted his car to perform.

Mike's niece was born with cerebral palsy. He learned how to replace her tracheotomy tube and how to perform CPR, should the need arise. He learned sign language with her (the tracheotomy tube made it impossible for her to speak), and they would "sing" together in sign language.

In the days following Mike's death, many teenagers came to comfort us and asked if they could do anything to help. Our response to their question was: "Don't ever do this. Don't commit suicide. Reach out to someone and ask for help!" Before Mike's memorial service, Mike's close friends met with us to share their grief, tell their stories about their friendship with him and discuss the tragedy of teen suicide. We talked about ways to prevent teen suicide. This was how the Yellow Ribbon Project came to life.

We decided to establish a foundation dedicated to eliminating suicide, a leading cause of death among teens.

Within days after Mike's death, we began printing pocket-sized cards that read:

YELLOW RIBBON PROJECT
In loving memory of Michael Emme

THIS RIBBON CARD IS A LIFELINE! It carries the message that there are those who care and will help. If you are in need and don't know how to ask for help, take this card to a counselor, teacher, clergy, parent or friend and say:

"I NEED TO USE MY YELLOW RIBBON!"

Someone, remembering Mike's beloved yellow Mustang, had the idea of attaching yellow ribbons to the cards, which we did. At Mike's memorial service we set out a basket containing five hundred of these yellow-ribbon cards. By the end of the service, the basket was empty (and Mike's Mustang was covered with one hundred yellow miniature roses, put there by his friends).

Mike's tragic death made us decide to help others, just as Mike did during his life. In the time since Mike's death, the Yellow Ribbon Project has touched—and saved—the lives of teens around the world. We receive many letters from teenagers about the Yellow Ribbon Project with comments such as:

"Your Web site has helped me recover from my depression."

"I've tried to commit suicide several times. This time I found the Yellow Ribbon card in my pocket and held onto it until a friend came by and I was able to give them the card. They recognized that I was suicidal and got me help."

"Thank you for being there to let those without hope know that there is always someone who cares."

Mike's final letter to us contained another important message. In that letter he told us, "I'll always be with you." Every time we speak to a group of teenagers or receive a letter from a teen or child who needs help, we know Mike's words are true.

Dale and Dar Emme

[EDITORS' NOTE: *This story, which was first printed in* A 3rd Serving of Chicken Soup for the Soul *in April 1996, has resulted in an even greater distribution of The Yellow Ribbon Project. The following are excerpts from some of the letters the Emmes received.*]

My name is Jessica and I am a senior in high school. I was very deeply touched by your story. I am a survivor of depression and suicidal impulses. I've struggled with this for the past five years and if I hadn't had someone who reached out to help me, I would not be here.

Last week a senior in high school shot himself. What if someone had stopped him and asked him how he was and really meant it? I think that would have made the difference between life and death.

So if you could please send information, suggestions and ribbons, I would greatly appreciate it. I've wanted to get the message out about teen suicide but never knew how. Thank you for helping me.

Jessica Magers

I found out about The Yellow Ribbon Project in A 3rd Serving of Chicken Soup for the Soul. *Your story really made me think about how much my friends and family mean to me, and if an occasion should arise when they do use their ribbon then I will be ever more grateful for your idea of creating The Yellow Ribbon Project. Thank you,*

Nicole Nero

Two months ago I broke up with my boyfriend who I loved very much. I could not deal with the pain and emptiness so I attempted suicide. I spent the night in I.C.U., the pills I took caused me to stop breathing. Because I am only sixteen, a straight-A student with everything going for me, this event shocked me and I realized I have a lot to live for and also my parents could not bear it if I were dead. So I am writing to ask if I could get two of your yellow ribbons. One for me and for my best friend. Thank you very much,

Jen Vetter

My Story

The journey in between what you once were and who you are now becoming is where the dance of life really takes place.

Barbara De Angelis

I never thought about killing myself; it just became a condition. Kind of like catching a cold. One minute you are fine, and the next minute you are sick. Whenever people would talk about suicide, I would think to myself, "I would never do that." Why would someone want to do something so final, so stupid?

For me, I just wanted the pain to stop. And it got to the point where I was willing to do whatever it took to make that happen. It started with the usual stuff. . . .

I am sixteen. I spend the summer with my mom and during the school year I live with my dad. I feel like an inconvenience to both of them. At my mom's I have no room. My mom isn't there for me when I need her because she always has something more important to do. At least, that is how it feels.

I was having trouble with my friends. The ones I had

not lost already to "different lifestyles" were unable to help me. In their own words, my problems were "too much" for them. The intensity of my pain scared them, like it did me.

Oh, yeah . . . did I mention my boyfriend, John, had dumped me that day? My first boyfriend had left me, too. He said I had become impossible to love and now John was gone, too. And it wasn't that I would be without him that mattered . . . it was me. What was wrong with me? Why is it so hard to love me and why is it that when it gets hard, everyone bails?

I was alone. All I had were the voices in my head telling me I blew it, I was too needy, I was never going to be loved once someone really got to know me. I felt that I wasn't even good enough to be loved by my own parents.

You know how, when you are really hurting, you feel like you can just call the person (the boyfriend, the friend) and tell him or her how much it hurts and they'll say, "Oh, I am so sorry; I didn't mean to hurt you; hang on, I will be right there"? Well, I called and I was crying, and I said it hurts too much, please come talk to me. He said he couldn't help me . . . and he hung up.

I went into my mom's bathroom and took a bottle of Tylenol PM, some tranquilizers and a couple pain pills I had left from an injury. Soon the pain would be over.

I will spare you the gruesome details of what followed. It was a whole new kind of pain. Physically, I puked until I couldn't move. Emotionally, I was more scared than I have ever been. I did not want to die. (Statistics show that immediately after "attempting" suicide, the person desperately wants to live . . . not die, which makes it even sadder to think about those who do succeed.) Luckily for me, I did not die. But I hurt my body (my stomach still aches). And I scared and hurt a lot of people. I scared myself, but I didn't die and I can't even begin to tell you how happy I am about that.

I cringe every time someone else finds out. I did not want to write this story, but I did want to help anyone else who might be thinking about it or who is in a lot of pain.

It has been a month since that night. I have laughed at least five hundred times, many of those real "pee your pants" kind of laughing. I have a therapist who really cares about me, and we are making real progress in building up my confidence. She is also helping my mom and dad be "better parents." I have realized that they really do care and that they are doing the best that they can. I have a new friend who has gone through some hard stuff herself. My intense feelings do not scare her, and we know what it means to "be there" for someone you care about. I have worked things out with some of my old friends and we are closer than ever. I have earned five hundred dollars and spent it all on myself . . . without guilt (well, maybe a little). And I am starting to forgive myself.

Oh, yeah . . . I met a guy. He is really sweet and he knows "my story." We have agreed to take things really slow.

These are only a few of the things I would have missed. Life gets really hard sometimes and really painful. For me, I couldn't feel everyone else's love because I had forgotten how to love myself. I'm learning now—learning how to accept, forgive and love myself. And I'm learning that things change. Pain *does* go away, and happiness is the other side. Although the pain comes back, so does the happiness. It is like waves in the ocean coming and going . . . coming and going . . . breathing in and breathing out.

Lia Gay

Just One Drink

There's a small cross by the side of Highway 128, near the town of Boonville. If this cross could talk, it would tell you this sad story:

Seven years ago my brother, Michael, was at a friend's ranch. They decided to go out for dinner. Joe arrived and volunteered to drive—after just one drink.

Lightheartedly, the four friends traveled the winding road. They didn't know where it would end—nobody did. Suddenly, they swerved into the opposite lane, colliding with an oncoming car.

Back home we were watching *E.T.* on video in front of a warm fire. Then we went to bed. At 2:00 A.M. a police officer woke my mom with the devastating news. Michael had been killed.

In the morning, I found my mother and sister crying. I stood there bewildered. "What's wrong?" I asked, rubbing my sleepy eyes.

Mom took a deep breath. "Come here . . ."

Thus began a grueling journey through grief, where all roads lead to nowhere. It still hurts to remember that day. The only thing that helps is telling my story, hoping you will remember it if you are tempted to get into a car with someone who has had a drink—even just one drink.

Joe chose the road to nowhere. He was convicted of manslaughter and served time. However, the real punishment is living with the consequences of his actions. He left us with an ache in our hearts that will never go away, a nightmare that will haunt him—and us—for the rest of our lives. And a small cross by the side of Highway 128.

Chris Laddish
Dedicated with love to the memory of Michael Laddish

Dead at 17

Agony claws my mind. I am a statistic. When I first got here, I felt very much alone. I was overwhelmed by grief, and I expected to find sympathy.

I found no sympathy. I saw only thousands of others whose bodies were as badly mangled as mine. I was given a number and placed in a category. The category was called "traffic fatalities."

The day I died was an ordinary school day. How I wish I had taken the bus! But I was too cool for the bus. I remember how I wheedled the car out of Mom. "Special favor," I pleaded. "All the kids drive." When the 2:50 P.M. bell rang, I threw my books in the locker. Free until tomorrow morning! I ran to the parking lot, excited at the thought of driving a car and being my own boss.

It doesn't matter how the accident happened, I was goofing off—going too fast, taking crazy chances. But I was enjoying my freedom and having fun. The last thing I remember was passing an old lady who seemed to be going awfully slow. I heard a crash and felt a terrific jolt. Glass and steel flew everywhere. My whole body seemed to be turning inside out. I heard myself scream.

Suddenly, I awakened. It was very quiet. A police officer was standing over me. I saw a doctor. My body was mangled. I was saturated with blood. Pieces of jagged glass were sticking out all over. Strange that I couldn't feel anything. Hey, don't pull that sheet over my head. I can't be dead. I'm only seventeen. I've got a date tonight. I'm supposed to have a wonderful life ahead of me. I haven't lived yet. I can't be dead!

Later I was placed in a drawer. My folks came to identify me. Why did they have to see me like this? Why did I have to look at Mom's eyes when she faced the most terrible ordeal of her life? Dad suddenly looked very old. He told the man in charge, "Yes—he is our son."

The funeral was weird. I saw all my relatives and friends walk toward the casket. They looked at me with the saddest eyes I've ever seen. Some of my buddies were crying. A few of the girls touched my hand and sobbed as they walked by.

Please—somebody—wake me up! Get me out of here. I can't bear to see Mom and Dad in such pain. My grandparents are so weak from grief they can barely walk. My brother and sister are like zombies. They move like robots. In a daze. Everybody. No one can believe this. I can't believe it, either.

Please don't bury me! I'm not dead! I have a lot of living to do! I want to laugh and run again. I want to sing and dance. Please don't put me in the ground! I promise if you give me just one more chance, God, I'll be the most careful driver in the whole world. All I want is one more chance. Please, God, I'm only seventeen.

John Berrio

"Gabby, You're Sooo Skinny"

I am a straight-A student. I am very involved in school activities and considered a "very together" teenager. Or at least, I was.

It all started innocently enough. I weighed about 125 pounds. I was not fat, but felt I could stand to lose a few pounds. A friend of mine had gone on a health kick and was getting great results from it—she was losing weight, she felt better and her friends were telling her how great she looked. I wanted to feel that way, too.

I began exercising and eating healthy snacks instead of the usual Coke-and-chips marathon watching the boob tube. Within a couple of weeks I had lost weight, I was feeling good, I cared more about what I wore and started feeling attractive in a way I had not experienced before. I would go to school and it seemed like everyone noticed. "Gabby, you look great," "Gabby, you look so beautiful," and "Gabby, you're so skinny." I don't think anything ever felt as good as those comments.

I was raised with the message that there is always room for improvement, so I figured if five pounds gets this much notice, just think what ten will do! If cutting back to

1,000 calories works, imagine 500! I figure that was the moment I took off down the road to anorexia.

My previous successes didn't feel as good to me as the success of this weight thing. I think it had something to do with the control I felt I had. I lost weight at a fast rate, and every time I lost a pound I was elated. It was a euphoria that, now in looking back, I realize I became addicted to. I lived for that feeling.

I remember the first day I went the whole day without eating. When I got into bed that night I felt this emptiness in my stomach. But I also felt thinness: a feeling I had come to connect with achievement and success. I remember thinking, *If I can go a whole day without eating, then why not two?*

There were many days I did just that. In fact, I could go three days without eating.

I don't remember exactly when it happened, but it was sudden and total: No one said nice things to me and no one was complimenting me. Instead of seeing the logical conclusion, which was that I was taking this too far, I started feeling that I was failing and needed to try harder. I needed to lose more weight; I would have to get serious now!

I had days where all I ate was an apple, and then I went to bed at night feeling like a failure, feeling fat. It got to the point that any food in my stomach felt like too much. It felt dirty and disgusting. I belittled myself for being so weak. My life was becoming a hell. I felt that if I could just control myself a little more, it would get better. The truth is, all happiness had long ago slipped away, and my whole being was devoted to the moments of success that I felt when I lost another pound.

A part of me knew this was probably wrong, but that part of me was out of reach. It was there, just not able to talk louder than my illness. I needed help, and yet there was no way I could ask for it. I could not even admit it to the people who tried so desperately to give it to me.

Teachers, school nurses, friends—they all suspected I had a problem. My concern was only to put them off and convince them I was fine. I wonder if they really believed me, or if they just knew they couldn't help until I was ready.

I remember one night my dad brought home steak and announced to me that I was going to eat it and he was going to watch me. He would not take no for an answer. I cried and begged him not to make me do this. This thing sitting on my plate had become my worst enemy. It was pure fat; one bite would ruin everything. I had to make him understand I could not eat this, and that if he really loved me, he would not make me. I was crying, begging him to let go of this crazy idea, but he wouldn't. He said he would sit there all night. I had no choice, NO CHOICE! But this was supposed to be my choice. The one thing I had control over. Those words pushed a button in me and I no longer cared about him or his feelings. All I felt were anger and hate. I hated him for making me do this, for making me feel my pain and face how distorted my reality had become. I hated him for making me eat that disgusting, evil food.

All my life I had done things for everyone else. The grades, the manners, the awards—everything for them, nothing for me. This eating thing, this losing weight had become *mine*. It represented me and *my* choices, and now my dad was trying to take that away from me, too!

As I lay in bed that night crying and feeling fat, I knew I needed help. I knew I was hurting people I loved.

After staying up all night, I came to the conclusion that it wasn't my dad I hated. I hated ME! I realized that I wasn't in control. For the first time in my life, I understood that this was *my* problem. I needed to take control of my life—not let the disease control it.

Things didn't change overnight. In fact, it was one long road to recovery. But slowly, with the help of friends and family, I began to heal. Now that I'm at my ideal weight, I have stopped weighing myself altogether. I no longer peruse fashion magazines, either—I may not be "in style," but I feel just right!

Gabriella Tortes
As told to Kimberly Kirberger

Already Perfect

Other people may be there to help us, teach us, guide us along our path. But the lesson to be learned is always ours.

Melody Beattie

Everyone can identify with the need to fit in. Each one of us struggles with self-esteem and self-worth to some degree. I spent much of my time striving to achieve perfection in every aspect of my life. What I did not realize was that in my desperate need to be perfect, I sacrificed the very body and mind that allowed me to live.

I was a happy kid with lots of friends and a supportive family. But growing up was really hard and even scary sometimes.

During my childhood, I was constantly involved in something that included an audience viewing my achievements or my failures. I was into acting by age seven, and progressed to training for and competing in gymnastics, horseback riding and dance—all of which required major commitment, discipline and strength. My personality thrived on the high energy required to keep up. I wanted everyone's praise and acceptance, but I was my own toughest critic.

After I graduated from high school and moved out on my own, my struggles with self-esteem and happiness increased. I began to put pressure on myself to succeed in the adult world. Meanwhile, I was feeling very inadequate and unsuccessful. I started to believe that my difficulties and what I perceived to be my "failures" in life were caused by my weight. I had always been a thin-to-average sized person. Suddenly, I was convinced that I was overweight. In my mind, I was FAT!

Slowly, my inability to be "thin" began to torture me. I found myself involved in competition again. But this time, I was competing against myself. I began to control my food by trying to diet, but nothing seemed to work. My mind became obsessed with beating my body at this game. I slowly cut back on what I ate each day. With every portion I didn't finish or meal I skipped, I told myself that I was succeeding, and in turn, I felt good about myself.

Thus began a downward spiral of my becoming what is known as anorexic. The dictionary defines it as "suppressing or causing loss of appetite, resulting in a state of anorexia." When taken to an extreme, anorexia can cause malnutrition and deprive the body of the important vitamins and minerals that it needs to be healthy.

In the beginning, I felt great—attractive, strong, successful, almost super-human. I could do something others couldn't: I could go without food. It made me feel special, and that I was better than everyone else. What I didn't see was that I was slowly killing myself.

People around me began to notice my weight loss. At first they weren't alarmed; maybe some were even envious. But then the comments held a tone of concern. "You're losing too much weight." "Elisa, you're so thin." "You look sick." "You'll die if you keep this up." All their words only reassured me that I was on the right path, getting closer to "perfection."

Sadly, I made my physical appearance the top priority in my life, believing that it was the way to become successful and accepted. As an actress, I am constantly being judged by my appearance. The camera automatically makes people appear heavier than they are. So I was getting mixed messages like, "Elisa, you are so skinny, but you look great on camera."

I cut back on my food more and more, until a typical day consisted of half a teaspoon of nonfat yogurt and coffee in the morning, and a cup of grapes at night. If I ate even a bite more than my allotted "crumbs" for the day, I hated myself and took laxatives to rid my body of whatever I had eaten.

It got to the point where I no longer went out with my friends. I couldn't—if I went to dinner, what would I eat? I avoided their phone calls. If they wanted to go to the movies or just hang out at home, I couldn't be there—what if food was around? I had to be home alone to eat my little cup of grapes. Otherwise, I thought I was failing. Everything revolved around my strict schedule of eating. I was embarrassed to eat in front of anyone, believing that they would think I was gluttonous and ugly.

My poor nutrition began to cause me to lose sleep. I found it hard to concentrate on my work or to focus on anything for any length of time. I was pushing myself harder and harder at the gym, struggling to burn the calories that I hadn't even eaten. My friends tried to help me but I denied that I had a problem. None of my clothes fit, and it was hard to buy any, since I had shrunk to smaller than a size zero!

Then one night, like so many nights before, I couldn't sleep, and my heart felt as though it might beat its way out of my chest. I tried to relax, but I couldn't.

The beating became so rapid and so strong that I could no longer breathe. The combination of starving myself and taking pills to get rid of anything that I did eat caused me to nearly have a heart attack. I stood up, and immediately fell down. I was really scared, and I knew I needed help. My roommate rushed me to the hospital, beginning the long road to my recovery. It took doctors, nurses, nutritionists, therapists, medications, food supplements . . . and most important, a new sense of what was really true about myself to get back on track with reality.

Recovering from what I did to my body and reprogramming the way I think about myself has been a very slow and extremely painful process. I still struggle with the effects of anorexia every day. Although it has been a couple of years since that hospital visit, it is by no means over for me. I must be honest with myself and stay committed to being healthy.

I had used my anorexia as a means of expression and control. I used it as my gauge for self-esteem and self-worth. It was my identity. Now I realize that the way to success lies in my heart, mind and soul, rather than in my physical appearance.

I now use my intelligence, my talents and acts of kindness to express myself. This is true beauty, and it has nothing to do with the size of my body. With my experience of trying to be "perfect" on the outside, I had sacrificed who I was on the inside. What I know now is, we are—each and every one of us—already perfect.

Elisa Donovan

No-Hair Day

Whatever you are doing, love yourself for doing it.
Whatever you are feeling, love yourself for feeling it.

Thadeus Golas

If you are turning sixteen, you stand in front of the mirror scrutinizing every inch of your face. You agonize that your nose is too big and you're getting another pimple—on top of which you are feeling dumb, your hair isn't blonde, and that boy in your English class has not noticed you yet.

Alison never had those problems. Two years ago, she was a beautiful, popular and smart eleventh-grader, not to mention a varsity lacrosse goalie and an ocean life-guard. With her tall, slender body, pool-blue eyes and thick blonde hair, she looked more like a swimsuit model than a high school student. But during that summer, something changed.

After a day of life-guarding, Alison couldn't wait to get home, rinse the saltwater out of her hair and comb through the tangles. She flipped her sun-bleached mane forward. "Ali!" her mother cried, "what did you do?" She discovered a bare patch of skin on the top of her daughter's scalp. "Did you shave it? Could someone else have done it while you were sleeping?" Quickly, they solved the mystery—Alison must have wrapped the elastic band too tightly around her pony tail. The incident was soon forgotten.

Three months later, another bald spot was found, then another. Soon, Alison's scalp was dotted with peculiar quarter-sized bare patches. After diagnoses of "it's just stress" with remedies of topical ointments, a specialist began to administer injections of cortisone, fifty to each spot, every two weeks. To mask her scalp, bloody from the shots, Alison was granted permission to wear a baseball hat to school, normally a violation of the strict uniform code. Little strands of hair would push through the scabs, only to fall out two weeks later. She was suffering from a condition of hair loss known as alopecia, and nothing would stop it.

Alison's sunny spirit and supportive friends kept her going, but there were some low points. Like the time when her little sister came into her bedroom with a towel wrapped around her head to have her hair combed. When her mother untwisted the towel, Alison watched the tousled thick hair bounce around her sister's shoulders. Gripping all of her limp hair between two fingers, she burst into tears. It was the first time she had cried since the whole experience began.

As time went on a bandanna replaced the hat, which could no longer conceal her balding scalp. With only a handful of wispy strands left, the time had come to buy a wig. Instead of trying to resurrect her once-long blonde hair, pretending as though nothing had been lost, Alison opted for a shoulder-length auburn one. Why not? People cut and dyed their hair all the time. With her new look,

Alison's confidence strengthened. Even when the wig blew off from an open window of her friend's car, they all shared in the humor.

But as the summer approached, Alison worried. If she couldn't wear a wig in the water, how could she lifeguard again? "Why—did you forget how to swim?" her father asked. She got the message.

After wearing an uncomfortable bathing cap for only one day, she mustered up the courage to go completely bald. Despite the stares and occasional comments from less-than-polite beachcombers—"Why do you crazy punk kids shave your heads?"—Alison adjusted to her new look.

She arrived back at school that fall with no hair, no eyebrows, no eyelashes, and with her wig tucked away somewhere in the back of her closet. As she had always planned, she would run for school president, changing her campaign speech only slightly. Presenting a slide show on famous bald leaders from Gandhi to Mr. Clean, Alison had the students and faculty rolling in the aisles.

In her first speech as the elected president, Alison addressed her condition, quite comfortable answering questions. Dressed in a T-shirt with the words "Bad Hair Day" printed across the front, she pointed to her shirt and said, "When most of you wake up in the morning and don't like how you look, you may put on this T-shirt." Putting on another T-shirt over the other, she continued. "When I wake up in the morning, I put on this one." It read, "No-Hair Day." Everybody cheered and applauded. And Alison, beautiful, popular and smart—not to mention varsity goalie, ocean lifeguard and now, school president with the pool-blue eyes—smiled back from the podium.

Jennifer Rosenfeld and Alison Lambert

Losing Hope

Wherever you go, there you are.

Buckaroo Bonzai

"Hope is the hat rack upon which I hang my dreams . . ."? Oh, please! I crumple up the paper and fling it across my bedroom. I can't believe I kept my hopeless seventh-grade attempts at poetry. I thought I was a poet that year. Obviously I wasn't, and never will be.

"Here they are," I mutter, pulling a stack of yearbooks from the depths of the drawer. They go all the way back to elementary school. *Lauren will like these. Best friends since first grade, she's not talking to me now, but I'm sure she'll want these . . . after . . .*

"You're hopeless, Carrie," she yelled at me over the phone Friday night. Because I don't see everything exactly her way, because I tell her things she doesn't want to hear. The way I think best friends should. Now I don't even have a best friend. And I can't stand losing her friendship.

I peer into the drawer, empty of yearbooks but still

containing the debris of my life. Now what would Josh want from me? According to him, nothing. "There's no hope, Carrie," he told me that night two weekends ago. The night he broke up with me, practically pushing me away as I begged him for another chance. No, he shook his head at me. No, it's over. No hope for us. He hasn't spoken to me since. I can't stand losing him, either.

I slip my hand into the pocket of my robe and finger the little container of pills. My stepfather takes these for his back, and I've heard his repeated warnings to my little brothers never to touch them, how dangerous pills like these can be. He never warned me, knowing that I'm old enough, knowing that I understand about things like dangerous pills.

A knock on my door makes my hand fly from the pocket. Of course, my mother barges right in before I can respond.

"Carrie," she says in her exasperated tone, "we're all waiting for you out by the tree. You know we can't open the presents until we're all together." The faint melody of a Christmas carol and the scent of hot cocoa waft into my room through the open door.

"Honestly, Carrie, can't you dress up a little for Christmas Eve? Or at least get that hair out of your eyes," she continues. "Sometimes I think you're hopeless." She sighs—loudly, dramatically, as if otherwise I wouldn't understand the depths of my hopelessness. "Well, hurry up."

With that, she closes the door and leaves me screaming silently after her: *Yes, Mom, I know I'm hopeless, like you always tell me. Every time I forget to empty the dishwasher, fold the laundry, get the hair out of my eyes, whatever.*

So they're all waiting for me. Mom, my stepfather, Dave, and Aaron and Mark. Waiting for me to join in the singing of carols and unwrapping of gifts. Sure, I'll go. I'll unwrap a few presents. Not that they'll mean a thing to me. But it's Christmas. I'm supposed to be happy. I can pretend. After all, I took drama class last semester.

Ah, school. Another one of the victorious arenas of my life.

"I'm sorry, Carrie, but it's hopeless," Ms. Boggio told me the last day before winter break. "You'd have to get an A on every test for the rest of the year to raise that D to a C." Then she left me alone in the biology lab, staring at my latest test, the latest record of my failures.

I tossed the test away. *I won't even have to show Mom,* I thought. *I won't have to hear that lecture again. The one about how I'm ruining my chances for college. That there will be no hope for my future if I keep going on this way. In fact, I'll never have to hear another lecture again. The problem will be solved before school starts in January.*

How about a note? Would they want one? I used to think I was some great writer. I'd spend hours filling notebook after notebook with my stories and poems, sometimes just my thoughts and ideas. That's when I felt most alive—writing and dreaming of being good at it, of having other people read my words. And having my words mean something to them. But that was before the hopelessness of being Carrie Brock swallowed me up.

"Just a lousy note," I remind myself. That's all I have to write now. Or ever. I've lost everything: my best friend and my boyfriend. Or I've messed it up: my grades, even my hair. I can't do anything right, and I can't stand facing the reminders of my failures anymore.

"Come on, Carrie," Aaron's voice cries through the door. "I want to open my presents."

Oh, all right. I'll do the note later. I drag myself up and tighten the belt on my robe. As I walk down the hall, the pills make a satisfying clicking noise in my pocket.

I sink into the couch and watch as Mark, my youngest brother, tears open his gifts, flinging wrapping paper everywhere. Then it's Aaron's turn. That's the tradition in our family. Youngest to oldest. Everyone oohs and aahs over Aaron's gifts.

"Your turn, Carrie," Mark informs me.

"Can you bring them?" I ask. "I'm tired."

Mark carries over a rectangular box. Clothes, of course. From Mom. I mumble the appropriate thanks. My gifts are few this year. Nothing from Lauren or Josh, of course. Trinkets from Aaron and Mark.

"Okay, I'm done," I say.

"No, wait, here's another one," Mark says, handing me a small package.

"Who's it from?"

"Me." My stepfather speaks up. Dave, the man who resides in the background of my life. A good guy, he treats me well. I've never regretted my mom marrying him.

I tear off the paper, revealing a book. But opening it, I find there are no words inside.

"It's blank," I say, looking up at Dave.

"Well, not quite. There's an inscription up front. But it's a journal, Carrie. For your words."

I flip to the front and find Dave's handwriting in one corner. I read the inscription silently.

> *To Carrie:*
>
> *Go for your dreams. I believe in you.*
>
> *Dave*

I look up at Dave again. He shrugs slightly, as if embarrassed. "Well, I know you want to be a writer, Carrie," he explains. "And I know you can do it."

His last words are almost lost in the noise my brothers are making, digging under the tree and coming up with my mother's presents. But Dave's words are not lost on me.

Somebody believes in me and in my dreams, even when I've stopped believing in them myself. When I thought I was beyond all hope. I clutch the journal to my chest and a feeling I haven't felt for a long time returns. I do want to be a writer. But most of all, I want to just be.

I watch the rest of the presents being opened, thinking there's something I need to do, but I can't quite figure out what. I can slip the pills back into the cabinet later, so that's not it. Then I know.

I grab a pen from the coffee table and open my journal. On that first blank page I write my words: "Hope is the hat rack I hang my dreams upon."

H'mm, I think. *Kind of sounds like a country song. Maybe it's not that bad after all.* I look up and smile at Dave, even though he's not looking my way. He's just given me the best Christmas present ever. I've gotten my dreams back. Maybe there's hope for me, after all.

Heather Klassen
Submitted by Jordan Breal

I Never Knew

The difference between holding on to a hurt or releasing it with forgiveness is like the difference between laying your head down at night on a pillow filled with thorns or a pillow filled with rose petals.

Loren Fischer

She was my best friend, and I loved her. She was the coolest girl in junior high and everyone wanted to be like her . . . and she chose me to be her best friend. Her name was Cindy. She was beautiful with her black hair and tall, thin body. While the rest of us in eighth and ninth grade were still looking amorphous, trying to take shape, Cindy was already beautifully poised in her adult body.

Her mother had died when she was a little girl. She was an only child, and she lived alone with her father. By the time we would get home from school every day, he would already be at work. He wouldn't come home until two or three in the morning, so we had free reign of the house. No parental supervision was the greatest thing we could ask for as teenagers. Her house was a big, two-story that was concealed by a large grove of orange trees. You couldn't see the house from the street, and we liked it that way. It added to the mystique and allure that we were always trying to create.

At school she was pretty much the center of attention. One whole corner of the quad was dedicated to Cindy and her "followers." If there was new music, clothes, hairstyles or even new ways to take notes or study, you could be fairly sure that it came out of that corner of the quad. Even the school faculty caught on to the power this girl held and convinced her to run for class president. Cindy and I were voted in as class president and vice president by a landslide.

By day, we were the acting liaison between students and faculty; by night, we hosted social activities at Cindy's house. If we weren't having a party, people would come just to hang out. Kids would be there for all kinds of reasons—to talk about relationships, their parents, to do their homework, or just because they knew someone they liked would be showing up.

After everyone left, I would usually spend the night. My mom wouldn't like it very much if it was a school night. Sometimes Cindy would come back to my house to spend the night, but my mom didn't like that much either because we would stay up all night laughing and talking. Cindy didn't like to be home alone.

That following summer, after I came home from vacation with my family, things were starting to change. Cindy looked thinner than usual with dark circles under her eyes, and she had started to smoke. The strikingly beautiful girl looked pale and gaunt. She said she missed me a lot. While it was a boost to my ego, I couldn't believe it could be entirely true. After all, there were always people trying to be close to her and get into her circle of friends.

My solution: two weeks at the beach. Our parents pitched in to rent a beach house for two weeks. My mom would be the only supervision. In Cindy's inimitable style, we collected a group of beach friends within a couple of days. We'd all hang out at this local café during the day, when we were not in the water or on the sand, and at night we'd hang out around this fire pit on the beach.

Cindy started to look like her old self, but better. She was tan. She looked great in a bikini, and all the guys on the beach wanted to be around her. But she was still smoking. She told me it calmed her nerves.

One night, Cindy came back to the beach house very late. She was all disoriented and noticeably excited. She told me she and this one guy had been drinking and smoking marijuana, and they had gotten together. She said that I had to try marijuana because it made everything better, clearer, in fact. She said she really liked this guy and wanted to run away with him. I knew she was just high, and she'd feel differently in the morning.

When school started that next year, things weren't the same, and I missed the old routine. Cindy wanted to get into different things than I wanted, and she started hanging around guys more and more. We would still hang out from time to time, but it wasn't as fun as it used to be. Cindy would get really serious and tell me that I just didn't understand how things were. I just thought that she was maturing faster emotionally than the rest of us, like she had physically.

One morning when I arrived at school, there were police cars all around and a lot of nervous activity in the halls. When I proceeded toward my locker, my counselor and another woman stopped me. I was asked to follow them to the office. My heart was pounding so fast and hard that I could hardly catch my breath. My head was racing with the different scenarios that might have caused this odd behavior.

When we all sat down in my counselor's office, the principal came in and took a seat. Was I in some kind of trouble? The principal began by talking about life and maturity and circumstances. Now my head was really spinning. (What was he trying to say?) And then my world froze in time with the words, ". . . and Cindy took her own life last night using her father's gun." I couldn't talk; I couldn't move. Tears started streaming from my eyes before my heart could even comprehend the pain. She was only fifteen years old.

As the suicide note explained, her father had repeatedly sexually abused her and she knew no other way out. Months after he was arrested, he finally confessed. The note also said something else. It said that the only family she ever knew and cared about was me. She left me a ring that her mother had left to her.

I cried for weeks. How is it that I never knew? We were closer than anyone and talked about everything; how come she never told me that? I was certain that I could have helped her, and I began to blame myself.

After weeks of grief counseling, I came to understand that the burden of Cindy's sexual abuse was too much for her to bear, especially when she started to become intimate with boys. The counselor explained to me that her shame was too great to talk about, even to her best friend. It dawned on me how alone she must have felt, and it suddenly became clear to me why she never wanted to spend the night alone in her own house.

My own suffering—weeks of pain and confusion—was eased greatly with all the help and support I received. Teachers, counselors, friends and family members all nurtured me. It was clear to everyone that this situation was going to change my life forever, but because I let help in, it subsequently add to my life an aspect of wisdom and compassion. I wish that Cindy could have known the relief that comes from letting others help you with your pain.

Cindy's suicide note also requested that she be cremated. The note said that I should spread her ashes wherever I wanted to. I chose the ocean off the beach where we had spent two weeks that summer.

On the day of the memorial, we rented a boat to take us out to sea. The boat was packed with friends and teachers, even though it was a rainy, overcast day. We stood on the bow and took turns sharing our experiences and love for our friend. When it came time for me to free her ashes, I hesitated. I didn't want to turn them loose in a sea that looked dark and menacing. I thought she had had enough of that in her own life.

My hesitancy gained attention, and both my mother and my counselor stepped up on the platform and put their arms around me. With their support I opened the lid and set my friend free. As some of the ashes hit the surface of the water, the sun broke through for a moment and sent beautiful rays of light that sparkled on the surface of the water. The clouds parted some more and soon the whole boat was bathed in warm sunlight. At that moment, I felt calmer than I had in weeks. Somehow I knew that the angels had come for my friend and that she would be all right—and so would I.

Rosanne Martorella

[EDITORS' NOTE: *Some of the critical signs to watch for if you think someone you know may be suicidal are:*
• *A sudden change in behavior (especially calmness after a period of anxiety or a lift in mood after a period of deep depression,*

which would indicate that the person now has the energy to act on suicidal thoughts).
- *Preoccupation with death.*
- *Giving away belongings.*
- *Direct or indirect threats to commit suicide. (It is particularly important to pay attention and take seriously any talk of suicide even if it seems like the person is "joking.")*

If you or someone you know is feeling suicidal or is showing any of the critical warning signs above, reach out to a professional you can trust (such as a school counselor) or call one of the hotlines listed below.]

800-SUICIDE: 800-784-2433

Yellow Ribbon Project: 303-429-3530, 3531, 3532
www.yellowribbon.org
Helps prevent teen suicide.

Youth Crisis Line: 800-843-5200, 24 hours
www.befrienders.org
Can refer you to a crisis hotline in your area.

A Call for Help

My dear friend Lindsay: She had been part of my life since kindergarten. We met over her ninety-six-pack of Crayolas, a big thing to a five-year-old. She was a constant fixture in my life. She was a born comedian, with more talent, creativity, laughter, love and curly red hair than she knew what to do with. The greatest thing about our friendship was that we completely understood each other. We always had a smile, a joke, a shoulder or an ear to lend one another. In fact, our favorite thing to do was to have our parents drop us off at a restaurant, where we would have these outrageously long talks over Mountain Dews, Diet Cokes and the most expensive dessert our baby sitting money would allow.

It was over one such talk in seventh grade where the subject of suicide came up. Little did I know that this would be a conversation that would forever change our relationship. We talked about how weird it would be if one of our friends ever committed suicide. We wondered how families could ever get over such a tragedy. We talked about what we thought our funerals would be like. This conversation was definitely the most morbid one we had ever had, but I did not think about it too much. I assumed that, at one time or another, everyone wonders who will cry and what will be said at their funeral. It never entered my mind that this talk was a cry for help from my beloved friend. Whenever this topic came up, I had the same frame of mind as my mother—we could never understand how one's life could get so desperate that the only alternative was death. However, we ended our talk with a laugh about how we were too "together" to ever do something so drastic, and we parted with a hug and a "Call me if you need anything."

I didn't think about our conversation until three weeks later, when I received a phone call from Lindsay. I immediately knew something was wrong when she did not begin the conversation with a bouncy hello and a good story. Today she came right out and asked me if she was important to my life and if she meant anything to this world. I answered with an energetic "Of course! I don't know what I'd do without you!" Lindsay then told me something that sent chills up my spine and neck. She told me that she felt lost, confused, worthless, and that she had a bottle of pills in her hand. She said that she was fully prepared to take them all, to end her life. *Was this the girl who sat next to me in English class and with whom I loved to get in trouble? Was this the girl who loved bright colors, laughing, and striking up conversations with anyone in the world? Was this my wonderful, funny friend who was so bubbly and light that she practically floated through life?*

My reality then came into check and I realized that this was my friend, and for that reason, I had to keep her on the phone. I then started the longest phone conversation in my life. Over the next three-and-a-half hours, Lindsay told me her troubles. And for three-and-a-half hours, I listened. She spoke of how she got lost in her large family (fifteen children, and she was the baby), how her self-confidence was low from her appearance (which I thought was beautiful and unique), how she was anorexic the summer before (I was too busy playing softball to notice), how she was confused about her future—whether or not she would follow her dreams or her parents' wishes, and how she felt completely alone. I kept telling her over and over how original, beautiful and important her dreams and personality were to our lives. By this time, we were both crying: she was frustrated, I was pleading for her life.

My mind then reached out at what I assumed was my final chance at helping Lindsay; I told her three simple things. I first told her that everyone has problems. It's a part of life. That overcoming these problems and moving onto greater heights is what life is all about. The second thing I told her was that if life was as bad as she said, then things couldn't possibly get worse. There wasn't room for any more failure—things had to improve. The final simple thing I told her was that I, or someone else close to her, would always be there, no matter what trials may come into her life. I told her that the fact that we were having this conversation, that she wanted me to know what was going on, proved my theory that she really wanted to live. If she wanted to end her life, she would have just done it. But, since she took time to call, her mind was saying "Help! I want to keep my life!" After I finished that last statement, I heard the best sound in the world—Lindsay flushing the pills down the toilet.

I then went to her house, and we talked about how she could start putting her life back together. We got her some help, and eventually, Lindsay overcame her issues. I am proud to say that Lindsay and I will be starting the eleventh grade together in the fall, she is getting excellent grades, and is a happy teenager. The road there wasn't easy, and we both slipped a few times. But, the important thing is that we raised ourselves up and arrived.

Jill Maxbauer

Tomorrow Came Again

My sister was twelve. My parents were separated. As for myself, I was eight. I really did not have a clue what my family was going through until that horrible, cold January night. How could I have had a clue? I mean, I was only eight years old. All I cared about was my afterschool snack, the cartoons on television and trying to stay up later than eight-thirty on school nights.

I remember that night like it was only milliseconds ago. My mother had asked me to carry the towels upstairs to the linen closet. After I moaned, groaned and procrastinated for about ten minutes, I finally agreed. I remember trying to peer over the tower of towels to make my way up the steep stairs safely. When I got to the closet, which just happens to be next to my sister's room, I heard her crying. Being the most concerned third-grader I could be, I opened the door a little bit wider, and I asked, "Shelley, what's wrong?"

She just looked at my confused expression, and then asked me to give her a hug. I was pretty much into the charade of showing that you hated your siblings, so I refused her request. She persisted and asked me once more. My shaky response was, "Why?"

Shelley explained to me that she had just swallowed an entire bottle of over-the-counter pills. I was not exactly sure at that point in time if this was a dangerous move on her part. But, I realized it must have been pretty serious. I ran down the stairs to my mother, crying the whole way. I told her exactly, word for word, what Shelley had just explained to me.

My mother raced up the stairs, two at a time. She burst into my sister's room, and she begged Shelley to get out of bed to tell her what happened. Shelley refused to tell my mother anything. My mother forced her out of bed, told her to get dressed, and they hurried to the hospital. My neighbor came over, and I cried myself to sleep. All I remember after that is waking up, and my neighbor was still there.

I later learned that Shelley was going to be all right, after she had gotten her stomach pumped. And especially after she had spent three months of her seventh-grade year in a rehabilitation center for adolescents. I never knew exactly why she had attempted suicide, and I never want to ask her. But what I do know is that life is our most precious gift, and I will never again pretend that I do not love my sister.

Ashley Hiser

It Happened to Me

Cancer. It's a funny word. It has two meanings. One of those meanings is the life-threatening disease we all know about. The other meaning isn't as accurate. We take it to mean something that happens to someone else, something that happens to your friend's aunt or someone in the newspaper. It's not something that happens to us, and it's definitely not something that happens to our own sister. But it happened to mine.

When I was about eight, every once in a while my eyesight would become blurry. I'd blink a few times and my eyes would go back to normal. I was taken to the eye doctor, and then for a CAT scan and various testing, but no one could find anything wrong. Eventually, it went away.

When my sister, Naomi, was about eight, she claimed to go blind when I hit her in the eye with an old nightshirt. I got in trouble, but when she was taken to the eye doctor, he couldn't find anything either. Eventually, she stopped complaining.

But when my sister, Tali, was about eight, she too began to complain that it was getting harder and harder to see out of one eye. My parents made an appointment with the eye doctor for about a month later, but they weren't too concerned.

But when my sister's complaints began to worsen, my parents began to get worried and made the eye doctor appointment sooner. When the appointment came, my parents were informed that it was possible that Tali had a form of cancer called melanoma. One of the places that this can form is the eye, though there is no known reason why it forms in a particular person. To ensure that the disease is completely removed from the body, the part of the body infected with the disease must be removed. In this case, it would be her eye. If it was proven, for certain, that she had melanoma, the doctors would have to work fast, or the disease could travel from her eye to her brain.

It was not time to worry yet, though, because all that was the worst-case scenario, and melanoma is very rare among children anyway. Nevertheless, I remember my mom coming home from the eye doctor and crying, along with my grandmother and my aunt and trying not to let my sister see. I remember thinking, *This isn't really happening. She can't really die, this will all blow over.* Maybe I was in shock, but it didn't feel like it. It was more like I had never even heard it, never even tried to acknowledge it was happening. Maybe it was crazy to feel like that, but maybe it was better that way, because I, the "unshaken one," was able to be the shoulder to cry on for everyone else. It makes it sound as if I was the brave one, but sometimes if you don't show your feelings on the outside, it means you're the most scared inside.

Well, Tali went in for her tests, and her X rays, and it was confirmed that she had cancer. Her eye would have to be removed immediately. We knew that if even one cancerous cell was left, the disease could fully return.

The operation took place soon after. My mother waited

in the hospital, while I stayed home and answered various phone calls. "No, we haven't heard anything yet," "Yes, she's still in surgery," "Yes, we'll notify you immediately." I still didn't believe it was happening. My sister was in surgery. . . . and I still thought I was dreaming.

We later got a call that she was out of surgery, and just awakening from the anesthesia. All had gone smoothly, and tests had shown that they probably got everything out. She would be fine.

Never during the entire experience did I acknowledge what was happening. People would stop to comfort me, and half the time it would take me a few seconds to realize why. Almost every day, I have people stop me in the halls and ask, "Hey, how's Tali doing?" and I answer, "She's fine, why do you ask?"

Even now, as I write this, she's jumping on the bed across the hall, screaming, "Hey Joanie, you done writing the wonderful story of my life yet?" And though it's a miracle, it seems quite normal that there is nothing wrong at all.

Joanie Twersky

Nintendo Master

When I first saw you, I thought—*Nintendo Master*. There was this intensity about you. Your piercing blue eyes and the way your hands moved rapidly along the control buttons were subtle hints of your expert skill.

You didn't appear too different from all of the other video-crazed teens out there, but you were. I guess the fact that it was summer, and we were both stuck in the oncology ward of the hospital cruelly betrayed the normality with which you tried to present yourself. Or maybe it was the fact that we were prematurely robbed of the innocence of childhood, and it comforted me to know that there was someone else out there just like me. I can only speculate, but all I know for sure is that I was drawn to your energy and zest for life.

That was the summer of my first post-cancer surgeries. The doctors were trying to fix my left hip joint, which had shattered under the intense bombardments of chemotherapy treatments. It wasn't the only thing that had shattered. I had misplaced my usual optimistic attitude about life and was surprised at how nasty I could be. This did not help to endear me to anyone in my presence.

My surgery had gone "well," the doctors said, but I was in excruciating pain.

I saw you again in physical therapy, realizing only then the extent of what cancer had done to you. I wanted to scream, "Let him go back upstairs and play his video games, you idiots!" But I just sat there in stunned silence. I watched you get up and start walking with the aid of the parallel bars. Prior to your entrance into the room, I had been sitting in my wheelchair, wallowing in self-pity—"Wasn't the cancer enough? Now my hip is screwed up, and I really don't care anymore. If I get up, it is going to kill."

You will never know me, but you are my hero, Nintendo Master. With such courage and poise, you got up on your one remaining leg. Some might have the audacity to call you disabled or even crippled, but you are more complete than many can ever wish to be. After you had your walk for the day, a walk that was perfectly executed on your part, and you were safely tucked into your bed and were enjoying your video games once again, I decided that it was about time that I get up and take a walk myself. You see, Nintendo Master, it dawned on me then that you had innately known what it takes most of us a lifetime to grasp—life is like a game, you can't win them all and yet the game goes on, forcing all to play it. Nintendo Master, you play it better than most!

Katie Gill

Owning the World

Character cannot be developed in ease and quiet. Only through experience of trial and suffering can the soul be strengthened, ambition inspired, and success achieved.

Helen Keller

I slowly came to understand what had been said. Instead of the expected dismissal of my illness and being told to choke down a series of medications, I was told I had leukemia. It was June 27, 1997. The weather was pleasant, and I was calm. From the smaller hospital in Kitchener, my mom and I proceeded directly to London to begin my own personal hell.

As my mom, dad and I sat listening in a vague stupor, what we could come to expect was explained to us in the simplest and nicest way possible. That information was repeated a lot during the next little while. It was a great deal to take in while under such shock. However, I decided right away that my case would be different. I would not lose all my hair, I would not puff up from steroids, I would not get mouth sores, and the chemotherapy would not be so hard on me as it is on other people. I was wrong.

The next couple of days were the most difficult I had faced in my life. To that point, most of my life had been no problem. I could dismiss whatever was wrong within a couple of days and never face very severe or life-changing consequences. But leukemia was a big deal that I would have to live with for an indeterminate length of time. I decided to complete this temporary obstacle with grace, maturity and an understanding of how much people were helping me, and how much I had to be grateful for.

Meanwhile, back at home people were slowly hearing the news. I started getting lots of cards and gifts. I knew they were meant to cheer me up, but they made me sad. I didn't want to be the center of bad attention. I didn't want people to know I was even sick. I wanted to get the chemotherapy, go home and be happy without everybody knowing. But the gifts and cards piled up, each one a painful reminder of what a difficult and daunting task lay before me.

When it was around time for it to fall out, I cut my shoulder-length black curly hair short. I didn't really care that much; I was too weak from the leukemia and the first strong dose of chemotherapy. My hair fell out about a week later. For the first little while I wore a wig or a hat all the time because I was so ashamed. Eventually, I came not to care if the nurses or my parents saw me without hair. It took quite a while longer for me to show a select group of my friends. I kept in contact with two of my best friends. I didn't have the energy or the strength to reassure them all firsthand.

I spent most of July in the hospital, waiting for my blood counts to come back high enough that I could return home. I completed a number of paintings, finding that painting helped to keep my spirits high and my mood cool, calm and collected. It was amazing therapy. I went home for a week in early August. I needed a break. I had to stay out of the sun, didn't have as much stamina as usual and wore a wig, but other than that it was the closest I would feel to normal for quite a while.

The following cycle of chemotherapy was the worst I have ever experienced. I had no idea what was in store for me. Up until then, I had handled all the chemotherapy with flying colors. At the end of August I was back in the hospital, only this time in pain. It was the worst pain I had ever felt. I wasn't allowed to have pain relievers because the doctors had to know if the pain changed in any way. An endless bombardment of seemingly unimportant questions, which in reality were quite significant, drove me insane. They put a tube down my nose to drain the stomach acid, and I suffered severe nausea and stomach pain for the next month. I finally went home feeling better. My bone marrow transplant was scheduled for October, earlier than anticipated. I went shopping, had my friends over, and had a great time. It was a very well-deserved break.

I was very fortunate to have two donors to choose from. Both my brother and my sister were perfect matches. The doctors chose my brother. We went to Toronto's special bone-marrow transplant unit confident and full of hope that this was finally coming to a close. The round of chemotherapy was strong enough to kill me if I hadn't had my brother's marrow to back me up. I did quite well in isolation. Except for the nausea. It just never went away. Everything I ate just came back up again. I went home promising to eat and drink as much as I could or a minimum of one-and-a-half liters a day. That proved to be extremely difficult.

Within a couple of days I was back in the hospital to get

hydrated and for treatment for shingles. The nausea still hadn't gone away. I was angry with myself for letting everybody down. We all had such high expectations for me after the bone-marrow transplant, and I wasn't meeting them. No matter how hard I tried, I could not bring myself to eat. On top of it, I had to take a great number of pills, which just made me more sick.

Even though the nausea continued, I was able to return home. It was torture. I got bronchitis and sinusitis and had no idea how it could possibly get worse. After a CT scan and routine clinic visit, I found out I had relapsed. The chemotherapy and bone-marrow transplant didn't work. The leukemia was back. All I had just been through was for nothing. This bad news came ten times harder than it had the first time. I had already been through all this, suffered the consequences, and lived through the trials and tribulations.

When a patient with AML relapses, the chances of long-term remission, or cure, with conventional treatments is about 20 percent. That news just never left my mind. However, I was able to remain secure in knowing that I was getting the newest and latest treatment. I was the eighth pediatric patient to try this new treatment through Sick Kids' Hospital, and so far it had worked quite well in adults. So I told myself it would be all right and started it along with another program my dad had heard about.

The medication my dad found was an experimental organic medicine that is injected into the lymph nodes. I had to do that every day for three months. It was up to me when to stop. It was as if a great weight had been taken off my shoulders when I finally felt confident enough to stop.

The hospital treatment was quite different. I had to endure a round of chemotherapy, followed by a dose of my brother's white blood cells, hoping that they would identify the leukemia as foreign "bad stuff" and destroy it. The first chemotherapy and batch of my brother's white blood cells proved inadequate. When I got my bone marrow checked there were still signs of leukemia. I went through the chemotherapy once more, knowing that if it didn't work this time I was as good as gone. They gave me the remaining batch of white blood cells, this time many more of them. My brother and I are such a close match that the blood cells hadn't attacked me enough, so, with the second and final round, they gave me the entire batch.

I am proud to say that I no longer show signs of any leukemia.

Slowly, day by day, I approach summer, regain my strength and remind myself of how valuable and fragile *everybody* is. It has been a long, hard fight, but I would not trade the lessons I have learned in those ten months for the world. I have learned to be brave. I have learned to be strong. And, most important, I have learned to persevere.

Liz Alarie

[EDITORS' NOTE: *We received the following from the author's parents:*

Two months later, Lizzie relapsed for the last time. Shortly after, she died at home. Lizzie lived her fifteen months of illness with radiant grace, maturity and ever-present gratitude. She accomplished her greatness here on Earth as a teacher. "Her world" witnessed her valiant actions, kind deeds and motivating stories such as this one. Lizzie's wish for mankind was simple: Begin now to live your life to the fullest—it is possible!

Ray and Mary Pat Alarie]

My Toughest Decision

Mistakes, mistakes, mistakes. Everyone makes them. No one saw mine coming.

Overall, I was a really good kid. At fifteen, I was a sophomore at a Catholic high school and a member of the National Honor Society. I played softball and ran cross-country. I had, and still have, aspirations of becoming a doctor. If someone would have told me that at the age of fifteen I would become pregnant, I would have said they were crazy. Why would anyone do something so foolish? It's still hard for me to believe, but it happened.

October 11, 1997, was the day my daughter was born. I took one look at her, and it was love at first sight. It was so overwhelming—a flood of emotions that I have never experienced. I loved her in a way that could only be described as unconditional. I looked at her, and in my heart I knew that I could not give her all the things that she needed and deserved to have, no matter how badly I wanted to. Physically, emotionally and in every other way, I was not capable of being a mother. I knew what had to be done. Putting all my emotions aside and doing what I felt was best for my daughter, I decided to give her up for adoption.

Placing my baby in the arms of her mother was the hardest thing I've ever had to do. My very soul ached. Even though I still get to see my daughter because I am blessed with having an open adoption, the pain is still there. I can feel it burning inside me every day, when I think about Katelyn. I only hope that when she gets older, she realizes how much I love her. I love her more than anything in the world.

Today is my daughter's first Christmas. I won't be there to share with her the joy of this season, or to play Santa and open her presents for her (she's only two months old). In fact, I won't be there to see her first step, or hear her first word. I won't be there to take pictures on her first day of kindergarten. When she cries for her mommy, it won't be me that she wants. I know in my heart that I made the right choice. I just wish with all my heart that it was a choice I never had to make.

Kristina Dulcey

I Am Not Alone

Here I stand, just another voice, lost in a crowd of noise. Though I am surrounded by familiar faces, I do not recognize anyone. I have never felt so alone. . . .

I am eighteen years old, and in love with the most wonderful person! He is cute, sweet and oh so charming. He makes me so happy. I have never felt so content. He is my best friend. When he looks in my eyes and says, "I love you," I just know we are forever. For us, life is a party.

Reality sets in and threatens to reveal the illusions of my fantasy world. *Where is he now?* I wonder desperately. *Where did I go wrong? Did I fall short of his expectations somehow? Or was he unable to meet mine? Was it that he never really loved me, and if so, did he lie?* WHY? The young man I thought I knew so well does not exist, is someone whose face I do not recognize. His voice sounds strange and distant. I see behind his disguise. I look past his smile and his promises. I see him for who he *really* is.

My stomach hurts lately, and I have trouble eating. I feel dizzy and nauseous. I get so tired, I can hardly stay awake. Yet even after a nap, I still feel cranky and irritable. Maybe it's just the flu. No, it is something else. I sense a truth I want to ignore.

My friend must know, too. I can tell by the way she watches me. I don't want to say anything because I am afraid. She brings me a pregnancy test and tells me, "You should take it just to be sure."

I pretend that I am not worried, that this is silly. "I know I am not pregnant." I keep saying it to reassure myself more than her. Then I go to the bathroom.

I watch two lines appear quickly. I can hardly breathe. I feel nothing really, except shock and denial. Tears will not come. I just stare in disbelief and then quietly call for my friend. I point at the test stick lying face up on the counter, the faint pink lines rapidly changing to a dark shade of maroon. As calmly as I can, I say, "This can't be right." She knows the test is right, and so do I. Tomorrow, I will go to the doctor. Right now, I just want to lie down.

"Positive. You are definitely pregnant." I look up and catch the nurse's eyes. It is real. There is no way to avoid the truth. She hands me a tissue as I cry. Now, my tears are endless. She listens as I lose myself in despair. I can't think. A million thoughts are colliding in my head, causing a mass of confusion. How will I tell him? He has to know.

I go to see him when I leave the clinic. He is sitting in his bedroom, with the light off. A small ray of light comes through the window, and casts shadows across his face. I turn my head away. I can't look him in the eye. I can feel my lips trembling as I try not to cry, but I will not allow him to witness the panic that grips me. I try to appear brave and unemotional as I tell this stranger I am carrying his child. He, too, seems unemotional. I feel his eyes upon me. Getting my words out is a struggle. I look up and try to smile, a weak attempt. This is not how I had imagined it would be. So, I wait for him to do, or say, something, anything to let me know I am not alone. Instead, his silence chills me. I know that things between us are changed forever; I turn and walk away. I want him to call to me, or run after me. I want him to hold me in his arms. As I am leaving, I vaguely hear him say, "I'm sorry."

I am outside now. The sun shines down upon me like a spotlight. I feel naked. The door shuts behind me, and I burst into tears. I cry for the young man on the other side of the door. I cry for the baby that is growing inside me. I cry because my heart is breaking. I suddenly feel my youth is ending.

Weeks go by, and every day I live in fear. I wish I had been more careful with my heart and my body. I wish I had never met him. I am too young to be a mother. I am scared. I feel sick and alone. Will my baby have a father? I sleep all day and cry all night. I wonder how it feels to laugh. I stare at myself in the mirror, looking for my smile, my happiness.

Now I see the beginning of this tiny creature on a screen. I hear a heartbeat separate from my own. I feel a new kind of love. A love that has confidence and guidance—the love of a mother. I lift my head up, and I stand strong for myself, for my unborn child and for the priorities instilled in me by my pregnancy.

Here I am amidst a crowd of noise, swimming against the current I have accepted as my reality, in a sea where familiar faces fade away, and I am not alone.

Sara Strickland

It's Tough to Be a Teenager

It's tough to be a teenager, no one really knows
What the pressure is like in school, this is how it goes.

I wake up every morning, and stare into this face
I wanna be good lookin', but I feel like a disgrace.

My friends they seem to like me, if I follow through with
    their dare,
But when I try to be myself, they never seem to care.

My mom, well she keeps saying, I gotta make the grade
While both my parents love me, it slowly seems to fade.

It seems like everyone I know is trying to be so cool
And every time I try, I end up just a fool.

I've thought about taking drugs, I really don't want to
    you know
But I just don't fit in, and it's really startin' to show.

Maybe if I could make the team, I'll stand out in the crowd
If they could see how hard I try, I know they would be
proud.

You see I'm still a virgin, my friends they can't find out
'Cause if they really knew the truth, I know they'd laugh
and shout.

Sometimes I really get so low, I want to cash it in
My problems really aren't so bad, if I think of how life's
been.

Sometimes I'm really lost, and wonder what to do
I wonder where to go, who can I talk to.

It's tough to be a teenager, sometimes life's not fair
I wish I had somewhere to go, and someone to *CARE*.

Tony Overman

Visionary

When I was fifteen, I stood in front of my English class and read an essay I had written. I talked about how excited all my friends were to be taking driver's education and getting driver's licenses. I was jealous. I knew that I'd always be walking everywhere I went or else dependent on others to drive me. I am legally blind.

Since I was four years old, I have had a condition called dry-eye syndrome. While I do have some sight, I never know when I wake up in the morning exactly how much vision I will have that day. The reason for this is that my eyes do not produce enough tears to lubricate my corneas. As a result, my corneas are scarred. Glasses cannot help me.

There are many things I cannot do. I can't drive, read the blackboard in school or read a book comfortably. But there are far more things I can do.

In high school, I played varsity basketball. My teammates gave me oral signals and I learned to gauge where the ball was by the sound of their voices. As a result, I learned to focus extremely well. I earned the sportsmanship award my senior year.

In addition to basketball, I was a representative to the student council. I also participated in a Model United Nations program, traveling to Washington, D.C., with my class to see our legislators in action. I graduated from high school with a dual curriculum in Jewish and general studies.

After graduation, I studied in Israel for two years. Today, I am a sophomore at Yeshiva University. I plan to go to law school and maybe rabbinical school.

Do I wish I could see like other people? Of course. But being blind hasn't limited me in any of the ways I consider really important. I'm still me. If I've had to be more dependent on my friends, at least I've learned who my friends really are.

Because I've had to struggle to find ways to learn that didn't include sight, I've made superior use of my other senses.

I don't know why God chose to give me only a little vision. Maybe he did it so that I would appreciate what I do have even more. Maybe he did it so that I would have to develop my other capabilities and talents to compensate. Or maybe he gave me this special "gift" because I am, in every other respect, so normal that he wanted to push me to excel. It worked.

There are many different ways to look at life. This is how I see it.

Jason Leib

Four Kisses

I am thirteen and going to a baseball game with my father. I bring binoculars, a little Dutch-boy haircut, my glasses, insecurity, a love for the game and a lack of serotonin in my brain. The fog is twisting around Candlestick Park, leaving the feeling of dampness, dirty water on my jacket and wetness on my glasses, making my perspective skewed like a funhouse mirror. My father wants more than anything else to teach me to keep score, but I am desperately trying to never learn anything new again, because the things I have learned in the last year have been all-around destructive: that I am clinically depressed, that a school day is too long, that I have obsessive-compulsive disorder, and that I am losing even more weight, and am down to eighty-five pounds.

My father grabs my hand. "Did you see that pitch? Right on the money, right on the money. Whoever says they're not going to take it all the way . . ." Asleep in the car on the way home, I can only vaguely hear the music he has on softly so as not to wake me. Something about going home, going home, going home. Mom is asleep in their bed with her red-and-gray quilt that smells just like she does.

My father stops in my room on his way to his. "Good night, Kater." He is standing in the one spot in my doorway where everything echoes. "Good night, Daddy. I love you. Can I have four kisses?" I need four of everything, because obsessive-compulsive disorder has me believing in plastic number power, power I can't have in other arenas. So I make my bed sixteen times and wash my hands until I have slammed the door to the cabinet under the sink just so, so that nobody dies or gets in a car wreck.

My father notes that I have been sleeping wildly. I am usually a still sleeper, the biggest moves I make are a shift from one side to the other, so that I go to sleep staring at the green light from my clock, and wake up with my face towards the wall. But starting last year, I have been waking up having kicked my quilt off, with my stuffed animals relegated unconsciously to the coldness of the floor.

The next day my father says, "Maybe you're getting better." He tries.

"I just want it to end."

"I know you do."

"But I really, really need it to end. Dad, I can't deal with it."

"You know how when you're cleaning out your desk or your room, you have to empty everything out, spread it all over the floor?"

"I guess." I wipe the tears from my face. I hate not being able to see.

"Well, you're there right now."

I hadn't noticed until now how foggy it is. We are walking across the street from a mortuary on the way back from my therapist. It is a Tuesday.

"What?" I asked, not understanding his point.

"Katie, you have everything spread out all over the floor. You have to wait, to pick it all up." This only makes me cry harder, because I am frustrated by the reality of the metaphor blown up, enlarged, unreachable.

My father and my mother are constant reminders to me of what I leave when I go to school for abbreviated days. They are what I stand to lose.

Graduation day. My father and my mother sit in the white plastic chairs; I am on an elevated platform. It is wood painted brown, and parts of it have chipped off so that the chairs that my eighth-grade class sits on are tipping and making plastic-to-wood noises through hollow speeches. Somewhere in the middle, I start to cry. For once it's okay, nobody jeers. I am leaving a part of my life on an uneven platform with my above-the-ears-but-growing-out haircut, bangs clipped back with golden barrettes, a white dress and wonderful parents.

My father drives me to my first day at high school. I haven't been to the therapist in three months. I am walking on legs and feet and ankles that I trust. A senior tells my older sister that I am strutting around school. I keep my bangs pulled away from my face. I hate not being able to see.

My father and I have begun to fight. He does not want me staying out too late. He is upset that my grades are lower than he expected. He always wants to know when I'll be home. When I argue with him, and he leaves, I almost don't know what to do with myself. My obsessive-compulsive power is gone. I am empty so that I can start over.

"Fall came today," my dad says, his first words to me that morning. Since the recent death of my friend's brother, I think of first words and last words more carefully than I should. There have been other first words on other mornings, mostly about the weather or the Giants and how they blew it in the seventh with two runners on, one of them in scoring position. I nod. I'm ineffectual with him that way, letting him bounce off me, because if I let him in, I would be admitting to something. I have thoughts now. And they are mine. My insides and my breaths and my friends and my words, they are all mine. I cling to them more and more.

When my father and I fight, it is loud and articulate. There's something cleansing about it, and it makes me shake. He tells me that he's proud of how well I can argue, that I can always get my point across. My father blames me when my mother gets sick, because it's the stress that I cause, manifesting itself in her.

I am finally sixteen. I have a best friend and contact lenses, a father, a mother and a past. I have beaten something. And that is what I have inside me: strength. I realize, midway through the first quarter of my junior year, that I don't know who bats cleanup for the Giants. I realize that the mortuary across from my old therapist was torn down to build a parking lot. I realize that I haven't talked to my father, sat down and talked to him, since I went away this summer by myself and came back with crisp white inspiration.

I finally have enough serotonin in my brain. I know what I need. I have respect for myself and what I went through. It used to be inexplicable. My father, my mother, a dry bedspread, a song about going home and the National League champion Giants went through it with me. I had built a fresh new me, but I had lost my father. And I wasn't willing to give him up.

I hear his sweaty-feet footsteps coming up the stairs in the house. I lie in my bed tonight, a sixteen-year-old at 110 pounds with long hair, a daughter, home by curfew. Warm and whole, stubborn, stronger, older, and I ask my father for one solitary kiss.

Kate Reder

No Matter What Happens

I remember a time when each day was long,
When the world was a playground and my life a song,
And I fluttered through years with barely a care,
Ignoring the future and what waited there.

School was intriguing and filled with delights.
I played away daytimes and dreamed away nights.
My parents assured me I had nothing to fear,
And that no matter what happened, they'd always be there.

Little I knew of a world outside home,
Where tragedy, sorrow and murder could roam.
All I saw were blue skies, rainbows and stars.
I looked past destruction of buildings and cars.

As a child, my biggest concern was just me;
I had to be happy, I had to be free.
And if I was content, I would not shed a tear,
And no matter what happened, I still would be here.

But as I grow up, darkness starts to set in;
My bright world has turned into concrete and tin.
I now see the violence I looked past before;
My friends start to die and my heart hits the floor.

Deadly diseases claim people I love,
There are landfills below me, pollution above.
I often think back to when life was a game.
But no matter what happens, it can't be the same.

There are days when I just want to break down and howl,
To give up completely, to throw in the towel,
But I hold my head high and I push my way through.
I have too much to give and so much to do.

And I make a vow that, though it'll be hard,
I'll go on with a smile and play every card.
I'll give all I can, help others and love.
No matter what happens, life will bloom again,
And the strength I don't have will come from above.

So come, take my hand, and through darkness we will
    sail—
If we all join together, we never can fail.
We'll remember to care, remember to feel,
And no matter what happens, our world we will heal.

Alison Mary Forbes
Submitted by Barry Weber

Hero of the 'Hood

When you have to cope with a lot of problems, you're either going to sink or you're going to swim.

Tom Cruise

By all odds, Mike Powell should never have survived. Addiction, drug pushing, prison or early death are the most likely cards dealt to street kids growing up in the "jungle" of South-Central Los Angeles—a violent combat zone of drug wars, gang slayings, prostitution and crime. But Mike's young life had a special purpose. For eight years, he braved terror and brutalization to keep his family of seven kids together. Incredibly, during that time, no one ever discovered that the only real parent the family had was just another kid.

When Mike was born, his father, Fonso, was in prison for drug dealing. Mike's fifteen-year-old mother, Cheryl, dropped out of school to support the baby. "Without you, my life could have been different," she later told Mike over and over. It was the guilty glue that would make Mike stick with her through the coming years of horror.

Fonso was released from prison when Mike was four, but instead of security, the six-foot-five, 300-pound Vietnam vet brought a new kind of fear into Mike's life. Fonso had severe psychological problems, and his discipline was harrowing. For minor infractions, such as slamming a door, he forced Mike to do pushups for hours. If the little boy collapsed, his father beat him. So fanatical was Fonso's insistence on school attendance that Cheryl had to hide Mike in a closet when he was sick.

Perhaps it was some dark premonition that drove Fonso to toughen up his young son and teach him self-reliance far beyond his years. Mike was barely eight when his father was murdered in a run-in with drug dealers.

Overnight, the protection and income Fonso had provided were gone. It was back to the streets for twenty-four-year-old Cheryl, who now had three kids: Mike; Raf, age four; and Amber, one year. Life was bitterly hard, and another baby was on the way.

It wasn't long before Cheryl brought home Marcel, a cocaine addict who terrorized the family even more than Fonso had. When Mike innocently questioned what Marcel had done with Cheryl's wages as a transit worker, Marcel broke the little boy's jaw so badly it had to be wired in place.

Marcel soon got Cheryl hooked on cocaine, and the two would disappear on drug binges, at first leaving the children locked in a closet but eventually just leaving them alone for weeks at a time. Cheryl had convinced Mike that if anyone found out what was happening, the children would be separated and sent to foster homes. Remembering his father's fierce admonitions to "be a man," the eight-year-old became consumed by the need to keep his family together, no matter what.

To make sure no one suspected anything, Mike began cleaning the apartment himself, doing laundry by hand

and keeping his sisters fed, diapered and immaculate. He scavenged junk shops for hairbrushes, bottles and clothes, whatever they could afford, and covered up for his mother's absences with an endless litany of excuses. Cheryl and Marcel were soon burning through everything the family had in order to buy crack—even money for rent and the children's food. When their money situation became desperate, Mike quietly quit elementary school at nine to support the family himself. He cleaned yards, unloaded trucks and stocked liquor stores, always working before dawn or late at night so the smaller children wouldn't be alone while awake.

As Cheryl and Marcel's drug binges and absences became longer and more frequent, their brief returns became more violent. Sinking deeper into addiction, Cheryl would simply abandon Marcel when his drugs ran out and hook up with someone who was better supplied. A crazed Marcel would then rampage through the slum apartment, torturing and terrorizing the children for information about where more money was hidden or where he could find their mother.

One night, Marcel put Mike's two-year-old sister in a plastic bag and held it closed. Without air, the toddler's eyes were bulging and she was turning blue. "Where's your mother?" the addict screamed. Sobbing, Mike and little five-year-old Raf threw themselves at Marcel again and again, beating on his back with small, ineffectual fists. In desperation, Mike finally sank his teeth into Marcel's neck, praying the savage tormentor would drop the plastic bag and pick on him instead. It worked. Marcel wheeled and threw Mike through the window, cutting him with shattered glass and breaking his arm.

Cheryl's parents, Mabel and Otis Bradley, loved their grandchildren deeply, but they worked long hours and lived a difficult multiple-bus commute away, and could see them only rarely. Sensing the family was struggling, Mabel sent toys, clothes and diapers, never dreaming that even the diapers were being sold by Cheryl for drug money. Although Mabel's constant phone calls and unconditional love became Mike's only anchor of support, he didn't dare tell her that anything was wrong. He feared his gentle grandmother would have a heart attack if she learned the truth—or worse, a violent confrontation with Marcel.

The family was forced to move constantly, sleeping in movie theaters, abandoned cars and even fresh crime scenes at times. Mike washed their clothes in public restrooms and cooked on a single-burner hot plate. Eventually, Cheryl and Marcel always caught up with them.

Despite the moves, Mike insisted the younger kids attend school, get good grades and be model citizens. To classmates, teachers and even their grandmother, the children always seemed normal, well-groomed and happy. No one could have imagined how they lived or that they were being raised by another child. Somehow Mike had managed to sort through the good intentions but brutal methods of his father, and blend them with the loving example of his grandmother, to form a unique value system. He loved his family deeply, and in return, the children loved, trusted and believed in him. "You don't have to end up on the street," he told them. "See what Mamma is like? Stay off drugs!" Secretly he was terrified that his mother would one day O.D. in front of them.

Over the next few years, Cheryl was jailed repeatedly for possession and sale of narcotics and other crimes, and was sometimes gone for up to a year at a time. Out of jail, she continued to have more children, making the family's financial situation increasingly critical. Hard as Mike tried, it was becoming impossible for him to care for three new babies and support a family of seven kids at the same time. One Christmas there was only a can of corn and a box of macaroni and cheese for all of them to share. Their only toys for the past year had been a single McDonald's Happy Meal figurine for each child. For presents, Mike had the children wrap the figurines in newspaper and exchange them. It was one of their better Christmases.

The young teenager now lived in constant anxiety, but still refused to fall into the easier world of drug dealing and crime. Instead, he braved the dangerous streets late at night selling doctored macadamia nuts, which, to half-crazed addicts, looked like thirty-dollar crack-cocaine "rocks." He knew he risked his life every time he took such chances, but he felt he had few choices. In the nightly siege of gang and drug warfare, the odds were against him, though. By age fifteen, Mike had been shot eight times.

Worse, his reserves of strength and hope were running dangerously low. For as long as he could remember, he had lived with relentless daily fears: *Will we be able to eat today? Will we all be on the street tonight? Will Marcel show up tomorrow?*

And after more than forty moves, it seemed they had finally hit rock bottom. "Home" was now the Frontier Hotel, a filthy dive on Skid Row where pimps and prostitutes stalked the halls and drug deals went down on the stairways. The kids had watched a murder in the lobby, and Mike was now afraid to leave them alone or to sleep. For the few nights they had been there, he had stayed up with a baseball bat to kill rats as they crawled under the door.

Sleep-deprived and overwhelmed by stress, Mike felt crushed by the responsibilities of his life. It was 2:00 A.M. His brother and sisters were huddled under a single blanket on the floor. Michelle, the youngest baby, was crying, but he had no food for her. The boy who had shouldered his secret burden for so many years suddenly lost hope.

Stumbling to the window in despair, Mike stood at the edge, steeling himself to jump. Silently asking his family to forgive him, he closed his eyes and took a last deep breath. Just then, a woman across the street spotted him and began screaming. Mike reeled back from the edge and fell into a corner, sobbing. For the rest of the night, he rocked the hungry baby and prayed for help.

It came a few days later on the eve of Thanksgiving 1993, shortly before Mike's sixteenth birthday. A church outreach group had set up a sidewalk kitchen nearby to feed the hungry, and Mike took the children there for free sandwiches. So impressed were the volunteers with him and the polite youngsters that they began asking gentle questions. A dam deep inside Mike finally broke, and his story spilled out.

Within days, the church group was at work trying to find the family permanent shelter, but no single foster home could take all seven children. Advised that the family would have to be separated "for their own good," Mike adamantly refused, threatening to disappear back into the jungle with the kids. The only person he trusted to keep the family together was his grandmother. Reluctantly, he finally told her of their life for the past eight years.

Stunned and horrified, Mabel Bradley immediately agreed to take the children, but the Los Angeles County social welfare system balked. Mabel was sixty-six, retired, and the children's grandfather was diabetic. How could the Bradleys possibly cope with seven youngsters? But Mike knew better. He hid the children and refused to negotiate any alternative except his grandparents. Finally the social workers and courts agreed, and an ecstatic Mabel and Otis Bradley were granted permanent legal custody of the children. Somehow every child had survived unscathed. Nothing short of miracles, it seemed—and Mike's unfathomable strength and love— had kept them together.

Mabel has since returned to work and now willingly commutes more than one hundred miles a day, while Otis cares for the children. Mike works as many jobs as he can to help support the family, but smart, willing and honest as he is, only minimum-wage jobs are available. More than anyone, he realizes the value of an education and is working on his GED.

His dream is to someday start a small company that can simultaneously employ and counsel street kids like himself who are without the traditional education and skills to make it in the normal work world, but who don't want to be forced back to street life because they can't find work.

Mike is also dedicated to reaching other inner-city kids through his music. A talented singer and songwriter, he writes inspirational rap with his own unique message of hope. Having seen so many kids die in his young life, he wants desperately to reach those who might live. "Surviving is against the odds, but it happens, and we have to get that message out. If a thousand people hear me and two kids don't get shot, don't deal, don't die, then we've done something."

There is little time to sing right now, though, for Mike and his family are still struggling themselves. But Raf, Amber and Chloe are now stepping proudly into Mike's big shoes to do their part at home. They are the three oldest street babies he raised—and taught to live with courage and hope.

They remember well all of Mike's words, whispered fiercely to them over and over during the bad times, during the many moves when, each time, they had to leave everything behind: "Whatever you have, be grateful for it! Even if you have nothing, be grateful you're alive!

Believe in yourself. Nobody is stopping you. Have a goal. Survive!"

Mike Powell will have his company for street kids some day. And there will be time, later, for the rest of his dreams, too. Mike is, after all, only nineteen.

Paula McDonald

The Mom I Never Had

I still remember the first time I heard that my mom had been admitted to the hospital for drug-related problems. I was angry, scared, sad and confused, and I felt betrayed. Questions ran through my mind. How could she do this to me? How could she do this to her family? Was it my fault? I felt that it was; that I had done something wrong. As if I had fought with her too much the day before. As if I had rebelled enough to drive her over the edge.

I think back to when I was younger, and I don't really remember my mom being there when I needed her. I never talked to her about the guys I liked, or shared my feelings if I was upset. In turn, she never confided in me when she was sad or needed someone to talk to. My life was never "normal" like all the other girls in my class. Why didn't my mom take me shopping? Why didn't my mom ever come to basketball games, teacher conferences or orthodontist appointments? Then it hit me. My mother, an R.N. who worked in the emergency room for numerous years—a great nurse, and friend to all—was a drug addict. My dad tried to convince me that everything would be okay, that if she moved away for a while, we would all be fine. But I knew deep in my heart that I needed my mother.

The next few days while my mother was in de-tox were hell. It still hadn't sunk in. I had no one to talk to, and there were so many unanswered questions. I watched home videos of when I was a little girl and wished everything would be "normal." I know now that it was never normal.

Then my mom called from the hospital. I remember her voice so soft and weak. She said she was sorry for everything. I wanted to tell her to come home, that I loved her and everything would be okay from now on. Instead, I kept telling her that it wasn't her fault, and between my sobs I said good-bye. You see, I wasn't supposed to cry. I was supposed to be the strong one.

The next day, we went to visit her. I didn't want to be alone with her. I didn't want to talk to her because I was afraid of what she might say. It was weird having those feelings toward my own mother. I felt like she was a stranger, someone I didn't know.

She came home on a Tuesday. We talked for a while and she said she wanted me to come to meetings with her. I said that I would, not knowing what kind of people I would meet or what they would be like. So I went, and the meetings really helped me understand that what my mom was dealing with was a disease, and that no one was at fault. I also met some great people who helped me understand things even further.

I was still unsure, though. At meetings, I heard all this talk about relapse and how to prevent it. What if my mom relapsed? How would I deal with this a second time? I remember when my mom was using drugs, she would stay in her bedroom for long periods of time. One day, after noticing that my mom hadn't come downstairs for a while, I got frightened. I tried to tell myself that even if she slipped, we would get through it, but I didn't really believe we could. I forced myself to go upstairs and see what she was doing. I was scared as I opened the door to her bedroom, afraid of what I might see. But I wasn't disappointed. I found her in her bed, reading a prayer book. I knew then that my mom was going to make it!

She had pulled through, and because of it, we were able to begin the mother-daughter relationship that we never had. I finally had my mom.

Becka Allen

Good Night, Dad

"You afraid of heights?" my dad asked, as I climbed up the seemingly unstable ladder to the second-story rooftop. I was up there to help him fix our TV antenna.

"Not yet," I replied, as he climbed up after me with tools in hand.

I didn't have much to do up there on the roof—mostly I just held the antenna still and handed my dad tools—so I began to talk to him as he worked. I could always talk to my dad. He was more like a big kid than an actual adult. In fact, he looked much younger than his forty-one years. He had straight black hair and a mustache, with no signs of graying or balding. He stood at a strong six feet and had dark green eyes that seemed to always be laughing at some secret joke. Even my friends, whom he'd make fun of without mercy, loved him. Most of my peers would be embarrassed to have their dad hang around with them, but not me; in fact, I took great pride in him. No one else had a dad as cool as mine.

After he finished working on the antenna, we went inside, and I began to get ready for bed. As I entered my room, I looked over and saw my dad working intently at his computer in his office, which was adjacent to my bedroom. As I watched him, I had the most incredible urge to just poke my head in and tell him that I loved him. I quickly brushed that urge away and continued on into my room. I couldn't possibly say to him "I love you"; I hadn't said that to him or anyone else since I was seven, when my mom and dad would come and tuck me in and kiss me good night. It just wasn't something a man said to another man. Still, as I walked in and closed my bedroom door behind me, the feeling continued to grow inside of me. I turned around, opened my door and poked my head into my dad's office.

"Dad," I said softly.

"Yes?"

"Um . . ." I could feel my heartbeat rising. "Uh . . . I just wanted to say . . . good night."

"Good night," he said, and I went back to my room and shut the door.

Why didn't I say it? What was I afraid of? I consoled myself by saying that maybe I'd have the courage to say it later; but even as I told myself that, I knew it might never happen. For some reason I felt that was going to be the closest I'd ever come to telling my dad I loved him, and it made me frustrated and angry with myself. Deep within me, I began to hope he'd know that when I said "Good night," I really meant to say "I love you."

The next day seemed like any other. After school, I began to walk with my best friend to his house, as I frequently do; however, his mom surprised us by picking us up in the parking lot. She asked me whose house I was going to, and when I said "Yours," she paused and said, "No, I have this feeling that your mom probably wants you home right now." I didn't suspect anything; I figured she had something she wanted to do with her own family, and so I shouldn't butt in.

As we pulled up to my house, I noticed a lot of cars in front and quite a few people I knew walking up our front steps.

My mom greeted me at the front door. Her face was streaming with tears. She then told me, in the calmest voice she could manage, the worst news of my life. "Dad's dead."

At first, I just stood there as she hugged me, unable to move or react. In my mind, I kept repeating *Oh God, no; this can't be true! Please . . .* But I knew I wasn't being lied to. I felt the tears begin to run down my face as I quickly hugged some of the people who had come over, and then I went upstairs to my bedroom.

As I got to my bedroom, I looked over into my dad's office. *Why didn't I say it?!* That was when I heard my little three-year-old brother ask, "Mommy, why is my brother crying?"

"He's just feeling a bit tired, honey," I heard my mom tell him as I closed my bedroom door behind me. She hadn't told him yet that Daddy wouldn't be coming home from work again.

Once in my room, I hurt so badly that my body went numb and I collapsed on the floor, sobbing. A few moments later, I heard a scream from downstairs and then my baby brother's voice crying out, "Why, Mommy?!" My mom had just told him what had happened. A few seconds later, she came into my room and handed my crying baby brother to me. She told me to answer his questions while she stayed downstairs to greet people who came over. For the next half hour I tried to explain to him why Heavenly Father wanted our dad back with him, while I simultaneously tried to pull myself back together.

I was told that my father had died in an accident at work. He worked in construction and somehow, he had been knocked off the crane he was inspecting. Some workers nearby said they didn't hear him shout or anything, but had run over to him when they heard him land. He was pronounced dead on arrival around eleven o'clock that morning, April 21, 1993.

I never really told my dad I loved him. I wish I had. I miss him very much. When I see him again after this life, I know that the first thing I'm going to say to him is "I love you." Until then, "Good night, Dad."

Luken Grace

A Name in the Sand

I sit on the rocky edge of a boulder, letting my feet dangle in the stillness of the water, and gaze out at the rippling waves crawling into shore like an ancient sea turtle. A salty mist hangs above the water, and I can feel it gently kissing my face. I lick my lips and can taste the familiar presence of salt from the ocean water. Above my head seagulls circle, searching the shallow, clear water for food and calling out to one another. And in my hand rests. . . .

The sound of a hospital bed being rolled down the hallway outside my mother's hospital room brought me out of my daydreams. The ocean was gone and all that was left was a bare hospital room, its only decorations consisting of flowers, cards and seashells carefully arranged on a table next to my mother's bed.

My mother was diagnosed with cancer about a year ago, a year full of months spent in various hospitals, radiation therapy, doses of chemotherapy and other methods to try to kill the cancer eating away at her life. But the tumors keep growing and spreading, and all the treatments have done is weaken her already frail body. The disease is now in its final course and, although nobody has told me, I know my mother won't be coming home this time.

I tried to change my thoughts, and they once again returned to my daydreams. Everything seemed so clear and so real, the sound of the waves, the taste of salt, the seagulls, and the . . . what was in my hand? I glanced down at my hands and realized I was holding my mother's favorite shell. I placed it against my ear, and the sound of the ocean sent cherished memories crashing into my mind.

Every year, my mother, my father and I would spend our summer vacations in a little cabin down by the ocean. As a little girl, I would explore this stretch of sand with my parents. Walking hand-in-hand, they would swing me high into the air as we ran to meet the incoming surf. And it was there, in those gentle waves, where my parents first taught me how to swim. I would wear my favorite navy blue-and-white striped swimsuit, and my father's strong arms would support me, while my mother's gentle hands would guide me through the water. After many mouthfuls of swallowed salty ocean water I could swim by myself, while my parents stood close by, proudly and anxiously watching over me. And it was in those grains of sand, not on a piece of paper that could be saved and displayed on a refrigerator, that I first painstakingly wrote my name.

My family's fondest memories weren't captured on film and put in a photo album, but were captured in the sand, wind and water of the ocean. Last summer was the final time my family would ever go to the ocean all together. This summer was nearly over and had been filled with memories of various hospitals, failed treatments, false hopes, despair, sorrow and tears.

I glanced over at my mother lying in her hospital bed, peacefully asleep after the doctor had given her some medicine for her pain. I wanted to cry out to God, "Why, why my mother? How can I live without her to help me through my life? Don't take her away from my father and me!" My tears and sobs began to fade away, as the dripping of my mother's IV hypnotized me into a restless sleep.

* * * *

"Ashes to ashes, and dust to dust," droned the pastor, while my father and I spread my mother's ashes over the ocean water. Some of them fell into the water and dissolved, while others were caught in the wind and carried away. This was my mother's final wish—to be in the place she loved the most, where all her favorite memories live on.

As the funeral concluded and people began to drift away saying words of comfort to my father and me, I stayed behind to say my final farewell to Mother. I carried her favorite shell that brought her so much comfort while she was in the hospital and unable to hear the sounds of the ocean. I put it to my ear and the sound of the ocean seemed almost muted. I looked into the shell and was surprised to find a piece of paper stuck inside of it. I pulled the paper out and read its words:

To my daughter, I will always love you and be with you.

A name in the sand will never last,
The waves come rolling into shore high and fast.
And wash the lines away,
But not the memories we shared that day
Where we have trod this sandy shore,
Our traces we left there will be no more.
But, wherever we are,
The memories will never be far.

Although I may not be with you,
Know that my love for you will always be true.
Those memories will last forever,
And in them we shall always be together.
Hold them close to your heart,
And know that from your side I will never part.

As I crossed the beach, I stooped and wrote my mother's name in the sand. I continued onward, turning only to cast one last lingering look behind, and the waves had already begun to wash my lines away.

Elizabeth Stumbo

Train Tracks

"Alison, come on out and play," my best friend yelled through the screen door. Many summer mornings, I ran through the old house, my long red hair flying after me, to meet Manda on the rickety front steps.

"Watcha wanna do t'day?" she always asked.

"Oh, I dunno. Let's go play at the Ol' Station again."

The Ol' Station was once a train station in 1912, but it was no longer in use. The tracks were rusty, but trains used them all the same. A narrow gravel road cut through the old train tracks and was used to lead to the housing area in which Manda and I lived.

Playing at the Ol' Station was more than fun, it was an eight-year-old's dream. Imaginations ran wild, friendships blossomed, and the day's worries were forgotten at the Ol' Station. Manda and I loved to run down the train tracks searching for granite rocks and old money that might have been left from the station's productive days. When we were younger, we would dress in our mothers' clothes and pretend we were ladies of America's elite, waiting for a train of riches. When one of us became angry with the other, we would run down the tracks, either as far as we were allowed or until we couldn't breathe.

One day, in a fit of rage against Manda, I started sprinting down the tracks, when her foot caught and she tripped.

"Ouch! Oh my gosh, Alison, help me!"

I looked back to find Manda lying on the tracks, bawling like I'd never seen my tough friend bawl before. I ran back to her. "What's wrong? Are you okay?"

"I tripped and hurt my knee."

I looked at the badly skinned knee.

"It's just a little blood. Here, you hop on my back and I'll carry you home." So that's what we did—I gave her a piggyback ride home.

Over the years, Manda and I had gone our separate ways, but we still considered ourselves friends. Beginning our ninth-grade year, we had only one class together, and that was Algebra I. We both hated math with a violent passion and hated our teacher equally as much. Manda sat behind me, so I spent most of the class time passing notes to Manda that made fun of Mrs. Madlock, whom we'd nicknamed "The Green Heifer" due to her large build and green shirts.

"Guess what today is?" Manda asked me during class one day.

"September nineteenth?"

"Yeah, but today is soccer try-out day!" Manda had always wanted to play soccer. "I've practiced so hard, the coach would be an idiot not to put me on the team."

"Alison, turn around and shut up. You have all weekend to talk to Manda." Mrs. Madlock barked at me. Smiling at Manda, I turned around to learn about the exciting world of algebra.

That night, I went out of town to watch my brother's first football game of the season. I couldn't help but wonder if Manda had made the soccer team; after all, it had been her dream. I called Manda's house as soon as I got home from the football game, but no one answered.

Disappointed that Manda hadn't cared enough to call and tell me the results of the soccer try-outs, I went to the local car show alone. Aimlessly wandering through the maze of cars, wondering why Manda and I had grown apart, I heard a voice shout my name. I turned around to see Jenni Stovers, a girl I was friendly with from school.

"Alison, did you hear about Manda?" The look on her face was difficult to read.

"No," I said casually. "Did she make the soccer team?" Jenni's eyes swelled up with tears as she sympathetically looked at me.

"Alison, Manda was killed last night in an accident."

My mouth dropped and my stomach did a flip-flop, making me feel sick. "Wha . . . what happened?" I stammered.

"Her mother was driving her home from soccer try-outs, and the sun made it hard to see. They were crossing the tracks by your house, and a train smashed into them."

I looked at Jenni's sympathetic face and ran. I ran past Ol' Station, over the railroad crossing, and down the gravel road that seemed to stare angrily up at me like an evil monster ready to attack. I ran up the rickety porch step and through my house, my long red hair flying after me. Throwing myself upon my bed, sobbing into my pillow, I thought back to the carefree days of our childhood when Manda had tripped on the tracks.

"It's just a little blood. Here, you hop on my back and I'll carry you home."

Only this time, I couldn't carry her home.

Alison Hamby

Let's Go Dancing in the Rain

Spring break of 1999 was perfect—I got to spend the entire time with my friends just vegging and hanging out. Of course, there was that English project due the day I got back, which I put off until the Sunday before. I was sitting at my computer furiously making up an essay when my little sister walked in from softball practice eating a snow cone and laughing with a sticky smile.

"Whatcha working on?" she asked lightheartedly.

I smiled at her appearance and told her that it was just an English essay. I turned back and continued clacking away. From behind my shoulder she tried to start a conversation.

"So . . ." she began. "You know a kid in your grade named Justin? Justin Schultz?" She licked at a drip on her snow cone.

"Yeah, I know him," I replied. I had gone to elementary school with Justin. He had to be the greatest guy I knew. He never stopped smiling. Justin had tried to teach me to play soccer in the third grade. I couldn't get it, so he smiled and told me to do my best and cheer everyone else on. I'd kind of lost touch with him in the last year, but I told my sister yes, anyway.

"Well," she said, trying to keep her messy snow cone under control. "His church group went skiing this week." She paused to take a lick.

Lucky guy, I thought.

My sister swallowed the ice chips and continued, "So he went skiing and today he died."

I felt the blood drain from my face in disbelief. My hands froze on the keyboard, and a line of Rs inched across the screen. My jaw slowly dropped as I tried to process what she'd said. *Breathe,* something in my head screamed. I shook my head and whipped around to look at my sister.

She was still innocently munching on her snow cone, staring at it determinedly. Her eyes rose to mine and she leaned back, a little startled. "What?" she asked.

"Y-you're joking, right? Who told you that? I don't believe it. How? Are you sure?" I spit out a long string of questions.

"Claire," she stopped me. She began a little slower this time. "A girl on my softball team was house-sitting for them. Justin's parents called her today and told her, and she told me. Sorry, I didn't think you knew him." She sat very still waiting for my response.

Every memory I had of Justin flashed through my mind. I inhaled slowly. "No. No! NO!" I tried to scream. No words came out. I sat up clumsily and shakily ran from the room with my sister behind me yelling, "Wait! I'm sorry . . ."

I called one of our mutual friends right away. She told me between sobs that no one knew why he died. The thirteen-year-old was as healthy as a horse. He fell asleep on Saturday night in the hotel room, and when his room-mate tried to wake him up Sunday morning, Justin wasn't breathing. I didn't want her to hear me cry, so I quickly got off the phone.

I went to school the next day and put on the same strong mask. The principal gave an impersonal announcement about Justin's death that morning and almost immediately I could hear sobs throughout the classroom. That was the worst week of my life. I tried to be a shoulder for others to cry on, but inside I was the one crying.

On Wednesday evening my friend gave me a ride to Justin's viewing. What surprised me when we walked into the room was that Justin's parents weren't crying. They were smiling and comforting everyone. I asked them how they were holding up, and they told me that they were fine. They told me they knew that he wasn't hurting now, that he was with God and would wait for them in heaven. I cried and nearly collapsed. Mrs. Schultz stepped forward to hug me, and I cried on her beautiful red sweater. I looked into her eyes and saw her sympathy for a girl who'd lost her friend.

I went home that night with a deep sadness in my heart for Justin. I wrote a letter to him that I planned on giving him at his funeral. In the letter I wrote to him about how sad everyone was, how much we missed him, how wonderful his parents were and the things he'd never get to do on Earth. I closed it with:

> *Somehow I've always believed that once in heaven, tangible things really don't mean that much anymore. Well, before you get too used to your new life, take these things with you. The smell of grass thirty minutes after it's cut. The feel of freshly washed sheets. The heat of a small candle. The sound a bee makes. The taste of a hot Coke just poured and swirling with ice— hot, but partially cold. The feel of raindrops on your soaked face. But if you take nothing else with you, take your family's embrace.*

I paused and stared into my candle. I rearranged my pen in my hand and continued writing. *Tell you what, Justin. When I die, let's go dancing in the rain.* I smiled through tears and slid my letter into an envelope.

The next day was Justin's funeral. At the last minute, my ride had to cancel because of a schedule conflict, and I was left to sit alone in my house crying. I glanced down at my letter and smiled, "How am I going to get this to you now, Justin?" I laughed through my tears and kept crying.

Sometimes strange thoughts pop into my head, as if from somewhere else. Sitting on my bed fingering a tissue, one of those thoughts told me how to get it to him. *Smoke is faster than dirt.* I was startled by this, but after thinking about it, I realized I was to burn the letter, not bury it. I cried for an hour as I carefully burned the letter. I'd burn a corner, then blow it out under the running water in the sink, afraid of the flames. Eventually, the letter was gone and the white smoke streamed from my window. I waved it away and prayed to God that Justin would someday read my words in the smoke.

That night I dreamt about death and awoke at 2:38 A.M. to hear rain tapping on my window. Rare are the visible words from heaven, but those precious raindrops were my answer. I had told Justin that I wanted to go dancing in the rain. The slow rhythm on my window told me that Justin had heard me. In that moment, I knew that he felt no pain and that we would see each other again. And on that day, we will go dancing in the rain together.

Claire Hayenga

Emergency 911

I never thought the day would come. You stop by me as I get on the tennis bus. "Would you like a ride to practice?" you ask.

"No, Stephanie—but thanks, anyway." My parents would freak if they found out I got into a car with a sixteen-year-old driver.

You drive away after promising to come to our tennis match tomorrow. I wave out of the bus window as you head down the hill.

Five minutes later, our bus is slowing down as we pass a crash on our left side. Crashes are really cool, especially if they are really bloody and gory. The car, a red Honda Civic, looks like yours, but there are lots here in Valley Center. The side is all bashed in, and everyone's faces are covered in blood. People are walking around with cell phones, calling 911. The bus moves on to tennis practice.

My mom is working at the hospital tonight. She calls home to say that two girls from my school are dead, and one is in critical condition. The other was released earlier. I blow it off. The next morning, my mom comes home. She says that you are dead, Stephie, and so is Jenn. I don't believe her and go to school. When I get to school, I suddenly believe her. I start crying as my friends look at each other in amazement. I never cry, at least I haven't in about three years. But this is real. They have a room open for people who can't handle classes. But I'm Danni. Of course I can handle them. But I can't. I can't last five minutes through first period before I start bawling.

I spend the day in the memorial room making cards for your families. Reporters come up to me and ask me how I feel. I say words not befitting a girl. Your family comes in, Stephanie. I am surprised by how much your sisters look like you. I almost mistook your older one for you. But you weren't there. I laid roses in the quad for you. I wrote countless poems and cried countless tears. Did you know you had so many friends?

The memorial service was held today. The song they played was "Lately"—a song about death and learning to live again. It was our favorite. As I step off of the bus back at Ramona High School, the last chords of "Lately" can be heard.

I won all of my matches for you today. I met a guy the other day. You sent him from heaven, didn't you? His name is Tyler. He helped me through this. I wanted to be with you, and almost succeeded. But he helped me realize that life is worth living to the fullest. After all, that's what you did.

Each day I forget a little more, but in my heart will always be the memory of your love and kindness. Oh, and Stephanie: I don't think crashes are cool anymore.

Danni Villemez

11:21 A.M.

[AUTHOR'S NOTE: *I was a junior at Columbine High School and was in the choir room when the shootings began. I wrote this poem after the tragedy to help me deal with the pain and grief. My classmates and I are still struggling with the emotional trauma, but we continue to heal. We are so grateful to the officers, firefighters and others who saved people's lives that day. I would like to thank everyone throughout the world for their ongoing support and prayers as we begin to rebuild.*]

> I lie on my bed
>   numb,
>   unemotional,
>   non-feeling.
> Fear stains my memories as I reflect
>   on a placid morning in Littleton.
> A usual day in choir.
> We prepare for concerts,
>   blithely indulging in normal routine.
> Carefree . . . Content . . .
>   Unaware. . . .

A sudden blast startles us.
A chemistry explosion?
Deafening eruptions penetrate "Ave Maria."
Sinuous voices now punctuated by gunshots,
  the demonic splintering the angelic.

The choir hushes
  to the rhythm of pounding hearts.
Students scream through halls
  as terror burns itself on innocent faces.

Tick, Tick, Tick—11:21—
  lives are forever changed.
Shock . . . Hysteria. . . .
  Why?
The sound of bombs ignite horror through our veins
  and send chills
  that pinch the skin like needles.

Some run.
Some stand paralyzed in shock,
  numbness engulfing all other emotions.
Billows of powder now blanket the hall,
  creating ghostly images.
I look through the delicate webs of cotton
  and see the fruits of hatred.
Bullets shatter glass
  and invade bodies,
  as malice sears the souls of the perpetrators.

A student prays;
  another hides in stunned confusion;
  a teacher bleeds.

Like children
  we are helpless,
  longing to be in mama's arms.

Screaming . . . Frantic . . .
  Why?

Two faces
  are plastered against the window.
The horror in their eyes strips away
  my consciousness.
My first instinct is to run;
  I duck as bullets spray the halls.

Our school is now the grounds of warfare—
  mortal fighting
  in a field of bombs and bullets.
Weapons that have fallen into the wrong hands
  have only one purpose and they
  are killing us and all I hear is gunfire.
Crackling, Crackling,
Humming, bursting, screaming, ringing, what
  now,
Too much
Too soon
Too young
So scared
Help us.

I struggle to escape but am slowed
  as if trudging through water.
Through the front doors I see milky clouds
  that absorb the sun;
I see golden light and sunburned pavement.
I cannot get there fast enough.

I am almost to the door.
A bullet ricochets off the pane.
The glass swirls like a droplet on water,
  creating rings that shiver and spread,
  shattering as I dash through the door—

All is silent.
I have escaped hell.

There is a dark room
    where ten broken bodies lie,
    and where others play dead.
In the darkness of the library,
    angels embrace the lifeless,
    and their wings flicker light
    against a wall of helpless shadows.
God now wraps His arms
    around the school
    and gathers the souls of the lost,
    makes strong the souls of the weak,
    cries for the violence on Earth.

Time picks up and I am
    vulnerable, insecure.
A dog's bark screams like bullets.
Who to trust?
Our haven is destroyed,
    and we are scattered.

I sit immobilized,
    while anxiety and guilt wrap themselves around me
    and consume me.
Angry . . . Numb . . .
    Why?
Are there answers in silence . . . ?
Because I am asking you and you don't answer . . .

Or maybe the silence is just you listening.

Joanna Gates

Tears

I did not cry for Michigan.
It seemed before my time.
I did not cry for Jonesboro,
too far away to mind.
I did not cry for Palisades
even though it may be mine.
I did not cry for Conyers, Georgia
By then it all seemed fine.
But I poured my heart right through my eyes
The day they shot up Columbine.

The tears they fell for children lost
And children on the line.
My head fell quick into my hands
for parents who must pine.
My eyes stayed glossy to a screen
Watching kids of my own climb.

But,
What shook my body up the most,
What made it hard to breathe,

What bolted all my stomach down
And wouldn't let me leave.
What made me think about those boys
And try to empathize
Was the fright, the fear, the look of death
In one scared victim's eyes.

She described a scene so horror filled
So wrapped with movie cuts.
I thought about these kids and film,
what put them in their ruts.
I ruled out only media—
we all watch similar things
But combined with loneliness and fear
Who knows what games can bring?

One lesson to be learned from this,
The only one for which I'm sure,
Is that a gun manufacturer, movie title, music
    lyric, parent, anti-depressant, Internet,
    trench-coat, insult, or whatever else,
Is not the thing at fault.
And no gun policy, censorship, parent in jail,
    drug ban, Web-site check, dress code, sus-
    pension, or whatever else,
Would have removed their every thought.
We must take looks inside ourselves, accept-
    ing looks with love.
For what they didn't like in someone else,
Is what they saw in themselves.

Jamie Rowen

Can That Be?

[AUTHOR'S NOTE: *I would like to submit the enclosed poem by my daughter Kelly, who was a sophomore. Kelly was a beautiful, kind and loving teenager with a heart of gold. She loved to write short stories and poetry, and wanted to become a published author. Kelly's life came to a tragic end, however, on April 20, 1999 when she was shot and killed in the library at Columbine High School. Kelly touched many hearts along her life's journey. A former middle-school teacher described her as "a gentle soul who walked among us that would never be forgotten." Kelly will remain forever in the hearts of those who loved her. This is one of Kelly's poems written in December 1998. Thank you for keeping Littleton in your prayers.*

God Bless,
Dee Fleming]

> I step outside what did I hear?
> I heard the whispers and
> The cries of people's fear.
> The loneliness of wisdom,
> Can that be?

The sad, sad sorrow that I see,
That is past in the tree.
Is it true? Can it be real?
Can I let them know how I really feel?
The things that I have seen,
The things that I have felt,
The feelings of sorrow that
I hope will soon melt.
I walked through the distances
And thought how it should be,
Of the smiles and the laughter,
That is what I thought it should be.
But can that be?
I walked past the dark houses,
And crossed the open fields.
I walked to the tree to kneel
I took a deep long breath
Then I closed my eyes.
I counted to three,
Then I open my eyes,
I was in my room,
That was a surprise.
But then I had seen that it was just a dream.
I walked to the window and pulled on the string.
What a surprise to see the sunrise.
In the distance were children with laughter and happiness,
That was the thought that I like to see!
But of course can that really be?
Or can this be another dream?

Kelly Ann Fleming

Building Bridges

When written in Chinese, the word "crisis" is composed of two characters. One represents danger and the other represents opportunity.

John F. Kennedy

The day started out just like most other Tuesdays. I'm in a show choir called "Unclaimed Freight" at Columbine High School; we rehearse in the mornings before school. I got to school at 6:50 A.M., saw friends and said hello on my way in.

We went through the day normally until fifth period, which for me is Concert Choir. We were starting our warm-ups when a student in the choir came into the room and said there was a guy downstairs with a gun.

This student was known to be a jokester. But he had a pretty serious look on his face, and I saw kids running by when I looked out the window. The choir director told us all to chill out. He didn't want us to panic—there were 114 choir members. He was walking toward the door near the stairwell when two girls opened the door, and we heard two shotgun bursts. Half the choir hit the ground.

My first instinct was to run. I went out the opposite door that the two girls had come in, into a corridor that leads to the auditorium.

I saw a stampede of people running down the hallways. I heard screams. I decided I wasn't going to try and join the mob, so I ran into the auditorium. I stood at the back of the auditorium, wondering what refuge kids were finding behind plastic chairs. Then I heard the semi-automatic fire. At some point, somebody pulled the fire alarm down, so lots of kids in the east end of the school got out without a notion of what was happening.

I headed out the north door. I saw the fire doors at the north hallway—the main hallway—were closed, so I turned and ran for the front door. As I got closer I saw there were already bullet holes in the glass.

Seeing the bullet holes made me run even faster. I reached the front door and pushed it open. The bullets had weakened the glass, and shattered glass came showering out of the door all over me. I just kept running. I didn't even notice the blood all over me until much later. I later went to the hospital for stitches.

About fifteen kids followed me and got out the front door. I learned later that we barely made it out. Seconds later one of the shooters, Dylan, came into the main office and started spraying bullets.

I saw a friend, and we ran to her house. From her house we could see the front of the school. We watched the police, the firefighters, the paramedics, the SWAT teams from Denver and other areas, and the National Guard as they showed up. State patrolmen and sheriffs pulled up and got out of their cars with their guns. They stood behind trees and told kids to run.

The next few hours seemed to last forever. At first I thought a kid was in the school with a gun and that he may have shot a few kids, maybe injuring somebody, but

I hoped he hadn't caused much harm. As I watched the different teams of police show up and heard on the radio there were two gunmen, possibly three, I started to realize how big this really was.

A group of police drove a fire truck close to the building. They jumped out and ran inside. I found out later that lots of those guys weren't trained to be in the positions they were leading. They went in and risked their lives—they didn't even think about it, they just did it to save lives.

It scared me to death when later reports on the radio said that twenty-five kids were killed. I hadn't seen my best friend, Dustin, come out. I prayed he was all right. I didn't find out he was safe until much later. He had hidden in a bathroom in the kitchen and was evacuated with other kids who hid nearby.

It was a living nightmare. It was a bad day multiplied by the biggest number you can think of. The day seemed to go on for years—hours were days; everything was wrong.

The night of the shootings a lot of us went to a service at St. Francis Cabrini Catholic Church. It was really emotional for all of us because we knew our friends who should be there were gone forever. I couldn't even imagine that friends of mine—Cory, Rachel, Isaiah, Cassie—wouldn't be back at school. How could their lives end so violently? How could Eric's and Dylan's minds get so messed up?

For the longest time I didn't know what day it was, the day of the week, the date—it all just kind of ran together. I didn't eat anything for three days—I had a sick feeling inside. I kept crying. Every emotion ran through my head. I was sad, mad, confused, helpless and lost.

I spent a little time with my parents. I hugged them a lot and told them I loved them. But I needed to be with my friends, the people who had experienced this with me. People can say, "I know how you feel," but it's not true if you weren't there.

There were lots of counselors around. Media were everywhere. People showed up trying to get kids to come to their church. What touched me most were the people who came just to be available for us. They were there if we needed someone to talk to. They didn't force themselves on us at all.

We had lots of get-togethers on private property where the media couldn't get to us. We would just go and be together—the first week that's all we did. We didn't have to speak to each other—it was enough to share the silence with each other.

The first place that the faculty and students got back together was at a community church. The student body was sitting together waiting for the faculty. The choir decided we wanted to sing because before the tragedy we were practicing some very spiritual, very touching songs that had a high level of difficulty. We got up together and went up on the stage. The faculty still hadn't made it in, so I was "volunteered" to conduct.

We started singing "Ave Maria." I had chills and the hair on the back of my neck was standing up. We hadn't warmed up and the song has some very high notes for females. But they were just ripping them out—the sound was unbelievable.

As we sang "The Lord's Prayer," the faculty came into the sanctuary and started singing with us. Then the whole student body joined in. Here we were, together for the first time after a living nightmare, singing "The Lord's Prayer." As I conducted and heard the most beautiful sounds ever, I felt the love in that room. At that moment I knew we would be all right.

Charlie Simmons

Minutes Like Hours

You walk into the store
and stride down the aisle.
You pick me up and
try to look casual while
you carry me down
to the checkout line.
Pull out your wallet,
you soon will be mine.
Your friends are observing
every move that you make.
The clerk asks for ID—
you show him a fake.
You quickly walk down
to the front of the store.
Your friends are waiting for you
as you step out the door.
You hop in the car
and drive away from the shop.
Then you shut off the ignition,
and pop off my top.
You take a few drinks

and pass me around.
That's when you decide
to take a drive around town.
You turn on your car
and put your foot on the clutch.
I'm sober, you think,
I didn't have very much.
You pull onto the road
with me by your side,
Taking occasional sips
as you enjoy the ride.
Then the brakes on the car
in front of you squeal.
You try hard to stop,
but lose control of the wheel.
You skid off the road,
and you know you have crashed.
The dashboard is shattered,
the windshield is smashed.
Minutes like hours,
You're in treacherous pain,
that washes your senses,
envelops your brain.
The screams all around you
are faint to your ears,
as life flashes before you,
your hopes and your fears.
Minutes like hours,
you plead and you pray,
I'll never touch it again,
just let me live one more day.
Your mind starts to go dark,
it falls apart piece by piece.
And then you slip into blackness,
the pain has finally ceased.

Before you entered that store,
you should have thought twice,
for I am the substance
that cost you your life.

Vidhya Chandrasekaran

Fire and Rain

Leslie had the most incredible voice. When she sang everyone would get very quiet as if making a sound would stop this beautiful angel from singing. She played the drums, the piano and was strikingly beautiful. Her presence captivated me. Every time I looked at her or heard her voice, I knew that Leslie was going to do wonderful things with her life.

We used to sit by the piano for hours singing James Taylor and Carly Simon songs. She taught me how to harmonize. When we sang together nothing else mattered. It was always a way for me to achieve instant happiness.

I remember when Leslie met Mike. "This one is different," she would tell me. "He is so grown up, very mature." He wasn't like the high-school boys she was used to dating. She was so excited that he had asked her to pick him up at the airport. He had been out of town visiting relatives, and he couldn't wait an extra minute to see her. She borrowed her parents' car.

I was told two days later that Leslie was dead. She had had a couple beers before leaving for the airport. She had a six-pack in the back seat. It was assumed the beers were for their reunion. She drove off the side of the road and hit a boulder. They didn't find her until thirty-six hours later, although the search had started immediately after Mike reported her missing.

Sometimes I sit quietly, scared to make a sound. I only wish I that I could hear her singing. I softly hum the tune of "Fire and Rain." I am alone. My beautiful angel must be singing somewhere else.

Anonymous

The Last Song for Christy

Matt never did drugs. He spent his afternoons and nights riding his skateboard through backstreets of the small town that raised him. His friends would experiment with the usual substances, but not Matt.

Christy was his sister; six years older. She and Matt were close. They both liked tattoos and metal guitar riffs. Christy would paint incredible portraits and abstract images, and Matt would jam on his guitar. They shared stories and they always said "I love you" before bed.

When Matt and I started dating, the first family member I was introduced to was his sister, Christy.

"See this tattoo on my wrist. Christy has it, too. We got them together." He lit up whenever he talked about her.

Matt was at the peak of his skateboarding career, and Christy was still painting. She was beautiful. They looked a lot alike—black hair, blue eyes. Christy was petite—her makeup dark and interesting—her lips, red and passionate. She looked the part she played—the artist, the once-rebel who survived hell and was now back, living life while revisiting the shadows of her past with each stroke of her paintbrush.

When Matt was in junior high, the police took Christy away. His parents wouldn't tell him why, but he found out on his own. Heroin. She had been doing heroin, and they caught her. She was only eighteen. She spent the next several months in rehab while Matt waited, guitar riffs, skate tricks—waited.

When she finally did come home, things were different. Christy seemed distant and Matt didn't know what to say. A few months later, they came again—the police. Matt was sleeping, and they knocked down the door. His sister was screaming as they dragged her away, this time to prison.

I asked Matt what it was like, how that affected him. I tried to imagine hearing her scream. I wondered how it was possible for Matt to sleep when he knew his sister was cold and alone in her cell somewhere.

"I couldn't," he said. "I couldn't sleep."

"Did you visit her?" I asked.

Matt was silent.

"Did you ever talk to her about it, tell her how much it hurt you, tell her that you couldn't sleep, tell her that you were afraid?"

There was a long silence. "She's okay now. She's been clean for eight years. She's great. It's over. The drugs, it's all over." Matt spoke to the wind when he spoke of Christy's past. His voice would fade out into oblivion and then he'd change the subject.

When Christy was finally released from jail and then rehab, Matt's family decided to move. They moved south, away from Christy's reputation and the backstreets where Matt had conquered curbsides and half-pipes in the small town by the sea. Christy was clean and never again did Matt wake up to his sister's arrests, or a cold sweat after the nightmares that plagued him while she was away. She had been clean for six months, and then two years, and then four. Matt went to high school and Christy moved back up north to go to school.

"Were you afraid?" I asked.

"Nope. She was going back to school. I was glad. She was going to pursue her art. She was so talented, you know," Matt whispered.

I knew. I had seen her artwork. It hung in Matt's room, in his kitchen and bathroom. She had even painted straight on the walls. Matt let her paint all over them.

Matt and I dated during my senior year. He was my first serious relationship. Christy came down to visit Matt and the family pretty often, and whenever she came down, Matt would rush to be with her. She was the woman in his life, more than I ever was. Christy and Matt were best friends. They were like nothing I had ever seen. Matt would light up when Christy entered a room. He was so proud of her. She was his angel, his big sister, and everything she said was amusing, brilliant or just cool.

I got the call a few months ago. Even though Matt and I had broken up over a year before, we were still close friends. The call wasn't from him, though. It was from another friend.

"Becca, look . . . I thought I should tell you. Christy died. She overdosed. Heroin. I'm sorry."

The air went numb, and the murmur of the TV in the other room muted. I dropped the phone and stared at the wall for what seemed like hours.

"But she was clean. Ten years now! She was clean . . ." I mumbled softly, my voice tainting the wind that blew on that rainy afternoon. I called Matt. He was with his family up north, where it happened.

I drove up north to be with him at this difficult time. matt told me, "She wasn't supposed to die. She was going to be married in a couple of months. They had the date and everything. We found this picture of her. She was wearing wings. You should see it; she looks like an angel."

He wasn't crying. I searched the blues of his eyes for a tear, but he was hypnotized. The shock. The impossibility of his earth angel lost somewhere in the universe. It was too much.

"The last time I saw her, she was so happy. I had my guitar and I was playing for her, and she was laughing. She was so beautiful and so happy. She was going to be a makeup artist. She would have been the best." Matt was smiling, and I took his hand.

She didn't have to die. She was clean for ten years, and then one day she started up again. Her body couldn't take it. She passed out, and they couldn't revive her. They couldn't make her come back.

Matt spoke during the funeral. His words were soft and eloquent, and he looked out at Christy's friends and family and told them how much he loved her, how much he will always love her. He showed his tattoo, the one that he and his sister got together. Some laughed. Some cried.

The picture that Matt had mentioned to me was perched behind the podium, between lilies and roses. Matt was right. She did look like an angel—red lips and blue eyes, wearing white and angel wings.

That night, after the funeral, Matt and I went down to the cove where he and Christy used to laugh. "How could she do this? Why? Why did she have to do this?" he asked.

He cried. I cried, too.

I talked to Matt the other day. I asked him how he was doing.

"I'm okay," he said. "Most of the time. Sometimes I can't sleep. I'm waiting for Christy to come home or for her to call. Sometimes I have these nightmares. I play the guitar a lot, even more than I used to. I have to practice. I'm in a band now, and we play gigs and stuff. The last song of the set is always the best. That's the song I practice over and over again until it's perfect. It has to be just perfect because I play it for Christy. The last song is always for Christy."

Rebecca Woolf

Defining Myself

Without a struggle, there can be no progress.
Frederick Douglass

My dad died when I was four. My brother was two and my sister only one. Soon after, our family grew to five children, as I found myself with a half-sister and then a half-brother. We lived in the poorest part of the city; the projects were only a block away.

My mother, a widow in her twenties with five kids, couldn't handle it. She became an alcoholic and a drug user. Her expensive drug habit caused her to use all the money she could get her hands on for drugs. Although we were on welfare, she didn't use the money for the food we needed. Instead, she used the money to help support her drug habit. Her routine became a normal occurrence: she sent each one of us kids to the store with a food stamp. We'd buy something for a quarter or less, then give the change to her. We soon began to rely on the food given out by homeless shelters in order to eat. We would receive a bag and walk through a line as donated food, such as TV dinners or canned green beans, was dropped in our bags.

Not only were we deprived of a proper diet, but our poverty prevented us from experiencing the normal joys that kids look forward to, such as Christmas. Although we swallowed our pride when we had no choice but to seek food donations, it was hardest during the holidays. Each winter, our thin, hand-me-down clothing and holed shoes forced us to accept free clothes and a voucher for new shoes at the local church, which we then exchanged as Christmas gifts. Knowing that our clothes came from this organization made it impossible to believe in Santa, tainting our holiday spirit.

Soon, my mom began disappearing for days at a time. In a way, it was better when she wasn't around because we didn't have to live in fear of her mental and physical abuse, like the beatings and heartless name-callings. One night, after my mom threw a lamp at me, nailing me on the side of the head, and a plastic vase at my sister, hitting her in the eye, I made the toughest decision that I ever had to make. I called Child Protective Services, while my sisters cried beside me, begging me not to. Although my mom had been reported before for abuse and neglect, we had always been prepared, cleaning the house beforehand and lying about our situation. Since I was a good student and none of us were troublemakers, we were convincing. We made everyone believe that we had a great life. But while we could lie to everyone else, we could no longer lie to ourselves.

We were put into foster care. My sister and I were placed with an elderly couple in the country, my brother stayed in the city with another family, and my half-sister and half-brother went to live with their dads. We were permitted to visit with my mom once a week, that is if she showed up. When she did come to see us, which averaged about once every two months, she promised us that she was getting an apartment so that we could live together once again.

It's been four years now since I made that call. No one

has heard from my mom in over two and a half years. We don't even know if she's dead or alive. Although my brother walked down the wrong path for a while having stolen a car, he was released from detention center early for good behavior and vows to turn his life around. My sister has been adopted by a family who lives in a nice neighborhood. She's on a swim team and finally getting good grades. My half-sister still lives with her father. Her dad remarried a wonderful woman who treats her like her own daughter. Unfortunately, we lost contact with our little half-brother, and we haven't had any luck finding him. He'll be turning six soon.

And me? I'd like to say that I'm doing pretty well. I just turned sixteen, and I have finally found stability in my life, which has helped me excel and succeed in many areas. I've been on the honor roll for five years, and I'm involved in way too many school activities. I'm even in a volunteer group that promotes the fight against drugs and alcohol. I'm a good advocate of the anti-drug campaign because I know from firsthand experience what happens when drugs run your life: they ruin not only your own life, but the lives of those around you. I tell my story and amaze people with my positive attitude, despite all that I've been through. My adoptive mom says, "You've definitely made some sweet lemonade out of all the sour lemons you've been handed."

What I went through, all my hardships and pain, they're part of who I am. I'll always feel like I'm different, and I'll always have to fight the feelings that I wasn't good enough, not even for my own mom. But I'm not going to let those feelings define me. I will only let them make me stronger. And I know that I'm going to be somebody. Actually, I already am.

Morgan Mullens-Landis

7

MAKING A DIFFERENCE

It's important to be involved and stand up for what you believe in.

Ione Skye

The Leader

If only they knew how hard it is for me.
I'm turning sixteen, the world I begin to see.
My friends begin to change, right before my eyes,
and now they seem to laugh, and tell all sorts of lies.
They hang around together in groups of three or four;
the language they use . . . it isn't gentle anymore.
The kids that seem most lonely wind up in their pack,
and those that stand alone, they talk behind their back.
Somehow I feel rejected because I don't conform.
Those that step to their own beat don't seem to be the norm.
I've watched a few just fade away, with drugs and alcohol;
and many more have given up, too many to recall.
Alcohol is an option for everyone in my school.
I've lost a friend to booze again; I will not be a fool.
And sex, it seems so open, for everyone to explore.
Three girls I know that came to school don't come here
    anymore.
If only I could make a difference, what could I do or say?
I would go to school and try my best each and every day.
There is one thing I'd like to do before I graduate.
I'd like to touch them one by one before it is too late.

Tony Overman

Turning Up Your Light

Those who bring sunshine to the lives of others cannot keep it from themselves.

James M. Barrie

More than three decades ago, I was a sophomore at a large high school in Southern California. The student body of 3,200 was a melting pot of ethnic differences. The environment was tough. Knives, pipes, chains, brass knuckles and an occasional zip gun were commonplace. Fights and gang activity were weekly events.

After a football game in the fall of 1959, I left the bleachers with my girlfriend. As we walked down the crowded sidewalk, someone kicked me from behind. Turning around, I discovered the local gang, armed with brass knuckles. The first blow of the unprovoked attack immediately broke my nose, one of several bones to be broken in the pounding. Fists came from every direction as the fifteen gang members surrounded me. More injuries. A brain concussion. Internal bleeding. Eventually, I had to have surgery. My doctor told me that if I had been hit in the head one more time, I probably would have died.

Fortunately, they did not harm my girlfriend.

After I recovered medically, some friends approached me and said, "Let's go get those guys!" That was the way problems were "resolved." After being attacked, evening the score became a priority. A part of me said, "Yes!" The sweet taste of revenge was clearly an option.

But another part of me paused and said no. Revenge did not work. Clearly, history had demonstrated time and again that reprisal only accelerates and intensifies conflict. We needed to do something differently to break the counterproductive chain of events.

Working with various ethnic groups, we put together what we called a "Brotherhood Committee" to work on enhancing racial relationships. I was amazed to learn how much interest fellow students had in building a brighter future. Not all bought in to doing things differently. While small numbers of students, faculty and parents actively resisted these cross-cultural exchanges, more and more individuals joined in on the effort to make a positive difference.

Two years later, I ran for student body president. Even though I ran against two friends, one a football hero and the other a popular "big man on campus," a significant majority of the 3,200 students joined me in the process of doing things differently. I will not claim that the racial problems were fully resolved. We did, however, make significant progress in building bridges between cultures, learning how to talk with and relate to different ethnic groups, resolving differences without resorting to violence and learning how to build trust in the most difficult of circumstances. It's amazing what happens when people are on speaking terms with one another!

Being attacked by the gang those many years ago was clearly one of my toughest life moments. What I learned, however, about responding with love rather than returning hate has been a powerful force in my life. Turning up our light in the presence of those whose light is dim becomes the difference that makes the difference.

Eric Allenbaugh

The Most Mature Thing
I've Ever Seen

Every student at Monroe High School knew about it. Nobody did it. Nobody.

Lunchtime at Monroe High School was consistent. As soon as the bell that ended the last morning class started ringing, the students swarmed toward their lockers. Then those who didn't eat in the cafeteria headed with their sack lunches toward the quad. The quad was a large, tree-less square of concrete in the center of campus. It was the meeting-and-eating place.

Around the quad the various school cliques assembled. The druggies lined up on the south side. The punkers were next to them. On the east side were the brothers. Next to them were the nerds and brains. The jocks stood on the north side next to the surfers. The rednecks were on the west side. The socialites were in the cafeteria. Everybody knew their place.

This arrangement did create some tension. But for all the tension generated on the perimeter of the quad at lunchtime, it was nothing compared with the inside of the quad.

The inside was no-man's land.

Nobody at Monroe walked across the middle of the quad. To get from one side to the other, students walked around the quad. Around the people. Around the stares.

Everybody knew about it, so nobody did it.

Then one day at the beginning of spring, a new student arrived at Monroe. Her name was Lisa. She was unfamiliar to the area; in fact, she was new to the state.

And although Lisa was pleasant enough, she did not quickly attract friends. She was overweight and shy, and the style of her clothes was not . . . right.

She had enrolled at Monroe that morning. All morning she had struggled to find her classes, sometimes arriving late, which was especially embarrassing. The teachers had generally been tolerant, if not cordial. Some were irritated; their classes were already too large, and now this added paperwork before class.

But she had made it through the morning to the lunch bell. Hearing the bell, she sighed and entered the crush of students in the hall. She weaved her way to her locker and tried her combination three, four, five times before it banged open. Standing in front of her locker, she decided to carry along with her lunch all of her books for afternoon classes. She thought she could save herself another trip to her locker by eating lunch on the steps in front of her next class.

So Lisa began the longest walk of her life—the walk across campus toward her next class. Through the hall. Down the steps. Across the lawn. Across the sidewalk. Across the quad.

As Lisa walked she shifted the heavy books, alternately resting the arm that held her light lunch. She had grabbed too many books; the top book kept slipping off, and she was forced to keep her eye on it in a balancing act as she moved past the people, shifting the books from arm to arm, focusing on the balanced book, shuffling forward, oblivious to her surroundings.

All at once she sensed something: The air was eerily quiet. A nameless dread clutched her. She stopped. She lifted her head.

Hundreds of eyes were staring. Cruel, hateful stares. Pitiless stares. Angry stares. Unfeeling, cold stares. They bore into her.

She froze, dazed, pinned down. Her mind screamed, No! This can't be happening!

What happened next people couldn't say for sure. Some later said she dropped her book, reached down to pick it up, and lost her balance. Some claimed she tripped. It didn't matter how it happened.

She slipped to the pavement and lay there, legs splayed, in the center of the quad.

Then the laughter started, like an electric current jolting the perimeter, charged with a nightmarish quality, wrapping itself around and around its victim.

And she lay there.

From every side fingers pointed, and then the taunt began, building in raucous merriment, building in heartless insanity: "You! You! You! YOU!"

And she lay there.

From the edge of the perimeter a figure emerged slowly. He was a tall boy, and he walked rigidly, as though he were measuring each step. He headed straight toward the place where the fingers pointed. As more and more students noticed someone else in the middle, the calls softened, and then they ceased. A hush flickered over the crowd.

The boy walked into the silence. He walked steadily, his eyes fixed on the form lying on the concrete.

By the time he reached the girl, the silence was deafening. The boy simply knelt and picked up the lunch sack and the scattered books, and then he placed his hand under the girl's arm and looked into her face. And she got up.

The boy steadied her once as they walked across the quad and through the quiet perimeter that parted before them.

The next day at Monroe High School at lunchtime a curious thing happened. As soon as the bell that ended the last morning class started ringing, the students swarmed toward their lockers. Then those who didn't eat in the cafeteria headed with their sack lunches across the quad.

From all parts of the campus, different groups of students walked freely across the quad. No one could really explain why it was okay now. Everybody just knew. And if you ever visit Monroe High School, that's how it is today.

It happened some time ago. I never even knew his name. But what he did, nobody who was there will ever forget.

Nobody.

Chris Blake
Submitted by Leon Bunker

Broken Wing

*You were born with wings. Why prefer to crawl
through life?*

Rumi

Some people are just doomed to be failures. That's the
way some adults look at troubled kids. Maybe you've
heard the saying, "A bird with a broken wing will never
fly as high." I'm sure that T. J. Ware was made to feel this
way almost every day in school.

By high school, T. J. was the most celebrated troublemaker in his town. Teachers literally cringed when they
saw his name posted on their classroom lists for the next
semester. He wasn't very talkative, didn't answer
questions and got into lots of fights. He had flunked
almost every class by the time he entered his senior year,
yet was being passed on each year to a higher grade level.
Teachers didn't want to have him again the following
year. T. J. was moving on, but definitely not moving up.

I met T. J. for the first time at a weekend leadership
retreat. All the students at school had been invited to
sign up for ACE training, a program designed to have

students become more involved in their communities. T. J. was one of 405 students who signed up. When I showed up to lead their first retreat, the community leaders gave me this overview of the attending students: "We have a total spectrum represented today, from the student body president to T. J. Ware, the boy with the longest arrest record in the history of town." Somehow, I knew that I wasn't the first to hear about T. J.'s darker side as the first words of introduction.

At the start of the retreat, T. J. was literally standing outside the circle of students, against the back wall, with that "go ahead, impress me" look on his face. He didn't readily join the discussion groups, didn't seem to have much to say. But slowly, the interactive games drew him in. The ice really melted when the groups started building a list of positive and negative things that had occurred at school that year. T. J. had some definite thoughts on those situations. The other students in T. J.'s group welcomed his comments. All of a sudden T. J. felt like a part of the group, and before long he was being treated like a leader. He was saying things that made a lot of sense, and everyone was listening. T. J. was a smart guy and he had some great ideas.

The next day, T. J. was very active in all the sessions. By the end of the retreat, he had joined the Homeless Project team. He knew something about poverty, hunger and hopelessness. The other students on the team were impressed with his passionate concern and ideas. They elected T. J. co-chairman of the team. The student council president would be taking his instruction from T. J. Ware.

When T. J. showed up at school on Monday morning, he arrived to a firestorm. A group of teachers were protesting to the school principal about his being elected co-chairman. The very first communitywide service project was to be a giant food drive, organized by the

Homeless Project team. These teachers couldn't believe that the principal would allow this crucial beginning to a prestigious, three-year action plan to stay in the incapable hands of T. J. Ware. They reminded the principal, "He has an arrest record as long as your arm. He'll probably steal half the food." Mr. Coggshall reminded them that the purpose of the ACE program was to uncover any positive passion that a student had and reinforce its practice until true change can take place. The teachers left the meeting shaking their heads in disgust, firmly convinced that failure was imminent.

Two weeks later, T. J. and his friends led a group of seventy students in a drive to collect food. They collected a school record: 2,854 cans of food in just two hours. It was enough to fill the empty shelves in two neighborhood centers, and the food took care of needy families in the area for seventy-five days. The local newspaper covered the event with a full-page article the next day. That newspaper story was posted on the main bulletin board at school, where everyone could see it. T. J.'s picture was up there for doing something great, for leading a record-setting food drive. Every day he was reminded about what he did. He was being acknowledged as leadership material.

T. J. started showing up at school every day and answered questions from teachers for the first time. He led a second project, collecting 300 blankets and 1,000 pairs of shoes for the homeless shelter. The event he started now yields 9,000 cans of food in one day, taking care of 70 percent of the need for food for one year.

T. J. reminds us that a bird with a broken wing only needs mending. But once it has healed, it can fly higher than the rest. T. J. got a job. He became productive. He is flying quite nicely these days.

Jim Hullihan

Passing the Dream

She sat on the bench, feeding the birds.
Just throwing crumbs, not saying a word.
I sat down with my beads and braids,
Proclaiming what a mess her generation had made.
I spoke of poverty, and the war in 'Nam.
What is the use of going on?

She replied softly:

"All my life, I have worked for change.
Today, I give you my dream.
You can make a difference, with the small things you do.
The future is entirely left to you.
If things go wrong and you feel down,
Open your eyes and look around.
Don't look for someone to blame.
Search for an inspiration, to rise again.
The changes you make may not always be seen.
But perhaps you can give a child the chance to dream.
So get to work, and maybe find
A small solution to help humankind.

All my life, I have worked for change.
Today I give you my dream."

Today I decided to take a walk.
I passed a teen loudly playing his boom box.
He turned his music down low
And we chatted for a minute or so.
He spoke of the homeless, and the streets filled with crime.
Couldn't my generation have found the time
To ease some of this discord
By feeding the hungry, and housing the poor?

I replied softly:

"All my life, I have worked for change.
Today, I give you my dream.
I hope you make our world a better place.
But you must work diligently; just keep pace
With the changes and dreams of the generation to come.
But with a little luck, a small battle may be won.
Someday, we will merge. And in time you will be
The older generation looking back to see
How you have answered all these questions you ask.
Fixing tomorrow is now your task.
All my life, I have worked for change.
Today, I give you my dream."

Penny Caldwell

The Gravediggers of Parkview Junior High

People are always blaming their circumstances for what they are. I don't believe in circumstances. The people who get on in this world are the people who get up and look for the circumstances they want, and, if they can't find them, they make them.

George Bernard Shaw

The most important lessons we are taught in school go beyond answering the questions on a test correctly. It is when the lessons change us by showing us what we are really capable of accomplishing. We can, with the use of band instruments, make beautiful music. We can, with the use of a paint brush and canvas, show people how we see the world. We can, with the hard work of a team, beat the odds and win the game. However, no multiple choice or true/false test will ever teach us the greatest lesson of all: We are the stuff of which winners are made.

Not long after the release of the film *Jeremiah Johnson,*

starring Robert Redford, our seventh-grade class was discussing the story. We talked about the fact that this rough and tough mountain man was also kind and gentle. We discussed his deep love of nature and his wishes to be part of it. Our teacher, Mr. Robinson, then asked us a most unusual question. Where did we think Jeremiah Johnson was buried? We were shocked when he told us the final resting place of the great mountain man was about 100 yards away from the San Diego Freeway in Southern California.

Mr. Robinson asked us, "So, do you believe this was wrong?"

"Yes!" we all chimed in.

"Do you feel something should be done to change it?" he asked with a sly grin.

"Yes!" we replied with an enthusiasm born of youthful innocence.

Mr. Robinson stared at us, and after a few moments of suspenseful silence, he asked a question that would change the way some of us viewed life forever. "Well, do you think you could do it?"

"Huh?"

What was he talking about? We were just a bunch of kids. What could we do?

"There is a way," he said. "It's a way filled with challenge and probably some disappointment . . . but there is a way." Then he said he would help us but only if we promised to work hard and pledge to never give up.

As we agreed, little did we know that we were signing on to the most adventurous voyage of our lives thus far.

We began by writing letters to everyone we could think of who could help us: local, state and federal representatives, the cemetery owners, even Robert Redford. Before long, we started getting answers that thanked our class for the interest, but "there was absolutely nothing that could be done." Many would have given up at that point. Had it not been for our promise to Mr. Robinson not to quit, we would have. Instead, we kept writing.

We decided that we needed more people to hear about our dream so we contacted the newspapers. Finally a reporter from the *Los Angeles Times* came to our class and interviewed us. We shared what we had been trying to do and how discouraging it was that no one seemed to care. We hoped that our story would raise public interest.

"Did Robert Redford ever contact you?" the reporter asked.

"No," we replied.

Two days later our story made the front page of the paper, telling how our class was trying to right an injustice to an American legend, and that no one was helping us, not even Robert Redford. Next to the article was a picture of Robert Redford. That same day, as we were sitting in the classroom, Mr. Robinson was called to the office to take a phone call. He came back with a glow on his face like we had never seen before. "Guess who that was on the phone!"

Robert Redford had called and said he received hundreds of letters every day and that ours somehow had never reached him, but he was very interested in helping us achieve our goal. Suddenly our team was not only getting bigger, it was getting more influential and powerful.

Within a few months, after all the proper documents were filed, our teacher and a few of the students went to the cemetery and observed the removal of the remains. Jeremiah Johnson had been buried in an old wooden casket that had been reduced to a few rotted boards, and nothing but a few bones were left of the mountain man. All were carefully gathered up by the cemetery workers and placed in a new casket.

Then a few days later, at a ranch in Wyoming, a ceremony was held in honor of Jeremiah Johnson, and his final remains were placed to rest in the wilderness he had loved so much. Robert Redford was one of the pallbearers.

From then on, throughout the school, our class was referred to as the "Gravediggers," but we preferred to think of ourselves as the "Dream Lifters." What we learned that year was not just about how to write effective letters, how our government works, or even what you have to go through to accomplish such a simple thing as moving a grave site. The lesson was that nothing can beat persistence. A bunch of kids at the beginning of our teenage years had made a change.

We learned that we were the stuff of which winners are made.

Kif Anderson

The Boy Who Talked with Dolphins

From what we get we can make a living, what we give, however, makes a life.

Arthur Ashe

It began as a deep rumble, shattering the predawn silence. Within minutes on that January morning in 1994, the Los Angeles area was in the grip of one of the most destructive earthquakes in its history.

At Six Flags Magic Mountain theme park, twenty miles north of the city, three dolphins were alone with their terror. They swam frantically in circles as heavy concrete pillars collapsed around their pool and roof tiles crashed into the water.

Forty miles to the south, twenty-six-year-old Jeff Siegel was thrown from his bed with a jarring thump. Crawling to the window, Jeff looked out at the convulsing city and thought of the creatures who mattered more to him than anything else in the world. *I've got to get to the dolphins,* he told himself. *They rescued me, and now they need me to rescue them.*

To those who had known Jeff from childhood, a more unlikely hero could not have been imagined.

Jeff Siegel was born hyperactive, partially deaf and lacking normal coordination. Since he couldn't hear words clearly, he developed a severe speech impediment that made it almost impossible for others to understand him. As a preschooler, the small, sandy-haired child was taunted as a "retard" by other kids.

Even home was no refuge. Jeff's mother was unprepared to deal with his problems. Raised in a rigid, authoritarian household, she was overly strict and often angry at his differences. She simply wanted him to fit in. His father, a police officer in their middle-class Los Angeles community of Torrance, worked extra jobs to make ends meet and was often gone sixteen hours a day.

Anxious and frightened on the first day of kindergarten, five-year-old Jeff climbed over the schoolyard fence and ran home. Furious, his mother hauled him back to school and forced him to apologize to the teacher. The entire class overheard. As the mispronounced and barely intelligible words were dragged out of him, he became instant prey for his classmates. To fend off the hostile world, Jeff kept to isolated corners of the playground and hid in his room at home, dreaming of a place where he could be accepted.

Then one day when Jeff was nine, he went with his fourth-grade class to Los Angeles' Marineland. At the dolphin show, he was electrified by the energy and exuberant friendliness of the beautiful animals. They seemed to smile directly at him, something that happened rarely in his life. The boy sat transfixed, overwhelmed with emotion and a longing to stay.

By the end of that school year, Jeff's teachers had labeled him emotionally disturbed and learning-disabled. But testing at the nearby Switzer Center for children with disabilities showed Jeff to be average-to-bright, though so anxiety-ridden that his math test score came out borderline retarded. He transferred from public school to the Center. Over the next two years he became less anxious, and his academic achievement improved dramatically.

At the start of seventh grade he returned, unwillingly, to public school. Tests now showed his IQ in the 130s, the gifted range. And years of therapy had improved his speech. But to his classmates, Jeff was still the same victim.

Seventh grade was unfolding as the worst year of Jeff's life—until the day his father took him to Sea World in San Diego. The minute the boy saw the dolphins, the same rush of joy welled up in him. He stayed rooted to the spot as the sleek mammals glided past.

Jeff worked to earn money for an annual pass to Marineland, closer to his home. On his first solo visit, he sat on the low wall surrounding the dolphin pool. The dolphins, accustomed to being fed by visitors, soon approached the astonished boy. The first to swim over was Grid Eye, the dominant female in the pool. The 650-pound dolphin glided to where Jeff sat and remained motionless below him. *Will she let me touch her?* he wondered, putting his hand in the water. As he stroked the dolphin's smooth skin, Grid Eye inched closer. It was a moment of sheer ecstasy for the young boy.

The outgoing animals quickly became the friends Jeff never had, and since the dolphin area was isolated at the far end of Marineland, Jeff often found himself alone with the playful creatures.

One day Sharky, a young female, glided just below the surface until her tail was in Jeff's hand. She stopped. *Now what?* he wondered. Suddenly Sharky dived a foot or so below the surface, pulling Jeff's hand and arm underwater. He laughed and pulled back without letting go. The dolphin dived again, deeper. Jeff pulled back harder. It was like a game of tug-of-war.

When Sharky surfaced to breathe, boy and dolphin faced each other for a minute, Jeff laughing and the dolphin open-mouthed and grinning. Then Sharky circled and put her tail back in Jeff's hand to start the game again.

The boy and the 300- to 800-pound animals often played tag, with Jeff and the dolphins racing around the pool to slap a predetermined point or give each other hand-to-flipper high-fives. To Jeff, the games were a magical connection that he alone shared with the animals.

Even when there were summer crowds of 500 around the pool, the gregarious creatures recognized their friend and swam to him whenever he wiggled his hand in the water. Jeff's acceptance by the dolphins boosted his confidence, and he gradually emerged from his dark shell. He enrolled in a course at a nearby aquarium and devoured books on marine biology. He became a walking encyclopedia on dolphins and, to his family's amazement, braved his speech impediment to become a volunteer tour guide.

In 1983 Jeff wrote an article for the American Cetacean Society's newsletter, describing his experiences with Marineland dolphins. He was unprepared for what followed. Embarrassed by the extent to which he'd been playing with the dolphins without the park's knowledge, Marineland management revoked his pass. Jeff returned home numb with disbelief.

For their part, Jeff's parents were relieved. They could see no benefit to the time their strange, misfit son was spending with dolphins until a day in June 1984 when Bonnie Siegel took an unexpected long-distance phone call. That evening she asked her son, "Did you enter some kind of contest?"

Sheepishly, Jeff confessed that he'd written an essay for a highly coveted Earthwatch scholarship worth more than $2,000. The winner would spend a month in Hawaii with dolphin experts. Now, telling his mother about it, he expected a tirade. Instead, she said quietly, "Well, you won."

Jeff was ecstatic. Best of all, it was the first time that his parents realized he might achieve his dream of someday sharing his love of dolphins.

Jeff spent the month in Hawaii, teaching dolphins strings of commands to test their memories. In the fall, he fulfilled another condition of the scholarship by giving a talk on marine mammals to fellow students at Torrance High School. Jeff's report was so enthusiastic that it earned him, at last, grudging respect from his peers.

After graduation, Jeff struggled to find work in marine research, supplementing the low pay with minimum-wage moonlighting. He also earned an associate's degree in biology.

In February 1992 he showed up in the office of Suzanne Fortier, director of marine-animal training at Six Flags Magic Mountain. Though holding down two jobs, he wanted to do volunteer work with Magic Mountain's dolphins on his days off. Fortier gave him the chance—and was immediately amazed. Of the 200 volunteers she'd trained in ten years, she'd never seen anyone with Jeff's intuitive ability with dolphins.

In one instance, her crew needed to move a sick 600-pound dolphin named Thunder to another park. The animal had to be transported in a nine-by-three-foot tank. During the journey, Jeff insisted on riding in the truck bed with Thunder's tank to try to calm the anxious animal. When Fortier later called from the cab of the truck to ask how Thunder was doing, Jeff replied, "He's fine now. I'm cradling him." *Jeff's actually in the tank with Thunder!* Fortier realized. For four hours, Jeff floated inside the cool tank, holding Thunder in his arms.

Jeff continued to amaze co-workers with his rapport with the animals. His favorite at Magic Mountain was Katie, a 350-pound, eight-year-old dolphin who greeted him exuberantly and swam with him for hours.

Once again, as at Marineland, Jeff could interact with the dolphins and find affection in return. Little did he dream how severely his love would be tested.

As Jeff struggled to reach Magic Mountain on the morning of the earthquake, freeways were collapsing, and caved-in roads often forced him to backtrack. *Nothing is going to stop me,* he vowed.

When Jeff finally reached Magic Mountain, the water in the twelve-foot-deep dolphin pool was halfway down, and more was draining from the crack in the side. The three dolphins there when the quake hit—Wally, Teri and Katie—were in a frenzy. Jeff lowered himself to a ledge five feet down and tried to calm them.

To ease the dolphins through the continuing tremors, Jeff attempted to distract them by playing games, but it didn't work. Worse, he had to reduce their food: The pool's filtration system had shut down, creating the additional risk that an accumulation of their body waste would further contaminate the water.

Jeff remained with the dolphins that night as temperatures fell into the thirties. He was still there through the next day, and the next, and the next.

On the fourth day a road opened, and staffers secured a truck to transfer Wally, Teri and Katie to the dolphin pool at Knott's Berry Farm. But first, someone had to get them into their transport tanks. Transporting a dolphin is normally a routine procedure, after it has been safely guided through a tunnel and hoisted on a canvas sling. But the water level in the connecting tunnel was too low for the animals to swim through. The three dolphins would have to be caught in open water and then maneuvered into canvas slings.

Staffer Etienne Francois and Jeff volunteered for the jobs. As much as he trusted the dolphins, Jeff knew the likelihood of getting hurt or bitten by them in an open-water capture was almost 100 percent.

Wally was easily removed from the pool, but Teri and Katie became erratic. Each time Jeff and Etienne closed in on Katie, the powerful dolphin fended them off with her hard, pointed beak.

For almost forty minutes the men struggled as Katie butted and whacked them with her thrashing tail. Finally, just before they maneuvered her into a sling, she sank her needle-sharp teeth into Jeff's hand. Ignoring the bleeding, Jeff helped capture Teri and hoist her into the transport tank.

When the dolphins reached Knott's Berry Farm, Katie was exhausted but calm. Later, Fortier told friends that Jeff's courage and leadership had been essential in safely transporting the dolphins.

Today, Jeff is a full-time dolphin trainer at Marine Animal Productions in Gulfport, Mississippi, where he organizes programs for schools.

One day, before he left for Mississippi, Jeff gave a demonstration to sixty children from the Switzer Center at one of the aquariums where he had taught. He saw that a boy named Larry slipped off to play alone. Realizing Larry was an outcast, as he himself had been, Jeff called him forward and asked the boy to stand next to him. Then Jeff plunged his arms into a nearby tank and hauled up a harmless but impressive three-foot horn shark. As the children gasped, he allowed Larry to carry the dripping creature proudly around the room.

After the session, Jeff received a letter reading: "Thank you for the magnificent job you did with our children. They came back glowing from the experience. Several told me about Larry getting to carry the shark. This was probably the happiest and proudest moment of his life! The fact that you were once a student here added to it. You are a model of hope that they, too, can 'make it' in life." The letter was from Janet Switzer, the Center's founder.

For Jeff, that afternoon held an even more gratifying moment. As he spoke, he saw his mother and father in the audience, watching intently. From the look on their faces, Jeff could tell they were proud of their son at last.

Jeff has never earned more than $14,800 a year in his life, yet he considers himself a rich man and an exceptionally lucky one. "I'm completely fulfilled," he says. "The dolphins did so much for me when I was a child. They gave me unconditional love. When I think about what I owe the dolphins . . ." His voice trails off momentarily, and he smiles. "They gave me life. I owe them everything."

Paula McDonald

To Track Down My Dream

It was the district track meet—the one we had been training for all season. My foot still hadn't healed from an earlier injury. As a matter of fact, I had debated whether or not I should attend the meet. But there I was, preparing for the 3,200-meter run.

"Ready...set..." The gun popped and we were off. The other girls darted ahead of me. I realized I was limping and felt humiliated as I fell farther and farther behind.

The first-place runner was two laps ahead of me when she crossed the finish line. "Hooray!" shouted the crowd. It was the loudest cheer I had ever heard at a meet.

"Maybe I should quit," I thought as I limped on. "Those people don't want to wait for me to finish this race." Somehow, though, I decided to keep going. During the last two laps, I ran in pain and decided not to compete in track next year. It wouldn't be worth it, even if my foot *did* heal. I could never beat the girl who lapped me twice.

When I finished, I heard a cheer—just as enthusiastic as the one I'd heard when the first girl passed the finish line. "What was that all about?" I asked myself. I turned around and sure enough, the boys were preparing for their race. "That must be it; they're cheering for the boys."

I went straight to the bathroom where a girl bumped into me. "Wow, you've got courage!" she told me.

I thought, "Courage? She must be mistaking me for someone else. I just lost a race!"

"I would have never been able to finish those two miles if I were you. I would have quit on the first lap. What happened to your foot? We were cheering for you. Did you hear us?"

I couldn't believe it. A complete stranger had been cheering for me—not because she wanted me to win, but because she wanted me to keep going and not give up. Suddenly I regained hope. I decided to stick with track next year. One girl saved my dream.

That day I learned two things:

First, a little kindness and confidence in people can make a great difference to them.

And second, strength and courage aren't always measured in medals and victories. They are measured in the struggles we overcome. The strongest people are not always the people who win, but the people who don't give up when they lose.

I only dream that someday—perhaps as a senior—I will be able to win the race with a cheer as big as the one I got when I lost the race as a freshman.

Ashley Hodgeson

From Crutches to a World-Class Runner

A number of years ago in Elkhart, Kansas, two brothers had a job at the local school. Early each morning their job was to start a fire in the potbellied stove in the classroom.

One cold morning, the brothers cleaned out the stove and loaded it with firewood. Grabbing a can of kerosene, one of them doused the wood and lit the fire. The explosion rocked the old building. The fire killed the older brother and badly burned the legs of the other boy. It was later discovered that the kerosene can had accidentally been filled with gasoline.

The doctor attending the injured boy recommended amputating the young boy's legs. The parents were devastated. They had already lost one son, and now their other son was to lose his legs. But they did not lose their faith. They asked the doctor for a postponement of the amputation. The doctor consented. Each day they asked the doctor for a delay, praying that their son's legs would somehow heal and he would become well again. For two months, the parents and the doctor debated on whether to amputate. They used this time to instill in the boy the belief that he would someday walk again.

They never amputated the boy's legs, but when the bandages were finally removed, it was discovered that his right leg was almost three inches shorter than the other. The toes on his left foot were almost completely burned off. Yet the boy was fiercely determined. Though in excruciating pain, he forced himself to exercise daily and finally took a few painful steps. Slowly recovering, this young man finally threw away his crutches and began to walk almost normally. Soon he was running.

This determined young man kept running and running and running—and those legs that came so close to being amputated carried him to a world record in the mile run. His name? Glenn Cunningham, who was known as the "World's Fastest Human Being," and was named athlete of the century at Madison Square Garden.

The Speaker's Sourcebook

For You, Dad

"Here we go!" Dad would say, and I'd climb on his back. "There! Look! See London Bridge?"

Lying on the floor with his arms outstretched, he was my Superman and together we were weaving our way around make-believe clouds. But like those clouds, my moments with Dad always vanished too quickly—because there was something stronger than love in Daddy's life, something that was stealing him away. It was an enemy I would end up fighting when he no longer could. . . .

"He's sick," my mother would say when Dad passed out. "It doesn't mean that he doesn't love you."

I knew he did. He could make us laugh with his funny faces and cartoon drawings. I loved him, and I wanted to believe Mom still did, too. As my little brothers and I grew, she explained that Dad hadn't always been "this way." He was just a little wild when they'd met in high school. And with his wavy hair and wide smile, I could understand how he'd captured Mom's heart.

But soon he must have been breaking it. Sometimes we didn't see him for weeks. One day, he called to say he wasn't coming home again. "I'm not far. We'll see each other on weekends," he said after he'd moved out. "I'll swing by and get you Saturday."

"Mom," I called out. "Can we go with Daddy?"

Grabbing the phone, Mom said, "No, John, you have to visit them at the house. You know I won't let them get into a car with you."

I thought of the commercials I saw on TV—the ones with the twisted metal and chalk outlines. And the words *Drunk driving kills*. Could that happen to Daddy? *Please God*, I'd pray at night, *help Daddy get well*. But too often, when he pulled into the driveway, we could smell the booze.

"Daddy, don't drive like that," I'd plead. Usually, he tried to shrug off my worries, but once he pulled me close, his eyes heavy with sadness. "I wish I wasn't like this," he said. "I wish I was a good dad."

I wished that, too. I hated alcohol for what it had done—to all of us.

At first, I was too embarrassed to tell my friends the truth about my dad. But as I started to see kids drinking, I couldn't hold back. "That's why my dad isn't around," I'd say, pointing to the bottles.

All Dad's visits were brief. In between hugs and kisses, he drew pictures for us, and we crammed in stories about school and friends. "I'm getting help," he'd say. Maybe my brothers, Justin and Jordan, believed it—but I didn't. And yet with all my heart, I wanted to believe. I can still feel the rocking of the porch swing and my father's arm around my shoulder.

"The day you turn sixteen," he once said, "I'm going to buy you a car." I nuzzled closer to him. I knew he'd give me the world if he could. But I understood that no matter how much he wanted to, he couldn't.

Then one night during my senior year of high school, I got a call at the store where I worked part-time. "Heather?"

Mom's voice was strained. I knew what was coming. "There's been an accident."

I raced to the hospital; Dad's motorcycle had hit a mini-van. Blood tests showed he'd been drinking and doing drugs that night. The other driver was fine, thank God.

"I love you, Daddy," I sobbed, sitting by his bed. Though he was unconscious, his heart monitor quickened at the sound of my voice. He had found a way to let me know he'd heard me, and that he loved me. But there was something I had to make sure that he knew.

"I forgive you," I choked. "I know you did your best."

Moments later, he was gone. An accident killed my father, but his death was not sudden.

Everyone told me I needed to grieve, and for a while, I did. But in a sense, I'd been grieving for Dad all my life. Now I needed to do something that would help me feel less powerless against the enemy that had stolen him.

I went to the library to find what I could on substance abuse. *Almost every family is affected. . . . Children may repeat the patterns*, I read. My heart broke even more. My father's life hadn't amounted to very much. Maybe his death could.

That afternoon, I picked up the phone and called the area schools. "I'd like to talk about substance abuse," I began. "I've lived with it in my own family, so I think I can help."

Before I knew it, I was standing before a sea of young faces ready to speak, in a presentation called "Drug-Free Me."

"People who do drugs and alcohol aren't bad," I began. "They've just made the wrong choice." Then I asked the kids to draw pictures of what they wanted to be. They drew firemen and doctors and astronauts.

"See all those pretty dreams? They can never come true if you turn to drugs and alcohol." Their eyes grew wide. *I'm reaching them*, I thought. But I knew it wasn't that simple—I'd have to keep trying every day if I really wanted to make a difference.

Since then, I've used cartoon characters to get the message to younger kids. I've organized a tuxedo-stuffing program, sticking statistics on drunk driving into pockets of prom-goers. And I've joined Mothers Against Drunk Driving and the National Commission on Drunk Driving.

Today, as a college junior, I do presentations at middle and high schools. I also speak at victim-impact panels, sharing stories of loss with people convicted of driving under the influence. Most people on the panel have lost loved ones to people like my father. But I was a victim, too, and maybe my story hits harder.

"It's hard to think of a faceless stranger out there you may kill," I tell the offenders. "So think about the people you are hurting now—like a child at home who will miss you forever if you die."

I'd been missing my father long before he was taken for good. I remember once he said that we, his children, were the only things he'd ever done right in his life. Daddy, because of you, I'm doing something very right in mine.

Heather Metzger
As told to Bill Holton
Woman's World Magazine

Somebody Loves You

Don't forget to be kind to strangers. For some who have done this have entertained angels without realizing it.

Hebrews 13:2

One miserable rainy night, a man named Mark decided to end his life. In his mid-fifties, Mark had never been married, had never experienced the joy of having children or spending holidays with his family. Both his parents had been dead for seven years. He had a sister but had lost contact with her. He held a menial job that left him unfulfilled. Wet and unhappy, he walked the streets, feeling as if there was nobody in the entire world that cared if he lived or died.

On that same soggy night, I was sitting in my room watching the rain hit my window. I was six years old, and my life revolved around my Star Wars action figure collection. I was dreaming of the day when I'd have earned enough money to add Darth Vader to my new collector's case. To help me make money, my father paid me to jog with him. Every day, at seven o'clock, we jogged together.

And every day, I was fifty cents closer to getting Darth Vader.

When I heard the doorbell ring, I jumped from my chair and raced out of my room to the top of the steps. My mother was already at the door.

Opening it, she found herself face-to-face with a very disheveled-looking man with tears streaming down his face. My mother, overcome by pity, invited the man inside, and he sat with my parents in our living room.

Curious, I snuck downstairs so that I could get a better look. I couldn't understand what they were saying, but the sight of the rumpled man, holding his head in his hands and crying, made my chest ache. I raced back upstairs to my room and stuck my hand into my money jar. Pulling out the Kennedy half-dollar I had earned that day, I ran back downstairs.

When I reached the door of the living room, I walked right in. The three adults looked at me in surprise as I quickly made my way over to the stranger. I put the half-dollar in his hand and told him that I wanted him to have it. Then I gave him a hug and turned and ran as fast as I could out of the room and back up the stairs. I felt embarrassed but happy.

Downstairs, Mark sat quietly with his head bowed. Tears streamed down his face as he tightly clutched that coin. Finally looking up at my parents, he said, "It's just that I thought nobody cared. For the last twenty years, I have been so alone. That was the first hug I have gotten in—I don't know how long. It's hard to believe that somebody cares."

Mark's life changed that night. When he left our house, he was ready to live instead of die. Although my family never saw Mark again, we received letters from him every once in a while, letting us know that he was doing fine.

Being a six-year-old kid, I hadn't thought about what I

was doing that night. I had just reacted to the sight of someone else's pain. On our morning jogs, my dad and I had talked about the importance of giving, but I hadn't had any idea of what it really meant. My life changed that night, too, as I witnessed the true healing power of giving. Even if it's only a gift of fifty cents.

Before Mark left, my parents asked him why he had knocked on our door. Mark said that as he'd walked the streets that rainy night, hopeless and ready to die, he had noticed a bumper sticker on a car. He'd stood in the driveway and wondered about the people who lived in the house where the car was parked. Then, in a fog of unhappiness, he had made his way to the front door. It's hard to imagine that a bumper sticker and fifty cents could change two people's lives, but somehow they did.

The bumper sticker on our car read: SOMEBODY LOVES YOU.

Wil Horneff

The Power of a Smile

There is so much in the world to care about.

Laura Dern

Waiting tensely in the small, single room of the Portland Blanchet House, I could hardly control the knot of nervous excitement forming in my gut. It was my first time here with the church youth group to help feed the homeless, and I'd been given the hardest job of all. Nineteen tables in careful rows crowded the room, and it was my job to stand in the center, where I could see every table, telling new people to come in and fill the seats as they emptied.

I was thrilled and eager to be actively doing something directly to help people in the community, but I was also very nervous and curious. What would these people be like? I knew I was doing good and that I could learn a lot from hands-on work, but along with that zealous enthusiasm to broaden my perspective there tugged the urgent voice of a sheltered little suburban girl, whispering for me to hide.

There was no turning back now; it was time. People trudged in, a huddled line of bundles and packs. Red or blue patches of near frozen skin showed here and there beneath ragged scarves and overcoats, muffled eyes peered around the room with an air of bewilderment.

The seniors, who were always the first to be served, quickly occupied the seats farthest from the draft coming from the open door. They immediately started filling the complimentary plastic bags with portable food items such as cookies and rolls. I watched with a kind of naive awe, searching their faces, wondering what were their reasons for living this way, imagining what it would be like to live on the city streets twenty-four hours a day.

I was fidgety, having little to do at this point except wait for the first round of people to finish their meal, so I focused on the advice of the house director: "Lots of 'em come here as much to see a friendly face as to eat the food, so don't be afraid to smile."

This I could handle. Smiling the warmest, most sincere smile I could muster, I caught the eyes of every person I could, and though few smiled back, I felt good about it.

One old man with flyaway tufts of white hair kept looking at me with an expression of far-off wonderment. Vague gray-blue eyes shone amidst the wrinkled sand-paper of his face, and a not-quite-all-there smile beamed out with childlike simplicity. I was greatly touched by his evident pleasure at alternately swallowing a spoonful of ice cream and staring at my face. When he motioned me to come over closer to him, I was only a little alarmed. His speech was slurred and gentle, and he appeared mildly senile. As he reached out one thick-skinned hand to take mine, I felt no threat in his grandfatherly presence.

"I just wanted to ask you," he murmured sweetly, "how much do I owe you for your smile?"

In a laughing rush, I told him, "nothing," and that aged

smile grew even more wide and amazed.

"Well, in that case, may I have another?"

I complied with a helpless blush. He told me that as long as he remembered that smile, he'd be doing just fine.

I thought, *Me, too.* Sometimes that's all it takes.

Susan Record
Submitted by Mac Markstaller

Pay Attention

Jason came from a good family with two loving parents, two brothers and a sister. They were all successful academically and socially. They lived in a posh neighborhood. Jason had everything a boy could desire. But he was always into some kind of mischief. He wasn't a bad kid who caused trouble, but he always wound up in the thick of things.

In first grade, Jason was labeled Special Ed. They tried to keep him out of the regular classes. In middle school, he was the "misfit troublemaker." In high school, although never officially tested, Jason was tagged with having attention deficit disorder (ADD). More often than not, his teachers kicked him out of class. His first report card had one C and the rest Ds.

One Sunday the family was enjoying brunch at the country club when a teacher stopped and said, "Jason is doing so well these days. We're pleased and delighted."

"You must be mixing us up with another family," said the father. "Our Jason is worthless. He is always in trouble. We are so embarrassed and just can't figure out why."

As the teacher walked away, the mother remarked,

"You know, honey, come to think of it, Jason hasn't been in trouble for a month. He's even been going to school early and staying late. I wonder what's up?"

The second nine-week grading period was finally up. As usual, Jason's mom and dad expected low grades and unsatisfactory marks in behavior. Instead, he achieved four As and three Bs and honors in citizenship. His parents were baffled.

"Who did you sit by to get these grades?" the dad asked sarcastically.

"I did it all myself," Jason humbly answered.

Perplexed and still not satisfied, the parents took Jason back to school to meet with the principal. He assured them that Jason was doing very well.

"We have a new guidance counselor and she seems to have touched your son in a special way," he said. "His self-esteem is much better and he's doing great this term. I think you should meet her."

When the trio approached, the woman had her head down. It took a moment for her to notice she had visitors. When she did, she leaped to her feet and began gesturing with her hands.

"What's this?" asked Jason's father indignantly. "Sign language? Why, she can't even hear."

"That's why she's so great," said Jason, jumping in between them. "She does more than hear, Dad. She listens!"

Dan Clark

Joe Camel

"I don't believe it. They are actually taking it down!"

"We really do make a difference!"

As we sit in the bleachers of our high school stadium, we're feeling elated as the huge Joe Camel billboard, positioned directly in sight of our school, is being disassembled—and we did it!

Have you ever raised your hand simply to be part of something, and then have it turn into a life-altering event? That's exactly what happened to Eddie, Marisol and me. We belong to a school club called Friday Night Live, which promotes alcohol- and drug-free friendships and activities. It's not easy resisting the temptation to drink and smoke when, wherever you turn, advertising companies are using big money trying to hook us into using their products. The message is loud and clear: Use this stuff and you are cool, beautiful and popular.

During one of our FNL meetings, Eddie said, "It really makes me mad that everywhere I go on this campus, I can see the Joe Camel billboard, and yet the big tobacco companies tell everyone they are not targeting teens. Yeah, right!"

There are other billboards, but this is the only one you

can see from our school. Our counselor, Ms. Bambus, asked if anyone would be interested in writing to the billboard company and asking them to take it down. What followed was an amazing process that landed us on the *Today* show, CNN and many local TV shows.

We did some research and found out that there was a group called Human Health Services. We asked them if there were any other groups that had done this before and what they did. They gave us a few examples and recommended writing a polite letter to the billboard company. It seemed like it would be more fun if we just marched over and ripped up the billboard, but logic won out and we contacted the company and simply explained our concerns. We also cited the code that does not permit tobacco and alcohol advertisements within sight of a school. The vice president of the company said he couldn't see that the billboard was doing any harm.

Eddie wrote an article about it for the school newspaper, which was picked up by the local city paper. From then on, we had national media coming to our campus. One day, when I was on my way to lunch, Channel 10 came up to me and said, "Irene, we've been looking for you. We heard you and your friends are taking on Joe Camel." They asked for permission to film us talking about how we got started and what we hoped to accomplish.

Five months after all the excitement, the billboard came down. It was replaced by an ice cream advertisement. We were glad that it was all over and were looking forward to getting on with just being teens.

During the time we were involved with this, my grandfather—a smoker who started in his teens—was diagnosed with cancer. Maybe there was a higher power calling me to raise my hand to help write the letter that day. I believe if we help people not to start smoking, that's one family that won't have to watch a loved one die from it. That's a big deal!

Meladee McCarty

Anything Is Possible

It's funny how life works out. One day I was a regular high school student worried about landing the right career, and a year later, I was the owner of a company committed to changing the world, one teenager at a time. You see, my whole life I have been driven, to do something, to be something. I've always wanted to succeed, and I've never let anything come in the way of my goals.

It all started when I was eight years old. I felt like my life was over. My dad had just told me that he was no longer going to live with us; he and my mom were getting a divorce. That night, my loneliest night ever, my whole life changed. I became the man of the house. Although I felt a lot of pain when he left us, my new, important role in the family left me no choice but to move on and assume new responsibilities. Because my dad's leaving left us broke, I knew that my first job would be to earn some money for the family. As an eight-year-old, making money was not such an easy task. But I was a determined kid and not easily dismayed. I partnered with my best friend to start a lawn mowing company. I was director of marketing and he was director of labor. Our instant success gave me newfound confidence.

My ambitions to be successful did not end with the grass-cutting business in my childhood years. My drive to achieve my goals carried with me into my teenage years, where I first began exploring various career possibilities, confident that my explorations would unleash a hidden passion and begin the path to my future career. I attacked each possibility with intensity and determination. But neither medicine nor archaeology left me satisfied, so I continued to search for my passion.

During the time that I spent devoted to discovering my career, I also took some time to help a friend, five years older than I, learn to read. While my career searches left me unsatisfied, I felt an extreme sense of accomplishment in helping my friend. For the first time in my life, I became consciously aware of the power of helping others, and it was an experience that changed my life forever, although I didn't realize it at the time.

Still frustrated by the lack of career direction in my life, I decided that the stock market held my future and once again jumped head first into exploring this profession. Luckily, this one stuck. Before I knew it, I had landed myself an internship at a successful stock brokerage and eventually, after a great deal of hard work and commitment, I was offered many positions throughout the country.

Excited about my offers, but not wanting to ignore my education, I put my job offers on hold to attend classes at the University of Texas. It was during one of my classes that I was forced to reexamine my money-driven career choice. A successful young entrepreneur, Brad Armstrong, asked me what I wanted to do when I "grew up," a question many teenagers are asked and never want to answer. Feeling confident I replied, "I'll graduate when I'm nineteen or twenty, work in New York or Chicago, and retire young—like you." My teenage American dream.

Then he said, "Fantastic! Let's say you make lots of money and retire old, say age thirty-five. What are you going to do then?"

Without hesitation I replied, "See the world!"

He smiled and said, "Okay, let's say you see the world and you're thirty-eight. What are you going to do with the rest of your life? What is your *goal in life*?"

I suddenly flashed back on the experience I had teaching my friend to read and remembered the great sense of accomplishment that I had felt. It was at that moment that I realized what my goal was. I wanted to help others. And I wanted to do it in a way that I knew how.

"Brad," I said thoughtfully. "I want to write a book and help my peers." I am always so frustrated with the unfair portrayal of all teenagers as lazy, unintelligent and violent. What about the millions of us who work hard to get through school, hold steady jobs, support our families and stay clear of trouble?

He replied, "So, why don't you write now? Share with them the methods you've learned to succeed. You can help a lot of people. Share your knowledge."

That night I couldn't sleep. Brad's question about my life mission kept repeating in my head. I made the toughest decision of my life. I decided to follow my heart and jump into life not knowing where I would land.

After a great deal of research and hard work, my book about a career and life success for young people was complete. But I still had a problem. I realized that the very people I would be trying to sell my book to, would probably not be able to afford it. To solve this problem, I created an educational publishing company, designed to get my book into schools across America, where students could read the book at no cost and learn the skills needed to reach their dreams.

While I was not an overnight success, I am happy to say

that my book did eventually catch on with students, educators and business leaders. It is most rewarding to know that I got to help so many people realize what they can do to make their lives successful, especially teenagers, who have been constantly reminded of their weaknesses.

I've learned firsthand that every person holds limitless potential and passion waiting to be unleashed, and I am living proof that goals really can be achieved. Truly anything is possible when you follow your heart. The sky is no longer the limit.

Jason Dorsey

A Challenge That I Overcame

I was nervous as I sat waiting in the hospital room, unsure of what Dr. Waites, the pioneer of diagnosing developmental dyslexia, was telling my parents about the test results.

It all began when I moved to Dallas in the fourth grade, and I noticed that I was behind in my reading at Saint Michael's School. Reading out loud, I had difficulty with half the sentences. My teacher, Mrs. Agnew, said my reading comprehension and ability to pronounce words was at a lower lever than other fourth graders. I was scared every time she called on me to read aloud because, although I would try my hardest, she would always have to help me with the words. Mrs. Agnew suggested that I be tested for dyslexia.

At first I was confused about why I was being tested; I had been in all honors classes at the public school I had previously attended. The test made me feel uncomfortable, and I was scared to answer the questions, in fear of facing failure.

The test results showed that I had developmental dyslexia. At first I felt discouraged by this diagnosis, but eventually, I became determined to master my disability. I got tutors and speech therapy. I even tried to conquer the disability myself. I would read difficult books, hoping to increase the confidence I had in myself. I began to read and comprehend the readings better. I even began to love reading, which is kind of ironic since I had once detested it so much.

I had finally overcome my learning disability. Dr. Waites confirmed this when I was tested again. He said that my dyslexia was at a minimum. I was overjoyed. But even though I had conquered one of the biggest challenges in my life, I still felt like something was missing.

The missing link was filled when I put on my candy-striped uniform for the first time and walked down the halls of the hospital as a volunteer, the same hospital where I had once sat, nervous and confused. Because I felt so lucky to have had access to this facility that had helped me so much, I wanted to give back by being a volunteer.

One day a little girl in a wheelchair asked me to read a book to her. I read the book very slowly so that she could understand the story and the words. When it became time for me to leave, the girl thanked me for reading to her. I walked out of her room with a huge smile on my face. Eight years ago I would have hesitated in reading a book to this little girl, but now I was confident. I had overcome my disability and was helping others to overcome theirs. I am determined to succeed in life, and in the process, help others face and conquer the challenges that I have overcome.

Arundel Hartman Bell

A Street Kid's Guide

When I was asked to address a high school graduation in a nearby community, my mind boggled.

"Me!" I gasped. "You want me?"

After they assured me they did, I felt honored. Just think of it! Me! A guy who never went to high school was being asked to speak to a group of kids on such an important occasion.

What will I say to them? What profound words can I impart that would stay with them, and perhaps help them with life's choices? The more I thought about it, the more I realized that if I was not careful, I stood a good chance of adding my name to a long list of boring, over-the-hill, has-been speakers that came before me. These kids didn't need that. They didn't need any more long-winded speeches of how it was done in the past, nor did they need to be deluged by a barrage of useless platitudes.

I thought and rethought all sorts of ideas, but came up with nothing. It wasn't until the night before the address that it suddenly dawned on me. *Don't tell these kids what you did. Tell them what you learned while you were doing it.*

As I gathered these new thoughts, I drifted back to my

past. I grew up—or rather, was dragged up—in dozens of foster homes and institutions. It was hard to tell where one home left off and another began. Through those same years, I fumbled my way through seven different grade schools. Somehow I missed the fourth grade entirely. But that really didn't matter. Nobody paid very much attention to me. I had no books, no pencils and no paper. And as far as anyone was concerned, I was passing through.

By the time I was eleven, I was in the fifth grade and unable to read. A nun took pity on me. She kept me after school every day to teach me what she could. For the brief time I was with her, I learned a lot. I wish I could have stayed with her, but I knew I couldn't. I was in "the system." I was sent where they wanted to send me, and stayed until they sent me someplace else. I learned early to obey any and all rules, and to never question authority. The system was designed to teach unquestioned discipline, but it was really containment and control. It worked very well.

By the time I was fourteen, I was finished with school— or, rather, it was finished with me. In either case, I was tossed out, told I couldn't be educated, and given a job.

At first this was very frightening. I was alone and on my own. There was no one to turn to if I got into trouble, no one to guide me or show me the way. It was hard. I had to become street smart in a hurry. I got tough quickly; I learned to show no fear and to keep my mouth shut. I chose my roads by trial and error. Whenever I stumbled, I got up and tried again. I was determined not to quit and not to be beaten. I did alright. I got through.

About a dozen or so years ago, a friend who knew about my past and the way I grew up encouraged me to write it down. He told me it was important for people to know what it's like to grow up the way I did. And so, with much stress and difficulty, I somehow found the strength to reach back forty years to relive all the pain and all the tears. I revisited the fear and the loneliness. I wrote my autobiography, *They Cage the Animals at Night*. It was reading this book, and responding to it, that prompted those in charge of the graduation ceremony to invite me to address their kids.

It was a warm June morning when I stood at the podium. All eyes were fixed upon me. The kids were dressed in their caps and gowns and sticky from nervous perspiration. From time to time, they'd glance over to the sections reserved for parents, family and friends. They were trying to locate the proud and smiling faces of those whom they belonged to. When they did, they would smile as a faint blush filled their cheeks. They were just as proud as their parents.

I began to speak. I told them I was honored to be addressing them, but not having been in high school, or graduating from anything, I didn't feel qualified. I then made an unusual request. I asked them if there was any way in which I could take part in their moment, if they might let me be one of them: a graduate. Their applause took me into their ranks, and their eyes took me into their hearts.

I choked back my tears as I said, "This is a street kid's guide on how to get from here to there." Maybe a word here or a line there that might help you get through a rough time: I hope so. . . .

A Street Kid's Guide
(How to get from here to there)

It's hard to get from here to there
If you never get out of bed.
You lie a lot to fool your friends
But you fooled yourself instead.

It's harder to get from here to there
If you set your goals too high;
Then nothing ever works out right;
Too soon, you no longer try.

But the hardest way to get from here to there
Is when all you ever do
Is count up the years, and miles to go.
Then you're through before you're through.

So how do you get from here to there?
Well, you first must believe you can
Let no one tell you differently—
It's your life and it's in your hands.

Then turn your dreams into your goals
And see what you need now
To satisfy the requirements:
The why, the where and how.

At first you're overwhelmed, of course;
There is so much you don't know.
But keep your faith, be strong and sure,
For you do have a way to go.

Take careful steps and do them right,
Take pride in each thing done.
Don't look too far ahead of yourself,
Just that next step yet to come.

Before you know it you'll be there, friend,
Your dream will then be real.
And you'll be standing where I am now,
Telling others how good it feels.

You'll tell them not to quit themselves,
To have faith, though it's hard to bear.
So they will know it can be done—
They, too, can get from here to there.

Jennings Michael Burch

Teenagers Today

I can't count how many times people have uttered, while shaking their heads in obvious disappointment, "I just don't know what is with teenagers today."

The other day I was in my car on my way to the farmers market with my friend Jan when we passed two teens standing by the side of the road with a car wash sign. My car was filthy and my heart was full, so I pulled over. There were teenagers everywhere. There was a group directing the cars and another group spraying them down. As sponges were wiped over every square inch of my dirty car, I sat enjoying the little water battles and the many silent scenarios that were so obviously taking place. I couldn't help but wonder how many crushes, how many new friendships and how many little insecurities were in the air on this beautiful Saturday afternoon. I was amazed at how forty to fifty teenagers had devoted their Saturday to washing cars, and I was curious what their motivation might be.

At the end of the assembly line I handed them a twenty-dollar bill and asked what they were raising money for. They explained to me that a friend of theirs, C. T. Schmitz, had recently died of cancer. He was only fifteen years old and six-feet-two. He had gone to school with a lot of the teenagers who were there that day and each of them had memories of a boy sweeter than any they had known. His friend Kevin had decided to put this car wash together because he wanted to honor his friend and also bring together his classmates with his boy scout troop. He told me that they wanted to plant a tree in front of their school and if they raised enough money they would put a plaque there also. Both would be in memory of their friend C. T.

They handed me a bag of homemade cookies with my receipt and we drove away. I asked Jan to read to me what the tag that was tied to the bag said. It said simply, "Thanks for helping us plant a tree for C. T."

Yeah! I don't know what *is* with teenagers today!

Kimberly Kirberger

An Open Heart

We had to take a malaria pill every week for eight weeks and get a shot of gamma globulin. We were told to bring old clothes, flashlights, bug repellent and an open heart.

I think the last item was the most important: an open heart. That is what those kids really needed.

Honduras is a small country in Central America. The majority of the population is dirt poor, hungry, homeless, parentless and in need. This is where I, along with eighteen of my peers, had committed to spending two weeks of our summer vacation.

I am sixteen years old. This trip was not the vacation trip most teens dream of. It was sponsored by Mrs. Patricia King, whose two sons were adopted into her family from this third-world country. Through her love we were able to help those in need.

We spent our time at an orphanage with children who won our hearts the very moment we met them. How could you not adore a child who wants only a multicolored pen for his fourteenth birthday? For two weeks we shared our souls with these children. We lived in their world, relying only on bare necessities. The heat was often unbearable and the smell of raw sewage was constant. Dirt clung to everything and we had to close our eyes and hold our breath to shower in the contaminated water. It was our job to repaint the boys' room and the hard iron bunk beds. We washed and braided the girls' hair and painted their nails. We exchanged hugs, high fives, kisses and eventually good-byes. We came home different—better.

We learned that the best of all blessings is to be able to give to others. I feel lucky that I'm sixteen and I know that we can make a difference. That's not just something that celebrities say on TV. Every day I am grateful that I learned an open heart is a happy heart.

Sandy Pathe

Mark's Choice

The question is not whether we will die, but how we will live.

Joan Borysenko

"What's wrong?" I still remember asking that question to my teammate as he sat in front of his locker more than twenty years ago. We had just finished polishing off another opponent our senior year and there he sat—head in hands—alone—in pain. He was tough, seventeen years old and a great athlete. His name is Mark Overstreet. The rest of our teammates had showered and left for home, but Mark was still fully dressed in his football uniform. When he raised his head to speak, I saw tears in his eyes. Now I knew something was wrong. This was a young man who took pride in making the opponents cry on the football field. "I don't know," he said silently. "It's as if all the injuries I've ever had are coming back. My whole body hurts. My legs feel like they weigh a hundred pounds each."

A week or so before, an outbreak of the swine flu had swept through our community. One by one, students lined up to take the vaccine to prevent the spread of the illness. I remember we all took the shot and thought nothing of it. When Mark received the vaccine, however, his body developed a very rare allergic reaction to the drug—so rare that his sudden illness was never correctly diagnosed until ten years later.

The next morning after our conversation in the locker room, Mark awoke to find his right foot asleep. No matter how much he tried to rub the foot to alleviate the "pins and needles" feeling, the circulation never returned. Concerned, Mark's mother decided to take him to the doctor. Mark's life was about to change forever.

Baffled by what he saw while examining Mark, the doctor somberly exclaimed, "I don't know what's wrong with you, Mark, but you are going to lose that foot." Shocked, his mother backed up against the wall. Stunned, Mark said, "What are you talking about? What's wrong with me?" The doctor did not know the answer and admitted Mark into the hospital for further tests.

While in the hospital, Mark's left foot fell asleep and, just like the right one, never woke up. Now, not only were both feet losing circulation, but things were getting worse. Finally, after many failed tests, the doctor entered his room to tell him the news. "Mark, whatever it is, it is killing you. It's spreading up to your heart. We have one plan. To hopefully stop the spread we want to amputate both your legs just below the knee. If that doesn't work, you have two weeks."

Two weeks. Two weeks for a young man who had never been sick a day in his life. "What is wrong with me?" Mark again asked. "We don't know," responded the doctor. Mark prepared for the operation not knowing his chances.

When the operation was over, Mark awoke to find the doctor by his bed. "I've got some good news and some bad news," he said. "The good news is, whatever it was, it's gone. The operation was successful. You are going to live. The bad news is, you are probably going to be in a wheelchair your whole life and in and out of hospitals, as well. I'm sorry."

It was at that moment that Mark made a decision—a choice that would shape his whole future. "No!" he responded. "I'm not staying in hospitals—I'm not staying in wheelchairs. I'm going to walk and I'm going to live life! This is just the beginning—not the end."

It took a year, but after learning to use wooden legs, Mark walked out of the hospital for the last time. Later, he decided that since he would never play football or baseball again, he would coach and teach others to play. While in college, Mark met Sharon and fell in love. Sharon didn't mind Mark's wooden legs. She loved him for who he was. After graduation they married and Mark began his first job teaching handicapped students and coaching high school football. Today, Mark and Sharon have four beautiful children and a lovely home. He is a high-school principal in southwest Missouri and my boss. Every morning Mark gets up, puts on his legs and goes to school to greet students and teachers alike. You would never know if he has had a bad day because he would never tell you.

The choice was his. He could still be back in that wheelchair, in and out of hospitals, feeling sorry about the bad break he suffered in high school, but, instead, he is changing lives and living a blessed one himself.

Tom Krause

8

GROWING UP AND SELF-DISCOVERY

Who in the world am I? Ah, that's the great puzzle.

Lewis Carroll

The Girl Next Door

Do you remember
Many years ago
When we were young,
How we used to play together
Every day?

It seems like yesterday—
The childhood world
Of clowns and cotton candy
And summer days
That never seemed to end
When we played hide 'n' seek
From four o'clock till dusk
Then sat outside on someone's stoop
And listened to the crickets
And slapped away mosquitoes
And talked about our dreams
And what we'd do when we grew up
Until our mothers called us in.

And do you remember
That one winter when it snowed
For days and days on end
And we tried to build an igloo
Like the Eskimos?
Or when we made a game
Of raking leaves
All up and down the street
Until we'd made the biggest pile
The world had ever seen
And then we jumped in it?
Or how about the time
We gathered honeysuckle
From your yard
And sold it to the neighbors?
And the grand day when finally
The training wheels came off our bikes
And we were free
To explore the whole world
In an afternoon
So long as we stayed
On our own street.

But those days passed by furtively
And we grew up, as children do
Until we reached a day when we
Assumed that we were too grown-up
To play amid the trees on summer nights . . .
and when I see you now
You've changed in ways I can't explain
You're like a rose that blooms before its time
And falls a victim to
The February frost.

Because the waist on your jeans is getting tight
Symbolic of a youth that's not your own
And your face is pale and green—
You don't look well.
I see you scowling at the street
From the window in your room,
It's so rare to see you smiling anymore.
And when a car pulls up outside
You run downstairs and out the door
With a suitcase in each hand
And the car speeds away
And the girl next door is gone.

And I long once more
For the summer days
When I stood on your porch
And banged on your door
And bade you come outside to greet
the afternoon's adventures.

Won't you come out to play, once more?
For we are still so young . . .

Amanda Dykstra

Wonder, to Me

One morning, I woke up later than usual. The night before had been difficult. My eldest daughter, Carla, and I had exchanged harsh words. At sixteen years old, she was challenging my parenting skills. I'm sure that I must have scolded her about the type of friends she was hanging around with, her choice of social activities, even the clothes she wore.

When I walked into the kitchen, I saw an unfamiliar piece of paper on the kitchen table. Carla had already left for school. I thought maybe this was some homework that she forgot. Instead, it was a poem she had written:

Wonder, to me,
Is the worst place to be.
Situations get complex,
You're afraid of what's next.
Starting out fresh and brand-new,
Stepping in another shoe.
Wondering how you'll turn out,
Having all sorts of doubt.
Turning over a new leaf,
Sometimes wanting to leave . . . sometimes do!

As I read her words, my heart ached for the pain she was feeling. I recalled my own youth and teenage struggles. Now I felt that I had let her down somehow. A single mom, raising five children on my own and working two jobs, I was dealing with my own set of problems. But she needed me! How could I reach her?

Suddenly, all my own selfish worries left me. I grabbed a piece of paper and penned a reply that I hoped would bring her some comfort.

That afternoon while I was at work, she came home and found the poem that I had left. That evening there were hugs and maybe a few tears. It seemed that perhaps I had made some progress in narrowing the generation gap.

Days and months passed. We still had the typical mother–daughter disagreements, but with a special bond of respect and understanding for each other. It wasn't until a year later that I realized the full impact of our special relationship.

It was Carla's graduation. I was sitting in the bleachers, so very proud to see my own daughter's name on the program for the class speaker. As she approached the podium, I felt a sense of accomplishment in knowing that, through it all, I must have done something right to have such a vivacious, beautiful daughter who was providing her classmates with advice for their future.

She talked about leaving the security of school and venturing out on your own. Then I heard her share the story of her own struggles, doubts and fears. She was telling the entire audience about that difficult day when she left the poem on the kitchen table. And then, the words of advice to her classmates ended with the reply that I had given her so many months ago.

Dearest Carla,

Wonder, to me, is a good place to be.
It helps you to think, it helps you to see.
Life's full of twists and turns will abound,
But wonder and insight can guide you around.
Explore what you may and fill up your mind,
And hold in your heart the mysteries you find.
Wonder is only saying you yearn
To know and select the things that you learn,
And making a choice in which way you turn.
The best path you take will always be right,
'Cause if you were wrong, you CAN make it right.
Each new step you take when you listen and hear
Will give you more courage and freedom from fear.
So wonder my child, rid of your doubt,
And you will rejoice with how you turn out.
And though you may fall and struggle, too,
Know that I've been there, and will always love you.

I sat there, stunned. The entire auditorium was silent, listening to her message. My eyes welled with tears; everything was a blur. When I finally blinked, I saw the entire roomful of people on their feet, cheering and applauding. Then she ended her speech with her own inspired summary of "You can turn YOUR wonder into wonderful!"

Jill Thieme

Growing

I'm leaving now to slay the foe—
Fight the battles, high and low.
I'm leaving, Mother, hear me go!
Please wish me luck today.

I've grown my wings, I want to fly,
Seize my victories where they lie.
I'm going, Mom, but please don't cry—
Just let me find my way.

I want to see and touch and hear,
Though there are dangers, there are fears.
I'll smile my smiles and dry my tears—
Please let me speak my say.

I'm off to find my world, my dreams,
Carve my niche, sew my seams,
Remember, as I sail my streams—
I'll love you, all the way.

Brooke Mueller

New Beginnings

June, 1996

Dear Graduate,

Well, this is it! Graduation is over and you're ready to begin life's journey! I know you have lots of mixed feelings. That's the weird thing about most of life's big moments—very rarely do they consist of one emotion. But that's okay. It helps to make the good times more precious and the not-so-good times bearable.

I've spent a lot of time trying to figure out what sage advice I could pass along. That's one of the hard parts about being a parent—determining what should be said and what should be left for you to discover. I finally decided just to offer a little insight to life's basic questions. Some people go through their whole lives without ever giving them any thought. Too bad—as you search for the answers, you can make some wonderful discoveries. They can also be frustrating; just when you think you've found the answer, you'll find the need to ask another question. (Which explains why even at my incredibly advanced age, I still don't have any answers!) At any rate, I hope that sharing this little piece of myself and my soul will somehow help to carry you through when the questions come along.

Who? It took me a while to realize that this is probably the most important question of all. Take time to discover who you are and be your own person. Strive to be honest, respectful and happy. When you are at peace with yourself, everything else will fall into place. Just be careful not to wrap your identity in possessions. Allow yourself to grow and change. And remember always that you are not alone—you have your family, your friends, your guardian angel and God (not necessarily in that order!).

What? This is a tricky one, and at first this question had me fooled. I thought the question was, "What will I do today?" However, I found that things really got interesting when I instead asked, *"What is my passion?"* Discover what it is that burns inside and keeps you going, then nurture it. Take it apart and build it back together. Do whatever you want with it, but never let it from your sight. Do it because that's what you love to do. The joy it brings you will keep you going through some of the doldrums of life.

When? This is the sneaky one. Do not ignore it. It will keep you balanced. Some things are best done now. Procrastination usually just creates more work. But keep in mind that there is a season for everything, and some things are better left for another day. As hard as it may be, remember to take time to rest and enjoy the miracle of each new day. With practice, you will learn the pleasure of doing some things now and the unique delight of waiting and planning for others.

Where? Surprisingly, this is the easiest one. You will always have the answer with you if you keep your home in your heart and put your heart into wherever you call home. Be an active part of your community and you will discover the special charm that will endear it to you.

Remember always that the simplest act of kindness can make an enormous difference, and that you *can* change the world.

Why? Never stop asking this one. It's the one that will keep you growing. Let it. Let it challenge you when you've become too complacent. Let it shout at you when you are making decisions. Let it whisper to you when you lose sight of who you are or where you want to be. But you also need to be careful with this one. Sometimes the answer does not come for years, and sometimes it doesn't come at all. Recognizing that basic fact can keep you sane and allow you to move on.

How? Ah, this is the one on which I can't advise you! This is the one you will answer in your own special way. But you've come so far in the past few years, I know that you'll do fine. Just remember to believe in yourself and in miracles. Remember that the greatest discoveries come after stumbling over questions. And please remember— always—that I love you.

Congratulations on your new beginning.

Love,
Mom

Paula (Bachleda) Koskey

How Much Does It Cost?

The six teenagers sank onto their beanbags in the group counseling room. Today there was none of the usual raucous punching and good-natured exchange of insults. I knew they didn't want to be at school this week any more than I, their counselor, did.

For three days they had received counseling, comfort, sympathy and lectures. Ministers and psychologists had come to the school at a time when the kids' world seemed to have ended. It had indeed ended for four of their schoolmates, who had died in a car accident on the way home from a keg party in celebration of graduation.

What was there left for me to say? Only that these six would go on living, barring a tragedy like this one—a tragedy that didn't have to happen.

My mind searched for words to fill the silence. Finally I said, "I remember a day when I was about your age, seeing a fancy Levi's jacket and jodhpurs in a store window. Since I was to be riding in the girls' rodeo competition the following month, I figured I simply couldn't live without that outfit. I went into the store, found the garments in my size and bought them without asking how much they cost. I practically had a heart attack when the clerk told me the price. There went all the spending money I had saved practically forever. In fact, I had to go home and rob my piggy bank and then go back to the store for my purchase."

At that point in my story, I paused long enough to note that the group members were staring at me with questioning eyes. After all, what did a stupid rodeo costume have to do with their grief?

So I babbled on. "Was the outfit worth that much? No way, I concluded during the following months, when I had to do without several things I needed or wanted, including a class ring."

My counselees continued to look at me with a so-what? expression.

"I did learn from that experience," I said finally. "I learned to ask, 'What does it cost?' before buying. During the years following, I've learned that looking at price tags is a good idea when it comes to actions, also."

I told them about a time when I went on a hike with friends without telling our parents where we would be. The price was heavy. My fellow hikers and I got lost, and it was many terrifying hours before we straggled back to town to face our frantic parents and the drastic punishments they decided we deserved.

Now it was the kids' turn to talk, and they did, relating some of the times when their bad judgment had not been worth the cost of the consequences.

I gently reminded the students at this point that their friends' graduation celebration had cost too much. I mentioned the frequency of teen tragedies, many involving alcohol and other drugs. Then I read them parts of an editorial about an accident that had occurred a few months earlier. The article had been written by the town's chief of police:

Close to a thousand people were there that day, all sitting in front of a smooth casket topped with flowers and a high school letter jacket. Jason was president of the senior class, a star athlete, a popular friend to hundreds, the only son of successful parents, but he drove into the side of a fast-moving freight train at the city square on a beautiful Sunday afternoon and was killed instantly. He was eighteen years old. And he was drunk.

You never get accustomed to or forget the horror on the faces of parents when you break the news to them that their child is forever gone from this earth.

We know there will be both youth and parents who don't like our enforcement posture. There will be verbal and maybe physical abuse against the officers. Some parents will complain about our enforcement of underage drinking laws. But we can live with that a lot easier than telling parents that their son or daughter has been killed.

Four of the six students were crying by the time I finished reading the editorial. Crying for Jason, crying for their dead schoolmates and their families, crying because of their own loss.

Then we talked about the four friends they had just lost.

"Can any good come out of our tragedy?" I asked. "Or do we just let it end like a sad movie?"

It was Mindy, the shyest member of the group, who suggested in a wispy voice, "Maybe we could make a pledge or something."

Ordinarily, the three boys in the group would probably have ridiculed the idea, but this day was different.

"Hey!" Jonathan said. "Not a bad idea."

"Something like pretending there's a price tag on things grown-ups think we shouldn't do, then maybe deciding if we're ready to take the chance anyway," Laurel added.

Paul said, "The problem with that is, we can't know for sure what that price would be. Maybe nothing bad will happen even if we take the risk."

"That's a point," I admitted. "Suppose instead of 'How much *will* it cost?' we asked ourselves, 'How much *might* it cost?' Then we'd at least look at the possible outcomes."

"I'll buy that," Kent said.

A week ago, these kids would have shrugged off such suggestions, but today—well, today they weren't quite the same people they had been last week.

Margaret Hill

No Longer a Child

Jordana was a twelve-year-old girl like every other; she worried about her clothes, hair and boys. She always had a smile on her face and a warm hug to share. What most people did not know about her was that this little girl had some very grown-up problems. Her father caused these problems. He had sexually abused her when she was five and physically abused her for years after. The emotional scars left her in hidden shambles. Her mother and father divorced when Jordana was eight, leaving her mother with sole custody.

When we met in seventh grade, years after the abuse had stopped, she seemed like every other twelve-year-old girl. We became instant best friends, gossiping about movie stars, rock bands and boys. Jordana seemed happy living with her mother and stepfather, and when I asked about her father she only told me that she did not see him anymore.

One June day, I found out one of her biggest secrets. It was hot that day after school, and we went in Jordana's backyard to tan in tank tops and shorts. It was then that I noticed cuts on her arms, mirrored by scars of cuts that had already healed. When I asked her where she received the cuts, she turned to me and began to cry stories of the past, horrors flowing from her lips as fast as the tears fell from her eyes. Jordana told me that she had cut herself because she felt so much anger towards her father. She told me about the nights of terror, about beatings and the bruises. I didn't know what to do so I just listened, consoled and counseled to the best of my ability.

Not until I had gone home did I realize what had just happened. Jordana had trusted me with information that she had hidden deep inside for a dozen years. She had chosen my hand to reach out to and pleaded silently for me to reach back.

As the weeks went on the cuts became more frequent, as if she was using her body as a personal canvas. I became increasingly scared. I was too young to handle this myself. I realized soon that I did not have the means to help her, and my decision lay before me like a shallow grave. That day after school when Jordana was at basketball practice I went to her house and knocked on the door and reached out the only way I knew how, "Mrs. Brown, I have something I have to tell you." It was then that I realized I was no longer a child.

Hilary E. Kisch

The Two Roads

There was a path
Deep in the woods.
Once it forked—
The bad, the good.

I chose to take
The left-hand path,
I did not know
I had no map.

Now this road that I travel
Is dirty and battered.
It's littered with dreams
That are broken and tattered.

Paved with wrongdoings
And dotted with hearts,
That were taken from people
And just torn apart.

Pain and regret
Are common here.

wherever you turn,
They're always near.

I want to cross
To the other path,
And leave behind
This painful wrath.

I thought I was forever
doomed to walk.
And all the gates
were tightly locked.

But as I continued,
A footbridge I could see.
A Bridge of Hope
called out to me.

Slowly I crossed
to the path of good.
Finally I was on the path
Of which I thought I
should.

Now hidden deep
Within the woods.
The one that forked;
Paths bad and good.

I once was wrong,
But now I'm right.
And before me
Glows a guiding light.

Altered by
A little step.
So close to falling
In darkened depths.

But I was finally
Pulled to hope.
I found that footbridge,
And learned to cope.

My simple mistake
Following the crowd.
Ignoring the heart
That speaks so loud.

The choices you make
Can change your life.
One will bring happiness,
The other brings strife.

Following the crowd,
Won't lead you to right.
If you follow your heart,
You'll be guided by light.

There was a path,
Deep in the woods.
Once it forked—
The bad, the good.

Heed my warning,
Because I know.
Follow your heart—
You know where to go.

Whitney Welch

Image Isn't Everything

On the first day of school, after I got out of my mom's car and mumbled a good-bye, I stared in awe at the huge buildings that seemed to tower over my head. This high school was definitely bigger than the one I had previously attended. Over the summer I moved from Midland, Texas, to St. Louis, Missouri. I had lived in Midland all my life, until the move.

This was my second year of high school, but my first year of school in St. Louis. I was really nervous about starting a new school and having people like me. I had decided the night before, while lying in my bed trying to fall asleep, that I would be much happier in a new school if I made friends that were so-called "popular." Getting in with the right group of people would make my life a whole lot better. I had to project the right image to the people at this school. I didn't care how much money it cost me, I was determined to buy an outfit everyone else would want to have. I bought a new outfit, new make-up, got a manicure and had my hair styled just so the first day would be perfect. I had the chance to start over in a new school, make new friends and build an image for myself. I wasn't going to waste this opportunity.

Scared, yet anxious to begin my new life, I walked up the stairs to the front door. The halls were packed with kids yelling and laughing and telling stories of their summer adventures. I found my way to the main office where I was to receive my schedule and fill out forms. I was on my way. *My first class was geometry, but where was that?*

I was standing in the hall looking confused, when a short, blond girl wearing glasses came up and asked, "Are you new? You look lost. Do you want me to help you find your class? My name is Diane. What's yours?" Even though she seemed a bit strange, definitely not the kind of person I wanted to be associated with, I decided to answer her anyway. I was, after all, lost.

After exchanging names, I followed her up the stairs and down a hallway on the right, making polite conversation the whole way.

When we reached my room she said, "Well, here you are. It was nice meeting you. I hope I see you again. Welcome to JFK, and I hope your day goes all right."

I said thanks and waved good-bye. Once inside the classroom, I saw one big group of people huddled around someone who seemed to be telling some sort of story. I walked over and got close enough to overhear. All eyes were glued to the guy in the middle of the circle who was wearing a letter jacket covered with patches. I decided that this guy was popular. He was talking about how he and some of his friends had gone up to someone's ranch outside of St. Louis and done some pretty wild and crazy things. A few minutes later the teacher told everyone to break it up and go find a seat. I managed to get one right next to the guy wearing the letter jacket. I said, "Hi, my name is April and I'm new here." He said, "Hi, I'm Johnny."

That class dragged on and on. Finally the bell rang. I turned to him and asked, "I'm not sure where my next class is, could you help me find it?" He looked at me and then said a quick no, turned back to his friends, and walked out of the classroom. As they were walking out I heard him say, "Did you guys see that new girl trying to get into our group? That outfit was way too weird." They all laughed and some of them turned around and stared at me. I slowly gathered my stuff, not believing what had just happened. I walked out of the classroom and found my next class, bewildered that I could have cared so much.

The same type of thing happened all day in all of my classes. At lunch, I ended up sitting by myself because I had snubbed people who had been nice to me and I had been snubbed by people who I had tried to be nice to. I didn't realize it then, but I had been really shallow just wanting to be friends with popular people.

Finally, sixth period came around and I was ready to go home and never come back. Before class started, someone came up behind me and said, "Hi, again. How was your first day?" It was that same girl who had showed me to my first class.

I told her my day had not been so great. She said she was sorry and offered to walk me outside. At that moment I realized how wrong I was in wanting to only be friends with popular people. Those people weren't even going to consider being my friends, but there were some other people who I'd already met today and liked and they liked me. Maybe I shouldn't decide whether a person is worth being my friend or not by their reputation, but by who they are. I said, "Thanks, I'd like that. I'm sorry I was kind of rude this morning." She said it was okay, she was new at school once, too. Walking with Diane made me realize how nice it would be to have a friend like her. On the way to class she asked me if I wanted to go out after school to hang out with some of her friends and get to know them better. I did go out with Diane and had a lot of fun.

As time went on I made friends with lots of different people, some of them from "the popular crowd" and some not. My standards were different though. The people I sought out for friends were the nice ones—period.

Jamie Shockley

Hi There, Ugly!

It wasn't easy to pay attention in French class. Our yearbooks had just been passed out, so while the teacher droned on, we were quietly signing books and passing them around the room.

Mine was somewhere at the back of the class. I couldn't wait to get it back. What would my friends say of me? Would there be words of praise? Admiration? When class was over, I quickly found my yearbook and flipped through it with anticipation. And then it caught my eye: Someone had written large words across the last page of my book: HI THERE, UGLY!

I had never really considered whether or not I was 'good looking,' but now I knew. I was ugly. If someone at the back of that grade-seven class thought I was ugly, there were probably many others who agreed. I studied myself in the mirror: big nose, pimples, slightly overweight, not muscular. Yes, it must be true, I thought. I'm ugly. I told no one any of this. There seemed to be no need. It was a fact: I was ugly.

Years went by. I married a woman who is a very beautiful person—inside and out. I would tell her, "You're the most beautiful girl in the world!" and I meant it. She would reply, "And you're so handsome." I never looked her in the eyes when she said this. I felt it was one of those things wives "have to say" to their husbands. I would simply look down and remember that the true verdict on my looks was tucked away in my grade-seven yearbook.

Finally one day my wife asked, "Why is it that you never look at me when I say that you're handsome?" I decided to tell her about the yearbook and my conclusions. "You can't believe that! It's wrong! Somebody who didn't even know you in grade seven can't be taken that seriously! I know you, I love you and I chose to marry you. I think you're handsome and I think I've proved that." So, was I going to believe my wife . . . or that old graffiti?

I thought about that question for a long time and about how God doesn't make junk. Who was I going to believe? I chose to believe my wife and God.

I still have a big nose. At age thirty-four, I even still get pimples! My hair has begun to recede and you could probably find people who would say that I am ugly. But I'm not one of them! As time goes on and I listen more and more to those who love me, I know that I am beautiful . . . or should I say, handsome.

Greg Barker

I Won't Be Left Behind

I run my fastest
But still get beat.
I land on my head
When I should be on my feet.
I try to move forward,
But I am stuck in rewind.
Why do I keep at it?
I won't be left behind.

The harder I am thrown,
The higher I bounce.
I give it my all,
And that's all that counts.
In first place,
Myself, I seldom find.
So I push to the limit—
I won't be left behind.

Some people tell me you can't,
Some say don't.
Some simply give up.
I reply, I won't.

The power is here,
locked away in my mind.
My perseverance is my excellence,
I won't be left behind.

Make the best of each moment,
The future is soon the past.
The more I tell myself this,
The less I come in last.
Throughout my competitions,
I've learned what winning is about.
A plain and clear lesson—
Giving up is the easy way out.

So every night before I go to bed,
I hope in a small way I have shined.
Tomorrow is a brand-new day,
And I won't be left behind.

Sara Nachtman

I Am Loni

To be nobody but yourself in a world that's doing its best to make you somebody else is to fight the hardest battle you are ever going to fight. Never stop fighting.

e. e. cummings

Why do I even try? If there's one thing I should have learned, it's, try or not, I'll probably screw up. Mom says, "Loni, a lady shouldn't say things like 'screw up.'" That just proves my point. I even screw up how to tell you that I screwed up.

I know, I have so much going for me. Don't even go there. Dad brags about my grades, and Mom's proud of the person I am and all my activities. Grandma goes on and on about my pretty face. *Yeah, too bad about the rest of me,* I think to myself.

I'm not, like, big enough to be featured as The Amazing Amazon Teen in *The Guinness Book of World Records,* but I am big enough not to like shopping with my friends. "How cu-u-u-u-ute!" they squeal over every rack of clothes. They know they'll fit into anything. I can't commit until I scan the plastic circle dividers to see how high the sizes go.

I pretend that clothes don't matter to me. That explains my semi-grunge look everyone takes for my chosen style. No outfit is complete without a sweater, flannel shirt or sweatshirt tied around my waist to cover up . . . oh . . . everything.

So, when we go to the mall, I'm the designated shopper. You know, like the designated driver who goes to a party but doesn't partake. I stand outside the changing rooms to *ooh* and *aah* when they emerge for the three-way mirror check. Only after a careful inspection do I reassure them that their thighs, legs, waist or bottom do not look too big in that outfit; otherwise, it would be taken as insincere.

It takes all I have not to roll my eyes when they hand me a piece of clothing and plead, "Can you see if this comes in a smaller size?" Give me a break. Where should I look? The children's department?

I really did screw up, though. Being a self-appointed good sport, I tried out for the volleyball team with my friends. Here's the bad part: I made it.

It seems I have a killer serve. I use it for self-defense. The harder I ram the ball, the less likely it will be returned and force me to clod around the court keeping it in play.

To make matters worse, we keep winning. This is the first winning season of any girl's sport in our school's history. Volleyball fever took over, and attendance soared. Just my luck. And those pep rallies. There's a thrill. Jumping around high-fiving while my name echoes over the PA system.

In our small town, making it to State Finals is newsworthy. Our team was pictured sitting in the bleachers in a "V for Victory" formation. I was the connecting bottom of the "V," front and center in all my glory.

"Loni Leads the Charge to State!" read the headline. Not

bad. I didn't even pretend to protest when Mom bought copies for the relatives. I was pleased when the team framed the picture and hung it in the tunnel between our locker room and the arena. It soon became our team gesture to blow kisses at our picture every time we passed it.

It was the night of the final game, and we had home-court advantage. The series was tied two games to two. I led the team's run for our triumphant entrance. Cheers stormed down the tunnel to meet us. We glanced at the banners posted along the walls, taking energy from the words.

YOU GO, GIRLS! YES YOU CAN! WE'RE #1!

We were ready to blow kisses at our picture when shock froze me. Two words were written in red on the glass. Two words that totally changed the headline.

"Loni THE BULL leads the charge to State!"

The horns drawn on my head completed the insult.

I felt myself emptying until I wasn't me anymore. I was nobody. The team bunched behind me.

"Who did this?"

"Who would be so mean?"

Their questions had no answers. They thought they were as upset as I was, but they were wrong. I wasn't upset at all. I was in shock.

So this is the truth, I thought. *This is who I am.*

And all the words around me didn't heal the hurt because nobody said the three words I needed to hear most: "That's not true."

The team moved me down the tunnel. There was no time to sort myself. What was real seemed like a dream, and I couldn't shake myself awake. The chants of "Loni! Loni!" sounded hollow. I let the cheers of the many be muted by the jeers of the few.

We won the coin toss and took to the court for my first serve. Around me the team was pumped and ready to go.

I rolled the volleyball in my palms to get its feel and mechanically went into my serving stance. All I could see were the words . . . THE BULL. THE BULL. THE BULL.

I tossed the ball up, but before my fist made contact the shout "OLE!" hit me. I stutter-stepped and missed the ball. I told myself not to look, but my eyes were drawn anyway. I couldn't pick out who it was. The team tried to buck me up with back slaps and "that's okays." But it didn't help.

I went through the rotations until I was at the net. My concentration scurried between the game and the bleachers. When the ball skimmed the air above my head, a loud snorting sound came from the front row.

"That's taking the bull by the horns!" someone yelled. The player behind me made the save and set up the ball for me to spike. But I wasn't looking at the ball. I was staring into the faces of the five high-school guys who were mocking me. My humiliation only fueled their taunts.

"Give me a B, give me a U, give me a double L, too. What's that smell? LONI! LONI! LONI!"

Why didn't someone shut them up?

The coach called a time-out. "Loni, can you get your head in the game?"

I shrugged.

"Why are you letting a few people who don't even know you decide for you who you are?"

I shrugged again.

"Loni, you're valuable as a person and to your team. Unkind words don't change who you are unless you decide they change you," she said.

Sounds good in theory, I thought, *but this is the real world.*

"I'm keeping you in, but if you can't work through this I'll pull you."

I nodded.

I walked past the boys to take my place in the game. With each step I took, they stomped their feet to shake the floor. I got the point. Very funny.

I also had to walk past my teammates, and in spite of my weak showing, they were still rooting for me. "You can do it." "You're the best."

Something in me gave way. The quote on a magnet on my grandma's refrigerator popped into my thoughts: "God don't make no junk."

I knew what I knew, and I knew myself—I wasn't junk. I felt my value to the very depths of my soul. Who was I anyway? What did some immature boys know about me? There were so many people who loved and supported me, and it was time to do my best for them and for myself.

And just like that, I was free of them. Oh, they continued to stomp their feet with each of my steps. I didn't like it, but it didn't matter. They were powerless over my life.

The game was close, and we played hard. The winning serve fell to me. It was my moment, and I took it. The ball went up, my fist came forward and hit it right on. It was a perfect power serve unreturnable by the other team. The crowd went wild. The pep band started beating out our school song. The team huddled around me.

Shouts of "Loni! Loni!" vibrated the arena. The funny thing is, the cheers didn't feed me like they used to. They were great, but the joy I felt, the freedom I felt, the sense of myself I had filled me more than any cheers.

There was more than one victory that day, and the game was not the most important one.

Loni Taylor
As told to Cynthia Hamond

Just Me

From the time I was little, I knew I was great
'cause the people would tell me, "You'll make it—just wait."
But they never did tell me how great I would be
if I ever played someone who was greater than me.

When I'm in the back yard, I'm king with the ball.
To swish all those baskets is no sweat at all.
But all of a sudden there's a man in my face
who doesn't seem to realize that I'm king of this place.

So the pressure gets to me; I rush with the ball.
My passes to teammates could go through the wall.
My jumpers not falling, my dribbles not sure.
My hand is not steady, my eye is not pure.

The fault is my teammates—they don't understand.
The fault is my coaches—what a terrible plan.
The fault is the call by that blind referee.
But the fault is not mine; I'm the greatest, you see.

Then finally it hit me when I started to see
that the face in the mirror looked exactly like me.

It wasn't my teammates who were dropping the ball,
and it wasn't my coach shooting bricks at the wall.

That face in the mirror that was always so great
had some room for improvement instead of just hate.
So I stopped blaming others and I started to grow.
My play got much better and it started to show.

And all of my teammates didn't seem quite so bad.
I learned to depend on the good friends I had.
Now I like myself better since I started to see
that I was lousy being great—I'm much better being me.

Tom Krause

An Athlete's Prayer

It was right before the big one and the football player said,
"Excuse me guys for just a sec while I go bow my head."
And in the quiet of that room
The football player prayed,
"Oh God if nothing hear me now
I know that fate is made."

"So help us Lord to win this game,
It's the big one, man, you see,
If we lose this game that's it for us ,
Please do this, Lord, for me."

And as his body knelt in prayer,
He looked up to the sky,
"And while I'm here, and have some time,
I need to ask you why?"

"They say you never help teams win,
Just do it once I pray,
We will pay you back in kinder deeds
Or in another way."

"The reason I can't help you win,"
The Lord just then replied,
"Is as you're asking me to win,
So is the other side."

"I'm everybody's father and
I must not take one side,
So games are played all on your own
Or they would all be tied."

"But that doesn't mean you shouldn't pray,"
He answered him with care,
"You can pray that players don't get hurt
And that all the calls are fair."

"And then I won't just watch the game,
I'll bless it with my care,
Because dear son you need to learn
That life's not always fair."

And while the player heard this voice,
He bowed his head in prayer,
"I pray for fairness," said the boy
"And for your tender care."

"You shall be blessed," the Lord replied,
"Your team and you the same,
And now will you excuse me boy,
I cannot miss this game."

Sandy Dow Mapula

Applying Myself

Those who dream by day are cognizant of many things, which those who dream only by night may miss.

Edgar Allen Poe

At thirteen years old, I was like any other kid my age. I liked computer and Nintendo games. I complained about too much homework, and I hated when my little brother ate the last Fruit Roll-Up in the box. I guess I looked like any other kid my age, too. I wore baggy pants and oversize T-shirts—you know, the typical middle-school prison garb. However, inside I harbored a secret that made me feel different and weird.

You see, I was diagnosed with ADD. This is the hip term for attention deficit disorder. I couldn't even get the cool-kid type where you're hyper. I had to get the dreamier, "space-cadet" type. I can look straight into your eyes and not hear a word you're saying. It's sort of like in the Charlie Brown TV specials. All the adults' voices in the cartoon sound like endless droning. "Mwop, mwop, mwop, mwop." I appear to be listening while all the while my mind is somewhere miles away.

After extensive and boring tests, the doctor explained to my mom that I was what they called "dual exceptional." It sounds pretty cool, doesn't it? No, it doesn't mean that I have any special dueling abilities like the swordsmen in *The Three Musketeers*. It also doesn't mean that I have a major psychiatric disorder like multiple personalities. That might be kind of cool in a weird sort of way. What "dual exceptional" means is that I am what they call "gifted." This means I'm pretty bright, and yet I'm also learning disabled. This makes school challenging for me.

Yes, you can be gifted and learning disabled at the same time. The two words are not a contradiction in terms. I once heard a comedian refer to the words "jumbo shrimp" as one of these conflicted phrases.

I've learned to accept the fact that I'm an enigma to some. Still, it is a bummer to be misunderstood. The whole syndrome can sometimes make me feel like I am on the outside looking in. Everyone else seems to be getting it, and I'm not.

What really burns me up, though, is when teachers don't get it. In middle school, I took Language Arts with Mrs. Smith. She had piercing brown eyes that made you feel like you had done something wrong. Her no-nonsense, rigid posture made her look as though she'd forgotten to take the wire coat hanger out of her dress. Her face was angular, stiff and white, like a freshly starched and laundered hanky. A smile rarely creased her well-powdered complexion. I could imagine only an intermittent smirk grazing those thin red lips as she X'd her way through someone's failing test paper with her glorious red marker.

I was enrolled in Mrs. Smith's gifted section. That first day, she not only set down the rules of her cellblock, but she handed out copies of them for us to memorize and be tested on the following day. I knew right away that I had better "advocate" for myself. This is just some big, fancy-shmancy term that means to stand up for yourself. In my case, trying to explain, for the umpteenth time, about my learning disabilities. Basically, I have lousy reading comprehension and my handwriting is the pits. So I told her that I have ADD and that I might need to take home some reading assignments because my concentration is better when I am in a quiet setting. I went on to explain to her about my "fine motor skill" problems, which make my handwriting look like chicken scratch. I asked her if I might be able to use my word processor at home to do written assignments.

As I explained all this to Mrs. Smith, she gave me a squinty-eyed look down her bespectacled nose and said, "You are no different from anyone else, young man. If I do for you, I have to do for all the others." She snorted once and then added, "I will not give you an unfair advantage over your peers!" And with that, the bell rang and a herd of students swept me away to my next period.

The comprehension packets were rough. You had to read them, digest them and write an essay on them, all within the forty-five-minute allotted time. Not only couldn't I finish the reading, I couldn't write my essay fast enough or neatly enough to be legible. The result was that each paper came back decorated by Mrs. Smith's flaming red pen. She was like the mad Zorro of red X's.

One day, after she had handed me back my fifth X'd-out paper of the term, I approached her desk for the second time.

"Would you mind very much if I completed the next packet at home, Mrs. Smith? I think I might do better where there is less distraction." Then I backed away from her desk as though I were within firing range of her loaded mouth.

Mrs. Smith bit her thin red lips as her trademark smirk spread across them. "It's against school policy, young man. No unfair advantages. I have treated all students the same in the thirty years I have taught here." Then she flared her nose, clicked her heels and turned away from me, in more ways than one.

So I did what any other kid would do in my situation: I smuggled the packet out of the classroom. I felt like I was doing something illegal, and yet my motives were pure. I had to prove to her, or rather prove to myself, that I could do the work under the right conditions.

I secretly unfolded the contraband on my bed that night. The story, which had seemed so confusing in class, became quite clear to me in the still of my room. I not only got it, I could even relate to it. It was the true story of Louis Braille. He lived in the 1800s and was blinded by a childhood accident. During this time, society shut off the blind from having much of an education. Many were left with the bleak future of becoming homeless beggars. Despite much misunderstanding of his disability, Louis Braille "advocated" for himself. He developed a reading system of raised dots for the blind, which enabled him to read on a par with his peers. A world of books and knowledge opened up to him that he and others like him were literally blind to before. I was like Louis in my classroom setting. I was being made to learn like the other students who were sighted in a way I wasn't.

That night I sat down at my word processor. My thoughts spilled out so fast that my fingers danced across the keyboard, straining to keep up. I explained myself in terms of Louis, in hopes that Mrs. Smith would finally understand me. Funny thing is, somewhere along the line I began to understand myself in a way I never had before.

I cited many other famous people who were in some way different in their learning styles and abilities throughout history. Hans Christian Andersen was said to have been learning disabled, and yet he wrote some of the best fairy tales of our time. I summed it all up by asking, "If I were a student with a vision impairment, would I be seated in the back of the room?" I questioned, "Would I have my glasses taken away from me so that I would not have an unfair advantage over other, glassless students?"

Mrs. Smith never looked at me as she handed my paper back facedown on my desk that day. She never even commented that my work was done on the word processor. As my eyes focused in on the white page, I found an A decorating the margin instead of her customary X. Underneath were her neatly red-penned words: "See what you can do when you apply yourself?"

I took the paper, tucked it away in my folder and shook my head. I guess some people will never get it!

C. S. Dweck

The Blank Page

The pencil moved ever so slightly in my hand as I stared at the blank page that would become my completed homework assignment: a five-paragraph essay on the meaning of life for Mr. Neal's English class.

I had no idea that a person's palms could sweat as much as mine were gripping that pencil. I almost needed sunglasses to shade the glare of the blank notebook paper. I had been sitting at my desk pondering the various aspects and meanings of life for nearly an hour. Thus far, I was clueless as to what to write. *What does Mr. Neal expect?* I wondered. *I am only fourteen.*

I thought about everything that had happened previously in my life. I began high school this year, ran cross-country and played girls' soccer. However, I was sure that the meaning of life had nothing to do with any of these things.

I stretched my arms above my head and looked around the room. My room was so *me*. The mark of Jenni was everywhere to be seen, from my posters and paintings of Europe to the many vibrantly colored CDs that littered my floor. My gaze then fell upon a photograph of me standing beside a girl. Our arms are raised above our heads in an imitation of cheerleaders and we both flash blindingly bright smiles. I froze. Immediately, tears began to well in my eyes. The girl in the photograph and I had been best friends for nearly two years when a sudden disagreement planted a rift in our friendship that still had not been mended. It saddened me beyond measure that an argument could put so much distance between such close friends.

The pencil now moved fluidly across the paper.

When I again looked up, I happened to glance at the varsity *A* I had received for completing cross-country season. Memories now rolled through my mind and flooded my brain: remembrances of long, loud bus rides; water fights with our archrival; memorable trips to various fast-food eateries after the races; the stinging words of many arguments; the tinkling giggles of many laughs gone by.

Again, the lead scraped the clean white paper.

As I went to bed that night, my homework assignment still incomplete, I ran over in my mind what I had written so far. Fitful dreams revealed new stories and thoughts to be explored.

In my dreams, I remembered when my family moved to the beach—tearful good-byes rang in my ears. I reexperienced the velvety voice of my former crush during our first phone conversation, which was a major breakthrough, even though it only lasted five minutes. I remembered how excited I felt after that conversation—I drifted on cloud nine. I relived how happy and proud I felt walking across the Albemarle High School stage to receive my varsity *A*. Even in my sleep, a lone tear's salty track burned my cheek: Albemarle, my life in the past and also now, beginning anew.

I awoke early the next morning to finish my essay. When it was complete it read as follows:

When you asked us to write about the meaning of life in a five-paragraph essay, Mr. Neal, I wondered how I would ever fill so much empty space. I sat thinking it over for nearly an hour before I even knew how to begin. When I began to write, however, the problem became not how to fill the space, but how to make use of what little I had.

There is so much more to life than cross-country meets, soccer games, and the transformation from middle-schooler to high-schooler. What matters most is what you make of your life. If how you feel from day-to-day is based upon what others think and how they judge you, then your life has no basis. If you are a person who wakes up in the morning and dreads the day ahead, then your life has no meaning.

However, if you wake up every morning eager to start the new day, then your life has meaning, for it has a purpose. My life certainly has a purpose. Every day is a struggle to survive: building new friendships, fixing old ones, learning how to deal with complicated emotions and accepting new surroundings. I find that every day is a journey of finding out who and what you are.

I believe that the question "what is the meaning of life" is too broad. I don't think that anyone will ever truly discover the exact reason why we were put here and what we must do now that we are here. Personally, I do not care to discover the reason. I prefer to leave each day to its own devices.

Every day is an adventure in discovering the meaning of life. It is each little thing that you do that day— whether it be spending time with your friends, running in a cross-country race or just simply staring at the crashing ocean—that holds the key to discovering the meaning of life. I would rather be out enjoying these simple things than pondering them. We may never really discover the meaning of life, but the knowledge we gain in our quest to discover it is truly more valuable.

My hand ached and my pencil was but a stub, by my essay was finished. I had discovered many things while writing this essay, although maybe not the exact meaning of life. *I don't need to find that out yet,* I thought, smiling. *I have things to do along the way.*

My notebook page, as well as my mind, was no longer blank.

Jenni Norman

Winner

You can complain because roses have thorns,
or you can rejoice because thorns have roses.

Ziggy

I am a winner.

I have beaten odds to get where I am today.

I have felt some pain every time I have walked another step forward, yet after having taken even one step back, I have known that regression and giving up were not options for me. I have felt the emptiness of separation as I have moved in the wrong direction.

I have learned the arts of persistence, tenacity and dedication. I know how it feels to watch my world and dreams shatter to a million pieces at my feet. I know what it is to run until there is nothing left inside of me, and then run some more.

I know how it feels to be loved, and I know how it feels when that love grows hard and cold.

I know how to be happy. I know how to smile and spread joy into lives of others with that same smile.

I have learned that one conversation can make or break

a fragile mind and heart, and thus I have learned to choose my words carefully.

I know that enthusiasm is the key to everything, and yet I know how it feels to completely lack enthusiasm.

I have learned that winning is not everything, but sometimes it feels like it is the most important thing. I have learned that other color ribbons only prove to make that blue so much sweeter. I know that my chief competitor is always myself.

I know that sometimes my best isn't good enough for others and that people can be cruel. I know that sometimes I get frustrated with myself, especially when others are frustrated with me.

I know how it feels to have something mean so much to me that it *is* me. I have experienced wrath, outrage and fury, but have still made it through the storm a survivor.

I know what it is to love. I know how to spread joy and how to extract it from even the darkest situations.

I know what hope is, and I rely on it as my last refuge. I know that darkness must exist if only to make those tiny bits of light seem that much brighter.

I know that success is self-made, and that luck is a relative term.

I know that I am strong.

I know that miracles do exist, angels do find us in our hour of need, and there is always something behind me, pushing me forward.

I believe in myself at all times, even when I think that I don't and even when I feel like no one else does.

I know how it feels to be lost. I also know how it feels to be picked out of a crowd. What it is like to be the winner, and how it feels when, for one moment, you are the star of the show.

Above all, though, I know that all of this has made me ME.

I know that being a winner is not about winning whatever race faces me in the moment. I recognize I am winning just by pushing myself every day and by waking up each morning feeling blessed by the day that lies ahead of me. Through this I am winning in the most important race ever, the race I entered at birth—this race we call life.

Amy Huffman

An Ode to Shoes

Shiny look-a-likes are they,
empty night time, full all day,
travel miles along the street,
though they only move two feet.

When I was thirteen
I stepped
Off my horse
Out of my tall, black leather boots
And into
Running shoes
Into high school
And high-school track
Into high heels and high-school parties
Strutting
Running
Away from the chaos
And back
Strutting
Swinging my legs, my hips
Just enough
Just so, to get the looks

Not the bad ones,
The good
Expensive boots
All the girls have them
Like all the boys have egos
Fake ones
Like fake plastic heels I would never wear
Call me ritzy
I'll call you cheap
In orange, green, and clear
Four-inch heels
little skirts
and I remember
When no one really cared
When our calves hadn't developed into
The sexy, sloping
Line we exploit
When I tied my LA Gears with
One pink shoe lace
And one chartreuse
Like my socks
Like the style
Before the decade turned
Spun into
Steve Maddens and Doc Martins
And Mary Janes
Each with two names
And we all had two faces
Sometimes more for more occasions
Meaning more shoes
Overflowing our closets like muddy water
Like the muddy circle
The track I run in the spring rains
In the new Nikes
Glossy white leather flushing to red-brown

That cracks and dries in the summer sun
The heat
That beats down in a country where
These shoes are manufactured
By small, brown fingers
Crescents of dirt under unkept nails
Working fine threads into my shoes
Working from dawn until dusk
In a place where nobody knows
Steve Madden or Doc Martin
Or any other doctor that the baby's mother cries for
And the children cry here
For a new pair of shoes
Here in
Distorted Reality
In crowded
Walk-in closets
Full of shoes.

Jessica Pinto

Happiness from Within

Finish each day and be done with it. You have done what you could; some blunders and absurdities have crept in; forget them as soon as you can. Tomorrow is a new day; you shall begin it serenely, and with too high a spirit to be encumbered with your own nonsense.

Ralph Waldo Emerson

Having been raised Catholic by parents who worked hard for every penny they earned, I was taught at an early age that money cannot buy happiness. As much as my parents and the church tried to teach me these values, I had to learn through my own experiences that happiness comes from within and cannot be measured by material possessions.

As a child, I would sit in church, trying to concentrate on the words of the priest, but my attention was soon diverted by the sparkle of the gold and diamonds worn by the Sunday churchgoers. As my eyes began to wander, I noticed men dressed in their tailored suits and monogrammed shirts, accompanied by women in their designer dresses with matching handbags and shoes.

My family, on the other hand, was the opposite of glamorous. Our hand-me-down clothes had been washed so many times that the colors had become dull and lifeless and the material frayed around the seams. Although our clothes revealed the money struggles of our large family, our faces were always washed, our hair neatly combed, and we each tossed our twenty-five cents in the basket even when there was a second collection. As my family piled into our big green and white VW bus after the service, I fantasized about the glamorous lives led by those driving their brand new BMWs, wishing I were more like them.

I continued these fantasies when I was an adolescent attending Catholic school. Since it was a private school, most of the children came from wealthy families. As a result, I constantly felt inferior to the rest of my classmates. Although I could hide my lack of wealth at school by wearing our mandated school uniforms, my poverty was embarrassingly apparent on weekends when my classmates wore designer jeans, and I had no choice but to wear my sister's outgrown jeans. Once, because I could not afford a birthday gift, I gave one of my own used CDs to a friend in school. When she opened the gift, her face twisted into a strange look as if she did not know whether to laugh or say thank you. It was times like these, when the other kids laughed at me and talked behind my back, that convinced me that if I only had the new clothes, the nice house and other such material possessions, then maybe I would have a chance to fit in. Then I would be happy.

I began to believe so much in the material world that I started my first job when I was fourteen so that I could afford those "things" that were going to make me happy. Soon I was working two jobs in order to fulfill my needs.

I began to purchase the clothes, the jewelry and the perfume. Each purchase was a sign of hope. Each time I thought, *This is it, this is really going to make me happy.* Within a few days, sometimes as little as a few hours, that feeling of emptiness came over me again. I would dream bigger and set my goals higher to purchase something even better. Each time I thought it was going to be different, but it never was.

Unfortunately, it took many of these disappointing and painful experiences, not to mention the amount of money spent, for me to realize that what I admired in other people was not about their clothes, their hairstyles or the car they drove. It was their self-confidence. I admired the way they carried themselves, their ability to take on new challenges and the way they looked people in the eye during conversations instead of staring down at their toes as I often found myself doing. I began to notice that it was the qualities that they possessed inside themselves that I was lacking. I knew then that I would never be a complete person until I started to do some work on the inside.

There was no lightning bolt or voice from God that brought me to this realization. I had to go all the way down the wrong road in life to realize that I was headed in the wrong direction. As a result, I now possess those qualities that I had always admired in other people. Long gone are the days of remedying my problems with new clothes and makeup. I confess I still get caught up in the excitement of shopping sprees, but there is a difference today: I know each time I put on a new outfit and look in the mirror, the same person will be underneath it all. I now carry myself with an air of confidence, and I can look people in the eye, for I have no reason to look down.

Dianna McGill

The Plaster Shell

Intense feelings of embarrassment and absurdity filled my entire body. These feelings were not helped by the fact that I was slathered in baby oil, clad in a T-shirt and lying in my basement, in fifty pounds of plaster. I stared down at the warm plaster that embraced my midsection and slowly crept up toward my chest, and I tried to remember why I had chosen to make a plaster cast of my entire body. For a moment, I simply concluded that I was an utter fool, but I soon remembered my motives. And while the plaster dried, I certainly had the time to think about it.

The insecurities of my freshman year in college, combined with my poor body image, made me feel like an oaf. Here I was surrounded by all these lithe, long girls who wore the latest fashions really well. Was there some mold that churned out these girls? And where in the world did I come from?

That was the beginning of the question that led me to my plaster ensconcement. It all began 506 years ago, when my forebears were thrown out of Spain. They migrated to Eastern Europe and developed the stocky, bosomy shape consigned to overstuffed chairs. Though my tall, slender parents seemed to have defeated this pernicious (certainly in my eyes) shape, it continued lurking in the depths of the family gene pool and flung itself into existence again with the arrival of their firstborn child—me. It gifted me with wide hips, a nonexistent waistline, powerful shoulders and ample breasts. Very reminiscent of a long line of intimidating German matriarchs.

Built to survive harsh winters and to breed children, I certainly wasn't near anything I saw in fashion magazines —or like any of my new college peers. I loathed my shape and cursed my past. Though I was always an independent person who disregarded the edicts of popularity and fashion, I could not ignore our culture's concepts of beauty. The rancor I had for my body made my freshman year of college really hard. Clothing seemed made for those generic stick figures I sat next to in class. That was when Dorothy, my slightly eccentric art teacher and mentor, originated the idea of body casting.

Consequently, on a lovely May morning, I found myself sitting in a dark basement, encased in plaster. I lost all sensation in my legs at approximately the same time that the plaster hardened. After an additional uncomfortable twenty minutes, I slipped out of my plaster shell. At first, I was rather depressed by the sight of the powder-white and headless torso lying on an old towel. It looked more like a sea creature stranded by the tide than a human shape. My eyes squinted, trying not to take in the entire picture of my shape, which was even more exaggerated by the plaster. I thought about how I would never be graceful or delicate, how two-piece swimsuits were absolutely out of the question and how I would never be conventionally beautiful or fashionably thin.

As I stared at the empty outer shell of myself, a great realization hit me—I realized that I had been completely wrong about my body image. For the past nineteen years, I had believed that my linebacker-like shape would discourage others from noticing my additional attributes. How would they ever see my love of science and books, my creativity or my offbeat sense of humor?

All this time I had wanted to be fashionably svelte, but that would not make me a better person. I recognized that confidence was much more important to others than a dainty appearance and that if I had confidence, they would notice my talents. More important, I realized that I did not actually want to be thin and bikini-clad. I was quite content using my powerful build to lug around sixty-pound scenery pieces, and I liked my one-piece, practical bathing suits. My physical appearance had shaped my personality in a largely positive way. It contributed to my dislike of conformity. It gave me my somewhat self-deprecating sense of humor. And it gave me that strong will that I cherish so much. The misconception I was holding all these years, along with the exaggerated body cast that lay there on my basement floor, was suddenly so hilarious to me. I laughed for five minutes straight.

The body cast currently resides in Dorothy's attic, under a large blanket. I never actually used it in any art piece; I felt it had served its purpose. The process of body casting had been far more important than the product.

Since that day three years ago, I have not resented my ancestral build. I have also discovered that being comfortable in my body has given me increased confidence and assertiveness, something many girls, and women, lack. Perhaps they should all be given the opportunity to make their own body casts. When the shell of the body is separate from the person, it is obvious that it is severely lacking. Without the wisdom, sense of humor and heart, it really has no shape at all.

Miriam Goldstein

"I think it's so cool that you don't care if you're cool."

Reprinted with permission of Dave Carpenter.

Out of Step

The roots of true achievement lie in the will to become the best that you can become.

Harold Taylor

I wanted to find my niche. I wanted to fit in so badly with some group, any group in high school. Sports didn't really work for me. I sucked at just about all of them. In fact, I dreaded those times in PE when the captains picked teams. Fights sometimes ensued between captains about who would have the misfortune of ending up with me on their team. I was the guy who had a full-scale neurotic episode if you threw the ball to him.

I did run track for awhile. This was a pretty good sport for me because it required very little coordination, and I already had some practice running: away from bullies, their girlfriends and any ball thrown in my general direction. But I wanted to run sprints and only the football players got to run sprints. I was relegated to middle distance—the half-mile, which really didn't work for me. It took about two minutes to run, and the extent of my ability to exert myself athletically was about thirty seconds.

But one day, a girl I liked and sometimes stalked (although we didn't call it stalking back then—just a playful crush) happened into the band office to sign up. Because I had a "playful crush" on Jaclyn, I was hiding behind a tree and noticed her sign up for the band. Okay, sure, the uniforms were pretty dorky and being in the band didn't exactly give you the best reputation in school (which in my case couldn't really get much worse), but I could learn to play the drums and there *was* Jaclyn. I would later learn that many of the greatest musicians of our time were motivated to music by some girl whose name they most likely don't remember anymore.

It was not just the band, but the marching band. I picked the drums for two reasons: (1) It seemed pretty easy, and (2) I thought it would make me look cool. I later found out that the drums are actually quite difficult and that little or nothing could make me look cool. I wanted to play snare drum, but because of my lack of experience I was relegated to the tenor drum.

The first thing to learn was how to hold the drum and play it. We all had to learn the cadence which, to this day, I can still perform with two pencils and a paper cup, which really wows them on job interviews. Holding the drum and playing it is not as easy as it might look. I did, after several private lessons, learn the cadence. Next, as if that weren't difficult enough, I had to learn how to play it while not only walking, but marching.

We were required to march the equivalent of five miles per practice day, while carrying our eighty-pound drums (it was then I wished I had picked the flute) and wearing our big, shiny, black military shoes, in the 104-degree summer heat. And then one day, they delivered the Shakos. For those of you who may not be familiar with high school marching band terminology, the Shako is that really tall, furry-looking hat that you wear with a strap around your chin. Now I was marching five miles a day in my shiny shoes, carrying my eighty-pound drum, playing the cadence about six thousand times, in 104-degree heat, and wearing a big tall, white, furry hat.

Finally, at the end of the summer, our uniforms arrived. The band uniform is a sacred attire. It is carefully sized to fit the individual, hand sewn, and acquired through twenty-seven or so fundraising activities such as car washes, bake sales and door-to-door sales of things like half-melted candy bars at inflated prices. It is cleaned after each use and worn with pride. It is also 100 percent wool. Add now to the excruciatingly painful military shoes, the eighty-pound drum, the silly hat and the 104-degree heat, what I estimate to have been about forty pounds of long-sleeved, neck-to-toe, pure wool.

I forgot to mention something. In addition to an inability to play sports, I was also not so good at marching. If you were not in step, the band director would yell in a loud and embarrassingly annoyed voice, "OUT OF STEP!" It was at this point that I began to question my decision to join the band. How do playing music and marching around in silly formations, all "in step," go together?

The day of our first competition finally arrived. It was the Mother Goose Parade, an annual Thanksgiving Day event in my town. High school bands from all over the county marched while all the people in town lined the streets in lawn chairs and watched them march by. Although the parade didn't start until 9:00 A.M., we had to meet at 6:00 A.M. to get our uniforms from the "band boosters"—those selfless, dedicated parents who provided comfort and assistance to the members of the band.

At 6:00 A.M., to this day, I am not really in existence. Oh sure, you can get me out of bed and dress me, and I will walk and talk, but inside my brain is fast asleep, waiting for a more reasonable hour. I was standing around waiting for my Shako to be cleaned when I noticed a big urn of coffee. *Coffee? That wakes you up, doesn't it?* I poured myself a cup—my first-ever cup of coffee. It tasted pretty bitter, but I had to wake up. I dumped in three sugars and three packets of that white, milky powder that is supposed to scientifically simulate cream. It still tasted bitter but drinkable. I just had to wake up so I could be "IN STEP." After about ten minutes, I was awake. I WAS REALLY AWAKE. I went over to the corner and put on my drum. I wanted to see how fast I could play the cadence. Pretty fast. I started marching around in circles until one of the band boosters came over with a look of concern on her face. She suggested I sit down and rest until it was time to line up. That's when I learned to play the cadence with pencils and a paper cup.

Finally, the moment of truth. They lined us all up and we waited for about forty-five minutes. I had my coffee, and I was raring to go. The drum major blew his whistle and off we went. I beat the cadence out with all my heart. I marched with the precision of a brigadier general. For about the first hour. Then, something happened. Suddenly all my energy drained away. I began to feel sleepy and I fell "OUT OF STEP." No one noticed at first and I tried to skip back into step. But nothing worked. Then I saw one of the band boosters talking to another one and pointing at me. They looked very concerned. They enlisted a third booster and suddenly, to my horror, they all three pointed at me and motioned for me to leave formation. I complied; after all, they had rank. I walked over to them as the band marched on. They told me what I already knew, I was "OUT OF STEP," and would have to stay out of the formation until the band passed the judging stand. I could rejoin the band after the judging stand, but only if I followed along on the side of the road.

I couldn't believe it. Now, I not only couldn't march with the band, but I had to climb over the lawn chairs, popcorn and arms and legs of my fellow townspeople for the next mile to keep up with the band, in my shiny shoes, carrying my drum and wearing my Shako. I would like to say this was the single most humiliating moment of my life, but unfortunately there were more to follow. But this one did rank pretty high up there on the list.

I never did learn to march "IN STEP." But it hasn't really come up that much in my adult life. I also never did find a niche in high school, but I got through it. As an adult, I have found several niches that I fit into quite nicely, and I look for new ones every day. And I always ask if there is any marching competition before signing up.

Tal Vigderson

The Essence of Adolescence

I yelled at Mom yesterday
'Cause she told me I'm going through
A difficult age
And I'm not.
So I slammed the door extra hard
When I got up to my room.
And then I yelled at God for a while
Just for good measure
'Cause he made it snow but
Wouldn't close school.
Besides
He parked that damn streetlight
Just where
He knew it would shine in my eyes
Every night when I'm trying to sleep.
And I yelled at the light, too
'Cause it's too bright
And besides
It lights up the snowman
That the kids next door made.
I was too old to make a snowman this year

But that's okay
I've always hated snowmen anyway.
I yelled at the snowman, too
Before I sat down at my desk
Where this old box was sitting . . .
It had a bunch of
Stupid treasures from when I was little.
Inside was a cotton ball
And some acorns, a dead bee
My eraser collection, and a pen
That had my name on it.
I picked up the box and
Threw it away
'Cause it's dumb to keep that sort of stuff
I put my phone and a romance novel
On the desk instead.
I have to keep my priorities straight.

Then I got home from school today
And I sat down at my desk
I looked for my box.
It wasn't on my desk or in the trash
'Cause today was garbage day
And I sat back down and I guess,
I started to cry.
It's too complicated being mad at the world.

Anne Gepford
Submitted by Katie Shaw

Teenagers' Bill of Rights

Our Rights with Friends:

We all have the right and the privilege to have friends. We can choose our friends based on our own likes and dislikes. We don't have to like the same people everyone else likes or not like someone because they aren't in our "group." Friendship is a personal thing.

We can ask from our friends that they be trustworthy. If we share something with them and ask them not to tell everyone, we can expect that they will keep it just between us. We will give them the same right. If they don't, they have betrayed our trust and our friendship.

It is okay to be honest with our friends. If they do something that hurts us or concerns us, we can talk to them about it. We will be open to their being honest also. This does not mean it is okay to be mean to each other, just that we can talk honestly about our feelings.

We have the right to be respected for the decisions we make. Some of our friends may not understand the choices we make, but they are our choices. In return, we take responsibility for them.

With Parents and Other Adults:

We have the right to have our feelings respected and not compared to the feelings of puppies . . . or any other such put downs. Our feelings are strong and sometimes confusing. It helps if you take our feelings seriously and listen to us before disregarding them.

We feel we have the right to make decisions (some, not all) for ourselves. If we make mistakes we will learn from them, but it is time for us to be more responsible.

Whenever possible, exclude us from your fights. We understand that fighting is part of every relationship, but it is painful for us to be involved. Don't put us in the middle of *any* problem you have with each other.

We agree to treat you with respect and ask that you respect us in return. This includes respecting our privacy.

With Everyone:

We have the right to be loved unconditionally, and our goal is to love you the same.

We have the right to speak our minds, love ourselves, feel our feelings, and strive for our dreams. Please support us by believing in us rather than fearing for us.

Lia Gay; Jamie Yellin;
Lisa Gumenick; Hana Ivanhoe;
Bree Able; Lisa Rothbard

Center Stage

Once upon a time, my life was as orderly as the inside of my locker. I took detailed notes, never talked out of turn, helped put away library books during my free periods, and went to track practice after school. But all that changed the day Mr. Soames made Sara McGee my partner in biology.

"If he thinks I'm touching this, he's dreaming," Sara whispered after Mr. Soames told us to make the first incision into the earthworms we were dissecting. She pushed her bangs—they were orange today as opposed to last week's green—out of her face and frowned.

I took the knife from her hand and split the earthworm neatly down its center.

"Thanks," she said. She rolled up her sleeves and her silver bangles clattered. "I know I'm a baby, but cutting open animals makes me sick."

I finished dissecting the worm, and when the period was over, Sara slipped her backpack over her shoulder and asked me to eat lunch with her.

"Okay," I said, surprised. I followed her to her locker,

where she opened a tube of tomato-red lipstick and thickly applied it.

"Want some?" she asked, but I shook my head "no."

"Just a tiny bit?" she asked again, and before I could stop her, she dabbed it on. Then she removed the tortoiseshell barrette I always wore and lifted my hair into a high ponytail, pulling two tendrils down on either side of my ears.

"Stunning!" she said, standing behind me so that I could see both of us in the little mirror that hung from a hook. Stunning? I wasn't so sure.

Soon, whenever Sara chewed Juicy Fruit gum in class, I did, too, even though I was careful not to get caught. I wore long skirts like Sara's, and dangle earrings. She hid in the stacks during study hall and read old magazines and, consequently, so did I. She took me to Papa Jimmy's and introduced me to double caffé lattes and biscotti dipped in chocolate. She liked to start arguments in world history class about personal freedom and even though I never could do that, I did find myself, miraculously, volunteering to read out loud in Mr. Bernard's English class.

It was Mr. Bernard, in fact, who pulled me aside and told me I had a flair for drama (we were reading *Romeo and Juliet*). He also said I should try out for the part of Laura in the junior class production of *The Glass Menagerie*.

"No way. I could never do that," I told Sara as soon as we left the room. Secretly, though, I was pleased he had asked.

"Of course you can. You'll be great," Sara said. "You have to try out!" She bugged me until I finally agreed.

At the audition, I read a scene with Joe Greenlaw, who I'd never said a word to before. I doubt he knew who I was, but I could recite his activities as if they were listed in alphabetical order under his picture in the yearbook: junior class vice president; photo editor for the Park Ridge

Banner; captain, debate team; soccer goalie.

After we finished, Mrs. Layton, the director, just smiled and said, "Thank you *very* much," and the next day the casting list was posted on the bulletin board and there was my name, second from the top, with Joe Greenlaw's just above it.

I had play rehearsal almost every night, and so I had to use all my free time to catch up on my schoolwork and hardly ever had time to go to Papa Jimmy's with Sara. Slowly, though, a strange thing began to happen. Homework and chores, babysitting, and even Sara started to fade in importance, but the time I spent at rehearsals was as vivid as the glow-in-the-dark stars on my bedroom ceiling.

Joe talked to me, calling "Laura" from way down the hall. This made me so happy that I didn't even mind when I saw Rachel Thompson, who had waist-long hair that was shiny as glass, put her arm across his shoulder. One night, during dress rehearsal week, we were standing together on the fire escape outside the auditorium watching the snow flakes gather on the iron railing. Joe told me that deep down inside he was really shy and that he was glad he could be himself with me. "Maybe we should do things together," he said. "Go running, go to a dance, I don't know." And then we heard Mrs. Layton calling for us, so we ran back inside.

The next day, Sara stood by my locker just before homeroom. "Hi," she said.

"Hi."

"I never see you anymore. Except in classes, and that doesn't count." She tugged on one of the four stud earrings that lined her ear.

"I know," I said. "It's the play. I'm really busy. It'll be over soon." I looked closely at Sara, past her makeup, and her jewelry, and the long black cape that covered her shirt and her thick, black hiking boots. She always seemed so bold, the way she stated her opinions as if they were facts, and looked anybody in the eye. But now she was quiet, more like the old me than Sara. I gave her a hug.

"Let's do something," she suggested. She looked at the poster on the bulletin board just behind us. It was a drawing of a flapper girl twirling a strand of pearls. "Let's get a bunch of people together and crash the Winter Carnival dance. We'll go to the thrift shop and get some beaded dresses."

A dance. I thought of Joe and of our conversation the night before. And even though I knew, deep down, that it would be a white lie to say he'd invited me to that particular dance, I told her I was busy. "I can't," I said. She looked at me and waited. "Joe Greenlaw asked me."

"Yeah, right," she said.

"I'm sorry," I told her. "He did." Sara picked up her backpack from between her feet and started to walk away.

"Sara!" I called after her.

"Let me know when you can fit me into your busy schedule," she hissed.

* * * *

This is the part of my story that is really embarrassing—the part that I wish I could tell in third person, as if it really belonged to somebody else. A week after the play was over Joe found me during sixth-period study hall. "I'm sorry," he said.

I looked at him, not understanding.

"Sara McGee asked me if it was true we were going to the dance together. I'm sorry. I'm going with Rachel."

I looked down at my feet. The new me was going away, like a picture on a computer screen that fades out. I was sure my ears were bright red.

"I'm sorry," Joe continued. "It's nothing personal." He turned and looked like he was leaving, but then he came back. He put his hand on my arm. "Don't be embarrassed," he said. "You know, I should have asked you. I wish I had." And then he left.

Now Sara passed me in the hall without speaking. I spent most of my free time studying or practicing my sprints. I went back to wearing my plain, comfortable clothes and threw away my makeup. And I only talked when teachers called on me. As if nothing had changed.

But that wouldn't be true. To Sara, I might have looked the same. Still, deep inside, where she couldn't see, there was another me. I was brave, I was fun. I got a standing ovation in the middle of a stage, and a boy regretted not asking me to a dance. And it was Sara I had to thank for introducing that girl to me.

Jane Denitz Smith

So I Am Told

I'm a fourteen-year-old girl with moss-colored hair,
    sparkles and funny clothes, who feels lonely
    sometimes.
I do not ask to be understood because *I* can't even
    understand myself.
I ask to be accepted,
I ask to be accepted as I am.
I do not want to be told what potential I have, or what
    my future holds.
I do not want to be told that I'm going nowhere in life
    because I skipped a math test.
I question my existence, my meaning.
I question what the "Real World" is, and why I'm not
    there.
I feel happy with no shoes on.
I feel lonesome in a crowded room.
Sometimes my heart bleeds and I cry,
Laughter echoes in my mind.
I am told to be different,
To be myself.
But then I am told what to wear and how to act.

I like to write and rumors hurt.
I don't know how to dance, but I try to anyway.
Please don't try to understand me, nor judge me too
   quickly.
My name doesn't matter,
My heart is open.

Alexei Perry

Automobile Ambivalence

Life consists not in holding good cards but in playing those you hold well.

Josh Billings

I know it sounds a little strange since I live in Detroit, the Motor City, but from the time I bought my first car as a new teenage driver I've been afflicted with an apparently unique condition. Automobile ambivalence.

When I got my driver's license I was excited beyond belief. I'd saved some money to buy a little unsightly, plodder of a vehicle, so appearance didn't matter to me. Of course, not having much money, appearance really couldn't matter. This was a classic clunker car.

It didn't matter what it looked like; I was no longer chaperoned. I could drive to school, and I could pick up my friends. (Okay, I admit some of my friends wouldn't be caught in my car for fear of picking up some strange germs or being convinced the whole thing was just going to fall apart, without warning, at any instant.)

On the other side of the carburetor, my not-that-much-older brother had a passion for cars. He subscribed to all the auto magazines, washed and waxed his car every Saturday morning and kept the inside of the vehicle pristine clean. Our two cars, sharing the driveway, were pretty much the Odd Couple of autos.

Fearing that some strange occurrence would happen to his car being parked too closely to mine, my brother put a blanket over his every night, kind of like one of those jackets the X-ray technician wears to avoid exposure to radiation. My brother was convinced my car was sending out some type of harmful emissions well beyond what came out of my broken muffler.

I admit that his car was clearly the Homecoming Queen, while mine was, well . . . mine was pretty much the end-of-the-bench junior varsity football player who got his uniform dirty because he fell in the mud on the way to the locker room after the game. Not much talent, not much speed, dirty as can be, but still able to move in the right direction. Most of the time.

When I first heard the term "all-purpose vehicle" I believed they were actually referring to my car. My vehicle was multifunctional: It served as a mobile closet, storage area for sports equipment, stockpile for nonperishable food items and a portable periodical section of newspapers and magazines. Every "purpose" was utilized when an impromptu basketball game was organized for the park after school and I needed my gym clothes, a pregame snack, a basketball and shoes.

My automobile ambivalence did create a few problems on the homefront. This was clear when my brother was required to borrow my car because his princess of a vehicle was in the shop for probably some type of face lift or tummy tuck.

I gave him the latest briefing as he sprayed a few layers of disinfectant throughout and laid a clean towel over the driver's seat. The info I provided included don't lock the door because the key won't open it, the driver's side window doesn't roll down, the trunk light remains permanently on and don't park in a position where you'll need to back up to leave. Getting the car to go in reverse is usually a fifty-fifty proposition. It's not worth playing the odds given the potential difficulties of having to enlist the services of a passerby to push your car into a position where you can actually drive away.

When my brother returned from his jaunt in my jalopy I knew that something was amiss when he threw down the keys and simply stared at me.

"Problem?" I meekly proposed.

"You didn't tell me it stalls at most stops!"

"I guess I forgot to mention that little peculiarity. However, if you pump the accelerator twice, pull the passenger-side seatbelt once, turn the radio to country music and roll down the rear passenger-side window, it should start right up."

He was as amused as the time I had to confess to him that I'd backed out of the garage into his car parked in the driveway. I had seen his pride-and-joy vehicle as I'd entered mine but, apparently, my short-term memory wasn't in full operation that morning. As I heard the sound of metal on metal, I knew it wasn't a good sign. I told him that maybe having Dad put up some traffic signals in our driveway would be a good idea. He wasn't amused.

One of the benefits of automobile ambivalence is there isn't an overwhelming disappointment when a little body damage occurs. Heck, with my car, I'd have been hard-pressed to notice anything. The dents and dings throughout made it resemble one of those antique-looking candelabras you hammered away at in seventh-grade shop class.

Before going to advise my brother of the two-car pile-up in the driveway I surveyed the injuries. I remember actually being somewhat pleased that I'd accidentally achieved some symmetry given that the previous huge dent on the rear driver's side now matched the new dent on the opposite side. I thought, for whatever reason, that maybe I'd now get better gas mileage. Kind of some new aerodynamic action. More wind resistant.

After having had this first car for a couple years, I recall feeling a little sentimental as we approached an important milestone—one hundred thousand miles. Despite my general ambivalence, I did love my car, warts and all. I recall thinking for this big event I'd do something really special. I first thought a drive-thru car wash would be nice, but I was a little hesitant since I felt some of the dirt and rust may actually be holding the whole darn thing together.

I finally decided on a drive-in movie. Just a teenager and his car. In years since, I've had more cars and my auto ambivalence remains. But you only have one first car and although it's no longer intact, my memories are.

Bob Schwartz

Minimaxims for My Godson

The purpose of life is a life of purpose.

Robert Byrne

Dear Sandy,

Your nice thank-you note for the graduation present I sent you a few weeks ago just came in, and I've been chuckling over your postscript in which you say that such presents are great but you wish someone could give you "half a dozen foolproof ideas for bending the world into a pretzel."

Well, Sandy, I must admit, I don't have any very original thoughts of my own. But through the years I've encountered a few ideas of that kind—not platitudes but ideas sharp-pointed enough to stick in my mind permanently. Concepts that release energy, make problem-solving easier, provide shortcuts to worthwhile goals. No one handed them over in a neat package. They just came along from time to time, usually from people not in the wisdom-dispensing business at all. Compared to the great time-tested codes of conduct, they may seem like pretty small change. But each of them has helped to make my life a good deal easier and happier and more productive. So here they are. I hope you find them useful, too.

1. *If you can't change facts, try bending your attitudes.* Without a doubt, the bleakest period of my life so far was the winter of 1942 to 1943. I was with the Eighth Air Force in England. Our bomber bases, hacked out of the sodden English countryside, were seas of mud. On the ground, people were cold, miserable and homesick. In the air, people were getting shot. Replacements were few; morale was low.

   But there was one sergeant—a crew chief—who was always cheerful, always good-humored, always smiling. I watched him one day, in a freezing rain, struggle to salvage a fortress that had skidded into an apparently bottomless mire. He was whistling like a lark. "Sergeant," I said to him sourly, "how can you whistle in a mess like this?"

   He gave me a mud-caked grin. "Lieutenant," he said, "when the facts won't budge you have to bend your attitudes to fit them, that's all."

   Check it for yourself, Sandy. You'll see that, faced with a given set of problems one man may tackle them with intelligence, grace and courage; another may react with resentment and bitterness; a third may run away altogether. In any life, facts tend to remain unyielding. But attitudes are a matter of choice—and that choice is largely up to you.

2. *Don't come up to the net behind nothing.* One night in a PTA meeting, a lawyer—a friend and frequent tennis partner of mine—made a proposal that I disagreed with, and I challenged it. But when I had concluded what I thought was quite a good spur-of-the-moment argument, my friend stood up and proceeded to

demolish it. Where I had opinions, he had facts; where I had theories, he had statistics. He obviously knew so much more about the subject than I did that his viewpoint easily prevailed. When we met in the hall afterward, he winked and said, "You should know better than to come up to the net behind nothing!"

It is true; the tennis player who follows his own weak or badly placed shot up to the net is hopelessly vulnerable. And this is true when you rush into *anything* without adequate preparation or planning. In any important endeavor, you've got to do your homework, get your facts straight and sharpen your skills. In other words, don't bluff—because if you do, nine times out of ten, life will drill a backhand right past you.

3. *When the ball is over, take off your dancing shoes.* As a child, I used to hear my aunt say this, and it puzzled me a good deal, until the day I heard her spell out the lesson more explicitly. My sister had come back from a glamorous weekend full of glitter, exciting parties and stimulating people. She was bemoaning the contrast with her routine job, her modest apartment and her day-to-day friends. "Young lady," our aunt said gently, "no one lives on the top of the mountain. It's fine to go there occasionally—for inspiration, for new perspectives. But you have to come down. Life is lived in the valley. That's where the farms and gardens and orchards are, and where the plowing and the work are done. That's where you apply the visions you may have glimpsed from the peaks."

It's a steadying thought when the time comes, as it always does, to exchange your dancing shoes for your working shoes.

4. *Shine up your neighbor's halo.* One Sunday morning, drowsing in a back pew of a little country church, I

dimly heard the old preacher urge his flock to "stop worrying about your own halo and shine up your neighbor's!" And it left me sitting up, wide-awake, because it struck me as just about the best eleven-word formula for getting along with people that I've ever heard.

I like it for its implication that everyone, in some area of life, has a halo that's worth watching for and acknowledging. I like it for the firm way it shifts the emphasis from self to interest and concern for others. Finally, I like it because it reflects a deep psychological truth: People have a tendency to become what you expect them to be.

5. *Keep one eye on the law of the echo.* I remember very well the occasion when I heard this sharp-edged bit of advice. Coming home from boarding school, some of us youngsters were in the dining car of a train. Somehow the talk got around to the subject of cheating on exams, and one boy readily admitted that he cheated all the time. He said that he found it both easy and profitable.

Suddenly, a mild-looking man sitting all alone at a table across the aisle—he might have been a banker, a bookkeeper, anything—leaned forward and spoke up. "Yes," he said directly to the apostle of cheating. "All the same—I'd keep one eye on the law of the echo, if I were you."

The law of the echo—is there really such a thing? Is the universe actually arranged so that whatever you send out—honesty or dishonesty, kindness or cruelty—ultimately comes back to you? It's hard to be sure. And yet, since the beginning of recorded history, mankind has had the conviction, based partly on intuition, partly on observation, that in the long run a man does indeed reap what he sows.

You know as well as I do, Sandy, that in this misty area there are no final answers. Still, as the man said, "I think I'd keep one eye on the law of the echo, if I were you!"

6. *Don't wear your raincoat in the shower.* In the distant days when I was a Boy Scout, I had a troop leader who was an ardent woodsman and naturalist. He would take us on hikes, not saying a word, and then challenge us to describe what we had observed: trees, plants, birds, wildlife, everything. Invariably, we hadn't seen a quarter as much as he had, nor half enough to satisfy him. "Creation is all around you," he would cry, waving his arms in vast inclusive circles, "but you're keeping it out. Don't be a buttoned-up person! Stop wearing your raincoat in the shower!"

I've never forgotten the ludicrous image of a person standing in the shower with a raincoat buttoned up to his chin. The best way to discard that raincoat, I've found, is to expose yourself to new experiences in your life *all your life.*

All these phrases that I have been recalling really urge one to the same goal: a stronger participation, a deep involvement in life. This doesn't come naturally, by any means. And yet, with marvelous impartiality, each of us is given exactly the same number of minutes and hours in every day. Time is the raw material. What we do with it is up to us.

A wise man once said that tragedy is not what we suffer, but what we miss. Keep that in mind, Sandy.

Your affectionate godfather,

Arthur Gordon

Finding a Vision

Six years ago, I went blind. Due to a severe herpes simplex virus in my eyes, I lost one of my most precious possessions: my eyesight. Tiny cold sores covered the surface of my eyes, scarring my cornea. I wasn't allowed to stand in direct sunlight or even in a brightly lit room. The light would penetrate my eyelids and cause too much pain. At the age of seventeen, I was unprepared to find myself in a dark world. Who would I be without my ability to see?

All I wanted throughout the entire summer was to be able to see people. What new cute bathing suit styles was everyone wearing? Who had cut their hair or dyed it purple? I would have a conversation with someone and realize that I had no idea what facial expressions he was making. I no longer had the ability to make eye contact, a privilege I had taken for granted before. I longed to talk with my eyes. I just wasn't whole without my vision.

My parents became my sole support system. Hoping for a miracle, they took me to an eye specialist every day. No one was sure if I would ever completely recover, and if so, how long the healing process would take. Meanwhile, Mom and Dad adjusted their own lives in order to keep my spirits up. They would take me to baseball games and out to dinner—anything to get me out of the house. However, going places was difficult. I had to wear eye patches and dark sunglasses to ease the pain of bright light. As a seventeen-year-old, this wasn't exactly the fashion statement I was trying to make.

My parents had to take care of me everywhere. At restaurants they ordered my food, arranged it on the table, and then explained where everything was on my plate so I could finally eat it. My fifteen-year-old brother took this opportunity to rearrange the food on my plate. My mom was amazing. Each day she would brush my hair and lay out a decent looking outfit so I could walk out of the house with a little bit of pride. She was determined to keep my self-esteem as high as possible. I relied on my mom to make me feel pretty. At an age when I should have been gaining my independence, I found myself becoming increasingly dependent on my parents.

I wasn't able to drive or visit my friends. Movies were completely out of the question. Life seemed to just go on without me, as if I was never there. Fortunately, I had a wonderful friend who knew how to make me feel special. Donny and I had dated a couple of times before I lost my vision, but at that time we were just friends. He would come to my house to sit and talk with me. If the TV were on, he'd watch and I'd listen. One time, Donny took me to a baseball barbecue and introduced me to all of his friends. I had never been so happy in my entire life. He didn't care that I couldn't see his friends. He held my hand proudly and led me around. I may not have been able to see all the people I met that day, but their voices are clear in mind. I can still separate whose laughter belonged to whom. When I close my eyes now and try to remember that day, I mostly see darkness. But I can still smell the sausage and brisket cooking on the grill. I can hear the happiness around me and Donny's voice saying, "This is my girlfriend, Talina."

I slowly began to make progress toward the end of the summer. Little by little, I was able to open my eyes. My vision was still blurred but this achievement called for a celebration. My parents were still concerned and Donny continued to stay by my side. Then I began to worry, *Will I have to start my senior year wearing my thick glasses that everyone still refers to as Coke bottles?* I didn't want to think about it. August crept up on me, though, and I started school with limited vision and thick glasses. As I walked through the halls, I struggled to look confident. I had a harder time cheering at pep rallies and football games. My lack of clear vision and concern with my physical appearance took the fun out of everything that I used to love. My level of self-confidence had diminished to an unrecognizable point.

At a time in my life when I expected my only concern to be to have fun, I was learning a powerful lesson. I could no longer rely on appearance to make me feel better about myself. I had to go deeper. With the support of my family and friends, I realized that feeling good about who I am on the inside is far more important. Believing that I can overcome the obstacles that I face is crucial. My identity wasn't my thick glasses. My identity was my inner strength. This inner strength allowed me to love life even when I was unable to see it. Losing my eyesight could not take away my ability to hear the voices of the people who love me. It could not steal away the fresh smell of morning or the lingering aroma of my mom's cooking. Most important, my loss could never take from me the feel of my boyfriend's hand around my own.

Six years later, I continue to need steroid eyedrops to keep the virus from reoccurring. The scar tissue is slowly improving. Recently, I began to wear both contacts, which is a huge accomplishment. A day doesn't go by that I am not thankful for my progress and the lesson I learned. I am incredibly thankful for my special friend who visited me, introduced me as his girlfriend and is now my husband.

I am currently preparing for my first year of teaching. I think about which of my personal qualities I might be able to share with my students. I know how difficult it is to grow up and I want my students to believe that I understand them. If I can't teach them anything else, I hope I can get across the lesson that changed my teenage experience: True beauty is not about what you *see* on the outside but what you feel, sense and love from within.

Talina Sessler-Barker

No More What Ifs

It was August 2, 1999, a day I would never forget. Indeed, it was my dad's fifty-third birthday, but something else about that day was also very special. I called my dad up to see if he would like to have lunch together for his birthday. He agreed, and half-an-hour later I arrived at his school. (He's an elementary principal.) He ordered us BLTs at a nearby restaurant.

We walked together to the small fast-food restaurant. As we neared the door, two young girls walked in: two beautiful goddesses. They recognized my father, and approached us. "Hey Mr. Margheim," they happily chimed.

My dad had been their elementary-school principal, so he introduced us. "Chance, this is Stephanie."

"Uh, hi," I said. I didn't catch her friend's name. I was under the assumption that they were both college students. My dad must have read my mind because he asked them their ages. Embarrassed, I rubbed my hands over my face, paranoid. *Do they know that I'm interested, am I obvious?*

"Juniors," they said in unison. *Perfect,* I thought. I am a senior.

The conversation pretty much ended there, unfortunately. They were both working, so I figured that it would be best not to talk to them too much. My dad and I sat down. He ate, I couldn't. My stomach was doing flips; I was secretly waiting for Stephanie to approach me, hair blowing, eyes sparkling . . .

I guess we waited for some time before my dad gave me the old nudge. "Gotta get back to work," he whispered.

As we left, Stephanie gave me the usual, "Bye, nice to have met you."

"You, too," I crooned, lowering my voice.

The car ride back was silent. I am usually the conversation starter, but I was too deep in thought. I stared out the car window, thinking. I thought to myself as I got out of the car and walked into my father's office. After much contemplation, I decided, I was going to ask this girl out! I gave my father a hug, wished him a happy birthday and left.

My mind was asking a million questions. *No more what ifs*, I said to myself. *I am tired of what ifs.*

I pulled into the parking lot of the fast-food restaurant, and sat in my car for a good half-hour, contemplating my move. I was nervous, very nervous, heart-popping-out-of-my-chest nervous. I literally felt like I was having a heart attack! I took a deep breath, prayed and walked into the restaurant. She was talking to someone, so I waited by the counter. Her eyes met mine, and she walked over to me. After what seemed like an hour of staring at her, I opened my mouth and let the words fall out.

"Umm, I know this is gonna sound crazy, but would you like to go out sometime?"

What a relief! I finally asked someone out! I studied her face, reading her reaction.

"Awww, that's nice, but I am serious with someone right now."

"Oh, yeah, okay, don't worry about it," I said, "that's fine." "It was a good try though, right?" We both laughed. Our chat ended with a friendly handshake, and a "see you later."

Surprisingly enough, I wasn't disappointed. True, I would have loved to come home that night telling everyone that I finally had a date; and yet, I felt great! I had finally faced my fear and bit the bullet. I was prouder of myself at that moment than I had ever been in my life.

For the first time in seventeen years, I had faced my fear. I went home that day, and for once, I didn't have to ask myself, *what if?*

Chance Margheim

All the More Beautiful

At seventeen, I wanted desperately to be an adult, and believed I was making progress. I shaved almost every other day, and had my own wheels. The only thing I needed was the girl.

I saw her from a block away. She was tall, with long brown hair. We went to the same public school, but she often wore this plaid skirt, like a private-school girl. I drove up from behind, in my car, the only place I didn't feel short, and something amazing happened. She looked back at me. It felt just like one of those cheesy movies, slow motion, hair flowing, a halo of light surrounding her. She followed me with her eyes as I passed. That day, I felt tall wherever I went.

My luck didn't stop there. It turned out that she and my cousin were friends. He gave me her name and number. That afternoon, my sweaty, shaking hand picked up the phone, and I spoke to Kristen for the first time. That weekend, I drove down the same street where our eyes first met, to pick her up for our first date, my first real date ever.

I pictured myself sitting next to this perfect girl, in her perfect living room, being interrogated by her perfect parents. I arrived, and all my expectations began to be challenged. There was no playful dog in the front yard, and no white picket fence to keep him from running away. Before I could knock on the door, Kristen opened it just enough to slip out. Then she smiled and all was perfect again. We went miniature golfing and laughed together for the first time.

After that night, we were inseparable, sickening all our friends. She made me feel like a big man, even though she called me her little guy. I had never felt so close to anyone before. But some mornings, when I'd pick her up for school and she'd slip out her door, something was different. She wouldn't have that perfect smile. She'd stare out the window and she seemed lost. I'd ask her what was wrong, and she'd say, "Nothing."

No answer could have been worse. It drove me crazy. I wanted to help. I wanted her to smile. Most of all, I wanted to be let inside. If I was an adult, it was time to start acting like one.

I confronted her; told her I knew there was something wrong. I knew she had problems at home, and I knew I could help if she'd just let me. Then she started to cry. I felt utterly helpless.

She put her arms around me and pressed her face into my chest. I felt her hot tears seeping through my shirt.

I soon learned that Kristen suffered from anxiety and depression. At home, she couldn't escape her past. Outside, with me, she could pretend all was perfect. When she started crying, she stopped pretending, and let me inside. I also stopped pretending. There were times when I didn't feel strong, when I didn't feel wise. There were times when I didn't feel like an adult.

During these past six years, Kristen and I have shared many laughs and tears together. I have had time to study her smile. I realize it is not perfect and, therefore, all the more beautiful. She continues to challenge and surpass all my expectations, teaching me more about life than I ever imagined there was to know. We talk about marriage and a family of our own, but we're in no hurry to grow up.

Marc Gaudioso

Return to High School

Don't be afraid to take a big step. You can't cross a chasm in two small jumps.

David Lloyd George

On September 15, 1998, two landmark events occurred that I'd been anticipating my entire life: I turned eighteen, and I began college. When my parents, my sister, our dog, four boxes, three oddly shaped duffel bags and our gray station wagon drew near to the university where I would spend the next four years of my life, I was terrified.

I fidgeted, played with my clothing and my hair, then tried to distract myself by passing a lost ant from hand to hand for fifteen minutes, before releasing it safely by the side of the road as we pulled up to the dorm. My ant-gazing left me nearly cross-eyed and largely unconsoled. By the time we reached the front steps, my fear had left an "anxiety wrinkle" in my forehead, one that I swear I can still see today.

Meanwhile, orientation passed in a blur, like racing down a water slide, from which I plunged into the first day of classes. I went to the wrong building for three of my classes and the wrong side of campus for another. As I race-walked from class to class, I kept thinking I saw high school classmates, and had to remind myself that most of them were now living on the other side of the country.

Only six months later, on the occasion of my sister's debut in the school musical, I would return home for spring break and revisit high school; again, I felt terrified. As a freshman in high school, I had felt like a shadow-person until I found my place on the stage, where the true me found expression in drama. In one of the great ironies of my high school years, I felt the freest when my words were scripted and my gestures rehearsed. Offstage, and out of the classroom, I had felt like an outcast before the unforgiving eyes of my peers. Now, as a visitor from college who had not quite escaped the ghosts of high school past, I was going to watch my sister act, dance and sing on stage.

I arrived at my old high school two minutes before the musical was to begin, intending to sneak in and out, like a shadow in the night. But I'd forgotten that the shows always started late, that there was an intermission, and that I'd have to wait for my sister at the end to congratulate her. I would see everyone, and in the garish light of the lobby, everyone would see me. I escaped temporarily into the ladies' bathroom and practiced relaxed smiles, only to discover that as the corners of my mouth went up, the anxiety wrinkle in my brow deepened. With a sigh, I went out to watch the show.

Taking my seat as the lights and sound dimmed and the overture began, I tried to sit serenely. But I fidgeted, just as I had during the last few minutes of that two-hour drive to college, only this time, I had no ants to save. As I watched my sister perform, I couldn't help feeling as though I should be up on that same stage. And in that moment, I genuinely missed high school, the place where, as a senior, I had finally nearly fit in. Now I was a freshman all over again.

When the musical ended, I wove through the crowd, hugging classmates who had never really known me, searching for my sister. As I passed several of my former classmates, I looked them over carefully. Like me, they looked pretty much the same, as uncomfortable as I. One of them, a girl who might have become a good friend if social status had not divided us, asked me if I felt out of place, no longer a high school student, no longer a member of the cast. "Of course," I wanted to say, but now this seemed trivial. In high school, I'd almost always felt out of place. Only now had the sensation become manageable, like holding your breath under water, knowing that any second, you can pop back up and take a deep breath of air.

So I laughed and said, "Tonight I'm just the sister." She laughed too, but it was an awkward laugh. Now, she also understood what it was like to feel out of place, and suddenly I understood something about her, about the rest of my classmates. That night, the last night of our past together, we were all the same. I squeezed her hand, and, then, I had no trouble smiling a real smile, with both forgiveness and regret, before saying good-bye.

As I left the theater, I saw a few figures in the distance. Thinking I recognized them, I raised my arm and prepared to call their names. Then one figure turned toward me; realizing my error, I laughed. I had mistaken my sister's classmates for two of my college friends. In that moment, I knew where I belonged. Taking a fond last look at my high school, and my past, I walked through the gates to my car. A streetlight rose from behind a hedge, and my shadow pulled back and let me by.

Sierra Millman

Inspirations

Courage is the discovery that you may not win,
    and trying when you know you can lose.

Honor is standing for what you believe—
    not for what you know.

Life isn't about living without problems.
Life is about solving problems.

If you plow the field every day—
    the only thing that grows is resentment.

Compassion is passion with a heart.

The only thing in the whole universe people need to
    control are their attitudes.

How a person wins and loses is much more important
    than *how much* a person wins and loses.

If you only do what you know you can do—
    you never do very much.

There are no failures—
    just experiences and your reactions to them.

Getting what you want is not nearly as important
as giving what you have.

Going on a journey with a map requires following
directions—
going on a journey without one requires following
your heart.

Talent without humility is wasted.

If you don't want it bad enough to risk losing it—
you don't want it bad enough.

When life knocks you down you have two choices—
stay down or get up.

Tom Krause

The Days of Cardboard Boxes

Enjoy yourself. These are the good old days you're going to miss in the years ahead.

Anonymous

Cardboard boxes played a significant role in my childhood days. Don't get me wrong; toys were wonderful, too, but nothing could out-do a cardboard box and a few kids to go along with it—especially my two best neighborhood friends, Chris and Nick, brothers who lived three blocks away.

Summer was always the perfect time to have a cardboard box. The long, lazy days offered sufficient time to experience the true essence of a box and to truly bond with it. However, in order to bond with a box, we first had to find one. The three of us would pile into the back of my parents' truck, briefly jockeying for the coveted wheel seats, then sing the "Na Na Na" song (any song we only knew some of the words to but sang anyway) while we waited for my mom to find her keys. None of us dared to suggest that we ride in the front of the truck; that was for sissies.

Finally, after an infinite number of "Na Na Na" songs, Mom drove us to a box place, and there it was! The most beautiful box we had ever seen. It was a refrigerator box, most definitely the best kind to have. Refrigerator boxes could journey to far better places than any other box, and their ability to be anything was simply phenomenal. The furniture warehouse/showroom had thrown this glorious bounty out the back door like it was useless. We had arrived in time to rescue it from the nefarious jaws of a trash truck.

We watched with anticipation as Mom slid the box to the back of the truck. We crawled into the box for the ride home, sheltered from the wind and the bugs that seemed to aim right for the tonsils during mid-"Na."

Arriving back in the neighborhood was an experience that made our heads swell. Everyone who was outdoors could see us, and word would soon spread that Nick, Chris and Eva possessed a refrigerator box. You see, anyone who owned a refrigerator box held an esteemed position. We would be legends. We would take our box where no kids had ever gone before.

We unloaded our treasure and carried it with great care into the back yard. Chris said we should spend a few minutes of quiet time to gather our thoughts, and then we could discuss our ideas for this magnificent being. We did so for about five seconds. Then suddenly, as if an unknown force opened our voice boxes, we broke into song:

> *Na na na na*
> *Our box is groovy*
> *Na Na Na*
> *And so are we!*

Okay, it was a short song. But it was beautiful. And I'm sure it would have touched the hearts of those fortunate enough to hear it.

It was time to make our decision. "Let's go to Zo in our box," I said.

"Who?" Nick and Chris gave me one of their looks.

"Where to go or where not to go, that is the question," I retorted.

Nick told me I didn't make any sense, and I explained that it was all very simple, that he and Chris just needed to learn how to think backwards. Chris decided Nick was right—I didn't make any sense.

"Zo is Oz backwards, you ignorant little twerps! We wanna go to Zo and do everything Dorothy does in Oz, but backwards." I was hollering at them because I knew they had better sense than they were using.

Chris looked first at me and then at the box as he contemplated my bright idea. I wondered if Chris and Nick were seriously ill because they should have known by then, from all our past experiences, that boxes (especially this one) could take us anywhere. We could be or do anything we wanted because of the power of the almighty refrigerator box. And we could be backwards about it too.

"You know, Eva is right," Chris said. "We have never done anything backwards before, so let's make this the first time. But we can go *anywhere* backwards, not just Zo."

At that moment in our young lives we understood clearly that we were going to go down in history. People all over the world would be talking about "The Three Backwards Box Kids." Other children would attempt to go where we had gone, but none of them could ever be like us because their imaginations were inferior to ours.

We made a solemn declaration that our box would be a time machine. We swore on chocolate peanut butter cups that this backward idea was here to stay (at least until the next box). And anyone who broke a promise made over chocolate peanut butter cups was basically considered immoral.

After we had traveled several years back in time, we were faced with a dilemma. We were visiting with a singer named Elvis who inquired about how we got to Graceland. We told him about our time machine, the backwards idea, the chocolate-peanut-butter-cup promise, and how we were going to go down in history. Elvis was all shook up about us, and he said that we were pretty neat kids . . . but . . .

"But what?" we pressed.

He wanted to know how we were eventually going to get home again if we could only go backwards.

In all our days, we had never been faced with a predicament such as this. We had also never broken a chocolate-peanut-butter-cup promise. We were, you know, up a creek. We could not capitulate. Life always had its ups and downs—this was just one of the very big downs that would take a long night of pondering. Luckily, our parents would not let us stay out all night to play our make-believe games.

Soon my mom called out the back door, breaking us out of our imaginary world and landing us abruptly in the backyard again. It was time for Nick and Chris to go home. The three of us quickly made plans to meet at eight o'clock the next morning to discuss solutions to get us out of the disaster we were in. As I ran the few feet to my back door, Nick and Chris took off running the three blocks toward their home. Time could not be squandered. We only had until morning before we would be back in the reality of our imaginary world again.

At 7:33 the next morning, the phone broke the silence, and I stumbled out of bed with a hangover from thinking too much. When I answered the phone, Nick demanded to know if I had covered the box with plastic the night before like we were supposed to do, in case of rain. I looked out the window to see that it had rained, a very hard and drenching rain. With deep regret in my heart, I told Nick I hadn't, but the responsibility belonged to all of us, so it wasn't completely my fault.

Nick and Chris came over, and silence replaced our usual banter. Our box had only been with us for one day. Now we were stuck in the real world because our box was dead.

The soggy cardboard couldn't just be left out in the yard to rot away. It had been a good box while it lasted, and it deserved proper respect. So we dragged it to the side of the street where the garbage was picked up. The day before we had saved it from a trash truck that would have taken its life too early; now it was time for our box to go. Although it was a natural death, it could have been prevented. This reality would be a weight we would carry for all our childhood days.

The three of us sat next to our dead box so we could be there when the trash truck came. We even made up a "Na Na Na" requiem, and we sang with all our might as the truck hauled our box away. No one could have put more sincerity or emotion into a song than we did that day. Although we were mourning our box, we knew we must go on. We must find another box, and we must build another imaginary world with it.

I miss the cardboard-box days. However, just as we had to go on after the demise of our box, I had to go on and grow up. But my childhood imagination will always be a part of me. I will always believe in cardboard boxes.

Eva Burke

Rolling Down Summer's Hills

Every human being on this Earth is born with a tragedy, and it isn't original sin. He's born with the tragedy that he has to grow up. A lot of people don't have the courage to do it.

Helen Hayes

We run through the August night with only fireflies lighting our way, feeling the freedom of time that only children of summer ever know. The echo of our laughter sails through darkness, while we chase each other in tag. Soon we become silent, hunting through the tall, damp grass punctuated only by the beating of our hearts.

A hand pierces through the night, grabbing me. Our two bodies fall entwined into a huddled mass of legs and arms with her gaining the upper hand because I let her. She pins me down upon my back, her hands holding mine outstretched upon the moist grass. Straddling my chest with her knees, I sense her head slowly growing ever nearer. We're so close that I can feel the ins and outs of her breath upon my lips. She covers my mouth with her own and I am lost in the newness of my first kiss.

Before I can speak or think, she pulls away. Running off, she leaves me there dazed. That was how the night ended; this is how it began.

It's the summer of my thirteenth birthday, and I'm enjoying these majestic Pocono days. Our cabin overlooks the endless rolling hills carpeted by sweet-smelling grasses and black-eyed Susans. My younger brother Mikey and I climb to the highest point and then, lying down on our sides like two bowling pins, we close our eyes rolling wildly down to the bottom. It's a dizzying sensation to feel the world spin around and around this way. Sometimes I lose control and go careening off into some unplanned foreign destination.

And so it is when I first see Carly, hanging out among the other girls at Lake Wallenpaupack. I didn't know then that I'd go careening off sideways and smack straight into her world.

She hangs with this group of thirteen-year-old girls who've teamed up more out of convenience than common interest. Her long black hair falls in waves against her pale white skin, and she has this unique ability to smile at me with her eyes.

My posse looks like an odd assortment left over in some thrift-shop clearance box. First off, there's me. I had a major growth spurt this summer, and my limbs feel way too long. It's weird to suddenly tower over your own mother, the person you've looked up to your whole life. Now a good three inches taller than she, I can easily pat her on the head. Yet no matter how much I eat, my pants hang low on my gangly, 105-pound frame. Everything is changing around me and inside me. I can't even count on feeling comfortable in my own skin, which is now riddled with acne.

Then there's my ten-year-old brother, Mikey. He hasn't found any other kids his age around, and appears to be going through severe Nintendo withdrawal. It's my responsibility to watch out for all four fast-moving feet of him. We make an unlikely pair. Although only three years come between our ages, almost two feet separate our heights.

Finally there's Ron, who's fourteen, a full year older than I and so much more wise in the ways of the world. He shoves his Mets cap low on his head to shield his eyes from the sun and any parent's watchful gaze. In his left ear he sports a fake diamond stud, which denotes the coolness he envelops.

Ron and I sit on the dock, dangling our feet in the water's edge, while Mikey floats carelessly in his black inner tube. Once in a while we have the nerve to dart our eyes over to the girls who are taking turns diving into the water in their bright bikinis, giggling and trying to peek over at us as well.

Ron shares his experiences with women and I wonder how much of it is really true, but I listen closely just in case it is. Some of his stories are funny, and others are just really gross, but I tuck all of what he tells me safely away in the annals of my mind for future reference.

My only other experience hearing about sex was back in health class, and there it seemed like such a crude joke. There was this one jerk in the back of the room who'd laugh whenever the teacher mentioned anything sexual. He was the same guy who'd repeat over and over that there was going to be a "teste" on Monday and then die laughing at his own wit.

At home, my parents speak in strictly medical terms. The way they tell it, the whole thing sounds more like a painful procedure for wisdom teeth removal than a pleasurable experience. Here, sitting on the dock with Ron, it seems a lot more real. I watch Carly in her red two-piece. Her shining black hair reflects the noonday sun, and I wonder what it would be like to kiss those peach-colored lips. So far it's taken all the courage I can muster just to say hi as we pass each other every day at the lake.

Soon, night falls and Dad calls us around the dinner table to have an informal family meeting. He says he wants to talk about our "future." The cabin is hot and noticeably un-air-conditioned. The sweat on the back of my legs causes my skin to stick to the vinyl-covered dining chairs.

My dad sits at the head of the table with his elbows resting on the yellow Formica. He hasn't shaved since we arrived here, and the gray stubble on his cheeks and chin make him look old. My mother sits at the other end of the table still wearing the same swimsuit she wore earlier today down by the lake. She pulls the seat of her suit down over each thigh, fidgeting more than her usual calm demeanor allows. Mikey sits lazily dipping his Oreo cookies into a large glass of milk and then sucking them down over his wet lips.

My dad tells us he's been laid off from work—straight out with no beating around the bush. I can't say I'm shocked; we all saw the writing on the wall. Dad's a textile man, and the industry is dying. I know this because I've heard the hushed conversations between my mom and dad. With most labor now going overseas, there's just not enough work to keep the U.S. sewing factories alive. It's not as if Dad has a profession where he can just slip comfortably into a new opportunity. Finding another job at forty-six years old is rough.

Mikey just keeps sucking down his cookies. He's too young to understand that there is no magic that will make everything better, and that Dad doesn't have all the answers.

In between frantic thoughts, I hear Dad saying something about our home; using words like "scaling down" and "tightening belts." All I keep wondering is, *How is this going to affect me? Will I still be able to afford to go to the movies with my friends, or will I be left at home? And where will my home be?* I hear Dad saying something about our horrendous taxes and the possibility of moving to a smaller apartment.

I want to grab him and yell, "Stop! Don't you know you're ruining my life? I can't move . . . this is where all my friends are . . . this is where I go to school. We had a deal, remember? You would take care of me, and I would never have to worry about these kinds of things, because I'm just a kid."

And then this feeling gives way to a sickening rush of guilt for being so selfish. I look over at my parents who seem small and vulnerable. Who are these pathetic imposters whose words change everything for all of us, and how should I react to these strangers that I love so much? Should I lie and tell them everything will be okay? And is that what they need to hear, or is that really what *I* need to hear? I suddenly feel like the parent.

That night I run out to play tag with all those kids whose lives are still unchanged. I run through the night hoping to knock the wind out of myself—running to forget about my dad or maybe to stumble onto an answer that will save us. That's when Carly's arm reaches out to grab me. She kisses me, and I forget for one moment about all the uncertainty.

Then she's gone, and I lay there in the pitch-black darkness with my head spinning the same way it did when I rolled down those long summer hills. I feel that same dizzying disorientation lying there alone in the darkness, and I realize that sometimes there are no real answers, and life goes on.

C. S. Dweck

9

LETTERS FROM READERS

*T*o send a letter is a good way to go somewhere without moving anything but your
heart.

Phyllis Theroux

My Sister's First Love

Dear Chicken Soup for the Teenage Soul,

I am sending you a story my sister wrote for your consideration for a Chicken Soup *book. My sister, Jodi, underwent a very emotional, psychological and spiritual struggle as she dealt with the fact that her long-term boyfriend, Tim, was dying from an inoperable brain tumor. She helped Tim fight his cancer in every way imaginable, but unfortunately on Valentine's Day in 1997, Jodi sat by Tim's side as he took his last breath.*

Although her story is tragic, she was able to gain a whole new outlook on the meaning of life and death. She wrote this story about her experience, and it touched me deeply. The power of her words is simply breathtaking, and I wanted to share them with you, and, hopefully, others, as well.

Sincerely,
Kristi Vesterby

Immortal

*When someone dies, you don't get over it by
forgetting; you get over it by remembering, and
you are aware that no person is ever truly lost or
gone once they have been in our life and loved
us, as we have loved them.*

Leslie Marmon Silko

His dizziness and headaches began during the summer;
they worried me a little, but I never thought they would
amount to anything serious. I look back now and wonder
if he knew they were signs of what was to come. Tim and
I had been dating for over a year; we'd become best
friends. We were in that phase of our lives when we
thought nothing could go wrong. We were going to be
together forever and live our perfect high-school-
sweetheart love story with a white picket fence and all.
When his symptoms persisted, I think we both knew that
something was wrong, but I never could have imagined
just how wrong.

By basketball season, things were considerably worse.
It was his junior year, and Tim had hoped he would
finally be starting on the varsity team. I would sit in the
stands and cheer with the rest of my friends, but inside I
was constantly wondering who this impostor was that
was taking over Tim's body. He bobbled the ball as he'd
dribble up the court, or tip over on the backs of his heels
while attempting to play defense. His frustration
increased with each day of practice, so when his mother,
Ann, suggested he see a doctor, Tim agreed. The local
clinic scheduled an appointment for him to have a scan of
his brain the next time the "MRI-Mobile" came to Olivia,
our small, unequipped town. The scan later showed a

tumor growing on the base of Tim's brain, and from then on our lives were never the same.

We all sat crammed in an incredibly small room they called a doctor's office, waiting for the arrival of some overly busy neuro-oncologist. He was going to interpret the complicated X rays that were beyond the capability of the doctors at Prairie Family Practice. This room was as close to hell as I've ever been, and without even knowing what was ahead of me, it was difficult to find a way to pass the time. None of us wanted to think about why we were there, so we mostly occupied the passing minutes with the idle talk of basketball and history class. The oncologist finally graced us with his presence as he walked into our crowded room. He introduced himself and started discussing what we already knew from the scans. Tim had a tumor invading his brain stem. He went on to say that it was inoperable, which meant very little to me at the time. As he went into medical jargon, his words became mere background noise as I turned my attention toward Tim.

He sat in the chair directly across from me, listening to every word the doctor was saying. He was motionless; even his eyes seemed to be staring into a place that had somehow captured his whole being. Tim hated his eyes. He often joked about their "ugly" tint, which he called green-brown-yellow-orangish. I always had to remind him that despite their lack of definite color, his eyes were one of his best features. They disclosed his every emotion. All I had to do was look at them and I could actually see his love for me. His eyes revealed his kindness, his cocky and somewhat rebellious nature, and, of course, his spark of determination. Now they were vacant.

Ann, Tim's mother, asked a question, and I was thrown back into the conversation at hand. Dr. So-and-So answered by discussing the options that could be attempted to shrink the tumor. I wondered why none of his so-called options sounded promising. As this thought meandered through my mind, his mother, with a voice that attempted to hide the quivering, asked how long Tim was expected to live. Her words snuck up from behind me and grabbed my throat. I looked at her as though she was a murderer with no conscience. How could she ask such a question? Tim was not going to die, and she had no right to even suggest that he might. In a detached voice void of all emotion the doctor said, "One year to eighteen months with treatment."

As he spoke these words, the grip around my neck tightened to the point of choking me. I struggled for a breath, and the already tiny room closed even more. I needed space, and the first thought that crossed my mind was to run, not only from the room, but from the whole situation. I could escape now before I got hurt. I was confused and angry, but most of all I was consumed by the incredible fear of losing someone I loved so much.

I looked at Tim who sat motionless; he didn't say anything and neither did anyone else. The room was filled with an uncomfortable silence, and I could feel the pulse of my heart pounding in my ears. I was sure that everyone could hear me sucking in each breath. I don't remember what the doctor said before he left the room— I couldn't even look at this man who had just sentenced Tim to death. When we were alone, Ann crossed the room and gave Tim a hug. The rest of us sat and cried. Tim looked up and with a smile said, "I'm not going anywhere." It was his declaration of war.

I was nervous, and I didn't know what I should do. I was just the girlfriend; I didn't know if I had any business being a part of this ordeal. As I was thinking that this was a time their family should be alone, Ann left Tim's side and he motioned for me to come over. I sat down on his knee and, wrapping my arms around his neck, rested my forehead against his. When I opened my eyes they met his, and I saw the emotion in them that had been missing up to that point. Water welled up on the brim of his lids, and finally a single tear fell, gliding down his cheek in slow motion.

Tim had always had the fighter attitude, and I believed him completely when he said he was going to beat the odds that were stacked against him. The battle was on. He was going to do everything he could in order to conquer the cancer threatening to overtake the life that he wasn't done living. His life became a quest to find a physical cure. He viewed it as a challenge he needed to overcome, and there was no doubt in his mind that he would do it.

His battle was viewed as courageous; he became a local hero. Why is it that people with terminal illness are so respected for fighting for a cure until the end? Do they even have a choice? The focus always lies in finding a physical remedy. Do everything and anything you can to battle the disease. What have you got to lose? Don't give up. Rarely do you find people looking for a type of healing that restores the soul. I guess that's just not good enough. Death meant failure, and that was unacceptable. So along with everything else, I encouraged Tim to stay strong and fight. I wanted him to do whatever he could to beat the cancer. I didn't realize that it didn't have to be a war. Nobody had to be the loser. I wish I would have known that then.

He was bombarded by alternative healing options, some more "far out" than others, but all promising a miraculous cure. There was no way he could try all of them. Tim choked down over seventy pills a day: shark cartilage, herbal remedies, beta this and turbo that, each one offering a way to fight his growing tumor. He forced himself to drink glass after glass of carrot juice despite the thick texture, pungent odor and lingering aftertaste. He tried some positive-imagery techniques and then there was that magnetic contraption. The list goes on.

The traditional medical world was also involved in the battle, despite their lack of confidence in a cure. Surgery was out of the question because of the tumor's location, so the doctors suggested other treatment options. The Duke University brain-tumor team provided a protocol that involved heavy doses of radiation therapy, shooting directly at the base of his brain stem two times a day for several months. The tumor shrunk by half, but it wasn't annihilated; in fact, it was fighting back. Eventually chemotherapy, a word that had quickly became as taboo as profanity in church, was attempted as a last resort. It didn't work.

I was included in Tim's battle against cancer in almost every way possible, and the Orth family always made me feel welcome. I went where Tim went. I don't know if his parents always approved (or mine for that matter), but as long as it kept Tim happy, they didn't complain. I went along on all the hospital visits. I went on family trips. I spent more time at their house than I should admit, but it was worth it. I rapidly evolved from my "just a girlfriend" status to member of their clan. I loved them, and still do.

Tim's health declined rapidly during the last months of his life. His former physique was reduced to a loose layer of skin covering his skeleton. It was difficult to keep him comfortable, and he spent most of his days hunched on the reclining sofa in his living room. I spent most of my days in the seat beside him watching him sleep. Sometimes the selfishness in me would overpower my good sense, and I would wake him from a peaceful sleep so that I could talk to him.

In a matter of months I watched my boyfriend turn into an eighty-year-old man. He went blind, he couldn't walk, he couldn't remember, but he could still laugh. I experienced a crash course in Nursing 101, quickly learning all of the details involved in caring for someone who is terminally ill. However, I soon realized that my most important "job responsibility" was to keep a smile on Tim's face. It's difficult to maintain dignity when you can't do anything for yourself. He had to cope with issues of aging as a teenager. He was nineteen years old and had to deal with the fact that his girlfriend had to help him go to the bathroom. I cracked jokes and teased him about silly things to lighten his mood. I basically treated him like I always had; I was the person who didn't minister to him like he was dying. I made him laugh. It was the only thing I could do to help in a seemingly helpless situation, but it wasn't enough. I wanted to help him be at peace, even though I wasn't. One day after waking up from a regular afternoon nap, I noticed that Tim's eyes were focused in a dreamlike manner on something in the upper-right corner of the living room. He was mesmerized by what he was seeing, and the slight grin across his face suggested it was something awesome. It took me a few seconds to remember that Tim was blind because the tumor was slowly overtaking the optic nerve's space in his brain. I wondered what he could be looking at.

"Tim, what are you staring at?" I asked, though I wasn't sure I was ready to hear his answer.

"Just the light up there," he replied, continuing to stare ahead. The tears raced to my eyes, but I blinked to keep them from falling. I knew in my heart what he was seeing, but I wasn't satisfied with his vague answer. I wanted more.

"I can't see it. What is it like?" I asked.

"It's beautiful. You're not supposed to see it, though."

"Tell me about it," I probed with a combination of curiosity and fear. Tim didn't take his eyes off the spot in the corner of the room. He had several false starts before he was finally able to form the words he was searching for.

"I'm going up there . . . soon." The tears that had been welling in my eyes up to that point were released like floodgates. For the first time, I was grateful for Tim's blindness; I didn't want him to see me cry. I cleared my throat, in an attempt to get rid of the lump that had formed there, and took a deep breath, letting it out slowly to help me relax. This might be my last opportunity to talk to Tim about facing death, and I wasn't going to allow my emotions to let it slip away. I had so much I needed to tell him, for my own sake and for his. I wanted Tim to experience a peaceful death, and I did not want to be the one who was holding him back. I told him he could leave whenever he was ready. I explained that I would be okay after he left.

"I love you so much," I said, "and I am going to miss you more than you could possibly imagine. It will be so hard to live the rest of my life without you here, but I know that one day I'll see you again." Tim's attention was finally diverted from the heavenly focus. He reached over and held his hand out for me to hold. A smirk took over the peaceful expression that had been occupying his face and he let out a weak chuckle.

"That part is up to you," he said, completely amused with his insinuation that I had better be good while he was gone if I wanted to join him in eternity. He could never pass up a good smart remark. I laughed and cried. I felt a sense of relief. There was no way I could have said everything that needed to be said, and of course, everything didn't come out the way I intended it to. However, Tim and I were able to share an experience that offered us both a sense of closure. It was the closest to heaven that I have been in my lifetime, and I'll never forget it.

I left Tim's house on February 13 feeling disheartened. I always got a kiss from Tim before leaving; it was a custom

I'd grown used to. He would sit with his eyes closed and his lips puckered, waiting for me to bend down and say good night. Tonight things were different. Tim had slipped into a comalike state and was still incoherent as I prepared to leave. I bent down to kiss him good-bye, and his labored breathing was magnified. My lips touched his, and all hope for a response was lost. As I put on my coat and boots, I remembered that the next day was Valentine's Day. I had told him earlier that the best gift he could give me was for him to be at peace. As I closed the front door behind me, I wondered if he heard.

With a bunch of red and white balloons in hand, I entered the Orths' house the next morning. I knew he wouldn't be able to see the gift I'd brought, but I needed to bring something. Tim was lying lifeless in his high-tech hospice bed, but I could see his chest moving as he took each breath, and was relieved that he hadn't gone without me by his side. I spent the morning curled up next to him in his bed, holding his hand. Around 12:30, Tim took his last breaths. I don't recall the exact moment he died; I only remember opening my eyes and he was gone. His mother proclaimed, "Oh, Tim, no more seizures, no more headaches. Now you can see. Now you can laugh. Now you can run. Now you can fly! We love you!"

I didn't have any profound words; I'm not good with good-byes. I whispered, "See ya later."

Although Tim's life on earth ended on February 14, 1997, he continues to live on in so many other ways. Tim helped me to be the person that I am today. He taught me that the most important part of living is to find happiness in everything. I look back on all the memorable moments we shared together, and I recall his immortality. I remember all the fishless fishing trips. I remember eating popcorn and playing endless games of cribbage at my kitchen table. I remember cringing every time a song by Prince came on the radio because I knew he would sing along. I remember keeping my parents up all night with our outbursts of laughter, and I remember falling asleep on the couch listening to his heartbeat.

I know I will experience love again, but I will never find a replacement for what I had. Instead, I will take Tim with me as I continue to live my life. He will be with me when I graduate from college. He will be with me when my father walks me down the aisle at my wedding. He will be with me when I teach my first child to throw a softball. Eventually we will be together again when it's my time to leave this Earth.

Jodi Vesterby

Getting the Most Out of Life

I have gone through many difficult experiences in my life, barely squeezing around the obstacles in my way. But with those challenges came a great deal of learning. If I had to go back and do it all over again, I would not change a single thing. What I have come to learn is too valuable.

Marissa Angel

Dear Authors of *Chicken Soup for the Teenage Soul,*

I love your books! They are so wonderful!

When I started the first *Teenage Soul,* I was going through a really hard, depressing time, and suicide had popped into my head more than once. I read the stories about teenagers who had committed suicide, or attempted suicide, and they really made me think. I realized how incredibly stupid it would be for me to end my life for my own selfish reasons, just so I didn't have to face my problems and reality. I would have hurt so many people who love me. I thank you from the bottom of my heart for making me wake up and face my reality.

I'm fifteen years old, and I have cystic fibrosis. It's not contagious—I was born with it. This disease affects the lungs, the respiratory system and the digestive tract. I have been in the hospital several times, and it can be a lonely feeling. A part of me has felt alone all my life because of this disease. Sometimes my friends say, "Oh, I understand," but they don't really. No matter how hard they try, or how hard they want to, they can't understand what it's like to live with a life-threatening disease. I'm lucky, though: On the outside you can't tell anything is wrong with me. Some people with this disease aren't as lucky because they can look anorexic. Some die young, in their twenties. I am a very healthy cystic fibrosis kid. Sometimes I even forget I have it, but other times I can't help but be reminded.

During one of my first stays in the hospital, I made friends with a girl my age who had cancer. I remember her shiny bald white head in contrast to her bright blue hospital gown. We played together all the time, racing down the hospital corridors on our IV poles, kinda like scooters. The nurses would just laugh and let us have fun. I can't remember exactly why, but she went away and we didn't see each other anymore.

Later, I was moved to a different room. I shared it with another CF girl, Kate, who was sicker than I was. Even though I was in the hospital, the time we spent together was one of the best times of my life. It was cool just to have someone like me with the same illness. We would take our medicine together and have therapy together. She taught me how to blow smoke rings out of my nebulizer. We spent an endless amount of hours just talking and hanging out with one another. Our friendship was special. My health eventually improved, and I was able to go home. Kate was not so fortunate. She had to remain in the hospital. I lost contact with her after I left the hospital. The following summer I found out she had died. I was so sad not knowing how she died—or if she died alone. The whole time I was in the hospital I never really saw anyone come visit her, maybe a telephone call once in a while but that was it. She was only fourteen when she died. When I think about it sometimes it scares me to know that she died at fourteen and I am now fifteen. I get this lonely feeling that sometimes smothers me. None of my friends have to think about or wonder if they will live to see their sixteenth birthday. I do, almost every day. I think about Kate and the fact that she will never get to drive or freak out over SATs. She will never marry or have kids. I live in two worlds—one of which is very lonely and scary. But no matter how lonely or scary it may seem, I will survive. I've promised myself many times that I will live to see another day.

Today I enjoy playing soccer for my high school team. I long jump and throw the javelin. I act, sing and dance. I love to read and write, and I live my life to the fullest. From reading your books, I have learned that it's possible to do anything you want to, and that everyone is made of "Tough Stuff."

Sincerely,
Emily R. Monfort

Sharing an Intimate Moment

Dear Chicken Soup,

I have lived in Southern California my whole life. I was never part of the popular crowd in high school. I never had the best grades or kept up on my who-is-dating-who gossip. The only things that interested me were hanging out with my friends and being on time for my horseback riding lessons. I didn't set foot in an airport until I was sixteen and had my first boyfriend when I was seventeen.

I have never had much luck with guys. I don't like the idea of breaking up over something dumb and crying for a week about how much he hurt me, so I usually end things early. Just before my eighteenth birthday, I met the most beautiful guy. He was really sweet to me so I thought maybe he would be different from other guys. I really let myself like him; I trusted him.

On my eighteenth birthday, I went to school because I had two tests to take, one of which I failed. My friends had brought me balloons, but the wind took the biggest and prettiest one. Then the rain began to pour down on me. My birthday was not going very well, and worst of all, when I went to my boyfriend's house he broke up with me!

For the next day, I stayed in my room until my mom offered to take me to lunch. She presented me with Chicken Soup for the Teenage Soul. *Reading the stories made me feel so much better. Even though I didn't know the people who wrote the stories, I felt connected to them. They made me feel good inside.*

I have written about something that happened to me at summer camp that I would like to share with others in hopes that they too can get something positive from it. I hope it makes at least someone feel better, like others have done for me.

Sincerely,
Emily Ferry

Camp Confidence

"Mike! Camp question," Reese declared. "Now, the camp question, for those of you who don't know, is: Out of all the counselors at Meadow Oaks summer camp, who would you get together with?"

Mike sat for a second contemplating his decision. "Well, I could take the easy way out and say Monica," he grinned, "but I am not going to do that." He paused again before saying, "I would have to say the horse girl, Emily."

Okay, this is where I have to back up a bit. See, my name happens to be Emily. The conversation taking place above happened at a Meadow Oaks summer camp campout. It was two weeks before the end of camp, and my friend Reese and I had decided to attend the campout. When the kids were all asleep, the counselors made their way to the arts and crafts building where we all sat in a big circle and played Truth or Dare . . . without the dare.

The people in the circle ranged in age from sixteen to their early twenties. This game made me feel as if I was back in high school, but it was fun to find out what people thought about everyone else at camp.

Since Reese and I worked in the area of horses we didn't see or hear much of what went on with the other counselors. Mike certainly never came down to see us. We attended camp parties and staff events and had gotten to know a lot of the counselors, but we were still pretty much out of the loop. I had had a crush on Mike all summer, but he was a part of the really popular clique and I deemed him untouchable since he could pretty much have anyone he wanted. But during the last week of camp he paid more attention to me than before. Reese insisted he liked me, but I paid it no mind. Well, the campout certainly changed my view. This is where I return to the previous conversation.

". . . the horse girl, Emily," Mike said.

I sat in the darkness not sure what to think. Mike had just picked me out of all the other girls at camp. I sat for a minute while Reese chimed in my ear with, "I told you so." A few minutes later, Mike stood up and told me to follow him. I asked where we were going, and he said to follow. I heard the quiet oohs from the people in the circle as I stood and followed him to the back of the arts and crafts building.

He stood in front of me for a minute and turned his toe in, smiling like a little boy. "I can't believe I told all those people I like you," he said. I smiled at the sight of his twenty-three-year-old shyness, but when I began to say something back he pulled me close and kissed me sweetly. Now, at nineteen I had received my share of kisses, but something about Mike's kiss was different. It seemed more sincere than any I had gotten in the past. I felt as if I would float away.

Mike left for a teaching job in San Diego two days later. I have seen him a few times, but nothing ever came of our night at the campout. Circumstance wouldn't allow for it. But ever since that night I have walked with my head a little higher and looked in the mirror at a face I finally see as pretty . . . all because I was picked by one seemingly unattainable boy.

Emily Ferry

A Plea for All of Us

Dear Kimberly,

My parents have been foster parents for over ten years, but for about the past five years we've taken in mostly teenagers. Many are pregnant teens or unwed moms. It hasn't always been easy, but it's always been worth it, and I've learned a lot about people over the last several years. One of the things that has benefited me the most is learning to see where people are coming from. It's much easier to love someone, and much harder to get hurt, if you can understand the reasons that people act the way they do—whether it's fear, pain, or just plain not knowing any better. I wrote this poem from the perspective of my foster sisters, but I believe that, to some degree, all of us can relate. Very few people show all of their true selves, and everyone is crying out for someone to care enough to see past the outer shell to what's really there behind it. This is a plea to all of us from everyone around us who is hurting. Thanks, Kimberly.

Sincerely,
Rachel Bentley

Stone by Stone

I have a wall you cannot see
Because it's deep inside of me.
It blocks my heart on every side
And helps emotions there to hide.
You can't reach in,
I can't reach out.
You wonder what it's all about.

The wall I built that you can't see
Results from insecurity.
Each time my tender heart was hurt
The scars within grew worse and worse.
So stone by stone
I built a wall
That's now so thick it will not fall.

Please understand that it's not you,
Continue trying to break through.
I want so much to show myself,
And love from you will really help.
So bit by bit
Chip at my wall,
Till stone by stone it starts to fall.

I know the process will be slow,
It's never easy to let go
Of hurts and failures long ingrained
Upon one's heart from years of pain.
I'm so afraid
To let you in.
I know I might get hurt again.

I try so hard to break the wall,
But seem to get nowhere at all.
For stone upon each stone I've stacked,
And left between them not a crack.
The only way
To make it fall
Is imperfections in the wall.

I did the best I could to build
A perfect wall, but there are still
A few small flaws, which are the key
To breaking through the wall, to me.
Please use each flaw
To cause a crack,
To knock a stone off of the stack.

For just as stone by stone was laid
With every hurt, with every pain;
So stone by stone the wall will break,
As love replaces every ache.
Please be the one
Who cares enough
To find the flaws, no matter what.

Rachel Bentley

Life Is a Bumpy Road

Dear Kimberly,

Chicken Soup for the Teenage Soul was such a blessing for me. The quotes and stories really opened my eyes to all new perspectives in life. I am only twenty-three, and I have been incarcerated for seven years. This book has given me the courage to share my story with you.

When I was sixteen, I had my mind set on two things: having fun and being cool. One Saturday night, a friend and I knocked off from work at a local grocery store and could think of nothing better to do than ride around and get drunk. I never expected how drastically my life would change before that night ended.

After I was intoxicated, I came up with the "coolest" idea to show off in front of my older friend. "Hey man, let's go get my gun and find someone to scare by shooting at them." My friend didn't see anything wrong with the idea, so we went and got the gun. The alcohol, and now the gun, gave me all the "courage" I needed to show off. We finally passed a boy walking by himself along the road, and I just pointed the gun out of the window and started firing. He was fatally wounded and died right there on the side of the road.

I have now been paying for those actions for the past seven years as I sit in the Louisiana State Penitentiary serving a mandatory life sentence without parole. Like a lot of teens, I never worried about the consequences of my actions. I didn't care what happened tomorrow. I just wanted to have all the "fun" I could have today, but there was a price to pay. I'm afraid too many of us are making foolish decisions that come at such a high price, and we will never be able to clear ourselves of the consequences.

I am often asked what's the most important lesson I've learned, or what would I tell teens if I could only say one thing to them. It would be this: Life is a bumpy road with many regrets and very few second chances, so think before you act.

I have missed a lot of things in life. But reading all the stories in *Chicken Soup for the Teenage Soul* has taught me many things. I am thankful for the wonderful work y'all have done. Please keep up the awesome job. I can hardly wait for the new one to come out.

Thankfully yours,
Gary LeRoux

The Violence Needs to Stop

Dear *Chicken Soup for the Teenage Soul,*

I am not going to start out this letter like most. I am writing for one reason and one reason only: to get my point across. I have held in so much for the past two years—so much frustration, so much pain and so much confusion. Nobody seems to care that teens today are dealing with so many tough issues in our communities and schools. I am a teen with strong opinions about the world we live in. I have ideas about the changes that need to be made, but I don't even know where to begin. I feel like I have no one to talk to about it all. No one seems to want to listen. So I'm not used to expressing myself. I've learned to stay quiet, and that hurts.

Two years ago, during the summer before ninth grade, I was attacked and beaten up by two girls I didn't even know. I was hanging out in my hometown with my boyfriend and some of my friends when these girls started verbally harassing us. Supposedly I "looked" at them wrong. Suddenly things escalated and they were yelling—and I was punched in the face over and over. It all happened so fast and I don't remember much, but I do remember looking at my friends and my boyfriend while I was being punched. They just stood there and didn't do a thing. These girls were tough and powerful in our high school, so my friends must have been scared. I hit the ground and blacked out. When I woke up I was in so much pain it was overwhelming. I had bruises all over me, and I couldn't move my jaw. I couldn't understand how this could have happened to me.

I had always led a relatively easy life. Until that day, violence or hatred did not even exist in my world. But I now know that they exist everywhere—and their long-term effects are powerful.

After the attack, I became depressed and cried all the time. All I wanted to do was stay in my room where I was safe. Ninth grade was painful. I felt like I had been stabbed in the back by most of my friends. Whenever I saw them at school, they just looked away. Fortunately, my best friend, Michelle, was there for me and helped me to get back on my feet in more ways than one.

I started to notice the problems all around me. I became sensitive to the remarks of others and started to notice that certain kids at my school were continually picked on and harassed by older, more powerful kids. Fights broke out all the time, and it seemed like there were certain kids who would wait for any excuse to beat somebody up. The verbal harassment was brutal. Nobody was safe from the taunting and teasing. We even had police officers at our school, but their presence did little good. They seemed to be more interested in chatting with the teachers than patrolling the hallways, where all the trouble was going on.

I started to dread going to school. My grades dropped dramatically. I couldn't talk to anyone about what I was experiencing so I became more and more quiet. My parents and I finally talked about what I should do, and we all decided that changing schools would be the best thing for me. We decided that I would attend an alternative, independent-study program.

That decision seemed to jumpstart something inside of me. By this point, I was sick and tired of feeling depressed all the time. So I made a decision. I decided to get well. I wanted to be whole again, to experience my life to the fullest. And to be joyful. I tried to make the most of what was left of my freshman year by meeting people and reaching out. My success in making new friends gave me more energy and helped me to stop crying and start laughing and smiling once again.

Now that I am a junior in high school, I have spent a lot of time thinking about my experience and what changes need to be made to make the world a safer place for children. Ending violence in our schools is something that is extremely close to my heart, for obvious reasons, and something that I am very committed to in my lifetime. It's not fair that people have to walk home from school and be afraid for their lives. It's not fair that young teens go to school feeling scared inside and feeling like they need to "watch their back" because their peers make them feel like they're two inches tall and don't amount to anything. It's not fair that teens are afraid to speak their mind for fear that others might get mad and try to "throw down" and pick a fight. The truth is, teen violence is everywhere, and kids don't feel safe even in my small town.

I have a lot more time on my hands than the average teen since I am in an independent-study program, so I have spent the last year writing letters to people who might be able to help—congresspeople, community leaders, teachers and now you. I am trying to get the word out to as many people as possible that things need to change—and they can change. It is possible. We all need to stand up and do something about it. Teens need role models, more counselors, conflict resolution skills and anger management classes. How hard would it be to take just an hour every other day to work on these issues in the schools? Kids need to come together and learn how to get along and try to make amends. We need a place where we can talk freely about our life, how our day is going, about our families and our friends, and about our feelings and emotions. We need help in coping with all our feelings and our fears. We need peer communication skills classes in our schools. We need community centers where teens can get together and help each other out. We need adults who can teach us how to help each other and teach us how to take a stand against violence and hatred.

Coincidentally, I happened to be watching UPN today and a show called *Teen Files* came on. It was about teen violence and was hosted by Leeza Gibbons. The show made an incredibly positive impression on me. I would do anything to be able to meet those courageous teens, to thank them for opening my eyes even further to the problem and for helping me to see ways to begin solving the problem. The solution is kindness. These teens are committed to leading a life of kindness and service to each other after all they have been through and seen. And that is what matters most—that we learn to treat each other with kindness and respect.

Two years ago I was brutally beaten by girls who didn't stop to think about the emotional and physical pain they were causing. I was left to feel hurt and alone. I am now committed to preventing my experience from happening to other teens. I am going to work to make all of our lives better, and I am starting with this letter. I want to make a difference, and I need help. Please help me to get my message out to other teens so that we may all begin to work together for safe streets and safe schools. Help me to be heard.

Sincerely,
Ashley Sims

[EDITORS' NOTE: *If you also want to make a difference in your community and work toward safer streets and schools, here are some resources that we have found to be both useful and inspiring:*

Be a Global Force of One! 202 Common Sense, Portable and Human Ways to Restore Our Communities, Our Schools and Ourselves. *John T. Boal, PacRim Publishing, March 1998.*

Can Students End School Violence? Solutions from America's Youth. *Jason Ryan Dorsey, Archstone Press, LLC, November 1999.*]

Cotton Candy

When you're young you're told to be more responsible and act mature. If I knew being mature meant realizing all the hardships both in the world and in my life, I would have stayed three years old.

Claudia Cicciarella

Dear *Chicken Soup for the Teenage Soul,*

I was only eight years old when I was forced to grow up. My childhood dreams quickly became adolescent responsibilities. In September of 1991 I realized that the world is full of suffering, and it took me seven years to realize that it is also full of overcoming it.

My parents had separated that year. My sisters and I spent the first few months after the separation with my mom at her friend's house. Eventually we settled into a condominium of our own. We lived with my mom during the week and my dad on the weekends. Fridays were so hard. It was always so difficult to say good-bye to my mom. I could see the pain and anger in her eyes each time we would leave. My heart would ache tremendously. It always seemed like she looked at me as if it was the last time she would ever lay eyes on me. That made me even sadder.

One weekend, I decided not to say good-bye; I guess I was just trying to spare myself the pain. I got in the car with my father and we left, but as we were pulling away, I caught her sorrowful eyes as she watched us drive out of her life.

That weekend, my dad took us to a carnival at our synagogue. He seemed to be acting kind of strange, but we just tried to enjoy ourselves anyway. My dad was strict when it came to eating sugar, but on this day he let us eat cotton candy. I remember being flawlessly happy at that moment and my sisters' faces smiling at me with big bites of pink cotton in their mouths and joy in their eyes. Unfortunately, the happiness ended when we got home. My father sat us all down in the family room. As he spoke, his voice quivered in an obvious attempt to contain some unimaginable pain. He told us to always remember how happy we were that day and to never lose that. He then told us that our mother had committed suicide that morning.

The unbearable and intense pain I felt that day stayed with me for several years, and as the sorrow turned to anger, I learned to hate. I was furious with the idea that my mother had abandoned us. We were left to go through the turmoil of adolescence alone and unguided, to raise ourselves. From this loss, I learned not to trust anyone, for no one stays around forever. I constantly tested my friends' loyalty by pushing them away to see if they would come back. In the end, I always ended up alone. I hated everyone for leaving me—my friends, my mother, and even God. I was too bitter and too empty to realize that life can go on, but somewhere in the hollowness of my heart I finally found the strength to move forward. Heart Warrior Chosa once said, "In the darkest hour the soul is replenished and given strength to continue and endure."

I was touched by Jack Cavanaugh's story, "I'll Be Back,"* in *Chicken Soup for the Teenage Soul* about a boy who had lost his leg in a car accident. The boy, who was once the starting center on his high-school varsity basketball team, was hospitalized, had three operations, and ended up getting a prosthetic leg. He kept his spirits up and shunned anyone who told him that he would never play again. With determination, he did play basketball again. He wasn't bitter or angry, and he never pitied himself. He thanked God for saving his life, rather than hating God for taking his leg.

That's when I realized that I have everything it takes to overcome my anger and loneliness. God gives every soul the strength to endure; what was blinding me was my negative frame of mind. I now believe that anyone who experiences the kind of pain I did is also given the potential to overcome it. Seven years ago my mother died, and it is only recently that I have been able to overcome my anger, and trust my family, my friends and God once again. One day I hope to again feel as happy as I was with my first taste of cotton candy.

Thanks so much,
Michelle Sander

---

*"I'll Be Back," by Jack Cavanaugh, Chicken Soup for the Teenage Soul, pp. 279–286.

Bonding with Notebooks

Today could be the day that my mom realizes I'm growing up and gives me some more responsibility.

Jenny Gleason

Dear *Chicken Soup for the Teenage Soul,*

I have always been a real fan of your books and the important lessons of love and understanding that are shared in each of the stories. They have helped me to see things that were not so clear to me. I have received a great deal of comfort from reading many of the stories.

I had been going through some difficult times not so long ago dealing with the pressures of growing up and trying to communicate with my parents, particularly my mother. Our relationship had suffered because of this. When I would get frustrated or angry it seemed like we would end up in some sort of confrontation with each other and not talk about what we were really feeling. I feel like I have overcome those obstacles now, but not without a certain turn of events.

A while back I ran away from home so that I could be far enough away to vent my anger and release some of the pain bottled up inside of me. I stayed away for many hours, well into the night, before I finally decided to return home. When I walked through the front door of my house, I immediately saw all the pain, anger and disappointment on my parents' faces, especially my mother's. For days after the incident, my mom and I were on unfirm ground, to say the least. Everything we did or said was filled with tension until we both eventually snapped. We knew we desperately had to have a talk. We agreed to have breakfast together the next morning. That morning will remain etched in my memory forever. It was a turning point in both of our lives and our relationship.

We decided to go to a local café. On our way to the table I noticed that my mother had two notebooks and some pens. I asked her what they were for. She explained to me that sometimes it is easier to write down our feelings rather than try to talk about them. She then proceeded to hand me a notebook of my own and she kept one for herself. The "rules" for that talk were that she would pick a topic, and we would write down our feelings about the topic in the form of a letter. It could be as long or as short as we wanted. Our first topic was: "Why I am so angry." I had written a half page worth of stuff, and my mom filled up nearly three pages. I watched tears stream down her face as she wrote. I never realized anyone could hide so much anger and frustration. It could have been that I never paid much attention, either. Sometimes we think we are the only ones with problems, but I was reminded that morning that other people can be hurting just as much.

After she was finished writing we exchanged our notebooks and read what the other had written. As soon as I started reading my mother's words, I began to cry and so did she. When we were finished reading we discussed our feelings. Amazingly enough, it felt like all the anger I had welled up inside of me drained from my body. Our talk helped me realize so many things I had never thought of before, not only about my mother but about other people as well.

My mother and I continue to use our notebooks as a means of communicating our anger and frustrations, and our happiness also. We know that no matter how we feel about each other, our notebooks are a safe place to express it. We have made a pact that at the end of each letter we write, "I love you." Here are two of our more recent entries:

> Dear Mom,
>
> I just wanted you to know that some things I do are not meant to hurt or spite you. When I yell at you it's not because I hate you. And when I tell you I hate you, you should know that I really don't, although at times I feel like you hate me. Sometimes you just make me really mad and frustrated, and I don't know what to do with it. Like when you tell me you don't believe me even though I'm not lying, or when you do things that invade my privacy without my permission that you know I won't like. For instance, the other day you searched my room without me knowing or being there. I just wanted to hate you so much then. Then today you yelled at me, and it made me so mad. I really don't think there is much more to say right now. I love you.
>
> Katie

And my mother's response to my letter:

> Dear Katie,
>
> I realize that you get mad and frustrated, but I do, too. I don't want you to think that since I am an adult I

*don't have feelings. As much as you think that I might
like it, I don't like yelling at you. I just wish you would
help out a little more with the family and around the
house. It would make things easier on me. Some things
I do, like searching your room or not believing you, are
not done to be mean. I only do those things if I have
good cause. Sometimes you worry me, but it's just
because I care. Although you might not think so, you
yell at me as much as I yell at you. It hurts my feelings
as well. Sometimes I just want to cry. I'm glad you told
me how you felt about all those things. I'll try to work
on my temper with you, and I'll try to be more patient
if you will return the same courtesy to me and help me
out a little around the house. If this is not okay, tell me
and we can try to work something out. I love you.*

Mom

We gained a special gift that day at the restaurant and
we continue to be blessed with each other's everlasting
love and patience. I am now a firm believer that we all
need to express our feelings in order to live healthy lives.
Thank you so much for letting me share this with you.

Sincerely,
Katie Benson

Never Count Me Out

I understand I am not perfect and life won't always wait for me. I say "life is what I make it!" I dream of tomorrow, not of yesterday. I try to be successful and bold and brave. I hope tomorrow creates a new foundation because I am young and making my own roads.

Deanna Seay

Dear *Chicken Soup for the Teenage Soul,*

I am writing to thank you for your books. They have given me the confidence to overcome any obstacle—and I have faced a lot of them. My mom tells me I am the kind of person who has always had plenty of challenges, and when I didn't encounter enough I could be counted on to create some of my own.

My first challenge was not self-chosen, however. I was born with my umbilical cord wrapped around my neck. I wasn't breathing. After the doctors were able to resuscitate me, they discovered that something else was wrong. My right leg was twice the size of my left one, with barely any muscle tissue. They assured my mother that it was not too serious and that it would eventually work itself out and grow to the size of a "normal" leg. Unfortunately, it never did.

When I was in sixth grade, my family moved to Washington State. Adjusting to the move was difficult enough, yet suddenly I was experiencing back pain that wouldn't go away. I saw a doctor who took X rays and noticed something very uncommon. My spinal cord had attached to a piece of tissue that was pulling my back out of alignment. It would require surgery.

The surgery was agonizing. It was a complicated procedure, and I went through a lot of pain. The doctors found nerve endings that were damaged, and for some reason I lost the ability to urinate and had to be hooked up to a catheter. It was one of the most unpleasant experiences I have ever faced and one I never could have gotten through without the support of my family. They were always by my side.

After the surgery, I had to slowly regain mobility in my legs. The nurses and my mom would help me to slowly walk the halls until I could walk further and further every day. I was determined to grow strong once again. Finally, they sent me home.

I was told that I was going to need help walking for a while, but I wasn't about to just accept that as the final word. The first morning I woke up in my own bed, I decided I wasn't going to need anybody's help. I wanted to go downstairs and say good morning to my mom—on my own. I swung my legs to the side of my bed, and I fell to the floor. I pulled myself up and walked to the stairs, holding onto the walls for support. When I reached the stairs I told myself there was no going back. I held onto the railing and slowly walked down the steps, one at a time. Finally, I reached the bottom. When my mom saw me, she was so shocked and so proud that she started crying. It was in that moment that I decided I would never let my physical challenges get in the way of my accomplishments.

Much to my parents' chagrin, as my physical therapy sessions were coming to a close my football career was just getting started. I had always wanted to play football, but when I found myself all padded up for my first practice I was terrified. I almost quit. I made it through practice that day, though, and when I got home my dad had me watch the movie Rudy with him. It is about a guy who beats all the odds against him to become a star football player at the University of Notre Dame. That movie changed my life.

I'm now sixteen and have been playing for our high school team, despite my physical challenges and my size. I am only 5'3" and 125 pounds, so I'm not much of an offensive threat. My coach lets me play in the games, though, and I've had so much fun with my teammates. My hard work and determination has earned me their respect, and they've even taken to calling me "Rudy." My goal is to attend Notre Dame and play on their football team. I hope they call me "Rudy."

Your books with stories of triumph and busting through barriers have reinforced my determination to get the most out of my life. Thank you for showing me that we all have within us the power to achieve beyond our wildest imaginations.

Sincerely,
Dan Mulhausen

More Chicken Soup?

Many of the letters, stories and poems that you have read in this book were submitted by readers like you who have read *Chicken Soup for the Teenage Soul* and the other *Chicken Soup for the Soul* books. In the future, we are planning to publish *Chicken Soup for the Teenage Soul IV, Chicken Soup for the Teenage Soul on Love and Relationships, Chicken Soup for the Teenage Boy's Soul* and *Chicken Soup for the Teenage Christian Soul*. We would love to have you contribute a story, poem or letter to one of these future books.

This may be a story you write yourself, or one you clip out of your school newspaper, local newspaper, church bulletin or a magazine. It might be something you read in a book or find on the Internet. It could also be a favorite poem, quotation or cartoon you have saved. Please also send along as much information as you know about where it came from.

Just send a copy of your stories or other pieces to us at this address:

Chicken Soup for the Teenage Soul
P.O. Box 936
Pacific Palisades, CA 90272
e-mail: *stories@iam4teens.com*
Web site: *www.iam4teens.com*

Who Is Jack Canfield?

Jack Canfield is a bestselling author and one of America's leading experts in the development of human potential. He is both a dynamic and entertaining speaker and a highly sought-after trainer with a wonderful ability to inform and inspire audiences to open their hearts, love more openly and boldly pursue their dreams.

Jack spent his teenage years growing up in Martins Ferry, Ohio, and Wheeling, West Virginia, with his sister Kimberly (Kirberger) and his two brothers, Rick and Taylor. The whole family has spent most of their professional careers dedicated to educating, counseling and empowering teens. Jack admits to being shy and lacking self-confidence in high school, but through a lot of hard work he earned letters in three sports and graduated third in his class.

After graduating college, Jack taught high school in the inner city of Chicago and in Iowa. In recent years, Jack has expanded this to include adults in both educational and corporate settings.

He is the author and narrator of several bestselling audio- and videocassette programs. He is a regularly consulted expert for radio and television broadcasts and has published numerous books—all bestsellers within their categories—including more than twenty *Chicken Soup for the Soul* books, *The Aladdin Factor, Heart at Work, 100 Ways to Build Self-Concept in the Classroom* and *Dare to Win*.

Jack addresses over one hundred groups each year. His clients include professional associations, school districts, government agencies, churches and corporations in all fifty states.

Jack conducts an annual eight-day Training of Trainers program in the areas of building self-esteem and achieving peak performance. It attracts educators, counselors, parenting trainers, corporate trainers, professional speakers, ministers and others interested in developing their speaking and seminar-leading skills in these areas.

For further information about Jack's books, tapes and trainings, or to schedule him for a presentation, please contact:

The Canfield Training Group
P.O. Box 30880 • Santa Barbara, CA 93130
phone: 800-237-8336 • fax: 805-563-2945
e-mail: *speaking@canfieldgroup.com*
Web site: *www.chickensoup.com*

Who Is Mark Victor Hansen?

Mark Victor Hansen is a professional speaker who, in the last twenty years, has made over four thousand presentations to more than two million people in thirty-three countries. His presentations cover sales excellence and strategies; personal empowerment and development; and how to triple your income and double your time off.

Mark has spent a lifetime dedicated to his mission of making a profound and positive difference in people's lives. Throughout his career, he has inspired hundreds of thousands of people to create a more powerful and purposeful future for themselves while stimulating the sale of billions of dollars worth of goods and services.

Mark is a prolific writer and has authored *Future Diary, How to Achieve Total Prosperity* and *The Miracle of Tithing*. He is the coauthor of the *Chicken Soup for the Soul* series, *Dare to Win* and *The Aladdin Factor* (all with Jack Canfield) and *The Master Motivator* (with Joe Batten).

Mark has also produced a complete library of personal empowerment audio- and videocassette programs that have enabled his listeners to recognize and better use their innate abilities in their business and personal lives. His message has made him a popular television and radio personality with appearances on ABC, NBC, CBS, HBO, PBS, QVC and CNN.

He has also appeared on the cover of numerous magazines, including *Success, Entrepreneur* and *Changes*.

Mark is a big man with a heart and a spirit to match— an inspiration to all who seek to better themselves.

For further information about Mark, please contact:

Mark Victor Hansen & Associates
P.O. Box 7665
Newport Beach, CA 92658
phone: 949-759-9304 or 800-433-2314
fax: 949-722-6912
Web site: *www.chickensoup.com*

Who Is Kimberly Kirberger?

Kimberly is an advocate for teens, a writer for teens, a mother of a teen, and a friend and confidante to the many teens in her life. She is committed to bettering the lives of teens around the globe through her books and the outreach she does for teens on behalf of her organization, Inspiration and Motivation for Teens, Inc.

Kim's love for teens was first expressed globally with the publication of the bestselling *Chicken Soup for the Teenage Soul*. This book was a true labor of love for Kim, and the result of years of friendship and research with teens from whom she learned what really matters. After the success of the first *Teenage Soul* book, and the outpouring of hundreds and thousands of letters and submissions from teens around the world, Kim went on to coauthor the *New York Times* #1 bestsellers *Chicken Soup for the Teenage Soul II* and *Chicken Soup for the Teenage Soul III, Chicken Soup for the Teenage Soul Journal, Chicken Soup for the Teenage Soul Letters* and *Chicken Soup for the College Soul*. Kim's empathic understanding of the issues affecting parents led her to coauthor the recent release *Chicken Soup for the Parent's Soul*.

In October 1999, the first book in Kim's *Teen Love* series was released. *Teen Love: On Relationships* has since become a *New York Times* bestseller. Her friendship and collaboration with Colin Mortensen of MTV's *Real World Hawaii* produced the much-loved *Teen Love: A Journal on Relationships* and *Teen Love: On Friendship*. She recently released *Teen Love: A Journal on Friendship*.

Her nonprofit organization, Soup and Support for Teachers, is committed to teens and teachers having available to them inspiring and supportive reading materials.

When she is not reading letters she gets from teens, Kim is offering them support and encouragement in the forums on her Web site, *www.iam4teens.com*. She also enjoys nurturing her family, listening to her son's band and hanging out with her friends.

For information or to schedule Kim for a presentation, contact:

I.A.M. 4 Teens, Inc.
P.O. Box 936
Pacific Palisades, CA 90272
e-mail for stories: *stories@iam4teens.com*
e-mail for letters and feedback: *kim@iam4teens.com*
Web site: *www.iam4teens.com*

Contributors

Some of the stories in this book were taken from previously published sources, such as books and magazines. These sources are acknowledged in the permissions section.

Most of the stories were contributed by readers of our previous *Chicken Soup for the Soul* books who responded to our requests for stories. If you would like to contact the, you can reach them at their e-mail addresses provided below.

Liz Alarie passed away since submitting her story at the age of fourteen. Her family, which includes her mom and dad, one sister and two brothers, reside in Petersburg, Ontario, Canada. They can be reached at RR#2, Petersburg, ON., Canada, N0B 2H0 or via e-mail at *ralarie@continuum.org*.

Becka Allen is a fifteen-year-old sophomore. She has always enjoyed writing and this is her first published story. She can be reached at *tallen@central.net*.

Dr. Eric Allenbaugh is a management consultant, a national keynote speaker and bestselling author of *Wake-Up Calls: You Don't Have to Sleepwalk Through Your Life, Love or Career*. Eric has been a guest on nearly 300 television and radio talk shows regarding leadership and life issues. His seminars are frequently described as "life changing." He can be reached at Allenbaugh Associates, Inc., in Lake Oswego, Oregon, at 503-635-3963 or via e-mail at *eric@allenbaugh.com*.

Adi Amar is a graduate of Verde Valley School in Sedona, Arizona and currently an Outdoor Education student at Garrett College in Maryland. Born in Israel, Adi (whose name means "jewel" in Hebrew) is passionate about rock climbing, hiking, sailing, journaling, and yoga. She has received considerable acclaim for her innovative photography. Her mother, Lana Grimm, coproduced and costarred in the award-winning video *The Spirit of Yoga* in Sedona, just three months before the near-fatal crash. Her mother's miraculous recovery inspired Adi to develop a new appreciation for life, and she plans to build her future career on a combination of her outdoor skills, photographic talents and genuine love for nature.

Kif Anderson is establishing a reputation as a unique speaker who blends magic, motivation and merriment to lift his audiences to new heights of inspiration. He writes a monthly column for the on-line magazine *Lighten Up! America* and is an author of many works on magic. Kif is presently working on his first major book, titled *Reaching Beyond Perceived Realities*. In 1991 he was honored with the distinguished Comedy Magician of the Year Award. Kif can be reached at

P.O. Box 577, Cypress, CA 90630, by e-mail at magicalmotivator @the mall.net, or by calling 562-272-7363.

Greg Barker is currently the pastor at Grace Lutheran Church in Victoria, British Columbia, Canada. He enjoys communicating the grace of God to people of all ages, especially to his confirmation class of seventh and eighth grade students. Greg and his wife, Teresa, are enjoying their first baby, Christopher. Greg can be reached at 1273 Fort St., Victoria, British Columbia, Canada V8V 3L4 or e-mail: *glc@islandnet.com.*

Andrea Barkoukis wrote her story while in high school at Gilmour Academy in Cleveland, Ohio. She loves to read, be with friends and write. She has always wanted to be a writer and hopes to pursue writing as a career. She can be reached via e-mail at *Heaven675@aol.com.*

Libby Barnes is a freshman in high school in Minnesota. She enjoys writing poems, songs, music, stories and also loves to sing. Although she has never been published before, she hopes that it's not the last opportunity she gets to share her writing. Libby dedicates "China's Story" to her friends, whom she loves with all of her heart. She wants to thank them for sticking with her through thick and thin.

Sarah Barnett is a student and freelance writer in Ft. Worth, Texas. She has written many poems and other works for various publications including The National Library of Poetry and the Iliad Press. Her story was told to continually remind herself and others that such a simple thing, brought on by a simple person, can conquer so much. There are no limits. She can be reached via e-mail at *Duchess305@aol.com.*

Eugene E. Beasley enjoys reading, traveling, biking, walking and communicating with people and nature. After thirty-nine years of teaching communication arts, he is now presently writing, teaching drivers education, religious pursuits and gardening. There is much Eugene has learned through experience that he wishes to share. Thus, he writes and examines. At the moment, he is preparing a memoir for his children and grandchildren to explore after he goes on to the "greater" adventure.

Michele Bender is a freelance writer in New York City. She has written for many publications, including the *New York Times, Glamour, Jump, Cosmopolitan, Cosmo Girl, Ladies' Home Journal, Fitness* and *Marie Claire.* She can be reached via e-mail at *Mbender878@aol.com.*

Katie Benson is a student at Central High School in Little Rock, Arkansas. She likes to play soccer, snow ski and spend time with her friends. Katie can be reached by e-mail at *Katrisha@hotmail.com.*

Rachel Bentley is one of eight adopted/permanent foster/birth sisters. She has spent over fifteen years helping her family minister to over forty foster kids, primarily troubled teen girls. Now in her twenties and married, Rachel still ministers to teenagers and is very outspoken on pro-family issues. She is also very involved in music and enjoys her eleven (so far!) nieces and nephews. She can be reached at *a2jc4life@yahoo.com.*

Sarah Bercot is currently a freshman in high school in Indiana. She has had poems published in three different compilation volumes and a cartoon published in *All About You.* Her recent letter to the magazine's editor sparked a local television appearance. Her passions include drawing, painting, writing and reading.

Shashi Bhat is fourteen years old and a student from Ontario, Canada. She enjoys writing, reading and both playing and listening to music. Shashi has had her stories and essays published in various newsletters.

Bryony Blackwood is a Kenyan-born British citizen living in Virginia. He spent two years in a boarding school overseas before returning to the states for college. Change and adjustment have become recurring themes in his life. The most important lessons those changes have taught him are that you are free to choose your own path in life and to shape that life to fit your dreams. Life really is what you make of it.

Chris Blake teaches English and communications at Union College, a Seventh-day Adventist college in Lincoln, Nebraska. Chris is the former editor of *Insight* magazine and the author of *In Search of a God to Love* (to be released in 1998.) He loves God.

Laura Bloor is a student in high school in Ohio. Her hobbies include playing tennis, piano, writing, listening to music and being an active participant in many school clubs. Her future aspirations include writing for *Rolling Stone* or aiding in communications for MTV Network. Her story is dedicated to Colleen, whom she hopes never gives up on such an emotionally and mentally challenging disease. She can be reached via e-mail at *LoBlo311@aol.com.*

Jason Bocarro is currently pursuing his doctorate at Texas A&M University. Originally from London, England, Jason has spent the last five years working with troubled youths in Nova Scotia, New Hampshire and Texas. He is the coauthor of the monograph *Alternatives to Incarceration: Prevention or Treatment* and is currently working on a new book, *Humorous Stories Within Education.* He can be reached at 306 First St., College Station, TX 77840 or by calling 409-846-8207.

Alicia M. Boxler is an honor roll student. She is involved with her school marching band, church, youth group and Youth Alive. Alicia enjoys spending time with her boyfriend, friends, shopping, talking on the phone and going to concerts.

Stacy Brakebush is eighteen years old and is starting college in the fall. She plans to major in psychology at Saddleback Community College and transfer wherever God leads her. She is a leader in AWANA's at her church to third and fourth grade girls. She dedicates her story to her grandfather, James Smith, who passed away. He was a true example of human compassion and kindness and a soldier for Christ.

Jessie Braun is currently a sophomore at Pomona College in Claremont, California. She feels privileged and honored to have been given the opportunity to work on both the first and second volumes of *Chicken Soup for the Teenage Soul*.

Jennings Michael Burch is an internationally recognized author and speaker. His autobiography, *They Cage the Animals at Night*, chronicles his childhood experiences living in orphanages and foster homes. He speaks to children and adults about family, values, kindness and honor. He strives to eliminate the ridicule of children by other children and succeeds. He can be reached at 2 Elm St., Chappaqua, NY 10514 or call by calling 914-238-3031.

Eva Burke is a student at Central Florida Community College and plans to transfer to the University of Central Florida to finish her degree in social work. Eva has been writing since she was a child, and her first love in writing has always been poetry. She can be reached at P.O. Box 14787, Gainesville, FL 32604.

Cambra J. Cameron is a sophomore at Lubbock Christian University where she is involved in Kappa Phi Kappa and Acappella Chorus. She is grateful to God, her family and her friends for their continuing to help and encourage her. And to "David" who will always hold a special place in her heart. Her e-mail address in *jcameron@itl.net*.

Martha Campbell is a graduate of Washington University School of Fine Arts, and a former writer-designer for Hallmark Cards. Since she became a free-lancer in 1973, she has had over two thousand cartoons published and has illustrated nineteen books. You can write her at P.O. Box 2538, Harrison, AR 72602 or call 870-741-5323.

Nathen Cantwell is a high-school student in Aberdeen, South Dakota. He lives with his parents and little brother, and he enjoys drawing, writing, hunting, fishing and golfing. He wrote the story "Angel" for his mother for a mother's day gift in 1998.

Dave Carpenter has been a full-time cartoonist since 1981. His cartoons have appeared in a variety of publications, including *Reader's Digest, Barron's, Harvard Business Review*, the *Wall Street Journal*, the *Saturday Evening Post, Better Homes and Gardens, Good Housekeeping, Forbes, Woman's World*, as well as numerous other publications. Dave can be reached at P.O. Box 520, Emmetsburg, IA 50536.

Don Caskey writes a column for the *Gwinnett Daily Post* in Lawrenceville, Georgia, and develops training and performance support systems for Synesis Corporation in Roswell, Georgia. For more of Don's stories and columns, visit *www.nbdigital.com*. Letters are welcome at 2180 Pleasant Hill Road A5-271, Duluth, GA 30096 or *caskey@nbdigital.com*.

Terri Cecil has always been driven by challenges and that is how she looked at the car accident in 1983 that left her unable to walk. Since that injury, Terri has graduated from the University of Louisville, maintained full-time employment, served as a community volunteer, competed on the 1996 Paralympic

Fencing Team and earned the national title of Ms. Wheelchair America for 1998. She enjoys traveling and speaking on the joy of diversity, the triumph of the human spirit and the need to eradicate what Terri considers to be the strongest handicap of all—prejudice of any kind. Terri can be reached at 596 Plymouth St., Apt. 1, Wilkes-Barre, PA 18702 or by calling 717-820-3272 or by e-mail: *TerriMWA98@aol.com*. She can also be reached at Pride Health Care, Inc., at 800-800-8586.

Vidhya Chandrasekaran is a freshman in high school in Rockford, Illinois. She hopes to pursue a career in medicine. She has been writing short stories and poetry most of her life, and her various works have been published in books and local newspapers. Vidhya has also enjoyed playing the violin and dancing for a number of years and plans to continue. She can be reached via e-mail at *Vidhya85@aol.com*.

Diana L. Chapman has been a journalist for fourteen years, having worked at the *San Diego Union, The Los Angeles* Copley Newspapers and the *Los Angeles Times*. She specializes in human interest stories and is currently working on a book involving health issues, since she was diagnosed with multiple sclerosis in 1992. She has been married for nine years and has one son, Herbert "Ryan" Hart. She can be reached at P.O. Box 414, San Pedro, CA 90733 or call 310-548-1192.

Dan Clark is the international ambassador of the "Art of Being Alive." He has spoken to over 2 million people worldwide. Dan is an actor, songwriter, recording artist, video producer and award-winning athlete. He is the well-known author of seven books, including *Getting High—How to Really Do It, One Minute Messages, The Art of Being Alive* and *Puppies for Sale and Other Inspirational Tales*. He can be reached at P.O. Box 8689, Salt Lake City, UT 84108 or by calling 801-485-5755.

David Coleman is known nationwide as "The Dating Doctor." He received the 1997 National Lecture Entertainer of the Year from the National Association for Campus Activities and the 1996 and 1997 Reader's Choice Lecture Program of the Year from *Campus Activities* magazine. He was nominated for six straight years and is currently the number-one ranked entertainer in America by *Campus Activities* magazine. David received his bachelor's degree from Bowling Green State University, Ohio. He is the author of a self-syndicated column on relationships and a book entitled *101 Great Dates*. He is currently working on two more books: *Prescriptions from the Dating Doctor: Answers to the Most Common Relationship Questions* and *When the Heart Is Unavailable: Putting a Stop to Revolving Door Relationships* (with Richard Doyle). David can be reached at *www.dating-doctor.com* or by calling 513-583-8000. He is represented in the college market by Umbrella Productions, Inc. at 407-649-6448.

Melissa Collette is most happy when she is spending time with her friends, listening to music, writing poetry and acting. She hopes to one day become an actress and work her way up to directing and producing. She lives by the saying, "Everything happens for a reason."

Danielle Collier is a freelance writer and published fiction writer. She has a B.A. from Columbia University and an M.F.A. from the Iowa Writers' Workshop. Her story is dedicated to her parents and brother. She can be reached at *booxbabe@yahoo.com*.

David Cooney's cartoons and illustrations are published in a variety of magazines including *USA Weekend, American Legion, Mutual Funds* and the *Chronicle of Higher Education*. Through the scientific journals that feature his work, his cartoons are seen in over fifty countries. David's cartoons are also published in *The New Breed*, a cartoon feature distributed by King Features Syndicate. His cartoons run in numerous newspapers under the title *Twisted View*. David lives with his wife Marcia and two children in the small Pennsylvania town of Mifflinburg. His Web site is *www.davidcooney.com* and he can be reached via e-mail at *david@davidcooney.com*.

Liz Correale is a New Jersey native who currently attends college in New England. She is a psychology major with high hopes of a career in governmental intelligence. Liz attributes much of her inspiration to her deep faith and her mother's lively sense of humor. She remains happy by writing, running and guessing what color her sister's hair will be this week—fuchsia or royal blue?

Cheryl Costello-Forshey is a freelance writer, poet and songwriter who resides in Ohio. Her poem, "Making Sarah Cry," appears in *Chicken Soup for the Teenage Soul II* and *Stories for a Teen's Heart*. Cheryl's poetry can also be found in other *Chicken Soup* books: *A 4th Course, A 5th Portion* and *College Soul*, as well as the upcoming book, *Stories for a Faithful Heart*.

Emily Crane is a student at Kansas State University. She is majoring in advertising and is a member of the Alpha Kappa Chapter of Alpha Xi Delta. Her poem is dedicated to her cherished sisters of the pink rose and written for Josh. She can be reached via e-mail at *crane_emily@hotmail.com*.

Nick Curry III was born in Korea and then adopted by an American family when he was four years old. This all-American boy was president of his class, played soccer and baseball, and "will golf for food"! He attends school in Orlando, Florida.

Leesa Dean is a recent graduate from Mount Baker High School in Cranbrook, British Columbia, Canada. She is planning to further her education in order to one day teach high-school English. Her hobbies include reading, writing, traveling, going on outdoor adventures and talking to people. Her life goals include having fun, saving the Earth and making a difference! She can be reached via e-mail at *leesadean@hotmail.com*.

Brad Dixon was born when his mother was twenty-two years old. She later divorced his father who then left him and his sister. Their mother remarried and they were raised by a man named "My Dad." He was his best friend growing up and laid down a foundation for him and his sister surrounded by love. Brad has had a nice life and is still learning.

Stacey Doerner is seventeen years old and will be a member of the high-school graduating class of 2000. She enjoys playing soccer, running, spending time with her friends and family as well as reading and writing. She has been elected class treasurer the past three years and is a member of the NHS. Currently, she is looking forward to graduating and attending college.

Elisa Donovan first garnered the attention of filmgoers when she co-starred as the tippity, completely misguided slave-to-fashion, Amber, opposite Alicia Silverstone in the feature film *Clueless*. She also stars in the television series "Clueless" that airs on UPN. Next, Elisa will emerge in the Paramount feature *A Night at the Roxbury*, slated for release in October. Elisa was born in Poughkeepsie, New York, and raised on Northport, Long Island. Elisa began acting at the age of seven and became engrossed with New York theater. Some of her theater credits include *The Baby, Mad Love, Mad Forest, Dark Hours, Chamber Music* and *Treading the Boards*. Other credits in television and film include *Blossom, Encino Woman, Beverly Hills, 90210* and *Powder Burns*. Elisa currently resides in Los Angeles.

Jason Dorsey is one of America's leading young speakers. Each year he reaches over 100,000 people of all ages, backgrounds and aspirations. His first book, *Graduate to Your Perfect Job*, and integrated curriculum are used across America. You may reach him by phone at 512-442-5170 or at *www.jasondorsey.com*.

Kristina Dulcey goes to a Catholic high school and enjoys playing softball. She dreams of becoming a plastic surgeon so that she can help people whose external appearances do not conform with what society deems as acceptable. She would like to specialize in reconstructive surgery rather than cosmetic as she feels cosmetic is "superficial." "After all," she says, "it's what is on the inside that counts."

C. S. Dweck is the author of I.A.M. 4 Teen's "Little Voice" column. His writing has appeared in such publications as *MH-18 Magazine, Real Kids, Real Adventures #12* and *The Market Guide for Young Writers, 6th Edition*. He aspires and perspires to have his own book published. Reach him by e-mail at *dweck@ptdprolog.net*.

Amanda Dykstra has always wanted to be a writer. This is her first published poem. She can be reached at *Minerva382@aol.com*.

Danielle Eberschlag is an OAC graduate and will be entering the University of Toronto. She enjoys writing poetry, short nonfiction stories and formal essays during her spare time. She can be reached via e-mail at *tayskiss_scottslove@themoffatts.com* or *hansonlives@hotmail.com*.

Dale and **Dar Emme** started the Yellow Ribbon Suicide Prevention Program after losing their youngest son, Mike, seventeen, to suicide in 1994 and are dedicated to saving lives. They are in high demand giving presentations, workshops and in-services to youth, parents, teachers, staff, churches and communities across America and internationally.

Emily Ferry is a nineteen-year-old college student at Moorpark Junior College.

She plans to transfer to CSUN to get her B.A. in Child Psychology. In her spare time she wants to write, sing for her brother's band, run her own restaurant and start a horseback-riding school. Although all of these might seem like a far-off, impossible fantasy she plans to try to do them all and hopes that a few of them will happen.

Alison Mary Forbes is a sixteen-year-old high-school junior. She plans to pursue a long-awaited theater degree in college. Much thanks to the wonderful Barry Weber for submitting her poem when she was too chicken to do it herself! Alison can be reached at P.O. Box 26353, Wauwatosa, WI 53226.

Sydney Fox was born on November 1, 1982 in Tulsa, Oklahoma. Her parents' ministry to the homeless and the poor moved the family to the Washington, D.C. area. Helping the needy sparked her writing desires. It transformed daily journal entries into inspirational anecdotes about poverty's struggles. She works in a camera store and hopes to couple photography with her writings. She loves drama, plays the violin and cello and sings. She's planning her future and college major.

Carol Gallivan lives in East Hartford, Connecticut, with her husband, Kevin, and their two teenage daughters, Kelly and Tracy. The greatest joys in her life are her relationships with God; her family; her niece and nephew, Renee and Eric; her dear friends; and the teenagers in her neighborhood.

Kelly Garnett is currently a sophomore, majoring in Elementary Education at Oakland University in Michigan. She would like to thank her family and friends that have always been an inspiration—and true "chicken soup" for her soul.

Joanna Gates is a senior at Columbine High School and will graduate in May 2000. She lives in Littleton, Colorado with her parents, brother and a variety of pets. Joanna is an aspiring artist and writer and plans to major in visual arts in college. She also enjoys spending time with friends, singing and basketball. She can be reached via e-mail at *jgates123@yahoo.com.*

Marc Gaudioso is an aspiring screenwriter in Hollywood, California. He has a B.A. in English with an emphasis in creative writing from the University of Southern California, where he wrote a number of short stories. He can be reached via e-mail at *slvrscrn76@aol.com.*

Zan Gaudioso is a freelance writer whose stories have appeared in newspapers across the country. Zan earned her degree in special education for the deaf and went on to teach sign language, as well as teaching deaf children and adults. She became part of a landmark program that was the first to utilize sign language in order to foster verbal language skills in autistic children. From there, with additional training, she went on to become a surgical nurse. With writing as an integral driving force in her life, she continued to write and be published in newspapers and in family medical journals. She currently lives with her fiancé and their dog, Delilah, in Pacific Palisades, California. She can be reached via e-mail at *justzan@usa.net.*

Lia Gay is eighteen and is leaving in the fall to start college at the University of Kansas, where she will major in journalism. Lia is a talented writer, whose stories in the first volume of *Chicken Soup for the Teenage Soul* were favorites with readers. Lia is certain to succeed at any writing project she undertakes and she is certain to succeed equally well at living life to the fullest. She would like any correspondence to be sent to her care of Kimberly Kirberger, by regular mail to: P.O. Box 936, Pacific Palisades, CA 90272 or by e-mail to: *letters@teenagechickensoup.com.*

April Joy Gazmen is an eighteen-year-old Filipina-American attending University of Houston-Downtown. Although she participates as a volunteer and in school activities, writing and reading are her passion. She is inspired by the following people who are always in her heart: Mama, Cza, Hawke, Chino, friends and teachers. To be published in *Chicken Soup for the Teenage Soul II* is a dream come true. She can be reached at *irelandnikita@hotmail.com.*

Celine Geday is fourteen years old and is an honor-roll student in Washington. She enjoys writing short stories, poems and essays, reading, acting, dancing, listening to music and skateboarding. She is working on fulfilling her dreams and furthering her talents in all of these areas. She can be reached via e-mail at *NJCCGEDAY@juno.com.*

Katie Gill had Hodgkin's disease when she was sixteen. She is now twenty-four and pursuing a graduate degree in education. Presently she is working on a book for teens with cancer and trying to establish support networks for adult survivors of teenage cancer. Katie can be reached at 4520 Ashbury Park Dr., North Olmsted, OH 44070.

Randy Glasbergen has had more than twenty-five thousand cartoons published in magazines, books and greeting cards around the world. He also creates *The Better Half,* which is syndicated to newspapers by King Features Syndicate. You can find more of Randy's cartoons online at *www.glasbergen.com.*

Miriam Goldstein's body cast now resides in her basement, slowly dissolving under the combined assault of dampness and insects. However, Miriam herself has no plans for dissolution in the immediate future. She is a native of Manchester, New Hampshire and is currently attending Brown University, where she is double-majoring in biology and English. She enjoys wandering through tide pools, swamps and woods, haphazardly hammering bits of wood together as a theater techie, making sounds that vaguely resemble music on the flute and tenor sax, meeting unconventional people, and tweaking the nose of popular culture. She despises conformity and intolerance. She can be reached by writing c/o Martin's Associates, 817 Elm St., Manchester, NH 03104 or by e-mail at *khory@juno.com.*

Danette Julene Gomez is currently pursuing a career in the fashion industry, however writing remains her true passion, one she indulges in whenever possible. This piece was inspired by the joy and unconditional love she has shared with the two people who mirror her soul: her sisters, Darlene and Desiree. She resides in Los Angeles, California and this will be the first time her work has been published. She can be reached via e-mail at *DGomez6457@aol.com*.

Andrea Gonsalves is a student in her final year of high school in Ontario, Canada. She plans to study English literature at a university and become a novelist. She enjoys writing daily, finding it to be an effective medium for making sense of a confusing world. She hopes to use her writing to help and inspire others. Andrea can be reached via e-mail at *gonsalvesa@usa.net*.

Arthur Gordon was born in Savannah, Georgia. He has been managing editor for *Good Housekeeping*, editor in chief for *Cosmopolitan* and editorial director for *Guideposts* and *Airforce Magazine*. He has written two books, *Reprisal* and *A Touch of Wonder*.

Luken Grace is currently serving a two-year mission in Venezuela until August of 1999. He is a 1996 graduate of Sinagua High School in Flagstaff, Arizona. As the third child of six children, he has always enjoyed writing stories and drawing. After he graduates from college, he plans on becoming an English teacher.

Jennie Gratton graduated from Central High School in Manchester, New Hampshire in 1999, where she was president of the drama club and played trumpet in the band. She is currently attending Northeastern University majoring in English and theater. She has been writing on her own for years, keeping a journal and writing poetry and short stories. Jennie hopes to pursue a career in writing or costume design, and can be reached via e-mail at *Butrcup123@aol.com*.

Lisa Gumenick is a fifteen-year-old freshman in Pacific Palisades, California. She lives with her mom, dad and sister. Her older brother attends Brown University. Lisa loves friends, talking, dancing and drawing.

Alison Hamby is a senior in high school, where she plays on the varsity basketball team and is drum major in the band. She enjoys writing in her free time.

Cynthia Hamond is a freelance writer. This is her second story for *Chicken Soup*. She enjoys her school visits, especially when the children react to that "A-ha" moment in a story. She and her husband, Bruce, have five children and one grandchild. Cindy volunteers at St. Henry's as a teacher and lector and visits the homebound. She can be reached at 1021 West River St., Monticello, MN 55362 or call 612-295-5049 or fax 612-295-3117.

Barbara Hauck is currently a sophomore in high school and enjoys her cat, athletics, music, math, computers, writing and drawing. A polo enthusiast, Barbara hopes to attend a college where she can play polo competitively.

Claire Hayenga was born in Forth Worth, Texas. Since then she has lived with her mother, father and younger sister in four different locations in the area. The arts greatly interest Claire, who is sixteen years old.

Andrea Hensley has worked for the Salvation Army Camps, a program that reaches out to children, for five summers. Currently, Andrea works as a substitute teacher in the Renton School District. Andrea can be reached at 12037 64th Ave. South, Seattle, WA 98178.

Jennifer Love Hewitt is best known for her starring role as Sarah Reeves on FOX's Golden Globe-winning drama series, *Party of Five*. Love has starred in such big-screen hits as *I Know What You Did Last Summer* and *Can't Hardly Wait*. Her upcoming projects include *I Still Know What You Did Last Summer*, *The Suburbans* (with Ben Stiller), and an ABC movie-of-the-week in which she will play her idol, Audrey Hepburn.

Margaret (Meg) Hill writes articles, short stories and young-adult books. Recent titles are *Coping with Family Expectations* (Rosen, 1990) and *So What Do I Do About Me?* (Teacher Ideas Press, Libraries Unlimited, Englewood, Colorado, 1993). Kirk is the pen name she uses when writing from the viewpoint of a teenage boy.

Ashley Hiser is a seventeen-year old senior in high school in Morristown, New Jersey. She is involved in many activities through her school such as president of the French Club, member of the French Honor Socdiety, secretary of the Junior Statesmen of America, coeditor in chief of her school newspaper and manager of her cross-country team. Ashley has achieved perfect attendance throughout her three years of high school and has also been on the honor roll. She volunteers through her church's youth ministry and she makes a trip to Appalachia every summer. Ashley also works part-time at GapKids twelve to fifteen hours per week.

Ashley Hodgeson, age fifteen, began her writing career with a winning personal hero essay in fifth grade. Her writing achievements sparked ambition in other areas: academics (4.0 GPA), speech, track (she has run since sixth grade) and science projects.

Wil Horneff has made a name for himself on stage, screen and television. After beginning his career on Broadway, Wil starred in the feature films *Born to Be Wild*, *The Sandlot* and the upcoming *Harvest*. On television, he gave an award-winning performance as Jody Baxter in the CBS remake of *The Yearling* and costarred in Stephen King's *The Shining*. Wil is currently a freshman at the University of Pennsylvania.

Katie E. Houston is a sophomore in Santa Barbara, California. She loves acting, singing, dancing and has been taking piano lessons for eight years. She enjoys writing, especially realistic fiction and poetry. Katie runs track (hurdles) and she would someday like to perform on Broadway or be an English/drama teacher.

Amy Huffman is a seventeen-year-old student in high school in St. Louis, Missouri. Her favorite pastime is horseback riding, but she also enjoys writing, reading, listening to music, and spending time with her friends and her boyfriend. She gives many thanks to her family and friends for their continual support and belief in her and her dreams. And special thanks to "Buddy," who has made many of those dreams realities.

Jim Hullihan is an internationally recognized film producer and leadership retreat designer whose motivational media assemblies programs annually appear before 4 million people. As the creator of America's first CD-ROM magazine for teens entitled *Sweet! Digizine,* Jim is the leading motivation expert in U.S. secondary education. He can be reached at 148 S. Victory, Burbank, CA 91502, or by calling 818-848-1980.

Robin Hyatt was eighteen years old when she went to Camp Virginia Jaycee for the first time. She learned a lot from that experience and was also given a wonderful chance to broaden her horizons. It was the first time that she had ever worked with people of any mental handicap. She volunteered three more times at Camp Jaycee until she graduated from Lynchburg College in 1996 with a Bachelor of Arts degree. Each time she went she looked at the world a little differently. She is currently working as the special events coordinator at the Alexandria Chamber of Commerce.

Amanda Johnson is sixteen years old and a junior in high school in Placerville, California. This is her first published work but she has been writing poems and children's stories for years. Aside from writing, she also takes Jazz and Ballet and performs in school and community theatre productions. Amanda loves children.

Bret Anthony Johnston is currently a Teaching-Writing Fellow at the Iowa Writers' Workshop. His work has twice been honored in the *Atlantic Monthly,* and has appeared in such magazines as *Glamour, Mid-American Review, Southwest Review* and *Shenandoah,* where one of his stories received the 2000 Jeanne Goodheart Prize for best fiction of the year. His stories have been anthologized in *Patterns of Exposition 16ed* and *Scribner's Best of the Fiction Workshops 1999.* He can be reached at *Bretjohnst@aol.com.*

Randal Jones is a professional speaker and resident of Re: Think. He teaches seminars on thinking skills and personal management, helping people live and work deliberately for maximum effectiveness and satisfaction. He can be reached at 4307 Lealand Lane, Nashville, TN 37204, or by calling 615-292-8585.

Laurie Kalb is a member of the Class of 2000 at the Annenberg School for Communication at the University of Pennsylvania. Writing has been a passion of hers since she was a little girl. She also enjoys running, sculpture and nature photography. Although the lifestyle of a bohemian poet will always be appealing, she ultimately hopes to utilize her interest in human behavior and interpersonal relationships to encourage others to believe in the power of their own voices. She can be reached via e-mail at *Laurie248@aol.com.*

Molly Karlin is currently a high-school senior in Connecticut. She is class valedictorian, drama club vice president, student council secretary, reporter for the school newspaper and an active member of chorus and the National Honor Society. She aspires to write and star in a successful film or play. She would like to dedicate her story to the friends who have stayed by her through hard times (you know who you are). She can be reached via e-mail at *Sky1414@aol.com*.

Andrew Keegan is one of Hollywood's most popular young actors. Last television season, he had roles on both *Party of Five* and *7th Heaven*. Andrew will star in the upcoming Touchstone Pictures film *Ten Things I Hate About You*, which is based on William Shakespeare's *The Taming of the Shrew*. In his free time, he donates countless hours to charities that help critically and terminally ill children.

Kendal Kelly was born on October 2, 1982, the second of four children. She lives in Bristow, Oklahoma, near Tulsa. She is a high-school junior with a GPA of 3.97. She runs cross country and track, and plans to take state championship before she graduates. She loves little kids and babies, and writes in her spare time. She plans to attend college.

April Kemp, M.S., is an award-winning motivational speaker and sales trainer. She is dynamic with a high-energy delivery style dedicated to the education of audiences nationwide. Along with her husband, April developed a motivational software product, "Motivational Mind Bytes." She can be reached at 800-307-8821.

Hilary E. Kisch, a resident of Toronto, Canada, has finished her first year of university as an English major. "No Longer A Child" is her first piece of work submitted to a publisher. Aside from her passion for writing, she enjoys singing, playing guitar, and participating in a variety of sports including rugby and wakeboarding. She would like to dedicate this piece to her mother and thank her friends, Meghan and Greg, for their continued support. She can be reached via e-mail at *Hilary79@excite.com*.

Heather Klassen is from Edmonds, Washington, and writes for children and teenagers. She has had two picture books published and over one hundred stories appear in magazines. She can be reached by e-mail at *tressen60@cs.com*.

Mary Ellen Klee is an acupuncturist working in Santa Monica, Calif. Since 1971, she has been a student and teacher of the Arica method and practice developed by Oscar Ichazo. She has had a home in Big Sur, Calif., for over 30 years and is a trustee of the Esalen Institute. Starting with a teenage diary, writing has been a hobby and refuge for most of her life.

Paula (Bachleda) Koskey is the happy mother of two wonderful hormone hostages (a.k.a. teenagers), HopeAnne and Luke, and one post teen (whew!), Jesse. She would like to thank her children for all their inspiration and encouragement—and Clairol for covering the gray. She maintains her balance by writing, walking, eating chocolate and believing in miracles. Paula is the author of a children's book entitled *Secrets of Christmas*. She can be reached by writing 1173 Cambridge, Berkley, MI 48072, or by calling 810-542-0376.

Jonathan Krasnoff is a junior at Kansas State University in Manhattan, Kansas. He is majoring in Public Relations and Print Journalism. Jon hopes to attend law school after graduation. This story is dedicated to the bonds of true friendship. He can be reached at *jdk9569@ksu.edu* or by writing to P. O. Box 1415, Manhattan, KS 66505-1415.

Tom Krause is a motivational speaker, teacher and coach. He is the founder of Positive People Presentations and speaks to teenagers, teaching staffs, any organization dealing with teen issues and business organizations in the area of motivation and stress reduction. He is the author of *Touching Hearts—Teaching Greatness*, "Stories from a coach to touch your heart and inspire your soul," a motivational book for teenagers and adults. He can be reached via e-mail at *justmetrk@aol.com*.

Theresa Jensen Lacey is a freelance writer who has authored four hundred newspaper/magazine articles and two Native American history books: *The Blackfeet* (1995) and *The Pawnee* (1996, Chelsea House). Lacey is the author of two YA novels (available), is working on a children's book and one on Native American women. The author is of Comanche and Cherokee descent. She can be reached at 112 Carney Rd., Clarksville, TN 37043, or by calling 931-358-5511, or by e-mail: *tcjl@hotmail.com*.

Chris Laddish is a freshman in San Rafael, Calif. He has always enjoyed writing and has won first place in the Philips Literary Writing contest two years in a row. He hopes to become a screenwriter or journalist. Chris enjoys mountain biking, in-line skating and exploring the Internet. He is the youngest of six children and has lived in San Rafael his entire life.

Alison Lambert is a member of the class of 2000 at the University of Pennsylvania in Philadelphia. She is a certified emergency medical technician with the Newtown Square volunteer fire company #1 in Newtown, Pennsylvania. Ali is also an ocean lifeguard in Long Beach Township, New Jersey. She can be reached by e-mail: *alambert@sas.upenn.edu*.

Thad Langenberg is a student in Shawnee Mission, Kansas. His poetry has been published by *Indian Lore* and by the Kansas State Poetry Society's *Sunflower Petals*. His poem demonstrates how a single act of warmth and kindness can preserve life. It is dedicated to people who think they mean nothing to the world. He can be reached via e-mail at *langy999@earthlink.net*.

Medard Laz is a popular speaker and author of the international bestseller, *Love Adds a Little Chocolate: 100 Stories to Brighten Your Day and Sweeten Your Life*, as well as nine other books. Medard was instrumental in the development of Marriage Encounter and he cofounded (with Suzy Yehl Marta) Rainbows for All God's Children, a support group for children and teens who have experienced a divorce or death in their families. This group has ministered to over 600,000 children in sixteen countries. He also founded Joyful Again! (with Charlotte

Hrubes), a support weekend for widowers and widows. Med is a highly sought-after speaker, giving presentations and workshops on a variety of marriage and family issues, as well as topics related to emotional and spiritual growth. Med lives in Chicago and is a priest of the Archdiocese of Chicago. He can be reached at 3600 S. 57th Ct., Cicero, IL, or by calling 708-656-9216, or by e-mail: *MedardLaz@aol.com.*

Jason Leib is twenty years old and an upper junior at Yeshiva University. He was born and raised in the Chicagoland area. He is legally blind. Despite the vision problem, he played six years of Little League. He also attends the Special Olympics where he competed in several different sporting events and won gold, silver and bronze medals in the events he played in. He attended Ida Crown Jewish Academy for high school where he played one year of junior varsity basketball and two years of varsity basketball. He received the Sportsmanship trophy award as well as an award from B'nai B'rith for basketball. Jason played basketball in the Maccabee games and won a silver medal. He also participated in intramural softball all four years of high school. Jason can be reached at 4000 Enfield, Skokie, IL 60076 or by calling 847-329-7078.

Gary LeRoux is twenty-five years old and lives in Louisiana. He is interested in reading and writing about juvenile issues. His writing skills mainly include letters and poetry concerning juvenile justice. He can be reached at P.O. Box 2103, Reserve, LA 70084.

Melissa Lew is a seventeen-year-old high-school senior in Fountain Valley, California. She lives with her parents and her older brother, Chris. She looks forward to graduating this year, but until then she is kept busy as the FVHS Colorguard Captain. She can be reached via e-mail at *MissaStar@aol.com.*

Brian Leykum is a freshman at New York University. He grew up on Long Island, but his family recently moved to Massachusetts. "My Friend Mike" is Brian's first published piece. He can be reached via a-mail at *CurlyJ81@aol.com.*

Phyllis Lin is a fifteen-year-old freshman in high school in Bartlett, Illinois. An aspiring writer, Phyllis writes for both her school academy newsletter and for her own pleasure. In her spare time, she enjoys going out with friends, reading and playing the piano. Phyllis can be reached at e-mail: *Phyllis911@yahoo.com.*

Kathryn Litzenberger is a member of the Class of 2000 in Cromwell, Connecticut. This is her first published work, though she has always loved to write. In her spare time she sings, acts, writes and spends time with her friends. She dedicates this story to those who encouraged her to reach for her dreams: her friends, her family, her teachers and to the little girl who inspired her story—Rikki. She can be reached via e-mail at *Jewel0442@aol.com.*

Laura Loken is now a seventeen-year-old student in Crosby, North Dakota. Her story, "Don't Cry, Dad," was written on Christmas Eve in 1998 when she was sixteen years old. She enjoys singing, writing music, working in a nursing home and hanging out with friends. She is active in FCCLA, Youth Alive and her church youth group. She can be reached via e-mail at *fire_blue62@hotmail.com.*

Nailah Malik is a multicultural storyteller, literacy advocate and young-adult librarian of the Los Angeles Public Library. Having triumphed over formidable personal challenges, she brings a warmth and passion to her presentations that inspire and empower others. Her emphasis on stories that have practical applications for learning and living has made her a highly sought-after trainer and weaver of tales, and a powerful motivational speaker for students and educators of grade schools, colleges and universities in California. She has earned a B.A. in drama and an M.L.S. from the University of Southern California, and a B.A. in Economics from the University of California, Santa Barbara. Nailah can be reached at P.O. Box 6026-282, Sherman Oaks, CA 91413, or by calling 213-857-8089.

James Malinchak, age twenty-seven, is the author of two books for students: *Teenagers Tips for Success* and *From College to the Real World.* He specializes in motivational and inspirational presentations for teenagers and college students worldwide and is being called "America's #1 Teen Motivator." For information on his talks or books, contact him at P.O. Box 3944, Beverly Hills, CA 90212, or call 954-796-1925, or e-mail *JamesMal@aol.com.*

Bonnie Maloney is a sophomore in high school in Attleboro, Massachusetts. She enjoys reading and writing, and plans to study these along with psychology in the future. She is currently employed at a local bank that operates in and out of school, and looks forward to going somewhere unexplored for college.

Sandy Dow Mapula is a native of El Paso, Texas. She is presently a nurse for Zach White Elementary School and loves to write in her spare time. Her two sons, Steven and Kevin, whom she describes as the joys of her life, provide her with the inspiration to write. She can be reached at 604 Tepic, El Paso, TX 79912 or by e-mail: *SMAPULA781@aol.com.*

Chance Margheim is a high-school student from Blacksburg, Virginia. He enjoys writing in his leisure time and takes much pride in his work. He plans to attend a college in the near future and major in the field of communications, where he will work in the area of public relations. He can be reached via e-mail at *chance@bburg.net.*

Jill Maxbauer is a junior in high school. There, she is involved with theater, music, athletic training, softball and the Safe & Drug Free Schools Committee. She is the youngest of three girls and is currently deciding where she would like to go to college.

Sarah McCann is a sixteen-year-old student in Bedford, Nova Scotia. Her first love is dancing, but she also enjoys writing, watching movies and drawing.

Meladee McCarty is a program specialist for the Sacramento County Office of

Education in California. She works to find educational support for students with severe disabilities. She is coauthor, with her husband, of four best-selling books, including *A 4th Course of Chicken Soup for the Soul*, which has sold over 1.5 million copies, as well as *Acts of Kindness: How to Make A Gentle Difference*. She can be reached at Learning Resources, P.O. Box 66, Galt, CA 95632, or by calling 209-745-2212, or by faxing 209-745-2252.

Paula McDonald has sold over a million copies of her books on relationships and gone on to win numerous awards worldwide as a columnist, inspirational feature writer and photojournalist. She lives on the beach in Rosarito, Mexico. She can be contacted in the United States by writing PMB 724, 416 W. San Ysidro Blvd., Ste. L, San Ysidro, CA 92173 or by e-mailing *eieiho@compuserve.com*.

Dianna McGill was born and raised in a small town about an hour north of New York City. Her parents moved from the Bronx about two years before she was born. She is the youngest of eight born to strict Irish Catholic parents. Her family overcame many adversities together financially, as well as emotionally, and they remain close. She is thirty-two years old and works as a senior client service rep in a very large insurance agency. Reading and writing are two of her favorite hobbies and she hopes to write a novel someday.

Kate McMahon resides in South Orange, New Jersey with her parents, Vincent and Elizabeth and her brother, Luke. She is a senior in high school, where Olive O'Sullivan instructs her in English. Kate is interested in pursuing studies in creative writing as well as sociology.

Shelly Miller is a freshman studying electrical engineering at UM-Rolla. She really enjoys being a sister in Kappa Delta sorority and is the founder of the Society for the Antidisestablishment of Fairy Pressing! Check it out on her homepage at *http://www.umr.edu/~michele/*.

Sierra Millman's teenage years form a collage of creative expression in academics and arts at the Branson School and Stanford University, where she pursues her passion for theater, dance and writing. An honor student, National Merit Finalist and member of the Cum Laude Society, Sierra's first play, *Eccentricities*, won grand prize at the Rocky Mountain Playwriting Festival; she has published essays and articles, with stories in development, a children's book out with an agent and new ideas percolating. She can be reached via e-mail at *smillman@leland.stanford.edu*.

Emily R. Monfort is a sophomore at South Eugene High School and International High School in Eugene, Oregon. She has never been published, but writing stories and poetry is one of her many hobbies. She plays soccer for her school, loves to snowboard, wakeboard and white-water raft with her family. She loves to read and, after finishing *Chicken Soup for the Teenage Soul*, she felt motivated to send in a story about a life experience that could be inspiring to others.

Chick Moorman is the director of the Institute for Personal Power, a consulting firm dedicated to providing high-quality professional development activities for educators and parents. His latest book, *Where the Heart Is: Stories of Home and Family*, celebrates family strength, love, tolerance, hope and commitment. It can be ordered for $14.95 from Personal Power Press, P.O. Box 5985, Saginaw, MI 48603, or by calling 1-800-797-4133.

Brooke Mueller is seventeen years old and has been a resident of Anchorage, Alaska, all her life. At age eight, she began writing, along with her other hobbies of drawing and playing the piano. She also enjoys the many experiences life in Alaska has to offer, such as moose and caribou hunting, fishing, and skiing.

Dan Mulhausen is a student just graduated from Southridge High in Kennewick, Washington. After his letter was written he had foot surgery in the winter of '98, then came back and competed in his senior year of football and tennis. In football his team made the playoffs for the first time in school history and in tennis he was named team cocaptain. He awaits a response from Notre Dame University. He can be reached by e-mail at *Rudy63@aol.com*.

Morgan Mullens-Landis was born Morgan Nicole Maylee Mullens on December 28, 1982 in Gainesville, Florida. Her dad died a few weeks before her fourth birthday in December 1986. She was put in foster care in October 1995. She became Morgan Amithyst Landis on July 20, 1998 when she was adopted by Brian and Jackie Landis. She can be reached via e-mail at *amirose46@hotmail.com*.

David J. Murcott is a freelance writer who resides in San Diego, California. He has written and edited stories for *A 5th Portion of Chicken Soup for the Soul*, *Chicken Soup for the Teenage Soul* and *Stone Soup for the World*. He can be contacted at 619-590-1461.

Amy Muscato is a high school student in New Jersey. She has varied interests including theater, singing, politics and forensics. After her graduation in June 1999, she looks forward to attending college. Amy has aspirations of a career in either politics or television news.

Sara Nachtman is sixteen years old and is a focused student, determined athlete, with much emotional experience with trying to keep up with her competition. Sometimes she gets discouraged when her progress is slow or tiresome. These are the times when Sara writes to keep her motivation high while keeping in perspective what is really important.

Kent Nerburn is an author, sculptor and educator who has been deeply involved in Native American issues and education. He has served as project director for two books of oral history, *To Walk the Red Road* and *We Choose to Remember*. He has also edited three highly acclaimed books on Native American subjects. Kent won the Minnesota Book Award in 1995 for his book *Neither Wolf Nor Dog: On Forgotten Roads*. The story *Like People First* appeared in Kent's book *Letters to My Son*. Kent holds a Ph.D. in Theology and Art and lives with his family in Bemidju, Minnesota.

Jenni Norman is a fifteen-year-old sophomore in Albemarle, North Carolina. In addition to running cross-country and playing soccer, she is a member of the debate club and the Albemarle athletic fellowship. She loves making her friends laugh, writing, staying glued to the TV during the World Cup, trips to the beach and traveling abroad—she has been to Austria, Germany, Hungary and the Czech Republic, and plans to travel to England and France. Most of all, she loves chasing her mischievous dachshund Oscar. She can be reached at P.O. Box 550, Albemarle, NC 28002.

Jennifer Orendach is a sixteen-year-old high school student in Allentown, Pennsylvania. She is extremely happy to have been given the opportunity to display her work to such a large amount of people. Her life has always revolved around using her writing to help others better understand her feelings. She would like to dedicate this piece to her family, her many friends, and the kind people at *Chicken Soup for the Soul*. She can be reached at P.O. Box 4065, Bethlehem, PA 18018.

Tony Overman is a nationally known motivational youth speaker. He founded the National Youth I Care Hotline and produced *Teen Talk*, a nine-part video series. Tony conducts training workshops for teachers and motivational assemblies for schools. He can be reached at 18965 F.M. 2252, Garden Ridge, TX 78266, or by calling 800-487-8464.

Sandy Pathe is a junior in high school in New Jersey. She plans to continue her trips to Honduras annually and hopes her story can motivate others to put themselves out there and lend a hand. Any questions or comments are welcome at *SungirlsR@aol.com* or call 732-449-0335.

Peer Resources is a leading authority in peer helping services, programs, and resources for children, teens and adults. They can be contacted by e-mail at *helping@islandnet.com* or visited at *www.islandnet.com/~rcarr/peer.html*. Write to 1052 Davie St., Victoria, BC V8S 4E3 or call 800-567-3700.

Rochelle M. Pennington is a nationally recognized author of poetry, drama and nonfiction. She is also the originator and author of the midwestern newspaper column, *Insight and Inspiration*. As a quotations specialist, Rochelle has worked with several bestselling authors providing quote recommendations to enhance their books, including H. Jackson Brown (*Life's Little Instruction Books*) and Jack Canfield (*Chicken Soup for the Soul*). She is currently coauthoring Mr. Brown's next book, *Life's Little Instruction Book à la mode*. Rochelle, who resides in rural Wisconsin with her husband and their children, spends her free time actively involved in Christian education and in volunteering Hospice Hope care to the terminally ill. Rochelle can be reached at N1911 Double D Rd., Campbellsport, WI 53010 or by calling 920-533-5880.

Alexei Perry is a fifteen-year-old girl with a passion for writing. She has delighted in playing with words since she was two years old. If you should chance to see a young girl scribbling on a piece of candy paper, table napkin, feather or birch bark it is likely to be Alexei. In her poetry, she documents the pain and promise of life. She can be reached at P.O. Box 51, Site 2, RR#1 Elora, Ontario, N0B 1S0, Canada.

Theresa Peterson is a high school student and an active member of her church. He spare time is spent reading, writing and having fun with her friends. She is a warmhearted person whose loyalty to her friends and family is admirable. She can be reached at P.O. Box 366, Woodstown, NJ 08098.

Jessica Pinto is a freshman majoring in English at the University of California, Santa Barbara. She was invited to appear on National Public Radio to read her poetry and had two poems published by the 1999 Marin Poetry Contest. She was accepted to the California State Summer School for the Arts in 1998 for creative writing, where she composed "Ode to Shoes." She can be reached at P.O. Box 202, Mill Valley, CA 94942.

John Powell, S.J., is a professor at Loyola University in Chicago. He is a popular lecturer, teacher and bestselling author who effectively brings together psychology and religion in a unified approach to personal growth and spiritual development. For more information about any of John Powell's books, please call Thomas More Customer Service at 1-800-822-6701.

Shad Powers is a freelance writer in Battle Creek, Michigan. He has written for magazines such as *All About You, Jump* and *U. Magazine*. He is currently a sports writer for the *Battle Creek Enquirer* and can be reached via e-mail at *ShadP40@aol.com.*

Kevin Randall has been a leadership trainer and public speaker for the past seven years, having spoken at the National Association for Campus Activities National Convention, NACA Great Lakes Regional Conference, and to high school students across Michigan. In 1997, Kevin developed his most requested presentation, entitled Leadership as a Lifestyle, and has presented this session to rave reviews at high schools, colleges and conferences nationwide. For more information about Kevin Randall or his leadership programs contact, *Randallkev@hotmail.com.*

Susan Record is currently a student at Brigham Young University studying humanities, music and art history. She works as an editorial assistant for the BYU Faculty Center and plans to graduate in April of 1999. She and Justin Record were married in November 1996. In her spare time she enjoys writing and working in the garden.

Kate Reder is seventeen years old and lives in San Francisco with her parents and her older sister, Libby. She is a senior in high school, where she is the editor of the newspaper and of a literary magazine. She recently spent a fabulous summer in a Native Alaskan village writing, thinking and doing community service.

Rick Reed is a business owner, franchise developer and motivational speaker, as well as a youth travel hockey coach. His story is dedicated to his loving wife, Amy, and his two awesome sons, Patrick and Calvin, to whom he commits his story as proof of a life lesson learned—one he hopes they can learn without direct involvement. He can be reached via e-mail at *RReed12879@aol.com.*

Daphna Renan is currently a freshman at Yale College. She moved six times before she entered sixth grade, and it was during these early years that she learned the significance of deep and enduring friendships. Daphna would like to thank those who have filled her life with love, laughter and learning.

Sheila K. Reyman is a certified community college instructor. The consultant/trainer for a family child care program, Sheila presents workshops throughout the state. She has also been invited to speak with teens regarding goal-setting and positive attitudes. She can be reached at P.O. Box 20987, Mesa, AZ 85277, or by calling 602-807-1965.

Rachel Rosenberg is fifteen years old. She wrote "Unrequited Love" in 1998 when she was fourteen. She has been writing since she was ten, and one day plans to be a writer. She also writes longer stories and poems. Rachel attends high school in Montreal, Quebec, and can be reached at *Rae_38@hotmail.com.*

Danielle Rosenblatt is a sixteen-year-old student who enjoys theater, dancing, running, writing and laughing with her friends. She plans to pursue writing as a career and hopes to publish her own book one day. Danielle would like to thank her family and friends who have filled her life with love and encouraged her to reach for her dreams.

Jennifer Rosenfeld is a career counselor and is currently authoring *Building Your Yellow Brick Road: Real Women Create Extraordinary Career Paths.* She would love to hear more inspiring career profiles and can be reached at 212-794-6050.

Lisa Rothbard is a seventeen-year-old senior in high school. She has been involved with the *Chicken Soup for the Teenage Soul* series since she was thirteen. She can be reached via e-mail at *Rothie99@hotmail.com.*

Meredith Rowe is currently a member of the class of 2002 at Stanford University. However, she calls McKinney, Texas, home, and graduated in May 1998 from McKinney High School. Meredith has been writing since she was seven years old and loves to contribute to the Internet, especially by designing Web pages. She would like to thank all those who made her publication possible by adding their input. She can be reached via e-mail at *cardinal02@hotmail.com.*

Jamie Rowen is currently a student at Swarthmore College in Pennsylvania, studying International Relations. She loves to write, especially children's stories. This is her first published poem and she dedicates it to the victims of the Columbine tragedy.

Kimberly Russell would like to thank her entire family for all of the continued support they have given her. She is leaving in the fall to attend Gettysberg College where she will probably major in pre-law. She would like any correspondence to be sent to her care of Kimberly Kirberger, by regular mail to: P.O. Box 936, Pacific Palisades, CA 90272 or by e-mail to: *letters@teenagechickensoup.com*.

Michelle Sander is the middle of three girls from a Northern California single-parent home. She graduated with honors from San Ramon Valley High School in June 2000, and began her higher education at the University of California, San Diego in the fall. She can be reached by e-mail at *dmsander@ucsd.edu*.

Harley Schwadron is a self-taught cartoonist living in Ann Arbor, Michigan and worked as a journalist and public relations writer before switching to cartooning full-time in 1984. His cartoons appear in *Barron's, Harvard Business Review, Wall Street Journal, National Law Journal* and many others. He can be reached at P.O. Box 1347, Ann Arbor, MI 48106 or call 313-426-8433.

Bob Schwartz is a freelance humor writer with a concentration in the area of family life. He has a weekly column in a Michigan newspaper and his humorous writings have appeared in many national magazines and regional parenting publications. He also provides a monthly humorous column on running for numerous regional running magazines. He lives in Huntington Woods, Michigan with his wife and three children and can be reached via e-mail at *rschwartz@s4online.com*.

Talina Sessler-Barker, age twenty-three, graduated in 1998 from the University of Texas where she was a member of the Longhorn Cheerleading Squad. She currently teaches language arts and coaches cheerleading at Leander Middle School, while seeking her masters of education degree from Southwest Texas University. Her goal is to help young people realize that true beauty lies within themselves. She resides in Leander, Texas with her husband Donny.

Jamie Shockley currently attends high school in Spring, Texas. She actively participates in band, tennis and student council. She enjoys reading and outdoor activities. Jamie hopes to attend University of Texas at Austin or A&M University at College Station after graduating high school. She plans to major in business or engineering.

Veronica A. Shoffstall is a member of the Baha'i faith, which teaches that all people are from one race and have been created noble by one God. She has been trying to make sense of the world through words all her life. Now in her mid-forties, she is trying to recapture the wisdom of her youth and learn the lessons expressed in her poem *After a While*, which she wrote at the age of nineteen. She can be reached at 229 East 25th Street, #4D, New York, NY 10010.

JoLynn Shopteese is eighteen years old and lives in Savage, Minnesota. She wrote "Forever Changed," as a speech that she was asked to give after a missions trip to Mexico. She is hoping that she can be leader on the same trip next year. In the fall, she will be a freshman at Bethel College. She is planning to major in Spanish and go into social work and maybe writing. She would like to thank her family, especially her mom for "putting up with her." She can be reached via e-mail at *volleyball13jo@mailexcite.com*.

Ashley Sims is seventeen and lives in Morro Bay, California. She enjoys writing in her spare time. She feels that writing allows people to get in touch with their emotions and to express them. She hopes that one day she can help make a positive difference in the world.

Patty Anne Sluys is an eighteen-year-old Christian homeschool graduate residing in Chilliwack, British Columbia. She enjoys hockey, people, photography, hairdressing, desktop publishing and especially writing. She has put out a teen magazine called the *Penpal Scene* for three years. (It features inspirational articles, poems, stories, advice and more. Send $1 for sample issue.) Patty can be reached at 49950 Patterson Rd., Chilliwack, BC V2P 6H3, Canada.

Jane Denitz Smith is the author of two young adult novels, *Mary by Myself* (1994), and *Charlie Is a Chicken* (1998), both published by HarperCollins Publishers, and both Harper Trophy paperbacks. She is also the author of a board book, *Baby and Kitty and Mommy and Daddy* (Workman Publishing, 1994) and has written several plays, as well as novels. She writes and teaches in Williamstown, Massachusetts, where she lives with her husband and three children.

Karina Snow lives with her husband, Mark, in Oceanside, California. She is a recent graduate of Brigham Young University and volunteers with the youth group in her church. Karina enjoys reading, cooking and playing with her two young children, Tori and Brett.

Marc St. Pierre is a seventeen-year-old high school senior. He enjoys listening to music and hanging out with his friends. Thanks, Aunt Linda.

Sara Strickland is an amateur writer. She enjoys writing short stories and writing poetry. She is a student and a model. This story is dedicated to Kyle, the most important lesson she ever learned. She can be reached via e-mail at *SJStrickland@webtv.net.*

Elizabeth Stumbo will graduate as a member of the class of 2000. She participates in sports, scenery for school and community theaters, and is editor of her high-school yearbook. She hopes to pursue a career in the arts and communications field. She can be reached at P.O. Box 338, Ogden, IA 50212.

Ruth Ann Supica is a fourteen-year-old student in high school in Overland Park, Kansas. She really enjoys writing and is thrilled to have her first published piece be in *Chicken Soup for the Teenage Soul III.* This story is dedicated to her best friend, Laura Halvorson, who has stood beside her for all fourteen years of her life; to Teresa Hogan, one of her biggest inspirations; and to her wonderful family. She can be reached via e-mail at *Rootie14@aol.com.*

Andrew Tertes authors enchanting books, stories and poetry intended to inspire passion for one's own personal journey. For news on Andrew's upcoming books for adults and children, write to Unicorn News, P.O. Box 3164, San Rafael, CA 94901, or call 888-434-6789.

Jill Thieme. Turning "Wonder into Wonderful" was only one of the many lessons in life that Mom taught us. When we didn't have money, Mom would tell us to "Make a Memory." For several years now our holidays and birthdays have become a tradition of special activities. We'll be happy to share our creative family outings with others if you write to us at P.O. Box 381, Bridgeport, MI 48722.

Erica Thoits is the *Teen People* contest winner. She loves to horseback ride and swim. Her favorite pastime is going out on the family's boat. She is an avid reader and has been writing ever since she could type. Her handwriting is too sloppy to handwrite things. She loves dogs and couldn't live without her thirteen-year-old dog, who is only one year younger than she is.

Julia Travis is a high-school junior in Livonia, Michigan, where she is class president and a member of the soccer team. Her work has been published in *A Celebration of Michigan's Young Poets—1999.* She would like to thank the friends who have always been there for her. She can be reached via e-mail at *Julesorama@aol.com.*

Becky Tucker is eighteen years old and leads an active life in her hometown of Lebanon, Oregon. She believes in God and thanks him for all the inspiration he has placed within her.

Kathryn Vacca is a seventeen-year-old senior in high school in Boulder, Colorado. She is the opinion editor of her high-school newspaper, as well as the captain of the dance team and the debate team. Dance is her first passion, but she enjoys writing and is looking forward to a career in journalism.

Terri Vandermark graduated from Johnson City High School in 1983. She spent her first five years after graduation as a PCA for the elderly and continues to enjoy helping others. Today she works full-time as parts crib attendant for Felchar Mfg., a division of Shop Vac Corp. She enjoys writing, reading *Chicken Soup for the Soul,* being in love with Randy and spending time with her special friend, Tonya. Her latest dream has come true—getting her story published in *Chicken Soup for the Teenage Soul.*

Glenn Van Ekeren is a dynamic speaker and trainer dedicated to helping people and organizations maximize their potential. Glenn is the author of *The Speaker's Sourcebook, The Speaker's Sourcebook II* and the popular *Potential Newsletter.* Glenn has a wide variety of written publications and audio and video presentations available. He can be reached at People Building Institute, 330 Village Circle, Sheldon, IA 51201, or by calling 1-800-899-4878.

Jodi Vesterby was raised in Olivia, Minnesota. She currently attends Concordia College in Moorhead, Minnesota, and will graduate in 2001 with a degree in English Education. While attending Concordia, she has been involved in Campus Ministry, Habitat for Humanity and Justice Journeys. She can be reached by e-mail at *pvesterby@thurstongenetics.com.*

Tal Vigderson was born in San Diego, California. Tal has an undergraduate degree in film from San Diego State University. He has had careers in photography, entertainment-marketing research and teaching in several grade levels, including special education in a junior high school in south central Los Angeles. Tal attended law school at Loyola of Los Angeles and passed the California Bar. He is currently working as an entertainment attorney in Los Angeles representing filmmakers, writers, directors, producers, Internet companies and major studios in various forms of transactional work. Tal likes to travel and enjoys tennis, hiking and photography. He can be reached via e-mail at *TOV3@aol.com.*

Danni Villemez loves riding her horse Cal-o-Kashif, also known as Marshmallow because he is so fat. She only likes to ride him bareback because he is so comfy. When she rides she has lots of thoughts come to her and she makes sure she writes them down afterward. It drives her trainer crazy seeing sheaves of paper all over the tack room. Riding helps her to relax and is a great opportunity for her to reflect and pray.

Sarah J. Vogt was born and raised in Columbus, Indiana. Currently, she resides in South Florida and works as a PC/network analyst for a major corporation. Sarah has an undergraduate degree from Florida Atlantic University in business administration. Computers are her hobby and her livelihood and writing is her passion. She can be reached at 80 Catalpa Way, Columbus, IN 47203.

Christine Walsh is a comedian and actress in the greater Boston area. She is a freelance writer who loves all genres of literature, but favors writing for children and adolescents the most because it encourages boundless creativity. This story is dedicated to Brad, the person who taught her how to believe in herself.

Camden Watts will graduate from high school in 1999. Camden enjoys staying busy with difficult courses, running cross country, swimming, playing soccer and dancing. She writes and draws for her school newspaper and for her nationally acclaimed literary magazine, *Opus.* Her best work comes from experiences written late in the evening.

Whitney Welch is thirteen years old and in the eighth grade in Prineville, Oregon. She loves writing, especially poems and reading. In addition to cross-country running and track, she is active in tap and jazz dance. She travels as much as possible with her family and to date has been to twenty-eight states and Washington D.C. She plans to have a career as a teacher.

Mary Jane West-Delgado is a physical therapist and author of short stories and cartoons. She is president of Toe Bumpers, Inc., creating fun and decorative safety products for the home. You can reach Mary Jane at 805-688-1372 or by e-mail at *delgado@terminus.com.*

Kristy White is a fifteen-year-old sophomore in high school in Grass Valley, California. She enjoys acting, writing and playing the piano. She can be reached via e-mail at *eleemosynary29@hotmail.com.*

Sharon Whitley is a former bilingual grade-school teacher who has also taught high-school special education. Her work has appeared in *Reader's Digest* (including eighteen international editions), *Los Angeles Times Magazine, Guideposts* and the *San Diego Union-Tribune.* She can be reached at 5666 Meredith Ave., San Diego, CA 92120, phone: 619-583-7346.

Tom Witte was a writer and graphic arts designer in Denver, Colorado. He wrote this poem for his nephew, Ben, on the occasion of his bar mitzvah. His "Message for Ben" was written with great love, and Ben is proud and honored to have it published in memory of Tom, who died of AIDS at the age of forty-six. Ben can be reached via e-mail at *BMR@one.net.*

Digby Wolfe had a writing career of fifty years that has been divided equally between theatre and the media. British-born Digby Wolfe is perhaps best known for being the co-creator of the landmark television hit, *Laugh-In.* A multiple Emmy nominee and winner, Digby is now the tenured Professor of Play and Screenwriting at the University of New Mexico in Albuquerque.

Cecile Wood is a British citizen, studying at the College of William and Mary in Virginia. She is currently doing a semester abroad in Buenos Aires, Argentina. She is grateful to *Chicken Soup for the Soul* for giving her a chance to share her stories.

Rebecca Woolf is a freelance writer and photographer who has written for *Chicken Soup for the Teenage Soul II* and *III, Teen Love: On Relationships, Teen Love: On Friendship, Teen Love: A Journal on Friendship, 19* (the popular UK magazine) and more. Keep your eyes out for Rebecca's first solo book of poetry titled, *Through Broken Mirrors: A Reflective Memoir.* Rebecca is the program director and newsletter editor for Lead the Star, a creative company devoted to inspiring creativity and strength in identity in young adults. To reach Rebecca, please e-mail her at *rebeccawoolf@leadthestar.com.*

Lynne Zielinski, mother of seven and "Nana" to thirteen grandkids, resides in Huntsville, Alabama. She believes that life is a gift from God and what we do with it is our gift to God. She tries to write accordingly. Lynne can be reached by calling 256-883-1592 or 256-880-9052.

All the More Beautiful. Reprinted by permission of Marc Gaudioso. ©2000 Marc Gaudioso.

Return to High School. Reprinted by permission of Sierra Millman. ©2000 Sierra Millman.

The Days of Cardboard Boxes. Reprinted by permission of Eva Burke. ©1996 Eva Burke.

Rolling Down Summer's Hills. Reprinted by permission C. S. Dweck. ©2001 C. S. Dweck.

My Sister's First Love. Reprinted by permission of Kristi Vesterby. ©1999 Kristi Vesterby.

Immortal. Reprinted by permission of Jodi Vesterby. ©1999 Jodi Vesterby.

Getting the Most Out of Life. Reprinted by permission of Emily R. Monfort. ©2001 Emily R. Monfort.

Sharing an Intimate Moment and *Camp Confidence.* Reprinted by permission of Emily Ferry. ©2001 Emily Ferry.

A Plea for All of Us and *Stone by Stone.* Reprinted by permission of Rachel Bentley. ©1999 Rachel Bentley.

Life Is a Bumpy Road. Reprinted by permission of Gary LeRoux. ©1998 Gary LeRoux.

The Violence Needs to Stop. Reprinted by permission of Ashley Sims. ©1999 Ashley Sims.

Cotton Candy. Reprinted by permission of Michelle Sander. ©2001 Michelle Sander.

Bonding with Notebooks. Reprinted by permission of Katie Benson. ©2001 Katie Benson.

Never Count Me Out. Reprinted by permission of Dan Mulhausen. ©1998 Dan Mulhausen.

More Great Books

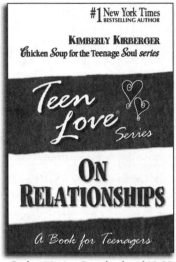

Code #7346 • Paperback • $12.95

Code #7664 • Paperback • $12.95

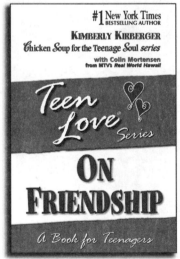

Code #8156 • Paperback • $12.95

Code #9128 • Paperback • $12.95

Available wherever books are sold.
To order direct: Phone 800.441.5569 • Online www.hci-online.com
Prices do not include shipping and handling. Your response code is CCS.